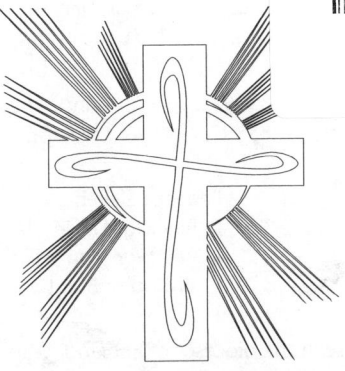

PARISH MASS BOOK

REVISED

YEAR C – Volume 1

McCRIMMONS
Great Wakering, Essex, UK

This edition published in 2024

Published by McCrimmon Publishing Co Ltd
10–12 High Street, Great Wakering, Essex, SS3 0EQ, UK
info@mccrimmons.com | www.mccrimmons.com

ISBN 978-0-85597-7931 A5 standard edition
ISBN 978-0-85597-7993 A4 Large-print edition

Concordat cum Originali	Rebecca Sleven
Nihil obstat	Rt Rev Mgr David Mason
Imprimatur	Rt Rev Mgr Alan Williams Bishop of Brentwood

Approved for use in the dioceses of England, Wales and Scotland.

The publishers wish to express their thanks to the following for their help in the preparation of this volume:
Helen Stimpson, Paul Moynihan, Rebecca Sleven and Martin Foster.

Cover illustration by The Benedictine Sisters of Turvey Abbey | Cover design: Helen Stimpson
Printed and bound by CPI, UK
Typeset in ITC Stone Serif and ITC Stone Sans.

H/BD

CONTENTS

ORDER OF MASS

ORDER OF MASS

In celebrating the Eucharist, the people of God assemble as the body of Christ to fulfil the Lord's command: 'do this in memory of me' (Luke 22:19).

At the Last Supper the Lord gathered his disciples, he spoke to them, took bread and wine, broke the bread, and gave them the Bread of life and the Cup of eternal salvation. In the Eucharist the Church to this day makes Christ's memorial and celebrates his presence in the same sequence of actions: we gather in Christ's name, in the Liturgy of the Word we listen as the word of God is proclaimed and explained, in the Liturgy of the Eucharist, we take bread and wine, give thanks, and receive the Body and Blood of Christ.

Christ is always present in his Church, particularly in its liturgical celebrations. In the celebration of Mass, Christ is really present in the very liturgical assembly gathered in his name, in the person of the minister who acts in the person of Christ, in the proclamation of his word and under the Eucharistic species. This presence of Christ under the appearance of bread and wine is called real, not to exclude other ways in which Christ is present, but because it is real *par excellence.*

cf Celebrating the Mass nn 18–19, 22;
General Instruction of the Roman Missal n 27;
Holy Communion and the Worship of the Eucharist Outside Mass n 6.

OUTLINE OF THE ORDER OF MASS

INTRODUCTORY RITES

Opening Song
Greeting
Penitential Act
Gloria (omitted during Advent and Lent)
Opening Prayer

LITURGY OF THE WORD

First Reading
Responsorial Psalm
Second Reading
Gospel Acclamation
Gospel
Homily
Profession of Faith
Prayer of the Faithful

LITURGY OF THE EUCHARIST

Preparation of Gifts
Prayer over the Gifts

EUCHARISTIC PRAYER

COMMUNION RITE

The Lord's Prayer
Rite of Peace
Lamb of God
Holy Communion
Prayer after Communion

CONCLUDING RITES

Blessing
Dismissal

INTRODUCTORY RITES

Where two or three are gathered in my name,
there am I in their midst.
(Matthew 18:20)

The Introductory Rites help the faithful come together as one, to establish communion and to prepare themselves properly to listen to the word of God and to celebrate the Eucharist worthily.

ENTRANCE SONG

ALL STAND

While the Entrance Song is sung, the Priest approaches the altar with the ministers and venerates it.

SIGN OF THE CROSS

▷ Music p 313

All make the Sign of the Cross as the Priest says

Priest: In the name of the Father, and of the Son, and of the Holy Spirit.
People: **Amen.**

GREETING

Priest: The grace of our Lord Jesus Christ,
and the love of God,
and the communion of the Holy Spirit
be with you all.

or

Priest: Grace to you and peace from God our Father
and the Lord Jesus Christ.

or

Priest: The Lord be with you.
People: **And with your spirit.**

A Bishop will say:

Bishop: Peace be with you
People: **And with your spirit.**

The Priest, or a Deacon, or another minister, may very briefly introduce the faithful to the Mass of the day.

PENITENTIAL ACT

Because of its emphasis on Easter and Baptism, the Blessing and Sprinkling of Water (page 62) may take place on Sundays, especially in Easter Time. When it is used it replaces the Penitential Act.

Otherwise, one of the following three forms of the Penitential Act is used. Each Penitential Act begins with the invitation to the faithful by the Priest:

Brethren (brothers and sisters), let us acknowledge our sins,
and so prepare ourselves to celebrate the sacred mysteries.

A brief pause for silence follows.

On certain days during the Church's year, for example Palm Sunday and the Easter Vigil, and during certain other celebrations, for example a Funeral Mass, Rite of Entry into the Catechumenate or Baptism, the Introductory Rites take a different form.

Penitential Act A

All: **I confess to almighty God**
and to you, my brothers and sisters,
that I have greatly sinned,
in my thoughts and in my words,
in what I have done and in what I have failed to do,

All strike their breast.

through my fault, through my fault,
through my most grievous fault;
therefore I ask blessed Mary ever-Virgin,
all the Angels and Saints,
and you, my brothers and sisters,
to pray for me to the Lord our God.

Penitential Act B

▷ *Music p 314*

Priest: Have mercy on us, O Lord.
People: **For we have sinned against you.**

Priest: Show us, O Lord, your mercy.
People: **And grant us your salvation.**

Penitential Act C

▷ *Music p 314*

After the silence the Priest or another minister invokes the gracious works of the Lord to which he invites the Kyrie eleison invocations, in sequence, as in the example below:

Priest or minister: You were sent to heal the contrite of heart:
Lord, have mercy. *or* Kyrie, eleison.
People: **Lord, have mercy.** *or* **Kyrie, eleison.**

Priest or minister: You came to call sinners:
Christ, have mercy. *or* Christe, eleison.
People: **Christ, have mercy.** *or* **Christe, eleison.**

Priest or minister: You are seated at the right hand of the Father to intercede for us:
Lord, have mercy. *or* Kyrie, eleison.
People: **Lord, have mercy.** *or* **Kyrie, eleison.**

The absolution by the Priest follows all of the options above

▷ *Music p 315*

Priest: May almighty God have mercy on us,
forgive us our sins,
and bring us to everlasting life.
All: **Amen.**

KYRIE

▷ Music p 315

The Kyrie, eleison (Lord, have mercy) invocations may follow:

Lord, have mercy. **Lord, have mercy.**		Kyrie, eleison. **Kyrie, eleison.**
Christ, have mercy. **Christ, have mercy.**	*or*	Christe, eleison. **Christe, eleison.**
Lord, have mercy. **Lord, have mercy.**		Kyrie, eleison. **Kyrie, eleison.**

GLORIA

▷ Music p 316

When indicated this hymn is sung or said:

All: **Glory to God in the highest,
and on earth peace to people of good will.
We praise you,
we bless you,
we adore you,
we glorify you,
we give you thanks for your great glory,
Lord God, heavenly King,
O God, almighty Father.**

**Lord Jesus Christ, Only Begotten Son,
Lord God, Lamb of God, Son of the Father,
you take away the sins of the world,
have mercy on us;
you take away the sins of the world,
receive our prayer;
you are seated at the right hand of the Father,
have mercy on us.**

**For you alone are the Holy One,
you alone are the Lord,
you alone are the Most High,
Jesus Christ,
with the Holy Spirit,
in the glory of God the Father.
Amen.**

COLLECT

▷ Proper

Priest: Let us pray.

All pray in silence for a while. Then the Priest says the Collect, to which the people respond:

People: **Amen.**

ALL SIT

LITURGY OF THE WORD

Did not our hearts burn within us as he spoke to us and explained the Scriptures to us?
(cf Luke 24:32)

In the Liturgy of the Word the assembly listens with hearts burning as the Lord speaks to it again and it responds with words of praise and petition.

By hearing the word proclaimed in worship, the faithful again enter into the unending dialogue between God and the covenant people, a dialogue sealed in the sharing of the Eucharistic food and drink. The proclamation of the word is thus integral to the Mass and at its very centre.

Celebrating the Mass nn 19, 152

FIRST READING

▷ Proper

The reader goes to the ambo and proclaims the First Reading, while all sit and listen.

To indicate the end of the reading, the reader acclaims:

Reader: The word of the Lord.
All: **Thanks be to God.**

▷ Music p 317

Following this reading, and the other readings it is appropriate to have a brief time of quiet as those present take the word of God to heart and begin to prepare a prayerful response to what they have heard.

RESPONSORIAL PSALM

The psalmist or cantor sings or says the Psalm, with the people making the response.

SECOND READING

On Sundays and certain other days there is a second reading.

To indicate the end of the reading, the reader acclaims:

Reader: The word of the Lord.
All: **Thanks be to God.**

▷ Music p 317

GOSPEL ACCLAMATION

ALL STAND

The assembly stands for the Gospel Acclamation to welcome the Gospel.
The Gospel Acclamation may not be omitted where there is more than one reading before the Gospel.

The Gospel Acclamation is

Alleluia.

GOSPEL

The assembly remains standing in honour of the Gospel reading, the high point of the Liturgy of the Word.

At the ambo the Deacon, or the Priest, sings or says:

▷ Music p 317

Deacon or Priest: The Lord be with you.
All: **And with your spirit.**

Deacon or Priest: A reading from the holy Gospel according to N.

The Deacon or Priest makes the Sign of the Cross on the book and, together with the people, on his forehead, lips, and breast.

All: **Glory to you, O Lord.**

At the end of the Gospel, the Deacon, or the Priest, acclaims:

Deacon or Priest: The Gospel of the Lord.
All: **Praise to you, Lord Jesus Christ.**

ALL SIT

HOMILY

The Homily is preached by a Priest or Deacon on all Sundays and Holydays of Obligation. On other days, it is recommended.

At the end of the Homily it is appropriate for there to be a brief silence for recollection.

ALL STAND

PROFESSION OF FAITH

On Sundays and Solemnities, the Profession of Faith will follow.

In Masses that include acceptance into the order of catechumens and in ritual Masses for the election or enrolment of names or for the Scrutinies, the Profession of Faith may be omitted.

On most occasions the form used is that of the Niceno-Constantinopolitan Creed. However, especially during Lent and Easter Time, the Apostles' Creed (page 12) may be used.

If the Profession of Faith is not said, the Prayer of the Faithful follows.

Niceno-Constantinopolitan Creed

▷ Music p 318

I believe in one God,
the Father almighty,
maker of heaven and earth,
of all things visible and invisible.

I believe in one Lord Jesus Christ,
the Only Begotten Son of God,
born of the Father before all ages.
God from God, Light from Light,
true God from true God,
begotten, not made, consubstantial with the Father;

through him all things were made.
For us men and for our salvation
he came down from heaven,

At the words that follow, up to and including 'and became man', all bow.

and by the Holy Spirit was incarnate of the Virgin Mary,
and became man.

For our sake he was crucified under Pontius Pilate,
he suffered death and was buried,
and rose again on the third day
in accordance with the Scriptures.
He ascended into heaven
and is seated at the right hand of the Father.
He will come again in glory
to judge the living and the dead
and his kingdom will have no end.

I believe in the Holy Spirit, the Lord, the giver of life,
who proceeds from the Father and the Son,
who with the Father and the Son is adored and glorified,
who has spoken through the prophets.

I believe in one, holy, catholic and apostolic Church.
I confess one Baptism for the forgiveness of sins
and I look forward to the resurrection of the dead
and the life of the world to come. Amen.

THE APOSTLES' CREED

Instead of the Niceno-Constantinopolitan Creed, the Apostles' Creed, may be used.

I believe in God,
the Father almighty
Creator of heaven and earth,
and in Jesus Christ, his only Son, our Lord,

At the words that follow, up to and including 'the Virgin Mary', all bow.

who was conceived by the Holy Spirit,
born of the Virgin Mary,
suffered under Pontius Pilate,
was crucified, died and was buried;
he descended into hell;
on the third day he rose again from the dead;
he ascended into heaven,
and is seated at the right hand of God the Father almighty;
from there he will come to judge the living and the dead.

I believe in the Holy Spirit,
the holy catholic Church,
the communion of saints,
the forgiveness of sins,
the resurrection of the body,
and life everlasting. Amen.

PRAYER OF THE FAITHFUL

Enlightened and moved by God's word, the assembly exercises its priestly function by interceding for all humanity.

Priest's Introduction

The Priest calls the assembly to prayer.

Intentions

As a rule the series of intentions is:

1 for the needs of the Church
2 for public authorities and the salvation of the whole world
3 for those burdened with any kind of difficulty
4 for the local community

Nevertheless, in particular celebrations such as Confirmation, Marriage, or a Funeral, the series of intentions may reflect more closely the particular occasion.

The Deacon, or a Reader, announces short intentions for prayer to the assembly.

After each intention there is a significant pause while the assembly prays, then the response is sung or said.

Example responses:

Deacon or Reader: We pray to the Lord.
All: **Lord, hear our prayer.**

or

Deacon or Reader: Let us pray to the Lord,
All: **Grant this, almighty God.**

or

Deacon or Reader: Let us pray to the Lord,
All: **Christ, hear us.** *or* **Christ, graciously hear us.**

or

Deacon or Reader: Let us pray to the Lord,
All: **Lord, have mercy.** *or* **Kyrie, eleison.**

After the final intention and response, there may be a period of silent prayer.

Priest's Prayer

Then the Priest says a concluding prayer to which all reply:

All: **Amen.**

ALL SIT

LITURGY OF THE EUCHARIST

Their eyes were opened and they recognised him in the breaking of bread.
(cf Luke 24:30–31)

At the Last Supper, Christ instituted the Sacrifice and Paschal meal that make the Sacrifice of the cross present in the Church. From the days of the Apostles the Church has celebrated that Sacrifice by carrying out what the Lord did and handed over to his disciples to do in his memory. Like him, the Church has taken bread and wine, given thanks to God over them, broken the bread, and shared the bread and cup of blessing as the Body and Blood of Christ (cf 1 Corinthians 10:16). *Celebrating the Mass n 174*

PREPARATION OF THE GIFTS

A hymn or song may be sung, or instrumental music played during the collection, the procession, and the presentation of the gifts. If there is no music, the Priest may speak the following words aloud and the people acclaim the response at the end of each prayer.

Priest: Blessed are you, Lord God of all creation,
for through your goodness we have received
the bread we offer you:
fruit of the earth and work of human hands,
it will become for us the bread of life.
People: **Blessed be God for ever.**

Priest: Blessed are you, Lord God of all creation,
for through your goodness we have received
the wine we offer you:
fruit of the vine and work of human hands,
it will become our spiritual drink.
People: **Blessed be God for ever.**

ALL STAND

The Priest completes additional personal preparatory rites, and the people rise as he says:

Priest: Pray, brethren (brothers and sisters),
that my sacrifice and yours
may be acceptable to God,
the almighty Father.

▷ *Music p 320*

People: **May the Lord accept the sacrifice at your hands**
for the praise and glory of his name,
for our good
and the good of all his holy Church.

PRAYER OVER THE OFFERINGS

▷ *Proper*

Then the Priest says the Prayer over the Offerings, at the end of which the people acclaim:

People: **Amen.**

EUCHARISTIC PRAYER

The Eucharistic Prayer, the centre and summit of the entire celebration, sums up what it means for the Church to celebrate the Eucharist. It is a memorial proclamation of praise and thanksgiving for God's work of salvation, a proclamation in which the Body and Blood of Christ are made present by the power of the Holy Spirit and the people are joined to Christ in offering his Sacrifice to the Father. The Eucharistic Prayer is proclaimed by the Priest celebrant in the name of Christ and on behalf of the whole assembly, which professes its faith and gives its assent through dialogue, acclamations, and the Amen. Since the Eucharistic Prayer is the summit of the Mass, it is appropriate for its solemn nature and importance to be enhanced by being sung.

Celebrating the Mass n 186

Eucharistic Prayers I to IV are the principal prayers and are for use throughout the liturgical year. Eucharistic Prayer IV has a fixed preface and so may only be used when a Mass has no preface of its own and on Sundays in Ordinary Time. Eucharistic Prayers I to IV and Eucharistic Prayers for Reconciliation I and II are printed in full, beginning on page 18.

PREFACE DIALOGUE

Priest: All:

The Lord be with you.
And with your spir - it.

Priest: All:

Lift up your hearts.
We lift them up to the Lord.

Priest: All:

Let us give thanks to the Lord our God.
It is right and just.

Priest: The Lord be with you.
People: **And with your spirit.**

Priest: Lift up your hearts.
People: **We lift them up to the Lord.**

Priest: Let us give thanks to the Lord our God.
People: **It is right and just.**

PREFACE

The Priest continues with the Preface.

SANCTUS

The Priest concludes the Preface with the people, singing or saying aloud:

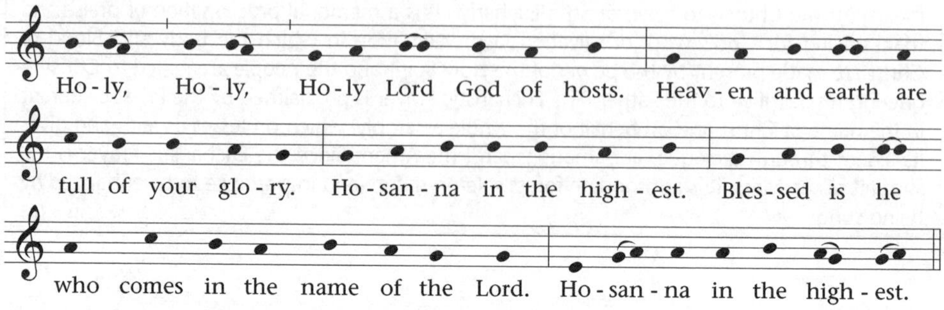
Ho - ly, Ho - ly, Ho - ly Lord God of hosts. Heav - en and earth are
full of your glo - ry. Ho - san - na in the high - est. Bles - sed is he
who comes in the name of the Lord. Ho - san - na in the high - est.

All: **Holy, Holy, Holy Lord God of hosts.**
Heaven and earth are full of your glory.
Hosanna in the highest.
Blessed is he who comes in the name of the Lord.
Hosanna in the highest.

or

San - ctus, San - ctus, San - ctus Dó - mi - nus De - us Sá - ba - oth. Ple - ni sunt cae - li
et ter - ra gló - ri - a tu - a. Ho - sán - na in ex - cél - sis. Be - ne - dí - ctus
qui ven - it in nó - mi - ne Dó - mi - ni. Ho - sán - na in ex - cél - sis.

ALL KNEEL

Texts for Eucharistic Prayers I to IV, Eucharistic Prayers for Reconciliation I and II and Eucharistic Prayers for use in Masses for Various Needs I to IV follow on page 18.

MEMORIAL ACCLAMATION

The Memorial Acclamation follows the words of Institution and the elevation of the host and chalice.

The Priest sings:

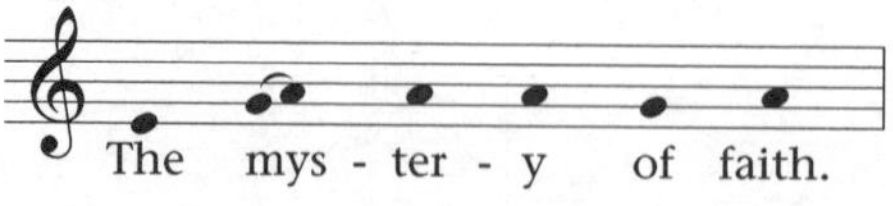
The mys - ter - y of faith.

And the people continue with one of the following acclamations.

Memorial Acclamation A

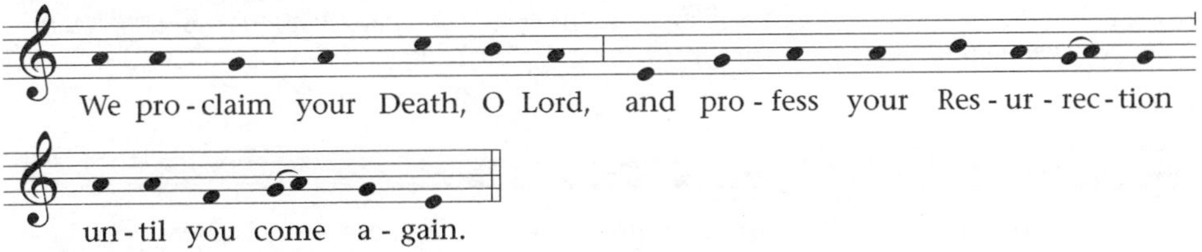
We pro - claim your Death, O Lord, and pro - fess your Res - ur - rec - tion
un - til you come a - gain.

Memorial Acclamation B

When we eat this Bread and drink this Cup, we pro - claim your
Death, O Lord, un - til you come a - gain.

Memorial Acclamation C

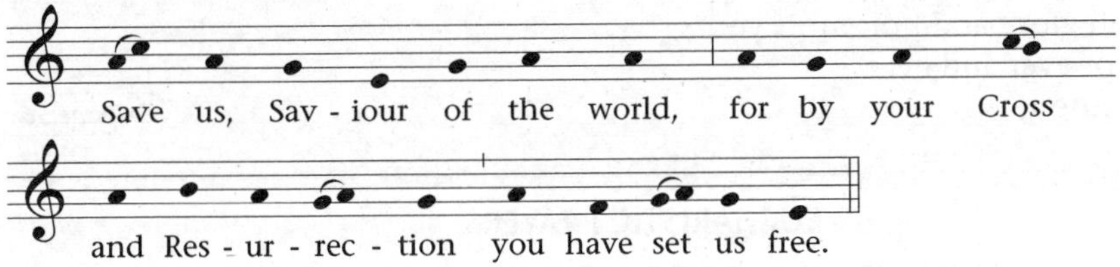
Save us, Sav - iour of the world, for by your Cross
and Res - ur - rec - tion you have set us free.

Priest: The mystery of faith.
People: **We proclaim your Death, O Lord,**
and profess your Resurrection
until you come again.

or

People: **When we eat this Bread and drink this Cup,**
we proclaim your Death, O Lord,
until you come again.

or

People: **Save us, Saviour of the world,**
for by your Cross and Resurrection
you have set us free.

DOXOLOGY AND GREAT AMEN

At the end of the Eucharistic Prayer, the Priest takes the chalice and paten with the host and, raising both, he alone sings (or says) the Doxology. The people acclaim 'Amen'.

Priest:

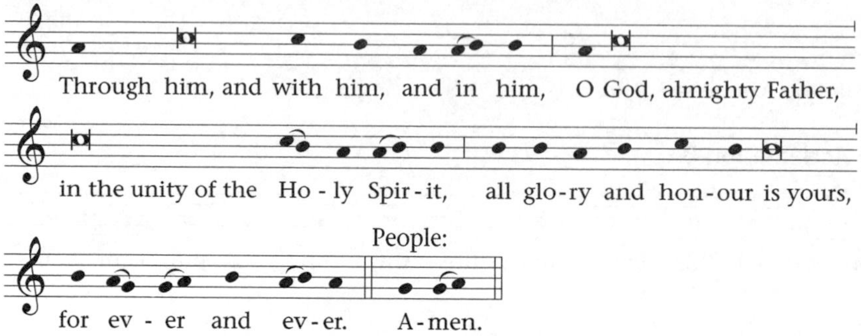
Through him, and with him, and in him, O God, almighty Father,
in the unity of the Ho - ly Spir - it, all glo - ry and hon - our is yours,
People:
for ev - er and ev - er. A - men.

Priest: Through him, and with him, and in him,
O God, almighty Father,
in the unity of the Holy Spirit,
all glory and honour is yours,
for ever and ever.

People: **Amen.**

▷ *page 56*

EUCHARISTIC PRAYERS

EUCHARISTIC PRAYER I

THE ROMAN CANON

On certain occasions, special forms of parts of the Eucharistic Prayer may be used.

Priest: To you, therefore, most merciful Father,
we make humble prayer and petition
through Jesus Christ, your Son, our Lord:
that you accept
and bless ✠ these gifts, these offerings,
these holy and unblemished sacrifices,
which we offer you firstly
for your holy catholic Church.
Be pleased to grant her peace,
to guard, unite and govern her
throughout the whole world,
together with your servant N. our Pope
and N. our Bishop,*
and all those who, holding to the truth,
hand on the catholic and apostolic faith.

* Mention may be made here of the Coadjutor Bishop, or Auxiliary Bishops

Commemoration of the Living

Remember, Lord, your servants N. and N.
and all gathered here,
whose faith and devotion are known to you.
For them, we offer you this sacrifice of praise
or they offer it for themselves
and all who are dear to them:
for the redemption of their souls,
in hope of health and well-being,
and paying their homage to you,
the eternal God, living and true.

Communicantes

In communion with those whose memory we venerate,
especially the glorious ever-Virgin Mary,
Mother of our God and Lord, Jesus Christ,
† and blessed Joseph, her Spouse,
your blessed Apostles and Martyrs,
Peter and Paul, Andrew,
(James, John,
Thomas, James, Philip,
Bartholomew, Matthew,
Simon and Jude;
Linus, Cletus, Clement, Sixtus,
Cornelius, Cyprian,
Lawrence, Chrysogonus,
John and Paul,
Cosmas and Damian)
and all your Saints;
we ask that through their merits and prayers,
in all things we may be defended
by your protecting help.
(Through Christ our Lord. Amen.)

Proper Forms of the *Communicantes*

On the Nativity of the Lord
and throughout the Octave
Celebrating the most sacred night (day)
on which blessed Mary
the immaculate Virgin
brought forth the Saviour for this world,
and in communion with those
whose memory we venerate,
especially the glorious ever-Virgin Mary,
Mother of our God and Lord, Jesus Christ, †

On the Epiphany of the Lord
Celebrating the most sacred day
on which your Only Begotten Son,
eternal with you in your glory,
appeared in a human body,
truly sharing our flesh,
and in communion with those whose
memory we venerate,
especially the glorious ever-Virgin Mary,
Mother of our God and Lord, Jesus Christ, †

On the Thursday of Holy Week at the Evening Mass of the Lord's Supper
Celebrating the most sacred day
on which our Lord Jesus Christ
was handed over for our sake,
and in communion with those
whose memory we venerate,
especially the glorious ever-Virgin Mary,
Mother of our God and Lord, Jesus Christ,

From the Mass of the Easter Vigil until the Second Sunday of Easter
Celebrating the most sacred night (day)
of the Resurrection of our Lord Jesus Christ
in the flesh,
and in communion with those
whose memory we venerate,
especially the glorious ever-Virgin Mary,
Mother of our God and Lord, Jesus Christ, †

On the Ascension of the Lord
Celebrating the most sacred day
on which your Only Begotten Son,
our Lord,
placed at the right hand of your glory
our weak human nature,
which he had united to himself,
and in communion with those
whose memory we venerate,
especially the glorious ever-Virgin Mary,
Mother of our God and Lord, Jesus Christ, †

On Pentecost Sunday
Celebrating the most sacred day of
Pentecost,
on which the Holy Spirit
appeared to the Apostles in tongues of fire,
and in communion with those
whose memory we venerate,
especially the glorious ever-Virgin Mary,
Mother of our God and Lord, Jesus Christ, †

Hanc Igitur

Therefore, Lord, we pray:
graciously accept this oblation of our service,
that of your whole family;
order our days in your peace,
and command that we be delivered from eternal damnation
and counted among the flock of those you have chosen.
(Through Christ our Lord. Amen.)

Proper Forms of the Hanc Igitur

On Maundy Thursday at the Evening Mass of the Lord's Supper
Therefore, Lord, we pray:
graciously accept this oblation of our service,
that of your whole family,
which we make to you
as we observe the day
on which our Lord Jesus Christ
handed on the mysteries
of his Body and Blood
for his disciples to celebrate;
order our days in your peace,
and command that we be delivered
from eternal damnation
and counted among the flock
of those you have chosen.
(Through Christ our Lord. Amen.)

From the Mass of the Easter Vigil until the Second Sunday of Easter
Therefore, Lord, we pray:
graciously accept this oblation of our service,
that of your whole family,
which we make to you
also for those to whom
you have been pleased to give
the new birth of water and the Holy Spirit,
granting them forgiveness of all their sins;
order our days in your peace,
and command that we be delivered
from eternal damnation
and counted among the flock
of those you have chosen.
(Through Christ our Lord. Amen.)

Be pleased, O God, we pray,
to bless, acknowledge,
and approve this offering in every respect;
make it spiritual and acceptable,
so that it may become for us
the Body and Blood of your most beloved Son,
our Lord Jesus Christ.

* On the day before he was to suffer,
† he took bread in his holy and venerable hands,
and with eyes raised to heaven
to you, O God, his almighty Father,
giving you thanks, he said the blessing,
broke the bread
and gave it to his disciples, saying:

TAKE THIS, ALL OF YOU, AND EAT OF IT,
FOR THIS IS MY BODY,
WHICH WILL BE GIVEN UP FOR YOU.

In a similar way, when supper was ended,
he took this precious chalice
in his holy and venerable hands,
and once more giving you thanks, he said the blessing
and gave the chalice to his disciples, saying:

TAKE THIS, ALL OF YOU, AND DRINK FROM IT,
FOR THIS IS THE CHALICE OF MY BLOOD,
THE BLOOD OF THE NEW AND ETERNAL COVENANT,
WHICH WILL BE POURED OUT FOR YOU AND FOR MANY
FOR THE FORGIVENESS OF SINS.

DO THIS IN MEMORY OF ME.

Memorial Acclamation

The Priest sings:

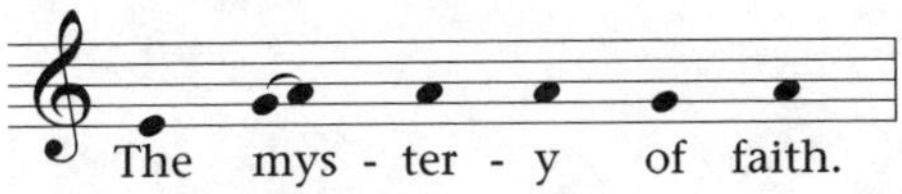

And the people continue with one of the following acclamations (overleaf):

* On the Maundy Thursday at the Evening Mass of the Lord's Supper, this part of the prayer begins:

On the day before he was to suffer,
for our salvation and the salvation of all,
that is today, †

Memorial Acclamation A

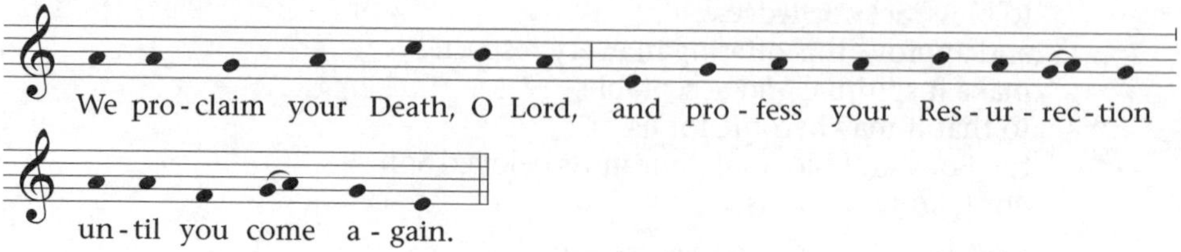
We pro-claim your Death, O Lord, and pro - fess your Res - ur - rec-tion
un-til you come a - gain.

Memorial Acclamation B

When we eat this Bread and drink this Cup, we pro-claim your
Death, O Lord, un - til you come a - gain.

Memorial Acclamation C

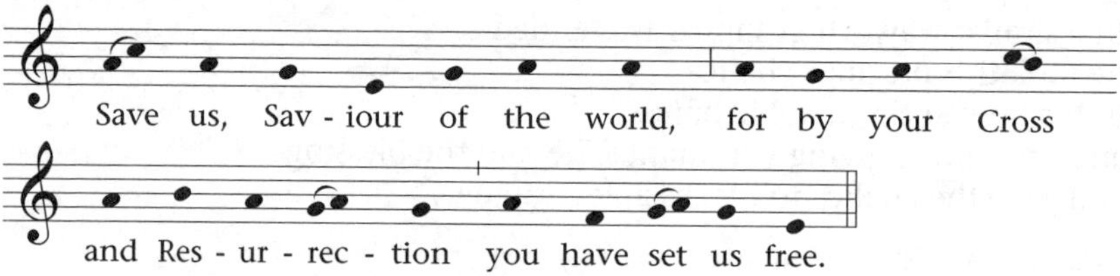
Save us, Sav - iour of the world, for by your Cross
and Res - ur - rec - tion you have set us free.

Priest: Therefore, O Lord,
as we celebrate the memorial of the blessed Passion,
the Resurrection from the dead,
and the glorious Ascension into heaven
of Christ, your Son, our Lord,
we, your servants and your holy people,
offer to your glorious majesty
from the gifts that you have given us,
this pure victim,
this holy victim,
this spotless victim,
the holy Bread of eternal life
and the Chalice of everlasting salvation.

Be pleased to look upon these offerings
with a serene and kindly countenance,
and to accept them,
as once you were pleased to accept
the gifts of your servant Abel the just,
the sacrifice of Abraham, our father in faith,
and the offering of your high priest Melchizedek,
a holy sacrifice, a spotless victim.

In humble prayer we ask you, almighty God:
command that these gifts be borne
by the hands of your holy Angel
to your altar on high
in the sight of your divine majesty,
so that all of us, who through this participation at the altar
receive the most holy Body and Blood of your Son,
may be filled with every grace and heavenly blessing.
(Through Christ our Lord. Amen.)

Commemoration of the Dead

Remember also, Lord, your servants N. and N.,
who have gone before us with the sign of faith
and rest in the sleep of peace.
Grant them, O Lord, we pray,
and all who sleep in Christ,
a place of refreshment, light and peace.
(Through Christ our Lord. Amen.)

To us, also, your servants, who, though sinners,
hope in your abundant mercies,
graciously grant some share
and fellowship with your holy Apostles and Martyrs:
with John the Baptist, Stephen,
Matthias, Barnabas,
(Ignatius, Alexander,
Marcellinus, Peter,
Felicity, Perpetua,
Agatha, Lucy,
Agnes, Cecilia, Anastasia)
and all your Saints;
admit us, we beseech you,
into their company,
not weighing our merits,
but granting us your pardon,
through Christ our Lord.

Through whom
you continue to make all these good things, O Lord;
you sanctify them, fill them with life,
bless them, and bestow them upon us.

Doxology and Great Amen

At the end of the Eucharistic Prayer, the Priest takes the chalice and paten with the host and, raising both, he alone sings (or says) the Doxology. The people acclaim 'Amen'.

Priest: Through him, and with him, and in him,
O God, almighty Father,
in the unity of the Holy Spirit,
all glory and honour is yours,
for ever and ever.

People: **Amen.**

Priest: People:

...for ev - er and ev - er.
A - men.

▷ page 56

EUCHARISTIC PRAYER II

This Eucharistic Prayer has its own Preface, but it may also be used with other Prefaces, especially those that present an overall view of the mystery of salvation.

On certain occasions, special forms of parts of the Eucharistic Prayer may be used.

Preface Dialogue

Priest: All:

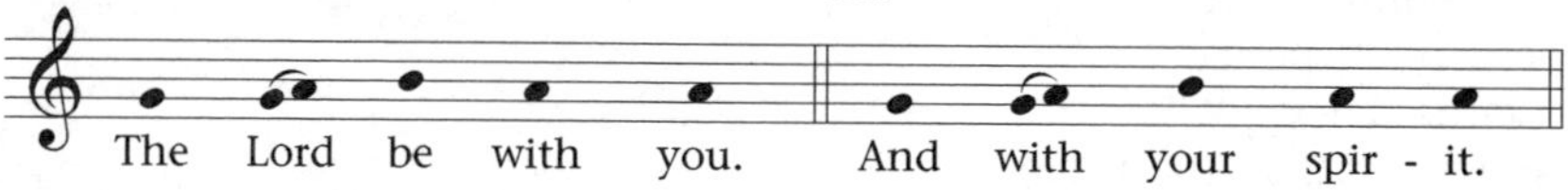
The Lord be with you.
And with your spir - it.

Priest: All:

Lift up your hearts.
We lift them up to the Lord.

Priest: All:

Let us give thanks to the Lord our God.
It is right and just.

Preface

Priest: It is truly right and just, our duty and our salvation,
always and everywhere to give you thanks, Father most holy,
through your beloved Son, Jesus Christ,
your Word through whom you made all things,
whom you sent as our Saviour and Redeemer,
incarnate by the Holy Spirit and born of the Virgin.

Fulfilling your will and gaining for you a holy people,
he stretched out his hands as he endured his Passion,
so as to break the bonds of death and manifest the resurrection.

And so, with the Angels and all the Saints
we declare your glory,
as with one voice we acclaim:

Sanctus

All:

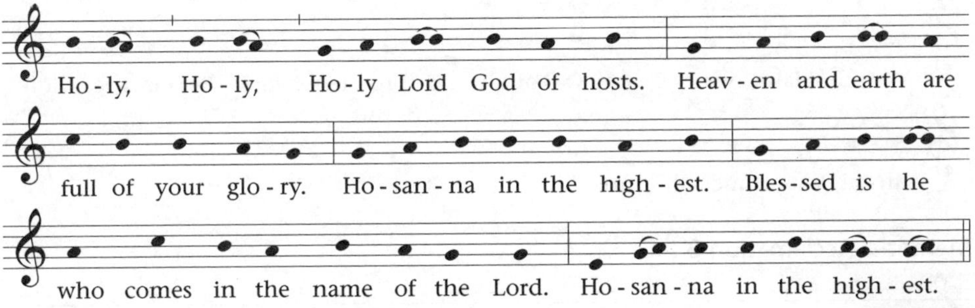
Ho - ly, Ho - ly, Ho - ly Lord God of hosts. Heav - en and earth are
full of your glo - ry. Ho - san - na in the high - est. Bles - sed is he
who comes in the name of the Lord. Ho - san - na in the high - est.

ALL KNEEL

Priest: You are indeed Holy, O Lord,
the fount of all holiness.
Make holy, therefore, these gifts, we pray,
by sending down your Spirit upon them like the dewfall,
so that they may become for us
the Body and ✠ Blood of our Lord Jesus Christ.

At the time he was betrayed
and entered willingly into his Passion,
he took bread and, giving thanks, broke it,
and gave it to his disciples, saying:

TAKE THIS, ALL OF YOU, AND EAT OF IT,
FOR THIS IS MY BODY,
WHICH WILL BE GIVEN UP FOR YOU.

In a similar way, when supper was ended,
he took the chalice
and, once more giving thanks,
he gave it to his disciples, saying:

TAKE THIS, ALL OF YOU, AND DRINK FROM IT,
FOR THIS IS THE CHALICE OF MY BLOOD,
THE BLOOD OF THE NEW AND ETERNAL COVENANT,
WHICH WILL BE POURED OUT FOR YOU AND FOR MANY
FOR THE FORGIVENESS OF SINS.

DO THIS IN MEMORY OF ME.

Memorial Acclamation

The Priest sings:

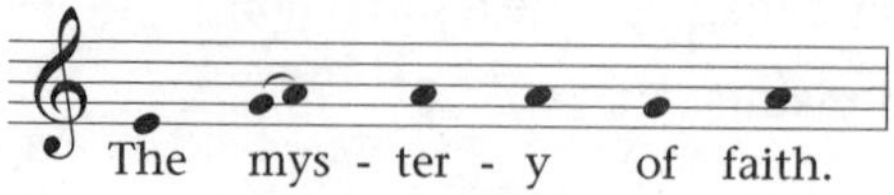
The mys - ter - y of faith.

And the people continue with one of the following acclamations:

Memorial Acclamation A

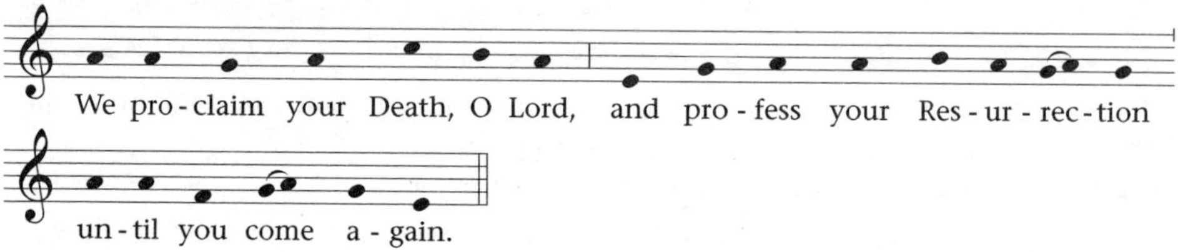
We pro-claim your Death, O Lord, and pro - fess your Res - ur - rec-tion
un-til you come a - gain.

Memorial Acclamation B

When we eat this Bread and drink this Cup, we pro-claim your
Death, O Lord, un - til you come a - gain.

Memorial Acclamation C

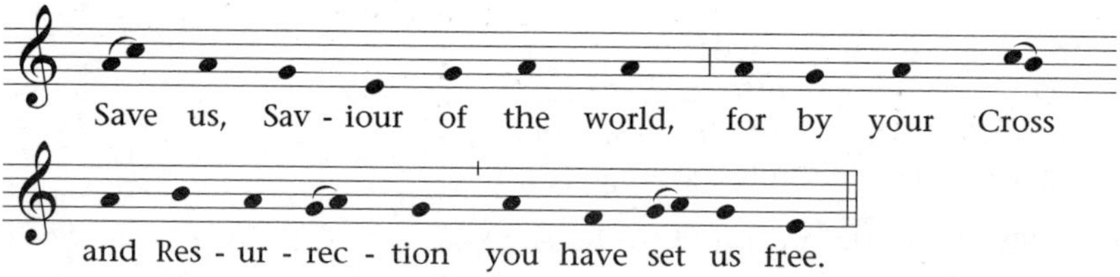
Save us, Sav - iour of the world, for by your Cross
and Res - ur - rec - tion you have set us free.

Priest: Therefore, as we celebrate
the memorial of his Death and Resurrection,
we offer you, Lord,
the Bread of life and the Chalice of salvation,
giving thanks that you have held us worthy
to be in your presence and minister to you.

Humbly we pray
that, partaking of the Body and Blood of Christ,
we may be gathered into one by the Holy Spirit.

Remember, Lord, your Church,
spread throughout the world,
and bring her to the fullness of charity,
together with N. our Pope and N. our Bishop *
and all the clergy.

In Masses for the Dead, the following may be added:

Remember your servant N.,
whom you have called (today)
from this world to yourself.
Grant that he (she) who was united with your Son in a death like his,
may also be one with him in his Resurrection.

Remember also our brothers and sisters
who have fallen asleep in the hope of the resurrection,
and all who have died in your mercy:
welcome them into the light of your face.
Have mercy on us all, we pray,
that with the Blessed Virgin Mary, Mother of God,
with blessed Joseph, her Spouse,
with the blessed Apostles,
and all the Saints who have pleased you throughout the ages,
we may merit to be coheirs to eternal life,
and may praise and glorify you
through your Son, Jesus Christ.

Doxology and Great Amen

At the end of the Eucharistic Prayer, the Priest takes the chalice and paten with the host and, raising both, he alone sings (or says) the Doxology. The people acclaim 'Amen'.

Priest: Through him, and with him, and in him,
O God, almighty Father,
in the unity of the Holy Spirit,
all glory and honour is yours,
for ever and ever.

People: **Amen.**

Priest: People:

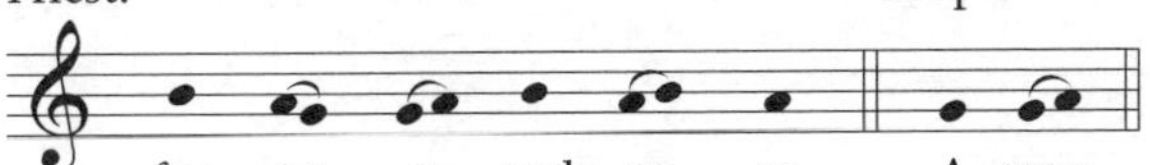

▷ page 56

---

* Mention may be made here of the Coadjutor Bishop, or Auxiliary Bishops

EUCHARISTIC PRAYER III

On certain occasions, special forms of parts of the Eucharistic Prayer may be used.

Priest: You are indeed Holy, O Lord,
and all you have created
rightly gives you praise,
for through your Son our Lord Jesus Christ,
by the power and working of the Holy Spirit,
you give life to all things and make them holy,
and you never cease to gather a people to yourself,
so that from the rising of the sun to its setting
a pure sacrifice may be offered to your name.

Therefore, O Lord, we humbly implore you:
by the same Spirit graciously make holy
these gifts we have brought to you for consecration,
that they may become the Body and ✠ Blood
of your Son our Lord Jesus Christ,
at whose command we celebrate these mysteries.

For on the night he was betrayed
he himself took bread,
and, giving you thanks, he said the blessing,
broke the bread and gave it to his disciples, saying:

TAKE THIS, ALL OF YOU, AND EAT OF IT,
FOR THIS IS MY BODY,
WHICH WILL BE GIVEN UP FOR YOU.

In a similar way, when supper was ended,
he took the chalice,
and, giving you thanks, he said the blessing,
and gave the chalice to his disciples, saying:

TAKE THIS, ALL OF YOU, AND DRINK FROM IT,
FOR THIS IS THE CHALICE OF MY BLOOD,
THE BLOOD OF THE NEW AND ETERNAL COVENANT,
WHICH WILL BE POURED OUT FOR YOU AND FOR MANY
FOR THE FORGIVENESS OF SINS.

DO THIS IN MEMORY OF ME.

Memorial Acclamation

The Priest sings:

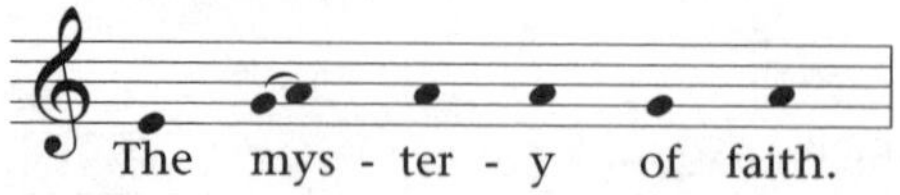

And the people continue with one of the following acclamations:

Memorial Acclamation A

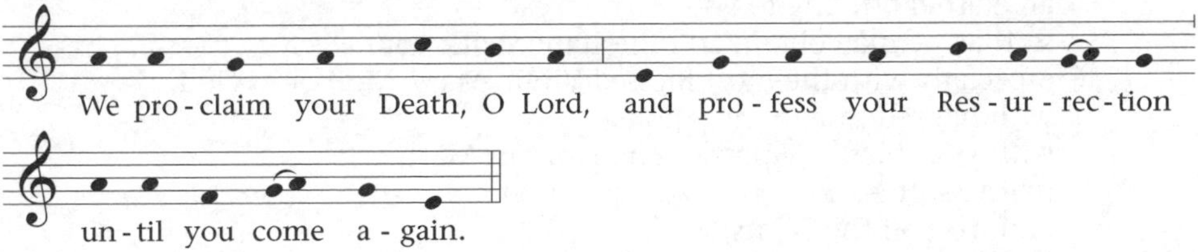
We pro - claim your Death, O Lord, and pro - fess your Res - ur - rec - tion
un - til you come a - gain.

Memorial Acclamation B

When we eat this Bread and drink this Cup, we pro - claim your
Death, O Lord, un - til you come a - gain.

Memorial Acclamation C

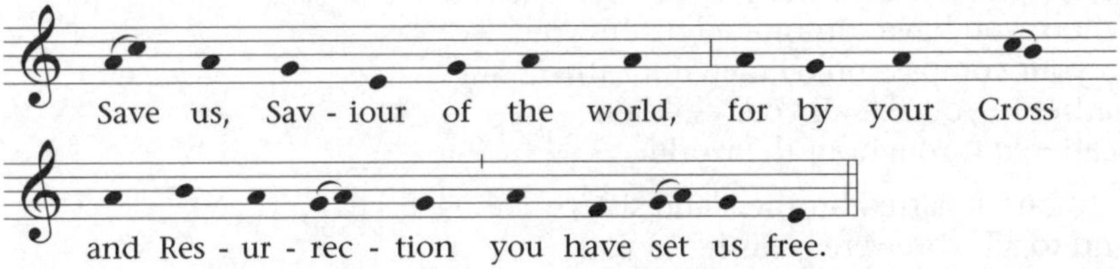
Save us, Sav - iour of the world, for by your Cross
and Res - ur - rec - tion you have set us free.

Priest: Therefore, O Lord, as we celebrate the memorial
of the saving Passion of your Son,
his wondrous Resurrection
and Ascension into heaven,
and as we look forward to his second coming,
we offer you in thanksgiving
this holy and living sacrifice.

Look, we pray, upon the oblation of your Church
and, recognizing the sacrificial Victim by whose death
you willed to reconcile us to yourself,
grant that we, who are nourished
by the Body and Blood of your Son
and filled with his Holy Spirit,
may become one body, one spirit in Christ.

May he make of us
an eternal offering to you,
so that we may obtain an inheritance with your elect,
especially with the most Blessed Virgin Mary, Mother of God,
with blessed Joseph, her Spouse,
with your blessed Apostles and glorious Martyrs
(with Saint N.: *the Saint of the day or Patron Saint*)
and with all the Saints,
on whose constant intercession in your presence
we rely for unfailing help.

May this Sacrifice of our reconciliation,
we pray, O Lord,
advance the peace and salvation of all the world.
Be pleased to confirm in faith and charity
your pilgrim Church on earth,
with your servant N. our Pope and N. our Bishop,*
the Order of Bishops, all the clergy,
and the entire people you have gained for your own.

Listen graciously to the prayers of this family,
whom you have summoned before you:
in your compassion, O merciful Father,
gather to yourself all your children
scattered throughout the world.

† To our departed brothers and sisters
and to all who were pleasing to you
at their passing from this life,
give kind admittance to your kingdom.
There we hope to enjoy for ever the fullness of your glory
through Christ our Lord,
through whom you bestow on the world all that is good. †

In Masses for the Dead, the following may be said:

† Remember your servant N.
whom you have called (today)
from this world to yourself.
Grant that he (she) who was united with your Son in a death like his,
may also be one with him in his Resurrection,
when from the earth
he will raise up in the flesh those who have died,
and transform our lowly body
after the pattern of his own glorious body.
To our departed brothers and sisters, too,
and to all who were pleasing to you
at their passing from this life,
give kind admittance to your kingdom.

---

* Mention may be made here of the Coadjutor Bishop, or Auxiliary Bishops

There we hope to enjoy for ever the fullness of your glory,
when you will wipe away every tear from our eyes.
For seeing you, our God, as you are,
we shall be like you for all the ages
and praise you without end,
through Christ our Lord,
through whom you bestow on the world all that is good. †

Doxology and Great Amen

At the end of the Eucharistic Prayer, the Priest takes the chalice and paten with the host and, raising both, he alone sings (or says) the Doxology. The people acclaim 'Amen'.

Priest: Through him, and with him, and in him,
O God, almighty Father,
in the unity of the Holy Spirit,
all glory and honour is yours,
for ever and ever.

People: **Amen.**

Priest: People:

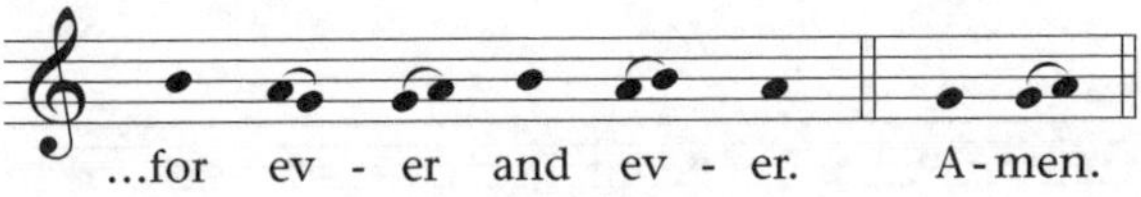
...for ev - er and ev - er.
A-men.

▷ page 56

EUCHARISTIC PRAYER IV

This Eucharistic Prayer has its own Preface which may not be replaced by another, because of the structure of the Prayer itself, which presents a summary of the history of salvation.
On certain occasions, special forms of parts of the Eucharistic Prayer may be used.

Preface Dialogue

Priest: All:

The Lord be with you.
And with your spir - it.

Priest: All:

Lift up your hearts.
We lift them up to the Lord.

Priest: All:

Let us give thanks to the Lord our God.
It is right and just.

Preface

Priest: It is truly right to give you thanks,
truly just to give you glory, Father most holy,
for you are the one God living and true,
existing before all ages and abiding for all eternity,
dwelling in unapproachable light;
yet you, who alone are good, the source of life,
have made all that is,
so that you might fill your creatures with blessings
and bring joy to many of them by the glory of your light.

And so, in your presence are countless hosts of Angels,
who serve you day and night
and, gazing upon the glory of your face,
glorify you without ceasing.

With them we, too, confess your name in exultation,
giving voice to every creature under heaven,
as we acclaim:

Sanctus

All:

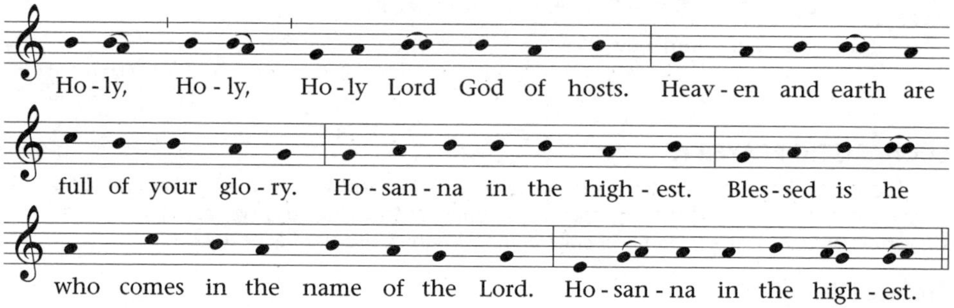
Ho - ly, Ho - ly, Ho - ly Lord God of hosts. Heav - en and earth are
full of your glo - ry. Ho - san - na in the high - est. Bles - sed is he
who comes in the name of the Lord. Ho - san - na in the high - est.

ALL KNEEL

Priest: We give you praise, Father most holy,
for you are great
and you have fashioned all your works
in wisdom and in love.
You formed man in your own image
and entrusted the whole world to his care,
so that in serving you alone, the Creator,
he might have dominion over all creatures.
And when through disobedience he had lost your friendship,
you did not abandon him to the domain of death.
For you came in mercy to the aid of all,
so that those who seek might find you.

Time and again you offered them covenants
and through the prophets
taught them to look forward to salvation.

And you so loved the world, Father most holy,
that in the fullness of time
you sent your Only Begotten Son to be our Saviour.
Made incarnate by the Holy Spirit
and born of the Virgin Mary,
he shared our human nature
in all things but sin.
To the poor he proclaimed the good news of salvation,
to prisoners, freedom,
and to the sorrowful of heart, joy.
To accomplish your plan,
he gave himself up to death,
and, rising from the dead,
he destroyed death and restored life.

And that we might live no longer for ourselves
but for him who died and rose again for us,
he sent the Holy Spirit from you, Father,
as the first fruits for those who believe,
so that, bringing to perfection his work in the world,
he might sanctify creation to the full.

Therefore, O Lord, we pray:
may this same Holy Spirit
graciously sanctify these offerings,
that they may become
the Body and ✠ Blood of our Lord Jesus Christ
for the celebration of this great mystery,
which he himself left us
as an eternal covenant.

For when the hour had come
for him to be glorified by you, Father most holy,
having loved his own who were in the world,
he loved them to the end:
and while they were at supper,
he took bread, blessed and broke it,
and gave it to his disciples, saying:

TAKE THIS, ALL OF YOU, AND EAT OF IT,
FOR THIS IS MY BODY,
WHICH WILL BE GIVEN UP FOR YOU.

In a similar way,
taking the chalice filled with the fruit of the vine,
he gave thanks,
and gave the chalice to his disciples, saying:

TAKE THIS, ALL OF YOU, AND DRINK FROM IT,
FOR THIS IS THE CHALICE OF MY BLOOD,
THE BLOOD OF THE NEW AND ETERNAL COVENANT,
WHICH WILL BE POURED OUT FOR YOU AND FOR MANY
FOR THE FORGIVENESS OF SINS.

DO THIS IN MEMORY OF ME.

Memorial Acclamation

The Priest sings:

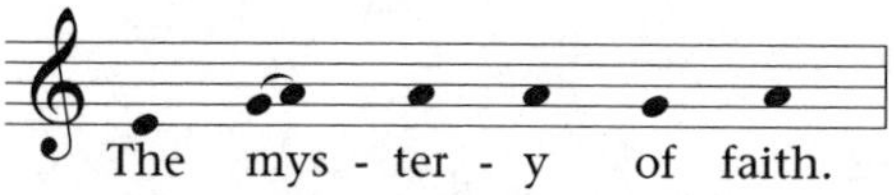
The mys - ter - y of faith.

And the people continue with one of the following acclamations:

Memorial Acclamation A

We pro - claim your Death, O Lord, and pro - fess your Res - ur - rec - tion
un - til you come a - gain.

Memorial Acclamation B

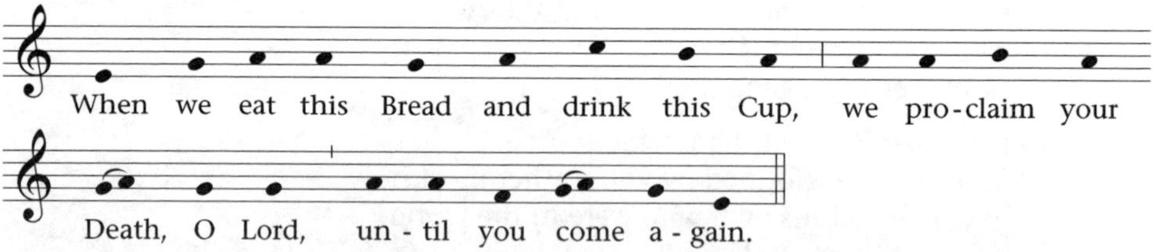
When we eat this Bread and drink this Cup, we pro - claim your
Death, O Lord, un - til you come a - gain.

Memorial Acclamation C

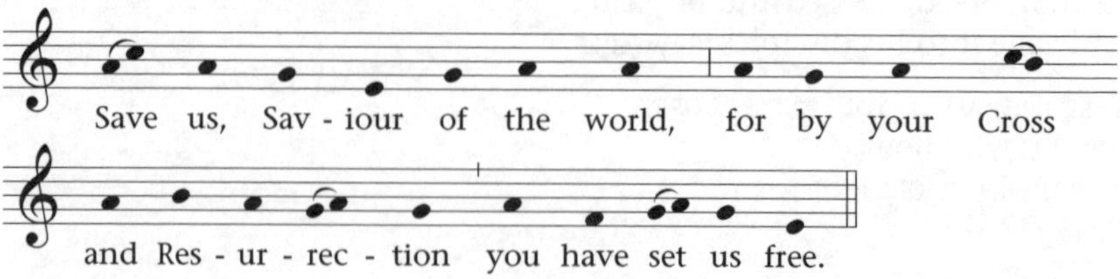
Save us, Sav - iour of the world, for by your Cross
and Res - ur - rec - tion you have set us free.

Priest: Therefore, O Lord,
as we now celebrate the memorial of our redemption,
we remember Christ's Death
and his descent to the realm of the dead,
we proclaim his Resurrection
and his Ascension to your right hand,
and as we await his coming in glory,
we offer you his Body and Blood,
the sacrifice acceptable to you
which brings salvation to the whole world.

Look, O Lord, upon the Sacrifice
which you yourself have provided for your Church,
and grant in your loving kindness
to all who partake of this one Bread and one Chalice
that, gathered into one body by the Holy Spirit,
they may truly become a living sacrifice in Christ
to the praise of your glory.

Therefore, Lord, remember now
all for whom we offer this sacrifice:
especially your servant N. our Pope,
N. our Bishop,* and the whole Order of Bishops,
all the clergy,
those who take part in this offering,
those gathered here before you,
your entire people,
and all who seek you with a sincere heart.

Remember also
those who have died in the peace of your Christ
and all the dead,
whose faith you alone have known.

To all of us, your children,
grant, O merciful Father,
that we may enter into a heavenly inheritance
with the Blessed Virgin Mary, Mother of God,
with blessed Joseph, her Spouse,
and with your Apostles and Saints in your kingdom.
There, with the whole of creation,
freed from the corruption of sin and death,
may we glorify you through Christ our Lord,
through whom you bestow on the world all that is good.

* Mention may be made here of the Coadjutor Bishop, or Auxiliary Bishops

Doxology and Great Amen

At the end of the Eucharistic Prayer, the Priest takes the chalice and paten with the host and, raising both, he alone sings (or says) the Doxology. The people acclaim 'Amen'.

Priest: Through him, and with him, and in him,
O God, almighty Father,
in the unity of the Holy Spirit,
all glory and honour is yours,
for ever and ever.

People: **Amen.**

Priest: People:

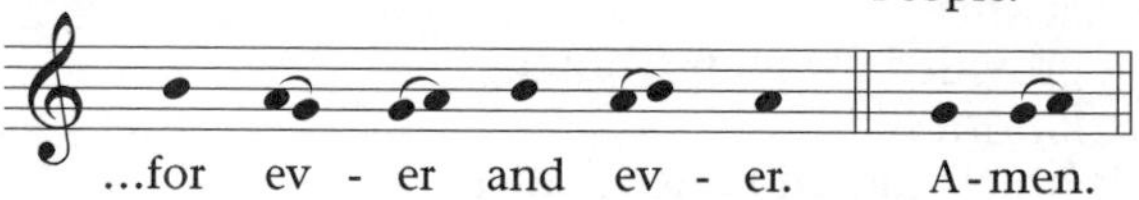

▷ page 56

EUCHARISTIC PRAYER FOR RECONCILIATION I

The Eucharistic Prayers for Reconciliation may be used in Masses in which the mystery of reconciliation is conveyed to the faithful in a special way, including Masses during Lent.

Although these Eucharistic Prayers have been provided with a proper Preface, they may also be used with other Prefaces that refer to penance and conversion, as, for example, the Prefaces of Lent.

Priest: The Lord be with you.
People: **And with your spirit.**

▷ Music p 15

Priest: Lift up your hearts.
People: **We lift them up to the Lord.**

Priest: Let us give thanks to the Lord our God.
People: **It is right and just.**

Priest: It is truly right and just
that we should always give you thanks,
Lord, holy Father, almighty and eternal God.

For you do not cease to spur us on
to possess a more abundant life
and, being rich in mercy,
you constantly offer pardon
and call on sinners
to trust in your forgiveness alone.

Never did you turn away from us,
and, though time and again we have broken your covenant,
you have bound the human family to yourself
through Jesus your Son, our Redeemer,
with a new bond of love so tight
that it can never be undone.

Even now you set before your people
a time of grace and reconciliation,
and, as they turn back to you in spirit,
you grant them hope in Christ Jesus
and a desire to be of service to all,
while they entrust themselves
more fully to the Holy Spirit.

And so, filled with wonder,
we extol the power of your love,
and, proclaiming our joy
at the salvation that comes from you,
we join in the heavenly hymn of countless hosts,
as without end we acclaim:

All: **Holy, Holy, Holy Lord God of hosts.**
Heaven and earth are full of your glory.
Hosanna in the highest.
Blessed is he who comes in the name of the Lord.
Hosanna in the highest.

▷ Music p 16

Priest: You are indeed Holy, O Lord,
and from the world's beginning
are ceaselessly at work,
so that the human race may become holy,
just as you yourself are holy.

ALL KNEEL

Look, we pray, upon your people's offerings
and pour out on them the power of your Spirit,
that they may become the Body and ✠ Blood
of your beloved Son, Jesus Christ,
in whom we, too, are your sons and daughters.

Indeed, though we once were lost
and could not approach you,
you loved us with the greatest love:
for your Son, who alone is just,
handed himself over to death,
and did not disdain to be nailed for our sake
to the wood of the Cross.

But before his arms were outstretched between heaven and earth,
to become the lasting sign of your covenant,
he desired to celebrate the Passover with his disciples.

As he ate with them,
he took bread
and, giving you thanks, he said the blessing,
broke the bread and gave it to them, saying:

TAKE THIS, ALL OF YOU, AND EAT OF IT,
FOR THIS IS MY BODY,
WHICH WILL BE GIVEN UP FOR YOU.

In a similar way, when supper was ended,
knowing that he was about to reconcile all things in himself
through his Blood to be shed on the Cross,
he took the chalice, filled with the fruit of the vine,
and once more giving you thanks,
handed the chalice to his disciples, saying:

TAKE THIS, ALL OF YOU, AND DRINK FROM IT,
FOR THIS IS THE CHALICE OF MY BLOOD,
THE BLOOD OF THE NEW AND ETERNAL COVENANT,
WHICH WILL BE POURED OUT FOR YOU AND FOR MANY
FOR THE FORGIVENESS OF SINS.

DO THIS IN MEMORY OF ME.

Priest: The mystery of faith. ▷ *Music p 17*
People: **We proclaim your Death, O Lord,**
and profess your Resurrection
until you come again.

or

People: **When we eat this Bread and drink this Cup,**
we proclaim your Death, O Lord,
until you come again.

or

People: **Save us, Saviour of the world,**
for by your Cross and Resurrection
you have set us free.

Priest: Therefore, as we celebrate

the memorial of your Son Jesus Christ,
who is our Passover and our surest peace,
we celebrate his Death and Resurrection from the dead,
and looking forward to his blessed Coming,
we offer you, who are our faithful and merciful God,
this sacrificial Victim
who reconciles to you the human race.

Look kindly, most compassionate Father,
on those you unite to yourself
by the Sacrifice of your Son,
and grant that, by the power of the Holy Spirit,
as they partake of this one Bread and one Chalice,
they may be gathered into one Body in Christ,
who heals every division.

Be pleased to keep us always
in communion of mind and heart,
together with N. our Pope and N. our Bishop.*
Help us to work together
for the coming of your Kingdom,
until the hour when we stand before you,
Saints among the Saints in the halls of heaven,
with the Blessed Virgin Mary, Mother of God,
the blessed Apostles and all the Saints,
and with our deceased brothers and sisters,
whom we humbly commend to your mercy.

Then, freed at last from the wound of corruption
and made fully into a new creation,
we shall sing to you with gladness
the thanksgiving of Christ,
who lives for all eternity.

Priest: Through him, and with him, and in him,
O God, almighty Father,
in the unity of the Holy Spirit,
all glory and honour is yours,
for ever and ever.

▷ Music p 18

People: **Amen.**

▷ page 56

EUCHARISTIC PRAYER FOR RECONCILIATION II

The Eucharistic Prayers for Reconciliation may be used in Masses in which the mystery of reconciliation is conveyed to the faithful in a special way, including Masses during Lent.

Although these Eucharistic Prayers have been provided with a proper Preface, they may also be used with other Prefaces that refer to penance and conversion, as, for example, the Prefaces of Lent.

Preface

Priest: The Lord be with you.
People: **And with your spirit.**

▷ Music p 15

Priest: Lift up your hearts.
People: **We lift them up to the Lord.**

Priest: Let us give thanks to the Lord our God.
People: **It is right and just.**

Priest: It is truly right and just
that we should give you thanks and praise,
O God, almighty Father,

* Mention may be made here of the Coadjutor Bishop, or Auxiliary Bishops

for all you do in this world,
through our Lord Jesus Christ.

For though the human race
is divided by dissension and discord,
yet we know that by testing us
you change our hearts
to prepare them for reconciliation.

Even more, by your Spirit you move human hearts
that enemies may speak to each other again,
adversaries may join hands,
and peoples seek to meet together.

By the working of your power
it comes about, O Lord,
that hatred is overcome by love,
revenge gives way to forgiveness,
and discord is changed to mutual respect.

Therefore, as we give you ceaseless thanks
with the choirs of heaven,
we cry out to your majesty on earth,
and without end we acclaim:

All: **Holy, Holy, Holy Lord God of hosts.**
Heaven and earth are full of your glory.
Hosanna in the highest.
Blessed is he who comes in the name of the Lord.
Hosanna in the highest.

▷ *Music p 16*

ALL KNEEL

Priest: You, therefore, almighty Father,
we bless through Jesus Christ your Son,
who comes in your name.
He himself is the Word that brings salvation,
the hand you extend to sinners,
the way by which your peace is offered to us.
When we ourselves had turned away from you
on account of our sins,
you brought us back to be reconciled, O Lord,
so that, converted at last to you,
we might love one another
through your Son,
whom for our sake you handed over to death.

And now, celebrating the reconciliation
Christ has brought us,
we entreat you:
sanctify these gifts by the outpouring of your Spirit,

that they may become the Body and ✠ Blood of your Son,
whose command we fulfil
when we celebrate these mysteries.

For when about to give his life to set us free,
as he reclined at supper,
he himself took bread into his hands,
and, giving you thanks, he said the blessing,
broke the bread and gave it to his disciples, saying:

TAKE THIS, ALL OF YOU, AND EAT OF IT,
FOR THIS IS MY BODY,
WHICH WILL BE GIVEN UP FOR YOU.

In a similar way, on that same evening,
he took the chalice of blessing in his hands,
confessing your mercy,
and gave the chalice to his disciples, saying:

TAKE THIS, ALL OF YOU, AND DRINK FROM IT,
FOR THIS IS THE CHALICE OF MY BLOOD,
THE BLOOD OF THE NEW AND ETERNAL COVENANT,
WHICH WILL BE POURED OUT FOR YOU AND FOR MANY
FOR THE FORGIVENESS OF SINS.

DO THIS IN MEMORY OF ME.

Priest: The mystery of faith. ▷ *Music p 17*

People: **We proclaim your Death, O Lord,**
and profess your Resurrection
until you come again.

or

People: **When we eat this Bread and drink this Cup,**
we proclaim your Death, O Lord,
until you come again.

or

People: **Save us, Saviour of the world,**
for by your Cross and Resurrection
you have set us free.

Priest: Celebrating, therefore, the memorial

of the Death and Resurrection of your Son,
who left us this pledge of his love,
we offer you what you have bestowed on us,
the Sacrifice of perfect reconciliation.

Holy Father, we humbly beseech you
to accept us also, together with your Son,
and in this saving banquet
graciously to endow us with his very Spirit,
who takes away everything
that estranges us from one another.

May he make your Church a sign of unity
and an instrument of your peace among all people
and may he keep us in communion
with N. our Pope and N. our Bishop *
and all the Bishops
and your entire people.

Just as you have gathered us now at the table of your Son,
so also bring us together,
with the glorious Virgin Mary, Mother of God,
with your blessed Apostles and all the Saints,
with our brothers and sisters
and those of every race and tongue
who have died in your friendship.
Bring us to share with them the unending banquet of unity
in a new heaven and a new earth,
where the fullness of your peace will shine forth
in Christ Jesus our Lord.

Priest: Through him, and with him, and in him,
O God, almighty Father,
in the unity of the Holy Spirit,
all glory and honour is yours,
for ever and ever.

▷ *Music p 18*

People: **Amen.**

▷ *page 56*

* Mention may be made here of the Coadjutor Bishop, or Auxiliary Bishops

EUCHARISTIC PRAYERS FOR USE IN MASSES FOR VARIOUS NEEDS

These Eucharistic Prayers have their own Prefaces which may not be replaced by another, because of the structure of the Prayers themselves.

I THE CHURCH ON THE PATH OF UNITY

Priest: The Lord be with you. ▷ Music p 15
People: **And with your spirit.**

Priest: Lift up your hearts.
People: **We lift them up to the Lord.**

Priest: Let us give thanks to the Lord our God.
People: **It is right and just.**

Priest: It is truly right and just to give you thanks
and raise to you a hymn of glory and praise,
O Lord, Father of infinite goodness.

For by the word of your Son's Gospel
you have brought together one Church
from every people, tongue, and nation,
and, having filled her with life by the power of your Spirit,
you never cease through her
to gather the whole human race into one.

Manifesting the covenant of your love,
she dispenses without ceasing
the blessed hope of your Kingdom
and shines bright as the sign of your faithfulness,
which in Christ Jesus our Lord
you promised would last for eternity.

And so, with all the Powers of heaven,
we worship you constantly on earth,
while, with all the Church,
as one voice we acclaim:

All: **Holy, Holy, Holy Lord God of hosts.** ▷ Music p 16
Heaven and earth are full of your glory.
Hosanna in the highest.
Blessed is he who comes in the name of the Lord.
Hosanna in the highest.

ALL KNEEL

You are indeed Holy and to be glorified, O God,
who love the human race
and who always walk with us on the journey of life.
Blessed indeed is your Son,
present in our midst
when we are gathered by his love,
and when, as once for the disciples, so now for us,
he opens the Scriptures and breaks the bread.

Therefore, Father most merciful,
we ask that you send forth your Holy Spirit
to sanctify these gifts of bread and wine,
that they may become for us
the Body and ✠ Blood
of our Lord Jesus Christ.

On the day before he was to suffer,
on the night of the Last Supper,
he took bread and said the blessing,
broke the bread and gave it to his disciples, saying:

TAKE THIS, ALL OF YOU, AND EAT OF IT,
FOR THIS IS MY BODY,
WHICH WILL BE GIVEN UP FOR YOU.

In a similar way, when supper was ended,
he took the chalice, gave you thanks
and gave the chalice to his disciples, saying:

TAKE THIS, ALL OF YOU, AND DRINK FROM IT,
FOR THIS IS THE CHALICE OF MY BLOOD,
THE BLOOD OF THE NEW AND ETERNAL COVENANT,
WHICH WILL BE POURED OUT FOR YOU AND FOR MANY
FOR THE FORGIVENESS OF SINS.

DO THIS IN MEMORY OF ME.

Priest: The mystery of faith.
▷ *Music p 17*

People: **We proclaim your Death, O Lord,
and profess your Resurrection
until you come again.**

or

People: **When we eat this Bread and drink this Cup,
we proclaim your Death, O Lord,
until you come again.**

or

People: **Save us, Saviour of the world,
for by your Cross and Resurrection
you have set us free.**

Therefore, holy Father,
as we celebrate the memorial of Christ your Son, our Saviour,

whom you led through his Passion and Death on the Cross
to the glory of the Resurrection,
and whom you have seated at your right hand,
we proclaim the work of your love until he comes again
and we offer you the Bread of life
and the Chalice of blessing.

Look with favour on the oblation of your Church,
in which we show forth
the paschal Sacrifice of Christ that has been handed on to us,
and grant that, by the power of the Spirit of your love,
we may be counted now and until the day of eternity
among the members of your Son,
in whose Body and Blood we have communion.

Lord, renew your Church (which is in N.)
by the light of the Gospel.
Strengthen the bond of unity
between the faithful and the pastors of your people,
together with N. our Pope, N. our Bishop,*
and the whole Order of Bishops,
that in a world torn by strife
your people may shine forth
as a prophetic sign of unity and concord.

Remember our brothers and sisters (N. and N.),
who have fallen asleep in the peace of your Christ,
and all the dead, whose faith you alone have known.
Admit them to rejoice in the light of your face,
and in the resurrection give them the fullness of life.

Grant also to us,
when our earthly pilgrimage is done,
that we may come to an eternal dwelling place
and live with you for ever;
there, in communion with the Blessed Virgin Mary, Mother of God,
with the Apostles and Martyrs,
(with Saint N.: *the Saint of the day or Patron*)
and with all the Saints,
we shall praise and exalt you
through Jesus Christ, your Son.

* Mention may be made here of the Coadjutor Bishop, or Auxiliary Bishops

Priest: Through him, and with him, and in him,
O God, almighty Father,
in the unity of the Holy Spirit,
all glory and honour is yours,
for ever and ever.

▷ Music p 18

People: **Amen.**

▷ page 56

II GOD GUIDES HIS CHURCH ALONG THE WAY OF SALVATION

Priest: The Lord be with you.
People: **And with your spirit.**

▷ Music p 15

Priest: Lift up your hearts.
People: **We lift them up to the Lord.**

Priest: Let us give thanks to the Lord our God.
People: **It is right and just.**

It is truly right and just, our duty and our salvation,
always and everywhere to give you thanks,
Lord, holy Father,
creator of the world and source of all life.

For you never forsake the works of your wisdom,
but by your providence are even now at work in our midst.
With mighty hand and outstretched arm
you led your people Israel through the desert.
Now, as your Church makes her pilgrim journey in the world,
you always accompany her
by the power of the Holy Spirit
and lead her along the paths of time
to the eternal joy of your Kingdom,
through Christ our Lord.

And so, with the Angels and Saints,
we, too, sing the hymn of your glory,
as without end we acclaim:

All: **Holy, Holy, Holy Lord God of hosts.
Heaven and earth are full of your glory.
Hosanna in the highest.
Blessed is he who comes in the name of the Lord.
Hosanna in the highest.**

▷ Music p 16

ALL KNEEL

Priest: You are indeed Holy and to be glorified, O God,
who love the human race
and who always walk with us on the journey of life.

Blessed indeed is your Son,
present in our midst
when we are gathered by his love
and when, as once for the disciples, so now for us,
he opens the Scriptures and breaks the bread.

Therefore, Father most merciful,
we ask that you send forth your Holy Spirit
to sanctify these gifts of bread and wine,
that they may become for us
the Body and ✠ Blood
of our Lord Jesus Christ.

On the day before he was to suffer,
on the night of the Last Supper,
he took bread and said the blessing,
broke the bread and gave it to his disciples, saying:

TAKE THIS, ALL OF YOU, AND EAT OF IT,
FOR THIS IS MY BODY,
WHICH WILL BE GIVEN UP FOR YOU.

In a similar way, when supper was ended,
he took the chalice, gave you thanks
and gave the chalice to his disciples, saying:

TAKE THIS, ALL OF YOU, AND DRINK FROM IT,
FOR THIS IS THE CHALICE OF MY BLOOD,
THE BLOOD OF THE NEW AND ETERNAL COVENANT,
WHICH WILL BE POURED OUT FOR YOU AND FOR MANY
FOR THE FORGIVENESS OF SINS.

DO THIS IN MEMORY OF ME.

Priest: The mystery of faith. ▷ *Music p 17*
People: **We proclaim your Death, O Lord,
and profess your Resurrection
until you come again.**

or

People: **When we eat this Bread and drink this Cup,
we proclaim your Death, O Lord,
until you come again.**

or

People: **Save us, Saviour of the world,
for by your Cross and Resurrection
you have set us free.**

Priest: Therefore, holy Father,
as we celebrate the memorial of Christ your Son, our Saviour,
whom you led through his Passion and Death on the Cross
to the glory of the Resurrection,
and whom you have seated at your right hand,
we proclaim the work of your love until he comes again
and we offer you the Bread of life
and the Chalice of blessing.

Look with favour on the oblation of your Church,
in which we show forth
the paschal Sacrifice of Christ that has been handed on to us,
and grant that, by the power of the Spirit of your love,
we may be counted now and until the day of eternity
among the members of your Son,
in whose Body and Blood we have communion.

And so, having called us to your table, Lord,
confirm us in unity,
so that, together with N. our Pope and N. our Bishop,*
with all Bishops, Priests and Deacons,
and your entire people,
as we walk your ways with faith and hope,
we may strive to bring joy and trust into the world.

Remember our brothers and sisters (N. and N.),
who have fallen asleep in the peace of your Christ,
and all the dead, whose faith you alone have known.
Admit them to rejoice in the light of your face,
and in the resurrection give them the fullness of life.

Grant also to us,
when our earthly pilgrimage is done,
that we may come to an eternal dwelling place
and live with you for ever;
there, in communion with the Blessed Virgin Mary, Mother of God,
with the Apostles and Martyrs,
(with Saint N.: *the Saint of the day or Patron*)
and with all the Saints,
we shall praise and exalt you
through Jesus Christ, your Son.

* Mention may be made here of the Coadjutor Bishop, or Auxiliary Bishops

Priest: Through him, and with him, and in him,
O God, almighty Father,
in the unity of the Holy Spirit,
all glory and honour is yours,
for ever and ever.

▷ Music p 18

People: **Amen.**

▷ page 56

III JESUS, THE WAY TO THE FATHER

▷ Music p 15

Priest: The Lord be with you.
People: **And with your spirit.**

Priest: Lift up your hearts.
People: **We lift them up to the Lord.**

Priest: Let us give thanks to the Lord our God.
People: **It is right and just.**

Priest: It is truly right and just, our duty and our salvation,
always and everywhere to give you thanks,
holy Father, Lord of heaven and earth,
through Christ our Lord.

For by your Word you created the world
and you govern all things in harmony.
You gave us the same Word made flesh as Mediator,
and he has spoken your words to us
and called us to follow him.
He is the way that leads us to you,
the truth that sets us free,
the life that fills us with gladness.

Through your Son
you gather men and women,
whom you made for the glory of your name,
into one family,
redeemed by the Blood of his Cross
and signed with the seal of the Spirit.

Therefore, now and for ages unending,
with all the Angels,
we proclaim your glory,
as in joyful celebration we acclaim:

All: **Holy, Holy, Holy Lord God of hosts.**
Heaven and earth are full of your glory.
Hosanna in the highest.
Blessed is he who comes in the name of the Lord.
Hosanna in the highest.

▷ Music p 16

ALL KNEEL

Priest: You are indeed Holy and to be glorified, O God,
who love the human race
and who always walk with us on the journey of life.
Blessed indeed is your Son,
present in our midst
when we are gathered by his love
and when, as once for the disciples, so now for us,
he opens the Scriptures and breaks the bread.

Therefore, Father most merciful,
we ask that you send forth your Holy Spirit
to sanctify these gifts of bread and wine,
that they may become for us
the Body and ✠ Blood
of our Lord Jesus Christ.

On the day before he was to suffer,
on the night of the Last Supper,
he took bread and said the blessing,
broke the bread and gave it to his disciples, saying:

TAKE THIS, ALL OF YOU, AND EAT OF IT,
FOR THIS IS MY BODY,
WHICH WILL BE GIVEN UP FOR YOU.

In a similar way, when supper was ended,
he took the chalice, gave you thanks
and gave the chalice to his disciples, saying:

TAKE THIS, ALL OF YOU, AND DRINK FROM IT,
FOR THIS IS THE CHALICE OF MY BLOOD,
THE BLOOD OF THE NEW AND ETERNAL COVENANT,
WHICH WILL BE POURED OUT FOR YOU AND FOR MANY
FOR THE FORGIVENESS OF SINS.

DO THIS IN MEMORY OF ME.

Priest: The mystery of faith.

▷ *Music p 17*

People: **We proclaim your Death, O Lord,**
and profess your Resurrection
until you come again.

or

People: **When we eat this Bread and drink this Cup,**
we proclaim your Death, O Lord,
until you come again.

or

People: **Save us, Saviour of the world,**
for by your Cross and Resurrection
you have set us free.

Priest: Therefore, holy Father,
as we celebrate the memorial of Christ your Son, our Saviour,
whom you led through his Passion and Death on the Cross
to the glory of the Resurrection,
and whom you have seated at your right hand,
we proclaim the work of your love until he comes again
and we offer you the Bread of life
and the Chalice of blessing.

Look with favour on the oblation of your Church,
in which we show forth
the paschal Sacrifice of Christ that has been handed on to us,
and grant that, by the power of the Spirit of your love,
we may be counted now and until the day of eternity
among the members of your Son,
in whose Body and Blood we have communion.

By our partaking of this mystery, almighty Father,
give us life through your Spirit,
grant that we may be conformed to the image of your Son,
and confirm us in the bond of communion,
together with N. our Pope and N. our Bishop,*
with all other Bishops,
with Priests and Deacons,
and with your entire people.

Grant that all the faithful of the Church,
looking into the signs of the times by the light of faith,
may constantly devote themselves
to the service of the Gospel.
Keep us attentive to the needs of all
that, sharing their grief and pain,
their joy and hope,
we may faithfully bring them the good news of salvation
and go forward with them
along the way of your Kingdom.

Remember our brothers and sisters (N. and N.),
who have fallen asleep in the peace of your Christ,
and all the dead, whose faith you alone have known.
Admit them to rejoice in the light of your face,
and in the resurrection give them the fullness of life.

* Mention may be made here of the Coadjutor Bishop, or Auxiliary Bishops

Grant also to us,
when our earthly pilgrimage is done,
that we may come to an eternal dwelling place
and live with you for ever;
there, in communion with the Blessed Virgin Mary, Mother of God,
with the Apostles and Martyrs,
(with Saint N.: *the Saint of the day or Patron*)
and with all the Saints,
we shall praise and exalt you
through Jesus Christ, your Son.

Priest: Through him, and with him, and in him, ▷ *Music p 18*
O God, almighty Father,
in the unity of the Holy Spirit,
all glory and honour is yours,
for ever and ever.

People: **Amen.** ▷ *page 56*

IV JESUS, WHO WENT ABOUT DOING GOOD

Priest: The Lord be with you. ▷ *Music p 15*
People: **And with your spirit.**

Priest: Lift up your hearts.
People: **We lift them up to the Lord.**

Priest: Let us give thanks to the Lord our God.
People: **It is right and just.**

Priest: It is truly right and just, our duty and our salvation,
always and everywhere to give you thanks,
Father of mercies and faithful God.

For you have given us Jesus Christ, your Son,
as our Lord and Redeemer.

He always showed compassion
for children and for the poor,
for the sick and for sinners,
and he became a neighbour
to the oppressed and the afflicted.

By word and deed he announced to the world
that you are our Father
and that you care for all your sons and daughters.

And so, with all the Angels and Saints,
we exalt and bless your name
and sing the hymn of your glory,
as without end we acclaim:

▷ Music p 16

All: **Holy, Holy, Holy Lord God of hosts.**
Heaven and earth are full of your glory.
Hosanna in the highest.
Blessed is he who comes in the name of the Lord.
Hosanna in the highest.

ALL KNEEL

Priest: You are indeed Holy and to be glorified, O God,
who love the human race
and who always walk with us on the journey of life.
Blessed indeed is your Son,
present in our midst
when we are gathered by his love
and when, as once for the disciples, so now for us,
he opens the Scriptures and breaks the bread.

Therefore, Father most merciful,
we ask that you send forth your Holy Spirit
to sanctify these gifts of bread and wine,
that they may become for us
the Body and ✠ Blood
of our Lord Jesus Christ.

On the day before he was to suffer,
on the night of the Last Supper,
he took bread and said the blessing,
broke the bread and gave it to his disciples, saying:

TAKE THIS, ALL OF YOU, AND EAT OF IT,
FOR THIS IS MY BODY,
WHICH WILL BE GIVEN UP FOR YOU.

In a similar way, when supper was ended,
he took the chalice, gave you thanks
and gave the chalice to his disciples, saying:

TAKE THIS, ALL OF YOU, AND DRINK FROM IT,
FOR THIS IS THE CHALICE OF MY BLOOD,
THE BLOOD OF THE NEW AND ETERNAL COVENANT,
WHICH WILL BE POURED OUT FOR YOU AND FOR MANY
FOR THE FORGIVENESS OF SINS.

DO THIS IN MEMORY OF ME.

Priest: The mystery of faith.

▷ *Music p 17*

People: **We proclaim your Death, O Lord,**
and profess your Resurrection
until you come again.

or

People: **When we eat this Bread and drink this Cup,**
we proclaim your Death, O Lord,
until you come again.

or

People: **Save us, Saviour of the world,**
for by your Cross and Resurrection
you have set us free.

Priest: Therefore, holy Father,
as we celebrate the memorial of Christ your Son, our Saviour,
whom you led through his Passion and Death on the Cross
to the glory of the Resurrection,
and whom you have seated at your right hand,
we proclaim the work of your love until he comes again
and we offer you the Bread of life
and the Chalice of blessing.

Look with favour on the oblation of your Church,
in which we show forth
the paschal Sacrifice of Christ that has been handed on to us,
and grant that, by the power of the Spirit of your love,
we may be counted now and until the day of eternity
among the members of your Son,
in whose Body and Blood we have communion.

Bring your Church, O Lord,
to perfect faith and charity,
together with N. our Pope and N. our Bishop,*
with all Bishops, Priests and Deacons,
and the entire people you have made your own.

Open our eyes
to the needs of our brothers and sisters;
inspire in us words and actions
to comfort those who labour and are burdened.
Make us serve them truly,
after the example of Christ and at his command.

* Mention may be made here of the Coadjutor Bishop, or Auxiliary Bishops

And may your Church stand as a living witness
to truth and freedom,
to peace and justice,
that all people may be raised up to a new hope.

Remember our brothers and sisters (N. and N.),
who have fallen asleep in the peace of your Christ,
and all the dead, whose faith you alone have known.
Admit them to rejoice in the light of your face,
and in the resurrection give them the fullness of life.

Grant also to us,
when our earthly pilgrimage is done,
that we may come to an eternal dwelling place
and live with you for ever;
there, in communion with the Blessed Virgin Mary, Mother of God,
with the Apostles and Martyrs,
(with Saint N.: *the Saint of the day or Patron*)
and with all the Saints,
we shall praise and exalt you
through Jesus Christ, your Son.

Priest: Through him, and with him, and in him,
O God, almighty Father,
in the unity of the Holy Spirit,
all glory and honour is yours,
for ever and ever.

▷ *Music p 18*

People: **Amen.**

▷ *page 56*

COMMUNION RITE

The eating and drinking together of the Lord's Body and Blood in a Paschal meal is the culmination of the Eucharist. The themes underlying these rites are the mutual love and reconciliation that are both the condition and the fruit of worthy communion and the unity of the many in the one. *Celebrating the Mass n 200*

ALL STAND

LORD'S PRAYER

Priest: At the Saviour's command
and formed by divine teaching,
we dare to say:

All: **Our Father, who art in heaven,**
hallowed be thy name;
thy kingdom come,
thy will be done
on earth as it is in heaven.
Give us this day our daily bread,
and forgive us our trespasses,
as we forgive those who trespass against us;
and lead us not into temptation,
but deliver us from evil.

▷ *Music p 323*

Priest: Deliver us, Lord, we pray, from every evil,
graciously grant peace in our days,
that, by the help of your mercy,
we may be always free from sin
and safe from all distress,
as we await the blessed hope
and the coming of our Saviour, Jesus Christ.

All: **For the kingdom,**
the power and the glory are yours
now and for ever.

RITE OF PEACE

Priest: Lord Jesus Christ,
who said to your Apostles,
Peace I leave you, my peace I give you,
look not on our sins,
but on the faith of your Church,
and graciously grant her peace and unity
in accordance with your will.
Who live and reign for ever and ever.

All: **Amen.**

Priest: The peace of the Lord be with you always.

All: **And with your spirit.**

▷ *Music p 323*

SIGN OF PEACE

The peace is always exchanged, though the invitation which introduces it is optional.

Deacon or Priest: Let us offer each other the sign of peace.

And all offer one another the customary sign of peace: a handclasp or handshake, which is an expression of peace, communion, and charity.

If commissioned ministers are to assist at Communion, it is desirable that they are in place on the sanctuary by the end of the exchange of peace. (Celebrating the Mass n 206)

BREAKING OF BREAD

The Priest takes the host, breaks it over the paten, and places a small piece into the chalice. Meanwhile the following is sung or said:

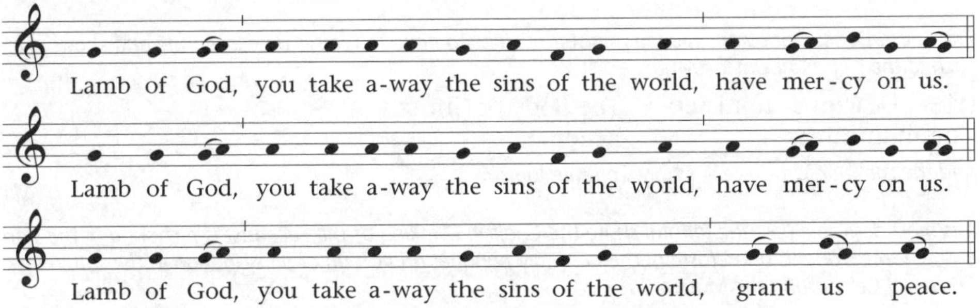
Lamb of God, you take a-way the sins of the world, have mer-cy on us.
Lamb of God, you take a-way the sins of the world, have mer-cy on us.
Lamb of God, you take a-way the sins of the world, grant us peace.

All: **Lamb of God, you take away the sins of the world,**
have mercy on us.

Lamb of God, you take away the sins of the world,
have mercy on us.

Lamb of God, you take away the sins of the world,
grant us peace.

The invocation may be repeated several times if the Breaking of Bread is prolonged. The final time always ends 'grant us peace'.

ALL KNEEL

INVITATION TO COMMUNION

After his private prayers of preparation the Priest genuflects, takes the host and, holding it slightly raised above the paten or above the chalice says aloud:

▷ *Music p 324*

Priest: Behold the Lamb of God,
behold him who takes away the sins of the world.
Blessed are those called to the supper of the Lamb.

All: **Lord, I am not worthy**
that you should enter under my roof,
but only say the word
and my soul shall be healed.

HOLY COMMUNION

Communion Song

The communion song begins while the Priest is receiving the Body of Christ and normally continues until all communicants have received communion.

Distribution of Communion

By tradition the Deacon ministers the chalice. Beyond this, no distinctions are made in the assignment of consecrated elements to particular ministers for distribution. (Celebrating the Mass n 211)

The communicants come forward in reverent procession. Before receiving Holy Communion standing they make a preparatory act of reverence by bowing their heads in honour of Christ's presence in the Sacrament.

The Priest, Deacon or commissioned minister of Holy Communion raises a host slightly and shows it to each of the communicants, saying:

Priest, Deacon or minister: The Body of Christ.
Communicant: **Amen.**

And the communicant receives Holy Communion.

It is most desirable that the faithful share the Chalice. Drinking at the Eucharist is a sharing in the sign of the new covenant, a foretaste of the heavenly banquet and a sign of participation in the suffering Christ. (cf Celebrating the Mass n 209)

When Communion is ministered from the chalice, the minister offers it to each of the communicants, saying:

Priest, Deacon or minister: The Blood of Christ.
Communicant: **Amen.**

And the communicant receives Holy Communion.

Period of Silence or Song of Praise

After the distribution of Communion, if appropriate, a sacred silence may be observed for a while, or a psalm or other canticle of praise or a hymn may be sung.

PRAYER AFTER COMMUNION

ALL STAND

Priest: Let us pray.

▷ **Proper**

All pray in silence for a while, unless silence has just been observed.
Then the Priest says the Prayer after Communion, at the end of which the people acclaim:

All: **Amen.**

CONCLUDING RITES

Go, make disciples of all the nations.
I am with you always; yes, to the end of time.
(Matthew 28:19, 20)

The purpose of the Concluding Rite is to send the people forth to put into effect in their daily lives the Paschal Mystery and the unity in Christ which they have celebrated. They are given a sense of abiding mission, which calls them to witness to Christ in the world and to bring the Gospel to the poor. *cf Celebrating the Mass n 217*

If they are necessary, any brief announcements to the people follow here.

BLESSING

Priest: The Lord be with you. ▷ Music p 325
People: **And with your spirit.**

On certain occasions, the following blessing may be preceded by a solemn blessing or prayer over the people. Then the Priest blesses the people, singing or saying:

Priest: May almighty God bless you:
the Father, and the Son, ✠ and the Holy Spirit.
People: **Amen.**

In a Pontifical Mass, the celebrant receives the mitre and says:

Bishop: The Lord be with you. ▷ Music p 325
All: **And with your spirit.**

Bishop: Blessed be the name of the Lord.
All: **Now and for ever.**

Bishop: Our help is in the name of the Lord.
All **Who made heaven and earth.**

On certain occasions the following blessing may be preceded by a more solemn blessing or prayer over the people. Then the celebrant receives the pastoral staff, if he uses it, and says:

Bishop: May almighty God bless you:
making the Sign of the Cross over the people three times, he adds:
the Father, ✠ and the Son, ✠ and the Holy ✠ Spirit.
All: **Amen.**

If any liturgical action follows immediately, the rites of dismissal are omitted.

DISMISSAL

▷ Music p 326

Then the Deacon, or the Priest himself says the dismissal sentence.

Deacon or Priest: Go forth, the Mass is ended.
People: **Thanks be to God.**

or

Deacon or Priest: Go and announce the Gospel of the Lord.
People: **Thanks be to God.**

or

Deacon or Priest: Go in peace, glorifying the Lord by your life.
People: **Thanks be to God.**

or

Deacon or Priest: Go in peace.
People: **Thanks be to God.**

At the Easter Vigil, on Easter Sunday, during the octave of Easter and on Pentecost, the dismissal takes the following form:

Deacon or Priest: Go forth, the Mass is ended, alleluia, alleluia.
People: **Thanks be to God, alleluia, alleluia.**

or

Deacon or Priest: Go in peace, alleluia, alleluia.
People: **Thanks be to God, alleluia, alleluia.**

Then the Priest venerates the altar as at the beginning.
After making a profound bow with the ministers, he withdraws.

APPENDIX TO THE ORDER OF MASS

✠ RITE FOR THE BLESSING AND SPRINKLING OF WATER

BLESSING OF WATER

After the greeting, the Priest, with a vessel containing the water to be blessed before him, calls upon the people to pray in these or similar words:

Priest: Dear brethren (brothers and sisters),
let us humbly beseech the Lord our God
to bless this water he has created,
which will be sprinkled on us
as a memorial of our Baptism.
May he help us by his grace
to remain faithful to the Spirit we have received.

And after a brief pause for silence, he continues:

Priest: Almighty ever-living God,
who willed that through water,
the fountain of life and the source of purification,
even souls should be cleansed
and receive the gift of eternal life;
be pleased, we pray, to ✠ bless this water,
by which we seek protection on this your day, O Lord.
Renew the living spring of your grace within us
and grant that by this water we may be defended
from all ills of spirit and body,
and so approach you with hearts made clean
and worthily receive your salvation.
Through Christ our Lord.

All: **Amen.**

or

Priest: Almighty Lord and God,
who are the source and origin of all life,
whether of body or soul,
we ask you to ✠ bless this water,
which we use in confidence
to implore forgiveness for our sins
and to obtain the protection of your grace
against all illness and every snare of the enemy.
Grant, O Lord, in your mercy,
that living waters may always spring up for our salvation,
and so may we approach you with a pure heart
and avoid all danger to body and soul.
Through Christ our Lord.

All: **Amen.**

or, during Easter Time

Priest: Lord our God,
in your mercy be present to your people's prayers,
and, for us who recall the wondrous work of our creation
and the still greater work of our redemption,
graciously ✠ bless this water.
For you created water to make the fields fruitful
and to refresh and cleanse our bodies.
You also made water the instrument of your mercy:
for through water you freed your people from slavery
and quenched their thirst in the desert;
through water the Prophets proclaimed the new covenant
you were to enter upon with the human race;
and last of all,
through water, which Christ made holy in the Jordan,
you have renewed our corrupted nature
in the bath of regeneration.
Therefore, may this water be for us
a memorial of the Baptism we have received,
and grant that we may share
in the gladness of our brothers and sisters
who at Easter have received their Baptism.
Through Christ our Lord.

All: **Amen.**

BLESSING OF SALT

Where the circumstances of the place or the custom of the people suggest that the mixing of salt be preserved in the blessing of water, the Priest may bless salt, saying:

Priest: We humbly ask you, almighty God:
be pleased in your faithful love to bless ✠ this salt
you have created,
for it was you who commanded the prophet Elisha
to cast salt into water,
that impure water might be purified.
Grant, O Lord, we pray,
that, wherever this mixture of salt and water is sprinkled,
every attack of the enemy may be repulsed
and your Holy Spirit may be present
to keep us safe at all times.
Through Christ our Lord.

All: **Amen.**

Then he pours the salt into the water.

SPRINKLING OF WATER

The Priest then sprinkles himself and the ministers, then the clergy and people, moving through the church, if appropriate.

Meanwhile, one of the following chants, or another appropriate song is sung.

Outside Easter Time

ANTIPHON 1 *Psalm 50:9*

Sprinkle me with hyssop, O Lord, and I shall be cleansed;
wash me and I shall be whiter than snow.

ANTIPHON 2 *Ezekiel 36:25–26*

I will pour clean water upon you,
and you will be made clean of all your impurities,
and I shall give you a new spirit, says the Lord.

HYMN *cf 1 Peter 1:3–5*

Blessed be the God and Father of our Lord Jesus Christ,
who in his great mercy has given us new birth into a living hope
through the Resurrection of Jesus Christ from the dead,
into an inheritance that will not perish,
preserved for us in heaven
for the salvation to be revealed in the last time!

During Easter Time

ANTIPHON 1 *cf Ezekiel 47:1–2, 9*

I saw water flowing from the Temple,
from its right-hand side, alleluia:
and all to whom this water came
were saved and shall say: alleluia, alleluia.

ANTIPHON 2 *cf Wisdom 3:8; Ezekiel 36:25*

On the day of my resurrection, says the Lord, alleluia,
I will gather the nations and assemble the kingdoms
and I will pour clean water upon you, alleluia.

ANTIPHON 3 *cf Daniel 3:77, 79*

You springs and all that moves in the waters,
sing a hymn to God, alleluia.

ANTIPHON 4 *1 Peter 2:9*

O chosen race, royal priesthood, holy nation,
proclaim the mighty works of him
who called you out of darkness into his wonderful light, alleluia.

ANTIPHON 5

From your side, O Christ,
bursts forth a spring of water,
by which the squalor of the world is washed away
and life is made new again, alleluia.

PRAYER

When he returns to his chair and the singing is over, the Priest says:

Priest: May almighty God cleanse us of our sins,
and through the celebration of this Eucharist
make us worthy to share at the table of his Kingdom.

All: **Amen.**

The Mass continues with the Gloria.
If the Gloria is not indicated, the Mass continues with the Collect. ▷ *page 9*

PREFACES

All the Prefaces within the scope of this volume are printed here, except those specific to a given Eucharistic Prayer (e.g. the Preface of Eucharistic Prayer II).

The Prefaces are printed in the order that the celebrations occur in the propers of this volume:

Advent • Christmas Time • Ordinary Time • Lent • Triduum • Easter
then
Prefaces from the Proper of Saints and other celebrations

ADVENT

This Preface is said in Masses of Advent from the First Sunday of Advent to 16 December.

PREFACE I OF ADVENT

THE TWO COMINGS OF CHRIST

It is truly right and just,
our duty and our salvation,
always and everywhere to give you thanks,
Lord, holy Father,
almighty and eternal God,
through Christ our Lord.

For he assumed at his first coming
the lowliness of human flesh,
and so fulfilled the design
you formed long ago,
and opened for us the way
to eternal salvation,
that, when he comes again
in glory and majesty
and all is at last made manifest,
we who watch for that day
may inherit the great promise
in which now we dare to hope.

And so, with Angels and Archangels,
with Thrones and Dominions,
and with all the hosts and Powers of heaven,
we sing the hymn of your glory,
as without end we acclaim:

Holy, Holy, Holy Lord God of hosts...

PREFACE II OF ADVENT

This Preface is said in Masses of Advent from 17 December to 24 December.

It is truly right and just,
our duty and our salvation,
always and everywhere to give you thanks,
Lord, holy Father,
almighty and eternal God,
through Christ our Lord.

For all the oracles of the prophets
foretold him,
the Virgin Mother longed for him
with love beyond all telling,
John the Baptist sang of his coming
and proclaimed his presence when he came.

It is by his gift that already we rejoice
at the mystery of his Nativity,
so that he may find us watchful in prayer
and exultant in his praise.

And so, with Angels and Archangels,
with Thrones and Dominions,
and with all the hosts
and Powers of heaven,
we sing the hymn of your glory,
as without end we acclaim:

Holy, Holy, Holy Lord God of hosts...

CHRISTMAS TIME

The following three Prefaces are said in Masses of the Nativity of the Lord and throughout Christmas Time with the exception of Masses that have a proper Preface.

PREFACE I OF THE NATIVITY OF THE LORD

CHRIST THE LIGHT

It is truly right and just,
our duty and our salvation,
always and everywhere to give you thanks,
Lord, holy Father,
almighty and eternal God.

For in the mystery of the Word made flesh
a new light of your glory has shone
upon the eyes of our mind,
so that, as we recognize in him
God made visible,
we may be caught up through him
in love of things invisible.

And so, with Angels and Archangels,
with Thrones and Dominions,
and with all the hosts
and Powers of heaven,
we sing the hymn of your glory,
as without end we acclaim:

Holy, Holy, Holy Lord God of hosts...

PREFACE II OF THE NATIVITY OF THE LORD

THE RESTORATION OF ALL THINGS IN THE INCARNATION

It is truly right and just,
our duty and our salvation,
always and everywhere to give you thanks,
Lord, holy Father,
almighty and eternal God,
through Christ our Lord.

For on the feast of this awe-filled mystery,
though invisible in his own divine nature,
he has appeared visibly in ours;
and begotten before all ages,
he has begun to exist in time;
so that, raising up in himself
all that was cast down,
he might restore unity to all creation
and call straying humanity
back to the heavenly Kingdom.

And so, with all the Angels, we praise you,
as in joyful celebration we acclaim:

Holy, Holy, Holy Lord God of hosts...

PREFACE III OF THE NATIVITY OF THE LORD

THE EXCHANGE IN
THE INCARNATION OF THE WORD

It is truly right and just,
our duty and our salvation,
always and everywhere to give you thanks,
Lord, holy Father,
almighty and eternal God,
through Christ our Lord.

For through him the holy exchange
that restores our life
has shone forth today in splendour:
when our frailty is assumed by your Word
not only does human mortality
receive unending honour
but by this wondrous union we, too,
are made eternal.

And so, in company with
the choirs of Angels,
we praise you, and with joy we proclaim:

Holy, Holy, Holy Lord God of hosts...

THESE PREFACES ARE SAID ON MORE SPECIFIC OCCASIONS DURING CHRISTMAS TIME

PREFACE I OF THE BLESSED VIRGIN MARY

THE MOTHERHOOD
OF THE BLESSED VIRGIN MARY

The following Preface is said on the Solemnity of Mary, the Holy Mother of God (1 January).

It is truly right and just,
our duty and our salvation,
always and everywhere to give you thanks,
Lord, holy Father,
almighty and eternal God,
and to praise, bless, and glorify your name
on the Solemnity of the Motherhood
of the Blessed ever-Virgin Mary.

For by the overshadowing of the Holy Spirit
she conceived your Only Begotten Son,
and without losing the glory of virginity,
brought forth into the world
the eternal Light,
Jesus Christ our Lord.

Through him the Angels praise your majesty,
Dominions adore and Powers
tremble before you.
Heaven and the Virtues of heaven
and the blessed Seraphim
worship together with exultation.
May our voices, we pray, join with theirs
in humble praise, as we acclaim:

Holy, Holy, Holy Lord God of hosts...

PREFACE OF THE EPIPHANY OF THE LORD

CHRIST THE LIGHT OF THE NATIONS

The following Preface is said in Masses of the Solemnity of the Epiphany. This Preface, or one of the Prefaces of the Nativity, may be said even on days after the Epiphany up to the Saturday that precedes the Feast of the Baptism of the Lord.

It is truly right and just,
our duty and our salvation,
always and everywhere to give you thanks,
Lord, holy Father,
almighty and eternal God.

For today you have revealed the mystery
of our salvation in Christ
as a light for the nations,
and, when he appeared
in our mortal nature,
you made us new by the glory
of his immortal nature.

And so, with Angels and Archangels,
with Thrones and Dominions,
and with all the hosts
and Powers of heaven,
we sing the hymn of your glory,
as without end we acclaim:

Holy, Holy, Holy Lord God of hosts...

THE BAPTISM OF THE LORD

The following Preface is said on the feast of the Baptism of the Lord.

It is truly right and just,
our duty and our salvation,
always and everywhere to give you thanks,
Lord, holy Father,
almighty and eternal God.

For in the waters of the Jordan
you revealed with signs and wonders
a new Baptism,
so that through the voice
that came down from heaven
we might come to believe in your Word
dwelling among us,
and by the Spirit's descending
in the likeness of a dove
we might know that Christ your Servant
has been anointed with the oil of gladness
and sent to bring the good news to the poor.

And so, with the Powers of heaven,
we worship you constantly on earth,
and before your majesty
without end we acclaim:

Holy, Holy, Holy Lord God of hosts...

ORDINARY TIME

The following Prefaces are said on Sundays in Ordinary Time.

PREFACE I
OF THE SUNDAYS IN ORDINARY TIME

THE PASCHAL MYSTERY
AND THE PEOPLE OF GOD

It is truly right and just,
our duty and our salvation,
always and everywhere to give you thanks,
Lord, holy Father, almighty
and eternal God,
through Christ our Lord.

For through his Paschal Mystery,
he accomplished the marvellous deed,
by which he has freed us
from the yoke of sin and death,
summoning us to the glory
of being now called
a chosen race, a royal priesthood,
a holy nation, a people
for your own possession,
to proclaim everywhere your mighty works,
for you have called us out of darkness
into your own wonderful light.

And so, with Angels and Archangels,
with Thrones and Dominions,
and with all the hosts
and Powers of heaven,
we sing the hymn of your glory,
as without end we acclaim:

Holy, Holy, Holy Lord God of hosts...

PREFACE II
OF THE SUNDAYS IN ORDINARY TIME

THE MYSTERY OF SALVATION

It is truly right and just,
our duty and our salvation,
always and everywhere to give you thanks,
Lord, holy Father,
almighty and eternal God,
through Christ our Lord.

For out of compassion for the waywardness
that is ours,
he humbled himself
and was born of the Virgin;
by the passion of the Cross
he freed us from unending death,
and by rising from the dead
he gave us life eternal.

And so, with Angels and Archangels,
with Thrones and Dominions,
and with all the hosts
and Powers of heaven,
we sing the hymn of your glory,
as without end we acclaim:

Holy, Holy, Holy Lord God of hosts...

PREFACE III
OF THE SUNDAYS IN ORDINARY TIME

THE SALVATION OF MAN BY A MAN

It is truly right and just,
our duty and our salvation,
always and everywhere to give you thanks,
Lord, holy Father,
almighty and eternal God.

For we know it belongs
to your boundless glory,
that you came to the aid of mortal beings
with your divinity
and even fashioned for us
a remedy out of mortality itself,
that the cause of our downfall
might become the means of our salvation,
through Christ our Lord.

Through him the host of Angels
adores your majesty
and rejoices in your presence for ever.
May our voices, we pray, join with theirs
in one chorus of exultant praise,
as we acclaim:

Holy, Holy, Holy Lord God of hosts...

PREFACE IV
OF THE SUNDAYS IN ORDINARY TIME

THE HISTORY OF SALVATION

It is truly right and just,
our duty and our salvation,
always and everywhere to give you thanks,
Lord, holy Father,
almighty and eternal God,
through Christ our Lord.

For by his birth he brought renewal
to humanity's fallen state,
and by his suffering cancelled out our sins;
by his rising from the dead
he has opened the way to eternal life,
and by ascending to you, O Father,
he has unlocked the gates of heaven.

And so, with the company
of Angels and Saints,
we sing the hymn of your praise,
as without end we acclaim:

Holy, Holy, Holy Lord God of hosts...

PREFACE V
OF THE SUNDAYS IN ORDINARY TIME

CREATION

It is truly right and just,
our duty and our salvation,
always and everywhere to give you thanks,
Lord, holy Father,
almighty and eternal God.

For you laid the foundations of the world
and have arranged the changing
of times and seasons;
you formed man in your own image
and set humanity over the whole world
in all its wonder,
to rule in your name over all
you have made
and for ever praise you
in your mighty works,
through Christ our Lord.

And so, with all the Angels, we praise you,
as in joyful celebration we acclaim:

Holy, Holy, Holy Lord God of hosts...

PREFACE VI
OF THE SUNDAYS IN ORDINARY TIME

THE PLEDGE OF THE ETERNAL PASSOVER

It is truly right and just,
our duty and our salvation,
always and everywhere to give you thanks,
Lord, holy Father,
almighty and eternal God.

For in you we live and move
and have our being,
and while in this body
we not only experience the daily effects
of your care,
but even now possess the pledge
of life eternal.

For, having received the first fruits
of the Spirit,
through whom you raised up Jesus
from the dead,
we hope for an everlasting share
in the Paschal Mystery.

And so, with all the Angels, we praise you,
as in joyful celebration we acclaim:

Holy, Holy, Holy Lord God of hosts...

PREFACE VII OF THE SUNDAYS IN ORDINARY TIME

SALVATION THROUGH
THE OBEDIENCE OF CHRIST

It is truly right and just,
our duty and our salvation,
always and everywhere to give you thanks,
Lord, holy Father,
almighty and eternal God.

For you so loved the world
that in your mercy you sent us the Redeemer,
to live like us in all things but sin,
so that you might love in us
what you loved in your Son,
by whose obedience we have been restored
to those gifts of yours
that, by sinning, we had lost
in disobedience.

And so, Lord, with all the Angels and Saints,
we, too, give you thanks,
as in exultation we acclaim:

Holy, Holy, Holy Lord God of hosts...

PREFACE VIII OF THE SUNDAYS IN ORDINARY TIME

THE CHURCH UNITED BY
THE UNITY OF THE TRINITY

It is truly right and just,
our duty and our salvation,
always and everywhere to give you thanks,
Lord, holy Father,
almighty and eternal God.

For, when your children were scattered afar
by sin,
through the Blood of your Son
and the power of the Spirit,
you gathered them again to yourself,
that a people, formed as one
by the unity of the Trinity,
made the body of Christ
and the temple of the Holy Spirit,
might, to the praise
of your manifold wisdom,
be manifest as the Church.

And so, in company with
the choirs of Angels,
we praise you, and with joy we proclaim:

Holy, Holy, Holy Lord God of hosts...

LENT

The following Prefaces are said on Sundays in Lent especially on Sundays where a more specific Preface is not prescribed.

PREFACE I OF LENT

THE SPIRITUAL MEANING OF LENT

It is truly right and just,
our duty and our salvation,
always and everywhere to give you thanks,
Lord, holy Father,
almighty and eternal God,
through Christ our Lord.

For by your gracious gift each year
your faithful await the sacred paschal feasts
with the joy of minds made pure,
so that, more eagerly intent on prayer
and on the works of charity,
and participating in the mysteries
by which they have been reborn,
they may be led to the fullness of grace
that you bestow on your sons and daughters.

And so, with Angels and Archangels,
with Thrones and Dominions,
and with all the hosts
and Powers of heaven,
we sing the hymn of your glory,
as without end we acclaim:

Holy, Holy, Holy Lord God of hosts...

PREFACE II OF LENT

SPIRITUAL PENANCE

It is truly right and just,
our duty and our salvation,
always and everywhere to give you thanks,
Lord, holy Father,
almighty and eternal God.

For you have given your children
a sacred time
for the renewing and purifying
of their hearts,
that, freed from disordered affections,
they may so deal with the things
of this passing world
as to hold rather to the things
that eternally endure.

And so, with all the Angels and Saints,
we praise you, as without end we acclaim:

Holy, Holy, Holy Lord God of hosts...

PREFACE IV OF LENT
THE FRUITS OF FASTING

The following Preface is said in Masses of the weekdays of Lent and on days of fasting.

It is truly right and just,
our duty and our salvation,
always and everywhere to give you thanks,
Lord, holy Father,
almighty and eternal God.

For through bodily fasting
you restrain our faults,
raise up our minds,
and bestow both virtue and its rewards,
through Christ our Lord.

Through him the Angels
praise your majesty,
Dominions adore and Powers
tremble before you.
Heaven and the Virtues of heaven
and the blessed Seraphim
worship together with exultation.
May our voices, we pray, join with theirs
in humble praise, as we acclaim:

Holy, Holy, Holy Lord God of hosts...

PREFACE III OF LENT
THE FRUITS OF ABSTINENCE

The following Preface is said in Masses of the weekdays of Lent and on days of fasting.

It is truly right and just,
our duty and our salvation,
always and everywhere to give you thanks,
Lord, holy Father,
almighty and eternal God.

For you will that our self-denial
should give you thanks,
humble our sinful pride,
contribute to the feeding of the poor,
and so help us imitate you in your kindness.

And so we glorify you with countless Angels,
as with one voice of praise we acclaim:

Holy, Holy, Holy Lord God of hosts...

THESE PREFACES ARE SAID ON MORE SPECIFIC OCCASIONS DURING LENT

THE TEMPTATION OF THE LORD

The following Preface is said on the First Sunday of Lent.

It is truly right and just,
our duty and our salvation,
always and everywhere to give you thanks,
Lord, holy Father,
almighty and eternal God,
through Christ our Lord.

By abstaining forty long days
from earthly food,
he consecrated through his fast
the pattern of our Lenten observance
and, by overturning all the snares
of the ancient serpent,
taught us to cast out the leaven of malice,
so that, celebrating worthily
the Paschal Mystery,
we might pass over at last
to the eternal paschal feast.

And so, with the company
of Angels and Saints,
we sing the hymn of your praise,
as without end we acclaim:

Holy, Holy, Holy Lord God of hosts...

APPENDIX

THE TRANSFIGURATION OF THE LORD

The following Preface is said on the Second Sunday of Lent.

It is truly right and just,
our duty and our salvation,
always and everywhere to give you thanks,
Lord, holy Father,
almighty and eternal God,
through Christ our Lord.

For after he had told the disciples
of his coming Death,
on the holy mountain
he manifested to them his glory,
to show, even by the testimony of the law
and the prophets,
that the Passion leads to the glory
of the Resurrection.

And so, with the Powers of heaven,
we worship you constantly on earth,
and before your majesty
without end we acclaim:

Holy, Holy, Holy Lord God of hosts...

THE SAMARITAN WOMAN

The following Preface is said on the Third Sunday of Lent, whenever the Gospel of the Samaritan Woman is read.

It is truly right and just,
our duty and our salvation,
always and everywhere to give you thanks,
Lord, holy Father,
almighty and eternal God,
through Christ our Lord.

For when he asked the Samaritan woman
for water to drink,
he had already created
the gift of faith within her
and so ardently did he thirst for her faith,
that he kindled in her the fire of divine love.

And so we, too, give you thanks
and with the Angels
praise your mighty deeds, as we acclaim:

Holy, Holy, Holy Lord God of hosts...

THE MAN BORN BLIND

The following Preface is said on the Fourth Sunday of Lent, whenever the Gospel of the Man Born Blind is read.

It is truly right and just,
our duty and our salvation,
always and everywhere to give you thanks,
Lord, holy Father,
almighty and eternal God,
through Christ our Lord.

By the mystery of the Incarnation,
he has led the human race
that walked in darkness
into the radiance of the faith
and has brought those born in slavery
to ancient sin
through the waters of regeneration
to make them your adopted children.

Therefore, all creatures of heaven and earth
sing a new song in adoration,
and we, with all the host of Angels,
cry out, and without end acclaim:

Holy, Holy, Holy Lord God of hosts...

LAZARUS

The following Preface is said on the Fifth Sunday of Lent, whenever the Gospel of the raising of Lazarus is read.

It is truly right and just,
our duty and our salvation,
always and everywhere to give you thanks,
Lord, holy Father,
almighty and eternal God,
through Christ our Lord.

For as true man he wept for Lazarus his friend
and as eternal God
raised him from the tomb,
just as, taking pity on the human race,
he leads us by sacred mysteries to new life.

Through him the host of Angels
adores your majesty
and rejoices in your presence for ever.
May our voices, we pray, join with theirs
in one chorus of exultant praise,
as we acclaim:

Holy, Holy, Holy Lord God of hosts...

THE PASSION OF THE LORD

This preface is said on Palm Sunday of the Passion of the Lord

It is truly right and just,
our duty and our salvation,
always and everywhere to give you thanks,
Lord, holy Father,
almighty and eternal God,
through Christ our Lord.

For though innocent
he suffered willingly for sinners
and accepted unjust condemnation
to save the guilty.

His Death has washed away our sins,
and his Resurrection
has purchased our justification.

And so, with all the Angels,
we praise you,
as in joyful celebration we acclaim:

Holy, Holy, Holy Lord God of hosts...

TRIDUUM

The following Preface is said in the Mass of the Lord's Supper.

PREFACE I OF THE MOST HOLY EUCHARIST

THE SACRIFICE AND THE SACRAMENT OF CHRIST

It is truly right and just, our duty and our salvation,
always and everywhere to give you thanks,
Lord, holy Father, almighty and eternal God,
through Christ our Lord.

For he is the true and eternal Priest,
who instituted the pattern of an everlasting sacrifice
and was the first to offer himself as the saving Victim,
commanding us to make this offering as his memorial.
As we eat his flesh that was sacrificed for us,
we are made strong,
and, as we drink his Blood that was poured out for us,
we are washed clean.

And so, with Angels and Archangels,
with Thrones and Dominions,
and with all the hosts and Powers of heaven,
we sing the hymn of your glory,
as without end we acclaim:

Holy, Holy, Holy Lord God of hosts...

EASTER

PREFACE I OF EASTER
THE PASCHAL MYSTERY

The following Preface is said during Easter Time. At the Easter Vigil, is said 'on this night'; on Easter Sunday and throughout the Octave of Easter, is said 'on this day'; on other days of Easter Time, is said 'in this time'.

It is truly right and just,
our duty and our salvation,
at all times to acclaim you, O Lord,
but (on this night / on this day /
in this time) above all
to laud you yet more gloriously,
when Christ our Passover
has been sacrificed.

For he is the true Lamb
who has taken away the sins of the world;
by dying he has destroyed our death,
and by rising, restored our life.

Therefore, overcome with paschal joy,
every land, every people exults
in your praise
and even the heavenly Powers,
with the angelic hosts,
sing together the unending hymn
of your glory,
as they acclaim:

Holy, Holy, Holy Lord God of hosts...

PREFACE II OF EASTER
NEW LIFE IN CHRIST

The following Preface is said during Easter Time.

It is truly right and just,
our duty and our salvation,
at all times to acclaim you, O Lord,
but in this time above all to laud you
yet more gloriously,
when Christ our Passover
has been sacrificed.

Through him the children of light
rise to eternal life
and the halls of the heavenly Kingdom
are thrown open to the faithful;
for his Death is our ransom from death,
and in his rising the life of all has risen.

Therefore, overcome with paschal joy,
every land, every people exults in your praise
and even the heavenly Powers,
with the angelic hosts,
sing together the unending hymn
of your glory,
as they acclaim:

Holy, Holy, Holy Lord God of hosts...

PREFACE III OF EASTER
CHRIST LIVING AND
ALWAYS INTERCEDING FOR US

The following Preface is said during Easter Time.

It is truly right and just,
our duty and our salvation,
at all times to acclaim you, O Lord,
but in this time above all to laud you
yet more gloriously,
when Christ our Passover
has been sacrificed.

He never ceases to offer himself for us
but defends us and ever pleads our cause
before you:
he is the sacrificial Victim
who dies no more,
the Lamb, once slain, who lives for ever.

Therefore, overcome with paschal joy,
every land, every people exults in your praise
and even the heavenly Powers,
with the angelic hosts,
sing together the unending hymn
of your glory,
as they acclaim:

Holy, Holy, Holy Lord God of hosts...

PREFACE IV OF EASTER
THE RESTORATION OF THE UNIVERSE
THROUGH THE PASCHAL MYSTERY

The following Preface is said during Easter Time.

It is truly right and just,
our duty and our salvation,
at all times to acclaim you, O Lord,
but in this time above all to laud you
yet more gloriously,
when Christ our Passover
has been sacrificed.

For, with the old order destroyed,
a universe cast down is renewed,
and integrity of life is restored to us in Christ.

Therefore, overcome with paschal joy,
every land, every people exults in your praise
and even the heavenly Powers,
with the angelic hosts,
sing together the unending hymn
of your glory,
as they acclaim:

Holy, Holy, Holy Lord God of hosts...

PREFACE V OF EASTER

CHRIST, PRIEST AND VICTIM

The following Preface is said during Easter Time.

It is truly right and just,
our duty and our salvation,
at all times to acclaim you, O Lord,
but in this time above all to laud you
yet more gloriously,
when Christ our Passover
has been sacrificed.

By the oblation of his Body,
he brought the sacrifices of old to fulfilment
in the reality of the Cross
and, by commending himself to you
for our salvation,
showed himself the Priest, the Altar,
and the Lamb of sacrifice.

Therefore, overcome with paschal joy,
every land, every people exults in your praise
and even the heavenly Powers,
with the angelic hosts,
sing together the unending hymn
of your glory,
as they acclaim:

Holy, Holy, Holy Lord God of hosts...

The following two Prefaces are said on the day of the Ascension of the Lord. They may be said on the days between the Ascension and Pentecost in all Masses that have no proper Preface.

PREFACE I OF THE ASCENSION OF THE LORD

THE MYSTERY OF THE ASCENSION

It is truly right and just,
our duty and our salvation,
always and everywhere to give you thanks,
Lord, holy Father,
almighty and eternal God.

For the Lord Jesus, the King of glory,
conqueror of sin and death,
ascended (today) to the highest heavens,
as the Angels gazed in wonder.

Mediator between God and man,
judge of the world and Lord of hosts,
he ascended, not to distance himself
from our lowly state
but that we, his members,
might be confident of following
where he, our Head and Founder,
has gone before.

Therefore, overcome with paschal joy,
every land, every people exults in your praise
and even the heavenly Powers,
with the angelic hosts,
sing together the unending hymn
of your glory,
as they acclaim:

Holy, Holy, Holy Lord God of hosts...

PREFACE II OF THE ASCENSION OF THE LORD

THE MYSTERY OF THE ASCENSION

It is truly right and just,
our duty and our salvation,
always and everywhere to give you thanks,
Lord, holy Father,
almighty and eternal God,
through Christ our Lord.

For after his Resurrection
he plainly appeared to all his disciples
and was taken up to heaven in their sight,
that he might make us sharers in his divinity.

Therefore, overcome with paschal joy,
every land, every people exults in your praise
and even the heavenly Powers,
with the angelic hosts,
sing together the unending hymn
of your glory,
as they acclaim:

Holy, Holy, Holy Lord God of hosts...

THE MYSTERY OF PENTECOST

The following Preface is said on Pentecost Sunday.

It is truly right and just,
our duty and our salvation,
always and everywhere to give you thanks,
Lord, holy Father,
almighty and eternal God.

For, bringing your Paschal Mystery
to completion,
you bestowed the Holy Spirit today
on those you made
your adopted children
by uniting them to your Only Begotten Son.
This same Spirit, as the Church
came to birth,
opened to all peoples
the knowledge of God
and brought together
the many languages of the earth
in profession of the one faith.

Therefore, overcome with paschal joy,
every land, every people
exults in your praise
and even the heavenly Powers,
with the angelic hosts,
sing together the unending hymn
of your glory,
as they acclaim:

Holy, Holy, Holy Lord God of hosts...

PREFACES FOR OTHER OCCASIONS

MYSTERY OF MARY AND THE CHURCH

This Preface is said on the Solemnity of The Immaculate Conception of the Blessed Virgin Mary

It is truly right and just,
our duty and our salvation,
always and everywhere to give you thanks,
Lord, holy Father,
almighty and eternal God.

For you preserved
the Most Blessed Virgin Mary
from all stain of original sin,
so that in her, endowed with the rich
fullness of your grace,
you might prepare a worthy Mother
for your Son
and signify the beginning of the Church,
his beautiful Bride without spot or wrinkle.

She, the most pure Virgin,
was to bring forth a Son,
the innocent Lamb
who would wipe away our offences;
you placed her above all others
to be for your people an advocate of grace
and a model of holiness.

And so, in company with the choirs
of Angels,
we praise you, and with joy we proclaim:

Holy, Holy, Holy Lord God of hosts...

MYSTERY OF THE PRESENTATION OF THE LORD

The following Preface is said on the feast of the Presentation of the Lord (2 February).

It is truly right and just,
our duty and our salvation,
always and everywhere to give you thanks,
Lord, holy Father,
almighty and eternal God.

For your co-eternal Son was presented on
this day in the Temple
and revealed by the Spirit
as the glory of Israel
and Light of the nations.

And so, we, too, go forth, rejoicing to
encounter your Salvation,
and with the Angels and Saints
praise you, as without end we acclaim:

Holy, Holy, Holy Lord God of hosts...

LATIN TEXTS OF THE ORDER OF MASS

CONFITEOR

Confiteor Deo omnipotenti et vobis, fratres,
quia peccavi nimis
cogitatione, verbo, opere et omissione:
mea culpa, mea culpa, mea maxima culpa.
Ideo precor beatam Mariam semper Virginem,
omnes Angelos et Sanctos,
et vos, fratres, orare pro me
ad Dominum Deum nostrum. Amen

KYRIE

Kyrie, eleison.
Kyrie, eleison.
Christe, eleison.
Christe, eleison.
Kyrie, eleison.
Kyrie, eleison.

GLORIA

**Gloria in excelsis Deo
et in terra pax hominibus bonae voluntatis.
Laudamus te,
benedicimus te,
adoramus te,
glorificamus te,
gratias agimus tibi propter magnam
gloriam tuam,
Domine Deus, Rex caelestis,
Deus Pater omnipotens.
Domine Fili unigenite, Jesu Christe,
Domine Deus, Agnus Dei, Filius Patris,
qui tollis peccata mundi, miserere nobis;
qui tollis peccata mundi,
suscipe deprecationem nostram.
Qui sedes ad dexteram Patris,
miserere nobis.
Quoniam tu solus Sanctus,
tu solus Dominus,
tu solus Altissimus,
Jesu Christe, cum Sancto Spiritu:
in gloria Dei Patris. Amen.**

CREDO

**Credo in unum Deum,
Patrem Omnipotentem,
factorem caeli et terrae,
visibilium omnium et invisibilium.
Et in unum Dominum Jesum Christum,
Filium Dei unigenitum,
et ex Patre natum ante omnia saecula.
Deum de Deo, lumen de lumine,
Deum verum de Deo vero,
genitum, non factum,
consubstantialem Patri:
per quem omnia facta sunt.
Qui propter nos homines
et propter nostram salutem
descendit de caelis.**

**Et incarnatus est de Spiritu Sancto
ex Maria Virgine; et homo factus est.**

**Crucifixus etiam pro nobis sub Pontio
Pilato;
passus et sepultus est,
et resurrexit tertia die, secundum Scripturas,
et ascendit in caelum,
sedet ad dexteram Patris.
Et iterum venturus est cum gloria,
iudicare vivos et mortuos,
cuius regni non erit finis.
Et in Spiritum Sanctum,
Dominum et vivificantem:
qui ex Patre Filioque procedit.
Qui cum Patre et Filio simul adoratur
et conglorificatur:
qui locutus est per prophetas.
Et unam, sanctam, catholicam
et apostolicam Ecclesiam.
Confiteor unum baptisma
in remissionem peccatorum.
Et exspecto resurrectionem mortuorum,
et vitam venturi saeculi. Amen.**

ORATE FRATRES

Orate fratres:
ut meum ac vestrum sacrificium
acceptabile fiat apud Deum
Patrem omnipotentem.

**Suscipiat Dominus sacrificium
de manibus tuis
ad laudem et gloriam nominis sui,
ad utilitatem quoque nostram
totiusque Ecclesiae sanctae.**

SURSUM CORDA

Dominus vobiscum.
Et cum spiritu tuo.

Sursum corda.
Habemus ad Dominum.

Gratias Agamus Domino Deo nostro.
Dignum et iustum est.

SANCTUS

**Sanctus, Sanctus, Sanctus Dominus
Deus Sabaoth.
Pleni sunt caeli et terra gloria tua.
Hosanna in excelsis.
Benedictus qui venit in nomine Domini.
Hosanna in excelsis.**

MYSTERIUM FIDEI

Mysterium Fidei.

1 **Mortem tuam annuntiamus, Domine,
et tuam resurrectionem confitemur,
donec venias.**

2 **Quotiescumque manducamus panem
hunc
et calicem bibimus
mortem tuam annuntiamus, Domine,
donec venias.**

3 **Salvator Mundi, salva nos,
qui per crucem et resurrectionem tuam
liberasti nos.**

PATER NOSTER

Praeceptis salutaribus moniti,
et divina insitutione formati,
audemus dicere:

**Pater noster, qui es in caelis:
sanctificetur nomen tuum;
adveniat regnum tuum;
fiat voluntas tua, sicut in caelo,
et in terra.
Panem nostrum cotidianum
da nobis hodie;
et dimitte nobis debita nostra,
sicut et nos dimittimus debitoribus
nostris
et ne nos inducas in tentationem;
sed libera nos a malo.**

Libera nos, quaesumus, Domine,
ab omnibus malis,...
...et adventum Salvatoris nostri Iesu Christi.

**Quia tuum est regnum,
et potestas, et gloria
in saecula.**

AGNUS DEI

**Agnus Dei, qui tollis peccata mundi:
miserere nobis.
Agnus Dei, qui tollis peccata mundi:
miserere nobis.
Agnus Dei, qui tollis peccata mundi:
dona nobis pacem.**

PROPER OF TIME

CONTENTS OF THE PROPER OF TIME

COMMON RESPONSORIAL PSALMS

The Responsorial Psalm should correspond to each reading and should, as a rule, be taken from the Lectionary In order, however, that the people may be able to sing the Psalm response more readily, texts of some responses and psalms have been chosen for the various seasons of the year or for the various categories of Saints. These may be used in place of the text corresponding to the reading whenever the Psalm is sung.

General Instruction of the Roman Missal n 61

The appropriate Common Responsorial Psalms are to be found at the beginning of each season.

ADVENT

ABOUT THE SEASON

Advent has a twofold character, for it is a time of preparation for the Solemnities of Christmas, in which the First Coming of the Son of God to humanity is remembered, and likewise a time when, by remembrance of this, minds and hearts are led to look forward to Christ's Second Coming at the end of time. For these two reasons, Advent is a period of devout and expectant delight.

Universal Norms on the Liturgical Year and the Calendar n 39

ABOUT THE READINGS

Each gospel reading has a distinctive theme: the Lord's coming at the end of time (First Sunday of Advent), John the Baptist (Second and Third Sunday), and the events that prepared immediately for the Lord's birth (Fourth Sunday).

The Old Testament readings are prophecies about the Messiah and the Messianic age, especially from the Isaiah.

The readings from an apostle serve as exhortations and as proclamations, in keeping with the different themes of Advent.

Introduction to the Lectionary n 93

COMMON RESPONSORIAL PSALMS FOR ADVENT

COMMON RESPONSE

R. **Come, Lord and set us free.**

COMMON PSALM 1 *Psalm 25(24):4-5b. 8-9. 10, 14. R.1b*

R. **To you, O LORD, I lift up my soul.**

1 O LORD, make me know your ways.
Teach me your paths.
Guide me in your truth, and teach me;
for you are the God of my salvation. R.

2 Good and upright is the LORD;
therefore he shows the way to sinners.
He guides the humble in right judgement;
to the humble he teaches his way. R.

3 All the LORD's paths are mercy and faithfulness,
for those who keep his covenant and commands.
The LORD's secret is for those who fear him;
to them he reveals his covenant. R.

COMMON PSALM 2 *Psalm 85(84):9ab, 10. 11-12. 13-14. R.8a*

R. Show us, O Lord, your mercy.

1 I will hear what the Lord God speaks;
he speaks of peace for his people and his faithful.
His salvation is near for those who fear him,
and his glory will dwell in our land. R.

2 Mercy and faithfulness have met;
justice and peace have kissed.
Faithfulness shall spring from the earth,
and justice look down from heaven. R.

3 The Lord will bestow his bounty,
and our earth shall yield its increase.
Righteousness will march before him,
and guide his steps on the way. R.

FIRST SUNDAY OF ADVENT

ENTRANCE ANTIPHON *cf Psalm 24:1–3*

To you, I lift up my soul, O my God.
In you, I have trusted; let me not be put to shame.
Nor let my enemies exult over me;
and let none who hope in you be put to shame.

▷ page 7

The Gloria is omitted.

COLLECT

Grant your faithful, we pray, almighty God,
the resolve to run forth to meet your Christ
with righteous deeds at his coming,
so that, gathered at his right hand,
they may be worthy to possess the heavenly Kingdom.
Through our Lord Jesus Christ, your Son,
who lives and reigns with you in the unity of the Holy Spirit,
God, for ever and ever. **Amen.**

FIRST READING *Jeremiah 33:14–16*

'I will cause a righteous Branch to spring up for David.'

A reading from the Prophet Jeremiah.

Behold, the days are coming, declares the Lord, when I will fulfil the promise I made to the house of Israel and the house of Judah.

In those days and at that time I will cause a righteous Branch to spring up for David, and he shall execute justice and righteousness in the land. In those days Judah will be saved, and Jerusalem will dwell securely. And this is the name by which it will be called: 'The Lord is our righteousness.'

The word of the Lord.
Thanks be to God.

RESPONSORIAL PSALM *Psalm 25(24):4-5b. 8-9. 10, 14. R.1b*

R. To you, O LORD, I lift up my soul.

1. O LORD make me know your ways.
Teach me your paths.
Guide me in your truth, and teach me;
for you are the God of my salvation. R.

2. Good and upright is the LORD;
therefore he shows the way to sinners.
He guides the humble in right judgement;
to the humble he teaches his way. R.

3. All the LORD's paths are mercy and faithfulness,
for those who keep his covenant and commands.
The LORD's secret is for those who fear him;
to them he reveals his covenant. R.

SECOND READING *1 Thessalonians 3:12–4:2*

'May the Lord establish your hearts for the coming of Christ.'

A reading from the first letter of Saint Paul to the Thessalonians.

Brothers and sisters: May the Lord make you increase and abound in love for one another and for all, as we do for you, so that he may establish your hearts blameless in holiness before our God and Father, at the coming of our Lord Jesus with all his saints.

Finally, then, brothers and sisters, we ask and urge you in the Lord Jesus, that as you received from us how you ought to walk and to please God, just as you are doing, that you do so more and more. For you know what instructions we gave you through the Lord Jesus.

The word of the Lord.
Thanks be to God.

ACCLAMATION BEFORE THE GOSPEL *Psalm 85 (84):8*

Alleluia, alleluia.
Show us, O LORD, your mercy,
and grant us your salvation.
Alleluia.

GOSPEL *Luke 21:25–28, 34–36*

'Your redemption is drawing near.'

The Lord be with you.
And with your spirit.

A reading from the holy Gospel according to Luke.
Glory to you, O Lord.

At that time: Jesus said to his disciples: 'There will be signs in sun and moon and stars, and on the earth distress of nations in perplexity because of the roaring of the sea and the waves, people fainting with fear and with foreboding of what is coming on the world. For the powers of the heavens will be shaken. And then they will see the Son of Man coming in a cloud with power and great glory. Now when these things begin to take place, straighten up and raise your heads, because your redemption is drawing near.

'But watch yourselves lest your hearts be weighed down with dissipation and drunkenness and cares of this life, and that day come upon you suddenly like a trap. For it will come upon all who dwell on the face of the whole earth. But stay awake at all times, praying that you may have strength to escape all these things that are going to take place, and to stand before the Son of Man.'

The Gospel of the Lord.
Praise to you, Lord Jesus Christ.

▷ *page 11*

PRAYER OVER THE OFFERINGS

Accept, we pray, O Lord, these offerings we make,
gathered from among your gifts to us,
and may what you grant us to celebrate devoutly here below
gain for us the prize of eternal redemption.
Through Christ our Lord. **Amen**

▷ *page 15*

Preface I of Advent, p 65.

COMMUNION ANTIPHON *Psalm 84:13*

The Lord will bestow his bounty, and our earth shall yield its increase.

▷ *page 58*

PRAYER AFTER COMMUNION

May these mysteries, O Lord,
in which we have participated,
profit us, we pray,
for even now, as we walk amid passing things,
you teach us by them to love the things of heaven
and hold fast to what endures.
Through Christ our Lord. **Amen.**

A solemn blessing or prayer over the people may be used. ▷ *page 59*

SECOND SUNDAY OF ADVENT

ENTRANCE ANTIPHON *cf Isaiah 30:19, 30*

O people of Sion, behold,
the Lord will come to save the nations,
and the Lord will make the glory of his voice heard
in the joy of your heart.

▷ *page 7*

The Gloria is omitted.

COLLECT

Almighty and merciful God,
may no earthly undertaking hinder those
who set out in haste to meet your Son,
but may our learning of heavenly wisdom
gain us admittance to his company.
Who lives and reigns with you in the unity of the Holy Spirit,
God, for ever and ever. **Amen.**

FIRST READING *Baruch 5:1–9*

'God will show your splendour.'

A reading from the Prophet Baruch.

Take off the garment of your sorrow and affliction, O Jerusalem, and put on for ever the beauty of the glory from God. Put on the robe of the righteousness from God; put on your head the crown of the glory of the Everlasting. For God will show your splendour everywhere under heaven. For your name will for ever be called by God: 'Peace of righteousness and glory of godliness'. Arise, O Jerusalem, stand upon the height and look towards the east and see your children gathered from west and east, at the word of the Holy One, rejoicing that God has remembered them. For they went forth from you on foot, led away by their enemies; but God will bring them back to you, carried in glory, as on a royal throne. For God has ordered that every high mountain and the everlasting hills be made low and the valleys filled up to make level ground, so that Israel may walk safely in the glory of God. The woods and every fragrant tree have shaded Israel at God's command. For God will lead Israel with joy in the light of his glory, with the mercy and righteousness that come from him.

The word of the Lord.
Thanks be to God.

RESPONSORIAL PSALM *126(125): 1-2b. 2c-3. 4-5. 6. R.3*

R. **What great deeds the Lord worked for us!**
Indeed, we were glad.

1 When the Lord brought back the exiles of Sion,
we thought we were dreaming.
Then was our mouth filled with laughter;
on our tongues, songs of joy. R.

2 Then they said among the nations,
'What great deeds the Lord worked for them!'
What great deeds the Lord worked for us!
Indeed, we were glad. R.

3 Bring back our exiles, O Lord ,
as streams in the Negeb.
Those who are sowing in tears
will sing when they reap. R.

4 They go out, they go out, full of tears,
bearing seed for the sowing;
they come back, they come back with a song,
bearing their sheaves. R.

SECOND READING *Philippians 1:3–6; 8–11*

'Be pure and blameless for the day of Christ.'

A reading from the Letter of Saint Paul to the Philippians.

Brothers and sisters: I thank my God in all my remembrance of you, always in every prayer of mine for you all, making my prayer with joy, because of your partnership in the gospel from the first day until now. And I am sure of this, that he who began a good work in you will bring it to completion at the day of Jesus Christ. For God is my witness, how I yearn for you all with the affection of Christ Jesus. And it is my prayer that your love may abound more and more, with knowledge and all discernment, so that you may approve what is excellent, and so be pure and blameless for the day of Christ, filled with the fruit of righteousness that comes through Jesus Christ, to the glory and praise of God.

The word of the Lord.
Thanks be to God.

ACCLAMATION BEFORE THE GOSPEL *Luke 3:4, 6*

Alleluia, alleluia.
Prepare the way of the Lord,
make his paths straight;
all flesh shall see the salvation of God.
Alleluia.

GOSPEL *Luke 3:1–6*

The Lord be with you.
And with your spirit.

A reading from the holy Gospel according to Luke.
Glory to you, O Lord.

'All flesh shall see the salvation of God.'

In the fifteenth year of the reign of Tiberius Caesar, Pontius Pilate being governor of Judea, and Herod being tetrarch of Galilee, and his brother Philip tetrarch of the region of Ituraea and Trachonitis, and Lysanias tetrarch of Abilene, during the high priesthood of Annas and Caiaphas, the word of God came to John the son of Zechariah in the wilderness.

And he went into all the region around the Jordan, proclaiming a baptism of repentance for the forgiveness of sins. As it is written in the book of the words of Isaiah the prophet, 'The voice of one crying in the wilderness:

"Prepare the way of the Lord, make his paths straight. Every valley shall be filled, and every mountain and hill shall be made low, and the crooked shall become straight, and the rough places shall become level ways, and all flesh shall see the salvation of God."'

The Gospel of the Lord.
Praise to you, Lord Jesus Christ.

▷ *page 11*

PRAYER OVER THE OFFERINGS

Be pleased, O Lord, with our humble prayers and offerings,
and, since we have no merits to plead our cause,
come, we pray, to our rescue
with the protection of your mercy.
Through Christ our Lord. **Amen**

▷ page 15

Preface I of Advent, p 65.

COMMUNION ANTIPHON *Baruch 5:5, 4:6*

Jerusalem, arise and stand upon the heights,
and behold the joy which comes to you from God.

▷ page 58

PRAYER AFTER COMMUNION

Replenished by the food of spiritual nourishment,
we humbly beseech you, O Lord,
that, through our partaking in this mystery,
you may teach us to judge wisely the things of earth
and hold firm to the things of heaven.
Through Christ our Lord. **Amen.**

▷ page 59

A solemn blessing or prayer over the people may be used.

THIRD SUNDAY OF ADVENT

ENTRANCE ANTIPHON *Philippians 4:4–5*

Rejoice in the Lord always; again I say, rejoice.
Indeed, the Lord is near.

▷ page 7

The Gloria is omitted.

COLLECT

O God, who see how your people
faithfully await the feast of the Lord's Nativity,
enable us, we pray,
to attain the joys of so great a salvation
and to celebrate them always
with solemn worship and glad rejoicing.
Through our Lord Jesus Christ, your Son,
who lives and reigns with you in the unity of the Holy Spirit,
God, for ever and ever. **Amen.**

FIRST READING *Zephaniah 3:14–18a*

'The Lord will exult over you with loud singing.'

A reading from the Prophet Zephaniah.

Sing aloud, O daughter of Sion; shout, O Israel! Rejoice and exult with all your heart, O daughter of Jerusalem! The LORD has taken away the judgements against you; he has cleared away your enemies. The King of Israel, the LORD, is in your midst; you shall never again fear evil. On that day it shall be said to Jerusalem: 'Fear not, O Sion; let not your hands grow weak. The LORD your God is in your midst, a mighty one who will save; he will rejoice over you with gladness; he will quiet you by his love; he will exult over you with loud singing. I will gather those of you who mourn for the festival, so that you will no longer suffer reproach.'

The word of the Lord.
Thanks be to God.

RESPONSORIAL PSALM *Isaiah 12:2–3. 4b-d. 5-6 response v 6*

R. Shout aloud and sing praise,
for great in your midst is the Holy One of Israel.

1 Behold, God is my salvation!
I will trust, and will not be afraid,
for the LORD is my strength and my praise,
and he has been my salvation.
With joy you will draw water
from the springs of salvation. R.

2 Give thanks to the LORD, invoke his name;
make known among the peoples his deeds;
proclaim that his name is exalted. R.

3 Sing to the LORD for he has wrought wonders;
let this be known through all the earth.
Shout aloud and sing praise, you who dwell in Sion,
for great in your midst is the Holy One of Israel. R.

SECOND READING *Philippians 4:4–7*

'The Lord is at hand.'

A reading from the Letter of Saint Paul to the Philippians.

Brothers and sisters: Rejoice in the Lord always; again I will say, rejoice. Let your reasonableness be known to everyone. The Lord is at hand; do not be anxious about anything, but in everything by prayer and supplication with thanksgiving let your requests be made known to God. And the peace of God, which surpasses all understanding, will guard your hearts and your minds in Christ Jesus.

The word of the Lord.
Thanks be to God.

ACCLAMATION BEFORE THE GOSPEL *Isaiah 61:1 (Luke 4:18)*

Alleluia, alleluia.
The Spirit of the LORD is upon me,
he has sent me to proclaim good news to the poor.
Alleluia.

GOSPEL *Luke 3:10–18*

The Lord be with you.
And with your spirit.

A reading from the holy Gospel according to Luke.
Glory to you, O Lord.

'And we, what shall we do?'

At that time: The crowds asked John, 'What, then, shall we do?' And he answered them, 'Whoever has two tunics is to share with him who has none, and whoever has food is to do likewise.' Tax collectors also came to be baptised and said to him, 'Teacher, what shall we do?' And he said to them, 'Collect no more than you are authorised to do.' Soldiers also asked him, 'And we, what shall we do?' And he said to them, 'Do not extort money from anyone by threats or by false accusation, and be content with your wages.' As the people were filled with expectation, and all were questioning in their hearts concerning John, whether he might be the Christ, John answered them all, saying, 'I baptise you with water, but he who is mightier than I is coming, the strap of whose sandals I am not worthy to untie. He will baptise you with the Holy Spirit and fire. His winnowing fork is in his hand, to clear his threshing floor and to gather the wheat into his barn, but the chaff he will burn with unquenchable fire.' So with many other exhortations he preached good news to the people.

The Gospel of the Lord.
Praise to you, Lord Jesus Christ.

▷ page 11

PRAYER OVER THE OFFERINGS

May the sacrifice of our worship, Lord, we pray,
be offered to you unceasingly,
to complete what was begun in sacred mystery
and powerfully accomplish for us your saving work.
Through Christ our Lord. **Amen**

▷ page 15

Preface I or II of Advent, pp 65–66.

COMMUNION ANTIPHON *cf Isaiah 35:4*

Say to the faint of heart: Be strong and do not fear.
Behold, our God will come, and he will save us.

▷ page 58

PRAYER AFTER COMMUNION

We implore your mercy, Lord,
that this divine sustenance may cleanse us of our faults
and prepare us for the coming feasts.
Through Christ our Lord. Amen.

▷ page 59

A solemn blessing or prayer over the people may be used.

FOURTH SUNDAY OF ADVENT

ENTRANCE ANTIPHON *cf Isaiah 45:8*

Drop down dew from above, you heavens,
and let the clouds rain down the Just One;
let the earth be opened and bring forth a Saviour.

▷ *page 7*

The Gloria is omitted.

COLLECT

Pour forth, we beseech you, O Lord,
your grace into our hearts,
that we, to whom the Incarnation of Christ your Son
was made known by the message of an Angel,
may by his Passion and Cross
be brought to the glory of his Resurrection.
Who lives and reigns with you in the unity of the Holy Spirit,
God, for ever and ever. **Amen.**

FIRST READING *Micah 5:2-5a*

'From you shall come forth one who is to be ruler in Israel.'

A reading from the Prophet Micah.

Thus says the LORD: You, O Bethlehem Ephrathah, who are too little to be among the clans of Judah, from you shall come forth for me one who is to be ruler in Israel, whose coming forth is from of old, from ancient days. Therefore he shall give them up until the time when she who is in labour has given birth; then the rest of his brothers shall return to the people of Israel. And he shall stand and shepherd his flock in the strength of the LORD, in the majesty of the name of the LORD his God. And they shall dwell secure, for now he shall be great to the ends of the earth. And he shall be their peace.

The word of the Lord.
Thanks be to God.

RESPONSORIAL PSALM *Psalm 80 (79):2ac, 3b, 15–16, 18–19 response v 4*

**R. Bring us back, O God;
let your face shine forth, and we shall be saved.**

1 O shepherd of Israel, hear us,
enthroned on the cherubim, shine forth.
Rouse up your might and come to save us. R.

2 God of hosts, turn again, we implore;
look down from heaven and see.
Visit this vine and protect it,
the stock your right hand has planted,
the son you have claimed for yourself. R.

3 May your hand be on the man at your right hand,
the son of man you have confirmed as your own.
And we shall never forsake you again;
give us life that we may call upon your name. R.

SECOND READING *Hebrews 10:5–10*

'Behold, I have come to do your will.'

A reading from the Letter to the Hebrews.

Brothers and sisters: When Christ came into the world, he said, 'Sacrifices and offerings you have not desired, but a body have you prepared for me; in burnt offerings and sin offerings you have taken no pleasure. Then I said, "Behold, I have come to do your will, O God, as it is written of me in the scroll of the book."

When he said above, 'You have neither desired nor taken pleasure in sacrifices and offerings and burnt offerings and sin offerings' (these are offered according to the Law), then he added, 'Behold, I have come to do your will'. He does away with the first in order to establish the second. And by that will we have been sanctified through the offering of the body of Jesus Christ once for all.

The word of the Lord.
Thanks be to God.

ACCLAMATION BEFORE THE GOSPEL *Luke 1:38*

Alleluia, alleluia.
Behold, I am the handmaid of the Lord;
let it be to me according to your word.
Alleluia.

GOSPEL *Luke 1:39–45*

The Lord be with you.
And with your spirit.

A reading from the holy Gospel according to Luke.
Glory to you, O Lord.

'Why is this granted to me that the mother of my Lord should come to me?'

In those days Mary arose and went with haste into the hill country, to a town in Judah, and she entered the house of Zechariah and greeted Elizabeth. And when Elizabeth heard the greeting of Mary, the baby leaped in her womb. And Elizabeth was filled with the Holy Spirit, and she exclaimed with a loud cry, 'Blessed are you among women, and blessed is the fruit of your womb! And why is this granted to me that the mother of my Lord should come to me? For behold, when the sound of your greeting came to my ears, the baby in my womb leaped for joy. And blessed is she who believed that there would be a fulfilment of what was spoken to her from the Lord.'

The Gospel of the Lord.
Praise to you, Lord Jesus Christ.

▷ *page 11*

PRAYER OVER THE OFFERINGS

May the Holy Spirit, O Lord,
sanctify these gifts laid upon your altar,
just as he filled with his power the womb of the Blessed Virgin Mary.
Through Christ our Lord. **Amen**

▷ *page 15*

Preface II of Advent, p 66.

COMMUNION ANTIPHON *Isaiah 7:14*

Behold, a Virgin shall conceive and bear a son;
and his name will be called Emmanuel. ▷ page 58

PRAYER AFTER COMMUNION

Having received this pledge of eternal redemption,
we pray, almighty God,
that, as the feast day of our salvation draws ever nearer,
so we may press forward all the more eagerly
to the worthy celebration of the mystery of your Son's Nativity.
Who lives and reigns for ever and ever. **Amen.** ▷ page 59

A solemn blessing or prayer over the people may be used.

CHRISTMAS TIME

ABOUT THE SEASON

After the annual celebration of the Paschal Mystery, the Church has no more ancient custom than celebrating the memorial of the Nativity of the Lord and of his first manifestations, and this takes place in Christmas Time.

Universal Norms on the Liturgical Year and the Calendar n 39

This solemnity of the Lord's birth [Christmas] celebrates the mystery of the incarnation by which the Word of God humbled himself to share in our humanity, in order that he might enable us to become sharers in his divinity.

Ceremonial of Bishops n 237

The ancient solemnity of the Epiphany of the Lord ranks among the principal festivals of the whole liturgical year, since it celebrates in the child born of Mary the manifestation of the one who is the Son of God, the Messiah of the Jewish people, and a light to the nations.

Ceremonial of Bishops n 240

ABOUT THE READINGS

For the vigil and the three Masses of Christmas both the prophetic readings and the others have been chosen from the Roman tradition.

The Gospel on the Sunday within the octave of Christmas, feast of the Holy Family, is about Jesus' childhood and the other readings are about the virtues of family life.

On the octave of Christmas, solemnity of the Mary, Mother of God, the readings are about the Virgin Mother of God and the giving of the holy Name of Jesus.

On the second Sunday after Christmas, the readings are about the mystery of the Incarnation.

On the Epiphany, the Old Testament reading and the Gospel continue the Roman tradition; the text for the reading from the apostolic letters is about the calling of all peoples to salvation.

On the feast of the Baptism of the Lord, the texts chosen are about this mystery.

Introduction to the Lectionary n 95

COMMON RESPONSORIAL PSALMS FOR CHRISTMAS

COMMON RESPONSE

R. Today we have seen your glory, O Lord.

COMMON PSALM – SEASON OF CHRISTMAS *Psalm 98(97):1. 2-3b. 3c-4. 5-6. R.3cd*

**R. All the ends of the earth have seen
the salvation of our God.**

1 O sing a new song to the LORD,
for he has worked wonders.
His right hand and his holy arm
have brought salvation. R.

2 The LORD has made known his salvation,
has shown his deliverance to the nations.
He has remembered his merciful love
and his truth for the house of Israel. R.

3 All the ends of the earth have seen
the salvation of our God.
Shout to the LORD, all the earth;
break forth into joyous song,
and sing out your praise. R.

4 Sing psalms to the LORD with the harp,
with the harp and the sound of song.
With trumpets and the sound of the horn,
raise a shout before the King, the LORD. R.

COMMON PSALM – EPIPHANY *Psalm 72(71):1-2. 7-8. 10-11. 12-13. R.cf. 11*

**R. All the kings of the earth shall fall
prostrate before you; all nations shall
serve you.**

1 O God, give your judgement to the king,
to a king's son your justice,
that he may judge your people in justice,
and your poor in right judgement. R.

2 In his days justice shall flourish,
and great peace till the moon is no more.
He shall rule from sea to sea,
from the River to the bounds of the earth. R.

3 The kings of Tarshish and the islands
shall pay him tribute.
The kings of Sheba and Seba
shall bring him gifts.
Before him all kings shall fall prostrate,
all nations shall serve him. R.

continued...

R. All the kings of the earth shall fall prostrate before you; all nations shall serve you.

4 For he shall rescue the needy when they cry,
the poor who have no one to help.
He will have pity on the weak and the needy,
and save the lives of the needy. R.

THE NATIVITY OF THE LORD — VIGIL MASS

25 DECEMBER

These readings are used at Masses on the evening of December 24, either before or after First Vespers (Evening Prayer I) of the Nativity.

ENTRANCE ANTIPHON *cf Exodus 16:6–7*

Today you will know that the Lord will come, and he will save us,
and in the morning you will see his glory.

▷ *page 7*

COLLECT

O God, who gladden us year by year
as we wait in hope for our redemption,
grant that, just as we joyfully welcome
your Only Begotten Son as our Redeemer,
we may also merit to face him confidently
when he comes again as our Judge.
Who lives and reigns with you in the unity of the Holy Spirit,
God, for ever and ever. **Amen.**

FIRST READING *Isaiah 62:1–5*

'The Lord delights in you.'

A reading from the Prophet Isaiah.

For Sion's sake I will not keep silent, and for Jerusalem's sake I will not be quiet, until her righteousness goes forth as brightness, and her salvation as a burning torch. The nations shall see your righteousness, and all the kings your glory, and you shall be called by a new name that the mouth of the LORD will give. You shall be a crown of beauty in the hand of the LORD, and a royal diadem in the hand of your God. You shall no more be termed Forsaken, and your land shall no more be termed Desolate, but you shall be called My Delight Is in Her, and your land Married; for the LORD delights in you, and your land shall be married. For as a young man marries a young woman, so shall your sons marry you, and as the bridegroom rejoices over the bride, so shall your God rejoice over you.

The word of the Lord.
Thanks be to God.

RESPONSORIAL PSALM *Psalm 89 (88):4–5. 16–17. 27, 29 response v 2a*

R. I will sing for ever of your mercies, O LORD.

1 'With my chosen one I have made a covenant;
I have sworn to David my servant:
I will establish your descendants for ever,
and set up your throne through all ages.' R.

2 How blessed the people who know your praise,
who walk, O Lord, in the light of your face,
who find their joy every day in your name,
who make your righteousness their joyful acclaim. R.

3 'He will call out to me, "You are my father,
my God, the rock of my salvation".
I will keep my faithful love for him always;
with him my covenant shall last.' R.

SECOND READING *Acts 13:16–17, 22–25*

The witness of Paul to Christ, the Son of David.

A reading from the Acts of the Apostles.

When Paul came to Antioch of Pisidia, he stood up in the synagogue, and motioning with his hand said: 'Men of Israel and you who fear God, listen. The God of this people Israel chose our fathers and made the people great during their stay in the land of Egypt, and with uplifted arm he led them out of it. And when he raised up David to be their king, of whom he testified and said, "I have found in David the son of Jesse a man after my heart, who will do all my will." Of this man's offspring God has brought to Israel a Saviour, Jesus, as he promised. Before his coming, John had proclaimed a baptism of repentance to all the people of Israel. And as John was finishing his course, he said, "What do you suppose that I am? I am not he. No, but behold, after me one is coming, the sandals of whose feet I am not worthy to untie."'

The word of the Lord.
Thanks be to God.

ACCLAMATION BEFORE THE GOSPEL

Alleluia, alleluia.
Tomorrow the wickedness of the earth will be destroyed:
the Saviour of the world will reign over us.
Alleluia.

GOSPEL *Matthew 1:1-25 Shorter form: Matthew 1:18–25 (Only read text with side line next to it).*

The Lord be with you.
And with your spirit.

A reading from the holy Gospel according to Matthew.
Glory to you, O Lord.

'Mary will bear a son, and you shall call his name Jesus.'

The book of the genealogy of Jesus Christ, the son of David, the son of Abraham. Abraham was the father of Isaac, and Isaac the father of Jacob, and Jacob the father of Judah and his brothers, and Judah the father of Perez and Zerah by Tamar, and Perez the father of Hezron, and Hezron the father of Ram, and Ram the father of Amminadab, and Amminadab the father of Nahshon, and Nahshon the father of Salmon, and Salmon the father of Boaz by Rahab, and Boaz the father of Obed by Ruth, and Obed the father of Jesse, and Jesse the father of David the king.

And David was the father of Solomon by the wife of Uriah, and Solomon the father of Rehoboam, and Rehoboam the father of Abijah, and Abijah the father of Asaph, and Asaph the father of Jehoshaphat, and Jehoshaphat the father of Joram, and

Joram the father of Uzziah, and Uzziah the father of Jotham, and Jotham the father of Ahaz, and Ahaz the father of Hezekiah, and Hezekiah the father of Manasseh, and Manasseh the father of Amos, and Amos the father of Josiah, and Josiah the father of Jechoniah and his brothers, at the time of the deportation to Babylon.

And after the deportation to Babylon: Jechoniah was the father of Shealtiel, and Shealtiel the father of Zerubbabel, and Zerubbabel the father of Abiud, and Abiud the father of Eliakim, and Eliakim the father of Azor, and Azor the father of Zadok, and Zadok the father of Achim, and Achim the father of Eliud, and Eliud the father of Eleazar, and Eleazar the father of Matthan, and Matthan the father of Jacob, and Jacob the father of Joseph the husband of Mary, of whom Jesus was born, who is called Christ.

So all the generations from Abraham to David were fourteen generations, and from David to the deportation to Babylon fourteen generations, and from the deportation to Babylon to the Christ fourteen generations.

Now the birth of Jesus Christ took place in this way. When his mother Mary had been betrothed to Joseph, before they came together she was found to be with child from the Holy Spirit. And her husband Joseph, being a just man and unwilling to put her to shame, resolved to send her away quietly. But as he considered these things, behold, an angel of the Lord appeared to him in a dream, saying, 'Joseph, son of David, do not fear to take Mary as your wife, for that which is conceived in her is from the Holy Spirit. She will bear a son, and you shall call his name Jesus, for he will save his people from their sins.'

All this took place to fulfil what the Lord had spoken by the prophet: 'Behold, the virgin shall conceive and bear a son, and they shall call his name Emmanuel'— which means, God with us.

When Joseph woke from sleep, he did as the angel of the Lord commanded him: he took his wife, but knew her not until she had given birth to a son. And he called his name Jesus.

The Gospel of the Lord.
Praise to you, Lord Jesus Christ.

▷ *page 11*

PROFESSION OF FAITH

All kneel at the words 'and by the Holy Spirit was incarnate.'

PRAYER OVER THE OFFERINGS

As we look forward, O Lord,
to the coming festivities,
may we serve you all the more eagerly
for knowing that in them
you make manifest the beginnings of our redemption.
Through Christ our Lord. **Amen**

▷ *page 15*

Preface I, II or III of the Nativity of the Lord, pp 66–67.

When the Roman Canon is used, the proper form of the Communicantes (In communion with those) is said, p 19.

COMMUNION ANTIPHON *cf Isaiah 40:5*

The glory of the Lord will be revealed,
and all flesh will see the salvation of our God.

▷ *page 58*

PRAYER AFTER COMMUNION

Grant, O Lord, we pray,
that we may draw new vigour
from celebrating the Nativity of your Only Begotten Son,
by whose heavenly mystery we receive both food and drink.
Who lives and reigns for ever and ever. **Amen.**

▷ page 59

A solemn blessing or prayer over the people may be used.

NATIVITY OF THE LORD - AT THE MASS DURING THE NIGHT

25 DECEMBER

ENTRANCE ANTIPHON *Psalm 2:7*

The Lord said to me: You are my Son.
It is I who have begotten you this day.

or

Let us all rejoice in the Lord, for our Saviour has been born in the world.
Today true peace has come down to us from heaven.

▷ page 7

COLLECT

O God, who have made this most sacred night
radiant with the splendour of the true light,
grant, we pray, that we, who have known the mysteries of his light on earth,
may also delight in his gladness in heaven.
Who lives and reigns with you in the unity of the Holy Spirit,
God, for ever and ever. **Amen.**

FIRST READING *Isaiah 9:2–7*[1]

'A son is given to us.'

A reading from the Prophet Isaiah.

The people who walked in darkness have seen a great light; those who dwelt in a land of deep darkness, on them has light shone. You have multiplied the nation; you have increased its joy; they rejoice before you as with joy at the harvest, as they are glad when they divide the spoil. For the yoke of his burden, and the staff for his shoulder, the rod of his oppressor, you have broken as on the day of Midian. For every boot of the tramping warrior in battle tumult and every garment rolled in blood will be burned as fuel for the fire. For to us a child is born, to us a son is given; and the government shall be upon his shoulder, and his name shall be called Wonderful Counsellor, Mighty God, Everlasting Father, Prince of Peace. Of the increase of his government and of peace, there will be no end, on the throne of David and over his kingdom, to establish it and to uphold it with justice and with righteousness from this time forth and for evermore. The zeal of the LORD of hosts will do this.

The word of the Lord.
Thanks be to God.

1 *Isaiah 9:1-6*

CHRISTMAS

RESPONSORIAL PSALM *Psalm 96(95):1–2a. 2b-3. 11–12a. 12b-13b. 13cd. response Luke 2:11*

R. Today a Saviour has been born to us;
who is Christ the Lord.

1 O sing a new song to the LORD;
sing to the LORD, all the earth.
O sing to the LORD; bless his name. R.

2 Proclaim his salvation day by day.
Tell among the nations his glory,
and his wonders among all the peoples. R.

3 Let the heavens rejoice and earth be glad,
let the sea and all within it thunder praise.
Let the field and all it bears rejoice. R.

4 Then will all the trees of the wood shout for joy
at the presence of the LORD, for he comes,
he comes to judge the earth. R.

5 He will judge the world with justice;
and the peoples with faithfulness. R.

SECOND READING *Titus 2:11–14*

'The grace of God has appeared for all people.'

A reading from the Letter of Saint Paul to Titus.

Beloved: The grace of God has appeared, bringing salvation for all people, training us to renounce ungodliness and worldly passions, and to live self-controlled, upright, and godly lives in the present age, waiting for our blessed hope, the appearing of the glory of our great God and Saviour Jesus Christ, who gave himself for us to redeem us from all lawlessness, and to purify for himself a people for his own possession who are zealous for good works.

The word of the Lord.
Thanks be to God.

ACCLAMATION BEFORE THE GOSPEL *Luke 2:10–11*

Alleluia, alleluia.
I bring you good news of great joy:
for unto us is born this day a Saviour, Christ the Lord.
Alleluia.

GOSPEL *Luke 2:1–14*

The Lord be with you.
And with your spirit.

A reading from the holy Gospel according to Luke.
Glory to you, O Lord.

'Unto you is born this day a Saviour.'

In those days a decree went out from Caesar Augustus that all the world should be registered. This was the first registration when Quirinius was governor of Syria. And all went to be registered, each to his own town. And Joseph also went up from Galilee, from the town of Nazareth, to Judea, to the city of David, which is called Bethlehem, because he was of the house and lineage of David, to be registered with Mary, his betrothed, who was with child. And while they were there, the time came for her to give birth. And she gave birth to her firstborn son and wrapped him in swaddling cloths and laid him in a manger, because there was no place for them in the inn.

And in the same region there were shepherds out in the field, keeping watch over their flock by night. And an angel of the Lord appeared to them, and the glory of the Lord shone around them, and they were filled with great fear. And the angel said to them, 'Fear not, for behold, I bring you good news of great joy that will be for all the people. For unto you is born this day in the city of David a Saviour, who is Christ the Lord. And this will be a sign for you: you will find a baby wrapped in swaddling cloths and lying in a manger.' And suddenly there was with the angel a multitude of the heavenly host praising God and saying, 'Glory to God in the highest, and on earth peace among those with whom he is pleased!'

The Gospel of the Lord.
Praise to you, Lord Jesus Christ.

▷ *page 11*

PROFESSION OF FAITH

All kneel at the words: 'and by the Holy Spirit was incarnate.'

PRAYER OVER THE OFFERINGS

May the oblation of this day's feast
be pleasing to you, O Lord, we pray,
that through this most holy exchange
we may be found in the likeness of Christ,
in whom our nature is united to you.
Who lives and reigns for ever and ever. **Amen**

▷ *page 15*

Preface I, II or III of the Nativity of the Lord, pp 66–67.

When the Roman Canon is used, the proper form of the Communicantes (In communion with those) is said, p 19.

COMMUNION ANTIPHON *John 1:14*

The Word became flesh, and we have seen his glory.

▷ *page 58*

PRAYER AFTER COMMUNION

Grant us, we pray, O Lord our God,
that we, who are gladdened by participation
in the feast of our Redeemer's Nativity,
may through an honourable way of life become worthy of union with him.
Who lives and reigns for ever and ever. **Amen.**

▷ *page 59*

A solemn blessing or prayer over the people may be used.

NATIVITY OF THE LORD — AT THE MASS AT DAWN

25 DECEMBER

ENTRANCE ANTIPHON *cf Isaiah 9:1, 5; Luke 1:33*

Today a light will shine upon us, for the Lord is born for us;
and he will be called Wondrous God,
Prince of peace, Father of future ages:
and his reign will be without end.

▷ page 7

COLLECT

Grant, we pray, almighty God,
that, as we are bathed in the new radiance of your incarnate Word,
the light of faith, which illumines our minds,
may also shine through in our deeds.
Through our Lord Jesus Christ, your Son,
who lives and reigns with you in the unity of the Holy Spirit,
God, for ever and ever. **Amen.**

FIRST READING *Isaiah 62:11–12*

'Behold, your salvation comes.'

A reading from the Prophet Isaiah.

Behold, the LORD has proclaimed to the end of the earth: Say to the daughter of Sion, 'Behold, your salvation comes; behold, his reward is with him, and his recompense before him.' And they shall be called The Holy People, The Redeemed of the LORD; and you shall be called Sought Out, A City Not Forsaken.

The word of the Lord.
Thanks be to God.

RESPONSORIAL PSALM *Psalm 97 (96):1, 6. 11–12.*

**R. Today a light will shine upon us;
for the Lord is born for us.**

1 The LORD is king, let earth rejoice;
let the many islands be glad.
The skies proclaim his justice;
all peoples see his glory. R.

2 Light shines forth for the just one,
and joy for the upright of heart.
Rejoice in the LORD, all you just;
to the memory of his holiness
give thanks. R.

SECOND READING *Titus 3:4–7*

'He saved us according to his own mercy.'

A reading from the Letter of Saint Paul to Titus.

Beloved: When the goodness and loving kindness of God our Saviour appeared, he saved us, not because of works done by us in righteousness, but according to his own mercy, by the washing of regeneration and renewal of the Holy Spirit, whom he poured out on us richly through Jesus Christ our Saviour, so that being justified by his grace we might become heirs according to the hope of eternal life.

The word of the Lord.
Thanks be to God.

ACCLAMATION BEFORE THE GOSPEL *Luke 2:14*

Alleluia, alleluia.
Glory to God in the highest,
and on earth peace among those with whom he is pleased!
Alleluia.

GOSPEL *Luke 2:15–20*

The Lord be with you.
And with your spirit.

A reading from the holy Gospel according to Luke.
Glory to you, O Lord.

'The shepherds found Mary and Joseph, and the baby.'

When the angels went away from them into heaven, the shepherds said to one another, 'Let us go over to Bethlehem and see this thing that has happened, which the Lord has made known to us.' And they went with haste and found Mary and Joseph, and the baby lying in a manger. And when they saw it, they made known the saying that had been told them concerning this child. And all who heard it wondered at what the shepherds told them. But Mary treasured up all these things, pondering them in her heart. And the shepherds returned, glorifying and praising God for all they had heard and seen, as it had been told them.

The Gospel of the Lord.
Praise to you, Lord Jesus Christ.

▷ page 11

PROFESSION OF FAITH

All kneel at the words: 'and by the Holy Spirit was incarnate.'

PRAYER OVER THE OFFERINGS

May our offerings be worthy, we pray, O Lord,
of the mysteries of the Nativity this day,
that, just as Christ was born a man and also shone forth as God,
so these earthly gifts may confer on us what is divine.
Through Christ our Lord. **Amen**

▷ page 15

Preface I, II or III of the Nativity of the Lord, pp 66–67.
When the Roman Canon is used, the proper form of the Communicantes (In communion with those) is said, p 19.

COMMUNION ANTIPHON *cf Zecharaiah 9:9*

Rejoice, O Daughter Sion; lift up praise, Daughter Jerusalem:
Behold, your King will come, the Holy One and Saviour of the world.

▷ page 58

PRAYER AFTER COMMUNION

Grant us, Lord, as we honour with joyful devotion
the Nativity of your Son,
that we may come to know with fullness of faith
the hidden depths of this mystery
and to love them ever more and more.
Through Christ our Lord. **Amen.**

▷ page 59

A solemn blessing or prayer over the people may be used.

NATIVITY OF THE LORD — AT THE MASS DURING THE DAY

25 DECEMBER

ENTRANCE ANTIPHON *cf Isaiah 9:5*

A child is born for us, and a son is given to us;
his sceptre of power rests upon his shoulder,
and his name will be called Messenger of great counsel.

▷ page 7

COLLECT

O God, who wonderfully created the dignity of human nature
and still more wonderfully restored it,
grant, we pray,
that we may share in the divinity of Christ,
who humbled himself to share in our humanity.
Who lives and reigns with you in the unity of the Holy Spirit,
God, for ever and ever. **Amen.**

FIRST READING *Isaiah 52:7–10*

'All the ends of the earth shall see the salvation of our God.'

A reading from the Prophet Isaiah.

How beautiful upon the mountains are the feet of him who brings good news, who publishes peace, who brings good news of happiness, who publishes salvation, who says to Sion, 'Your God reigns.' The voice of your watchmen—they lift up their voice; together they sing for joy; for eye to eye they see the return of the LORD to Sion. Break forth together into singing, you waste places of Jerusalem, for the LORD has comforted his people; he has redeemed Jerusalem. The LORD has bared his holy arm before the eyes of all the nations, and all the ends of the earth shall see the salvation of our God.

The word of the Lord.
Thanks be to God.

RESPONSORIAL PSALM *Psalm 98 (97):1. 2–3b. 3c-4. 5-6. response v 3cd*

R. **All the ends of the earth have seen
the salvation of our God.**

1 O sing a new song to the LORD,
for he has worked wonders.
His right hand and his holy arm
have brought salvation. R.

2 The Lord has made known his salvation,
has shown his deliverance to the nations.
He has remembered his merciful love
and his truth for the house of Israel. R.

3 All the ends of the earth have seen
the salvation of our God.
Shout to the Lord, all the earth;
break forth into joyous song,
and sing out your praise. R.

4 Sing psalms to the Lord with the harp,
with the harp and the sound of song.
With trumpets and the sound of the horn,
raise a shout before the King, the Lord. R.

SECOND READING *Hebrews 1:1–6*

'God has spoken to us by his Son.'

A reading from the Letter to the Hebrews.

Long ago, at many times and in many ways, God spoke to our fathers by the prophets, but in these last days he has spoken to us by his Son, whom he appointed the heir of all things, through whom also he created the world. He is the radiance of the glory of God and the exact imprint of his nature, and he upholds the universe by the word of his power. After making purification for sins, he sat down at the right hand of the Majesty on high, having become as much superior to angels as the name he has inherited is more excellent than theirs. For to which of the angels did God ever say, 'You are my Son, today I have begotten you'? Or again, 'I will be to him a father, and he shall be to me a son'? And again, when he brings the firstborn into the world, he says, 'Let all God's angels worship him.'

The word of the Lord.
Thanks be to God.

ACCLAMATION BEFORE THE GOSPEL

Alleluia, alleluia.
A hallowed day has shone upon us.
Come, O nations, and adore the Lord;
for today a great light has come down to earth.
Alleluia.

GOSPEL *John 1:1-18 Shorter form: John 1:1–5, 9–14 (only read text with side line next to it).*

The Lord be with you.
And with your spirit.

A reading from the holy Gospel according to John.
Glory to you, O Lord.

'The Word was made flesh, and lived among us.'

In the beginning was the Word, and the Word was with God, and the Word was God. He was in the beginning with God. All things were made through him, and without him was not any thing made that was made. In him was life, and the life was the light of men. The light shines in the darkness, and the darkness has not overcome it.

There was a man sent from God, whose name was John. He came as a witness, to bear witness about the light, that all might believe through him. He was not the light, but came to bear witness about the light.

The true light, which gives light to everyone, was coming into the world. He was in the world, and the world was made through him, yet the world did not know him. He came to his own, and his own people did not receive him. But to all who did receive him, who believed in his name, he gave the right to become children of God, who were born, not of blood nor of the will of the flesh nor of the will of man, but of God. And the Word became flesh and dwelt among us, and we have seen his glory, glory as of the Only Begotten from the Father, full of grace and truth.

John bore witness about him, and cried out, 'This was he of whom I said, "He who comes after me ranks before me, because he was before me."'

For from his fullness we have all received, grace upon grace. For the law was given through Moses; grace and truth came through Jesus Christ. No one has ever seen God; the only begotten God, who is at the Father's side, he has made him known.

The Gospel of the Lord.
Praise to you, Lord Jesus Christ.

▷ *page 11*

PROFESSION OF FAITH

All kneel at the words: 'and by the Holy Spirit was incarnate.'

PRAYER OVER THE OFFERINGS

Make acceptable, O Lord, our oblation on this solemn day,
when you manifested the reconciliation
that makes us wholly pleasing in your sight
and inaugurated for us the fullness of divine worship.
Through Christ our Lord. **Amen**

▷ *page 15*

Preface I, II or III of the Nativity of the Lord, pp 66–67.
When the Roman Canon is used, the proper form of the Communicantes (In communion with those) is said, p 19.

COMMUNION ANTIPHON *cf Psalm 97:3*

All the ends of the earth have seen the salvation of our God.

▷ *page 58*

PRAYER AFTER COMMUNION

Grant, O merciful God,
that, just as the Saviour of the world, born this day,
is the author of divine generation for us,
so he may be the giver even of immortality.
Who lives and reigns for ever and ever. **Amen.**

▷ *page 59*

A solemn blessing or prayer over the people may be used.

THE HOLY FAMILY OF JESUS, MARY AND JOSEPH

THE SUNDAY IN THE OCTAVE OF THE NATIVITY OF THE LORD OR, IF THERE IS NO SUNDAY, 30 DECEMBER.

When a Sunday does not occur between December 25 and January 1, this feast is celebrated on December 30 with only one reading before the Gospel.

ENTRANCE ANTIPHON *Luke 2:16*

The shepherds went in haste,
and found Mary and Joseph and the Infant lying in a manger.

▷ page 7

COLLECT

O God, who were pleased to give us
the shining example of the Holy Family,
graciously grant that we may imitate them
in practising the virtues of family life and in the bonds of charity,
and so, in the joy of your house,
delight one day in eternal rewards.
Through our Lord Jesus Christ, your Son,
who lives and reigns with you in the unity of the Holy Spirit,
God, for ever and ever. **Amen.**

There are two options for the readings before the Gospel, either of which may be used. The first option follows. The alternative readings are found on page 106.

First Option

FIRST READING *Sirach 3:2–6, 12–14*[2]

'He who fears the Lord honours his parents.'

A reading from the Book of Sirach.

The Lord honoured the father above the children, and he confirmed the judgement of the mother over her sons. Whoever honours his father atones for sins, and whoever glorifies his mother is like one who lays up treasure. Whoever honours his father will be gladdened by his own children, and when he prays he will be heard. Whoever glorifies his father will have long life, and whoever obeys the Lord will refresh his mother.

O son, help your father in his old age and do not grieve him as long as he lives; even if he is lacking in understanding, show indulgence; in all your strength do not despise him. For kindness to a father will not be forgotten, and against your sins it will be credited to you.

The word of the Lord.
Thanks be to God.

RESPONSORIAL PSALM *Psalm 128(127):1–2. 3. 4-5. R.cf. 1*

**R. Blessed are all who fear the Lord,
and walk in his ways.**

1 Blessed are all who fear the Lord,
and walk in his ways!
By the labour of your hands you shall eat.
You will be blessed and prosper. R.

continued...

2 *Sirach 3:3-7, 14-17a*

CHRISTMAS

R. Blessed are all who fear the Lord, and walk in his ways.

2 Your wife like a fruitful vine
in the heart of your house;
your children like shoots of the olive,
around your table. R.

3 Indeed thus shall be blessed
the husband who fears the Lord.
May the Lord bless you from Sion.
May you see Jerusalem prosper
all the days of your life! R.

SECOND READING *Colossians 3:12–21* *Shorter form: Colossians 3:12–17 (only read text with side line next to it).*

Family life in the Lord.

A reading from the Letter of Saint Paul to the Colossians.

Brothers and sisters: Put on, as God's chosen ones, holy and beloved, compassionate hearts, kindness, humility, meekness, and patience, bearing with one another and, if one has a complaint against another, forgiving each other; as the Lord has forgiven you, so you also must forgive. And above all these put on love, which binds everything together in perfect harmony. And let the peace of Christ rule in your hearts, to which indeed you were called in one body. And be thankful. Let the word of Christ dwell in you richly, teaching and admonishing one another in all wisdom, singing psalms and hymns and spiritual songs, with thankfulness in your hearts to God. And whatever you do, in word or deed, do everything in the name of the Lord Jesus, giving thanks to God the Father through him.

Wives, submit to your husbands, as is fitting in the Lord. Husbands, love your wives, and do not be harsh with them. Children, obey your parents in everything, for this pleases the Lord. Fathers, do not provoke your children, lest they become discouraged.

The word of the Lord.
Thanks be to God.

Alternative readings for use *ad libitum* in Year C

FIRST READING *1 Samuel 1:20–22, 24–28*

'Samuel, as long as he lives, is lent to the Lord.'

A reading from the First Book of Samuel.

In due time Hannah conceived and bore a son, and she called his name Samuel, for she said, 'I have asked for him from the Lord.'

The man Elkanah and all his house went up to offer to the Lord the yearly sacrifice and to pay his vow. But Hannah did not go up, for she said to her husband, 'As soon as the child is weaned, I will bring him, so that he may appear in the presence of the Lord and dwell there for ever.' And when she had weaned him, she took him up with her, along with a three-year-old bull, an ephah of flour, and a skin of wine, and she brought him to the house of the Lord at Shiloh. And the child was young. Then they slaughtered the bull, and they brought the child to Eli. And she said, 'Oh, my lord! As you live, my lord, I am the woman who was standing here in your presence, praying to the Lord. For this child I prayed, and the Lord has granted me my petition that I made to him. Therefore I have lent him to the Lord. As long as he lives, he is lent to the Lord.' And he worshipped the Lord there.

The word of the Lord.
Thanks be to God.

RESPONSORIAL PSALM *Psalm 84 (83):2–3. 5–6. 9–10. R.cf. 5a*

R. Blessed are they who dwell in your house, O Lord.

1 How lovely is your dwelling place,
O LORD of hosts.
My soul is longing and yearning
for the courts of the LORD.
My heart and my flesh cry out
to the living God. R.

2 Blessed are they who dwell in your house,
for ever singing your praise.
Blessed the people whose strength is in you,
whose heart is set on pilgrim ways. R.

3 O LORD God of hosts, hear my prayer;
give ear, O God of Jacob.
Turn your eyes, O God, our shield;
look on the face of your anointed. R.

SECOND READING *1 John 3:1–2, 21–24*

'We are called children of God; and so we are.'

A reading from the First Letter of Saint John.

Beloved: See what kind of love the Father has given to us, that we should be called children of God; and so we are. The reason why the world does not know us is that it did not know him. Beloved, we are God's children now, and what we will be has not yet appeared; but we know that when he appears we shall be like him, because we shall see him as he is.

Beloved, if our heart does not condemn us, we have confidence before God; and whatever we ask we receive from him, because we keep his commandments and do what pleases him. And this is his commandment, that we believe in the name of his Son Jesus Christ and love one another, just as he has commanded us. Whoever keeps his commandments abides in God, and God in him. And by this we know that he abides in us, by the Spirit whom he has given us.

The word of the Lord.
Thanks be to God.

ACCLAMATION BEFORE THE GOSPEL *Colossians 3:15a, 16a*

**Alleluia, alleluia.
Let the peace of Christ rule in your hearts;
let the word of Christ dwell in you richly.
Alleluia.**

or *cf. Acts 16:14b*

**Alleluia, alleluia.
Open our hearts, O Lord,
that we may pay attention to the words of your Son.
Alleluia.**

GOSPEL *Luke 2:41–52*

The Lord be with you.
And with your spirit.

A reading from the holy Gospel according to Luke.
Glory to you, O Lord.

Jesus is found by his parents sitting among the teachers.

The parents of Jesus went to Jerusalem every year at the Feast of the Passover. And when he was twelve years old, they went up according to custom. And when the feast was ended, as they were returning, the boy Jesus stayed behind in Jerusalem. His parents did not know it, but supposing him to be in the group they went a day's journey, but then they began to search for him among their relatives and acquaintances, and when they did not find him, they returned to Jerusalem, searching for him. After three days they found him in the Temple, sitting among the teachers, listening to them and asking them questions. And all who heard him were amazed at his understanding and his answers. And when his parents saw him, they were astonished. And his mother said to him, 'Son, why have you treated us so? Behold, your father and I have been searching for you in great distress.' And he said to them, 'Why were you looking for me? Did you not know that I must be in my Father's house?' And they did not understand the saying that he spoke to them. And he went down with them and came to Nazareth and was submissive to them. And his mother treasured up all these things in her heart. And Jesus increased in wisdom and in stature and in favour with God and man.

The Gospel of the Lord.
Praise to you, Lord Jesus Christ.

▷ *page 11*

PROFESSION OF FAITH

The Profession of Faith is said when this feast is celebrated on Sunday.

PRAYER OVER THE OFFERINGS

We offer you, Lord, the sacrifice of conciliation,
humbly asking that,
through the intercession of the Virgin Mother of God and Saint Joseph,
you may establish our families firmly in your grace and your peace.
Through Christ our Lord. **Amen.**

▷ *page 15*

Preface I, II or III of the Nativity of the Lord, pp 66–67.
When the Roman Canon is used, the proper form of the Communicantes (In communion with those) is said, p 19.

COMMUNION ANTIPHON *Baruch 3:38*

Our God has appeared on the earth, and lived among us.

▷ *page 58*

PRAYER AFTER COMMUNION

Bring those you refresh with this heavenly Sacrament,
most merciful Father,
to imitate constantly the example of the Holy Family,
so that, after the trials of this world,
we may share their company for ever.
Through Christ our Lord. **Amen.**

▷ *page 59*

A solemn blessing or prayer over the people may be used.

SOLEMNITY OF MARY, THE HOLY MOTHER OF GOD

1 JANUARY, OCTAVE DAY OF THE NATIVITY OF THE LORD

ENTRANCE ANTIPHON

Hail, Holy Mother, who gave birth to the King,
who rules heaven and earth for ever.

or *cf Isaiah 9:1, 5; Luke 1:33*

Today a light will shine upon us, for the Lord is born for us;
and he will be called Wondrous God,
Prince of peace, Father of future ages:
and his reign will be without end.

▷ *page 7*

COLLECT

O God, who through the fruitful virginity of Blessed Mary
bestowed on the human race
the grace of eternal salvation,
grant, we pray,
that we may experience the intercession of her,
through whom we were found worthy
to receive the author of life,
our Lord Jesus Christ, your Son.
Who lives and reigns with you in the unity of the Holy Spirit,
God, for ever and ever. **Amen.**

FIRST READING *Numbers 6:22–27*

'They shall put my name upon the people of Israel, and I will bless them.'

A reading from the Book of Numbers.

The LORD spoke to Moses, saying, 'Speak to Aaron and his sons, saying, Thus you shall bless the people of Israel: you shall say to them,

'The LORD bless you and keep you; the LORD make his face to shine upon you and be gracious to you; the LORD lift up his countenance upon you and give you peace.

'So shall they put my name upon the people of Israel, and I will bless them.'

The word of the Lord.

Thanks be to God.

RESPONSORIAL PSALM *Psalm 67(66):2–3. 5. 6, 8. R.2a*

R. May God be gracious and bless us.

1 May God be gracious and bless us
and let his face shed its light upon us.
So will your ways be known upon earth
and all nations learn your salvation. R.

2 Let the nations be glad and shout
for joy,
with uprightness you rule the peoples;
you guide the nations on earth. R.

3 Let the peoples praise you, O God;
let all the peoples praise you.
May God still give us his blessing
that all the ends of the earth may
revere him. R.

SECOND READING *Galatians 4:4–7*

'God sent forth his Son born of woman.'

A reading from the Letter of Saint Paul to the Galatians.

Brothers and sisters: When the fullness of time had come, God sent forth his Son, born of woman, born under the law, to redeem those who were under the law, so that we might receive adoption as sons. And because you are sons, God has sent the Spirit of his Son into our hearts, crying, 'Abba! Father!' So you are no longer a slave, but a son, and if a son, then an heir through God.

The word of the Lord.
Thanks be to God.

ACCLAMATION BEFORE THE GOSPEL *Hebrews 1:1–2*

Alleluia, alleluia.
At many times, long ago, God spoke to our fathers by the prophets,
but in these last days he has spoken to us by his Son.
Alleluia.

GOSPEL *Luke 2:16–21*

The Lord be with you.
And with your spirit.

A reading from the holy Gospel according to Luke.
Glory to you, O Lord.

They found Mary and Joseph, and the baby. And at the end of eight days, he was called Jesus.

At that time: The shepherds went with haste and found Mary and Joseph, and the baby lying in a manger. And when they saw it, they made known the saying that had been told them concerning this child. And all who heard it wondered at what the shepherds told them. But Mary treasured up all these things, pondering them in her heart. And the shepherds returned, glorifying and praising God for all they had heard and seen, as it had been told them. And at the end of eight days, when he was circumcised, he was called Jesus, the name given by the angel before he was conceived in the womb.

The Gospel of the Lord.
Praise to you, Lord Jesus Christ.

▷ *page 11*

PRAYER OVER THE OFFERINGS

O God, who in your kindness begin all good things
and bring them to fulfilment,
grant to us, who find joy in the Solemnity of the holy Mother of God,
that, just as we glory in the beginnings of your grace,
so one day we may rejoice in its completion.
Through Christ our Lord. **Amen.**

▷ *page 15*

Preface I of the Blessed Virgin Mary (on the Solemnity of the Motherhood), p 67.
When the Roman Canon is used, the proper form of the Communicantes (In communion with those) is said, p 19.

COMMUNION ANTIPHON *Hebrews 13:8*

Jesus Christ is the same yesterday, today, and for ever.

▷ *page 58*

PRAYER AFTER COMMUNION

We have received this heavenly Sacrament with joy, O Lord:
grant, we pray,
that it may lead us to eternal life,
for we rejoice to proclaim the blessed ever-Virgin Mary
Mother of your Son and Mother of the Church.
Through Christ our Lord. **Amen.**

▷ *page 59*

A solemn blessing or prayer over the people may be used.

SECOND SUNDAY AFTER THE NATIVITY

ENTRANCE ANTIPHON *Wisdom 18:14–15*

When a profound silence covered all things
and night was in the middle of its course,
your all-powerful Word, O Lord,
bounded from heaven's royal throne.

▷ *page 7*

COLLECT

Almighty ever-living God,
splendour of faithful souls,
graciously be pleased to fill the world with your glory,
and show yourself to all peoples by the radiance of your light.
Through our Lord Jesus Christ, your Son,
who lives and reigns with you in the unity of the Holy Spirit,
God, for ever and ever. **Amen.**

FIRST READING *Sirach 24:1–2, 8–12*[3]

The wisdom of God has dwelt in the chosen people

A reading from the Book of Sirach.

Wisdom will praise herself and will boast in the midst of her people. In the assembly of the Most High she will open her mouth, and in the presence of his forces she will boast: 'Then the Creator of all things commanded me, and the one who created me gave my tent a resting place. And he said, "Make your dwelling in Jacob and in Israel receive your inheritance." From eternity,

3 *Sirach 24:1-4, 12-16*

in the beginning, he created me, and for eternity I shall not cease to exist. In the holy tabernacle I ministered before him, and so I was established in Sion. In the beloved city likewise he gave me a resting place, and in Jerusalem was my dominion. So I took root in an honoured people, in the portion of the Lord, his inheritance.'

The word of the Lord.
Thanks be to God.

RESPONSORIAL PSALM *Psalm 147:12-13. 14-15. 19-20. R. John 1:14*

R. **The Word became flesh and dwelt among us.** *or* **Alleluia.** *(May be repeated two or three times)*

1 O Jerusalem, glorify the Lord!
O Sion, praise your God!
He has strengthened the bars of your gates;
he has blessed your children within you. R.

2 He established peace on your borders;
he gives you your fill of finest wheat.
He sends out his word to the earth,
and swiftly runs his command. R.

3 He reveals his word to Jacob;
to Israel, his decrees and judgements.
He has not dealt thus with other nations;
he has not taught them his judgements. R.

SECOND READING *Ephesians 1:3–6, 15–18*

'He predestined us for adoption as sons through Jesus.'

A reading from the Letter of Saint Paul to the Ephesians.

Blessed be the God and Father of our Lord Jesus Christ, who has blessed us in Christ with every spiritual blessing in the heavenly places, even as he chose us in him before the foundation of the world, that we should be holy and blameless before him. In love he predestined us for adoption to himself as sons through Jesus Christ, according to the purpose of his will, to the praise of his glorious grace, with which he has blessed us in the Beloved.

For this reason, because I have heard of your faith in the Lord Jesus and your love towards all the saints, I do not cease to give thanks for you, remembering you in my prayers, that the God of our Lord Jesus Christ, the Father of glory, may give you the Spirit of wisdom and of revelation in the knowledge of him, having the eyes of your hearts enlightened, that you may know what is the hope to which he has called you, what are the riches of his glorious inheritance in the saints.

The word of the Lord.
Thanks be to God.

ACCLAMATION BEFORE THE GOSPEL *cf 1 Timothy 3:16*

Alleluia, alleluia.
Glory to you, O Christ, proclaimed among the nations.
Glory to you, O Christ, believed in throughout the world.
Alleluia.

GOSPEL *John 1:1–18 Shorter form: John 1:1-5, 9-14 (only read text with side line next to it).*

The Lord be with you.
And with your spirit.

A reading from the holy Gospel according to John.
Glory to you, O Lord.

'The Word became flesh and dwelt among us.'

In the beginning was the Word, and the Word was with God, and the Word was God. He was in the beginning with God. All things were made through him, and without him was not any thing made that was made. In him was life, and the life was the light of men. The light shines in the darkness, and the darkness has not overcome it.

There was a man sent from God, whose name was John. He came as a witness, to bear witness about the light, that all might believe through him. He was not the light, but came to bear witness about the light.

The true light, which gives light to everyone, was coming into the world. He was in the world, and the world was made through him, yet the world did not know him. He came to his own, and his own people did not receive him. But to all who did receive him, who believed in his name, he gave the right to become children of God, who were born, not of blood nor of the will of the flesh nor of the will of man, but of God. And the Word became flesh and dwelt among us, and we have seen his glory, glory as of the Only Begotten from the Father, full of grace and truth. | John bore witness about him, and cried out, 'This was he of whom I said, "He who comes after me ranks before me, because he was before me."'

For from his fullness we have all received, grace upon grace. For the law was given through Moses; grace and truth came through Jesus Christ. No one has ever seen God; the only begotten God, who is at the Father's side, he has made him known.

The Gospel of the Lord.
Praise to you, Lord Jesus Christ.

▷ page 11

PRAYER OVER THE OFFERINGS

Sanctify, O Lord, the offerings we make
on the Nativity of your Only Begotten Son,
for by it you show us the way of truth
and promise the life of the heavenly Kingdom.
Through Christ our Lord. **Amen**

▷ page 15

Preface I, II or III of the Nativity of the Lord, pp 66–67.

COMMUNION ANTIPHON *cf John 1:12*

To all who would accept him,
he gave the power to become children of God.

▷ page 58

PRAYER AFTER COMMUNION
Lord our God, we humbly ask you,
that, through the working of this mystery,
our offences may be cleansed
and our just desires fulfilled.
Through Christ our Lord. **Amen.** ▷ page 59

A solemn blessing or prayer over the people may be used.

EPIPHANY OF THE LORD — VIGIL MASS

6 JANUARY
OR THE SUNDAY BETWEEN 2 JANUARY AND 8 JANUARY
This Mass is used on the evening of the day before the Solemnity.

ENTRANCE ANTIPHON *cf Baruch 5:5*
Arise, Jerusalem, and look to the East
and see your children gathered from the rising to the setting of the sun.
▷ page 7

COLLECT
May the splendour of your majesty, O Lord, we pray,
shed its light upon our hearts,
that we may pass through the shadows of this world
and reach the brightness of our eternal home.
Through our Lord Jesus Christ, your Son,
who lives and reigns with you in the unity of the Holy Spirit,
God, for ever and ever. **Amen.**

LITURGY OF THE WORD
The readings are as for the Mass During the Day (page 115 opposite).

PRAYER OVER THE OFFERINGS
Accept we pray, O Lord, our offerings,
in honour of the appearing of your Only Begotten Son
and the first fruits of the nations,
that to you praise may be rendered
and eternal salvation be ours.
Through Christ our Lord. **Amen.** ▷ page 15

Preface of the Epiphany of the Lord, p 67.

COMMUNION ANTIPHON *cf Revelation 21:23*
The brightness of God illumined the holy city Jerusalem,
and the nations will walk by its light. ▷ page 58

PRAYER AFTER COMMUNION

Renewed by sacred nourishment,
we implore your mercy, O Lord,
that the star of your justice
may shine always bright in our minds
and that our true treasure may ever consist in our confession of you.
Through Christ our Lord. **Amen.**

▷ page 59

A solemn blessing or prayer over the people may be used.

EPIPHANY OF THE LORD — MASS DURING THE DAY

6 JANUARY
OR SUNDAY BETWEEN 2 JANUARY AND 8 JANUARY

ENTRANCE ANTIPHON *cf Malachi 3:1; 1 Chronicles 29:12*

Behold, the Lord, the Mighty One, has come;
and kingship is in his grasp, and power and dominion.

▷ page 7

COLLECT

O God, who on this day
revealed your Only Begotten Son to the nations
by the guidance of a star,
grant in your mercy,
that we, who know you already by faith,
may be brought to behold the beauty of your sublime glory.
Through our Lord Jesus Christ, your Son,
who lives and reigns with you in the unity of the Holy Spirit,
God, for ever and ever. **Amen.**

FIRST READING *Isaiah 60:1–6*

'The glory of the Lord has risen upon you.'

A reading from the Prophet Isaiah.

Arise, shine, for your light has come, and the glory of the LORD has risen upon you. For behold, darkness shall cover the earth, and thick darkness the peoples; but the LORD will arise upon you, and his glory will be seen upon you. And nations shall come to your light, and kings to the brightness of your rising.

Lift up your eyes all round, and see; they all gather together, they come to you; your sons shall come from afar, and your daughters shall be carried on the hip. Then you shall see and be radiant; your heart shall thrill and exult, because the abundance of the sea shall be turned to you, the wealth of the nations shall come to you. A multitude of camels shall cover you, the young camels of Midian and Ephah; all those from Sheba shall come. They shall bring gold and frankincense, and shall bring good news, the praises of the LORD.

The word of the Lord.
Thanks be to God.

RESPONSORIAL PSALM *Psalm 72(71):1-2. 7-8. 10-11. 12-13. R.cf. 11*

R. All the nations on earth shall fall prostrate before you, O Lord.

1 O God, give your judgement to the king,
to a king's son your justice,
that he may judge your people in justice,
and your poor in right judgement. R.

2 In his days justice shall flourish,
and great peace till the moon is no more.
He shall rule from sea to sea,
from the River to the bounds of the earth. R.

3 The kings of Tarshish and the islands
shall pay him tribute.
The kings of Sheba and Seba
shall bring him gifts.
Before him all kings shall fall prostrate,
all nations shall serve him. R.

4 For he shall rescue the needy when they cry,
the poor who have no one to help.
He will have pity on the weak and the needy,
and save the lives of the needy. R.

SECOND READING *Ephesians 3:2–3a, 5–6*

'It has now been revealed that the Gentiles are fellow heirs of the promise.'

A reading from the Letter of Saint Paul to the Ephesians.

Brothers and sisters: I assume that you have heard of the stewardship of God's grace that was given to me for you, how the mystery was made known to me by revelation, which was not made known to the sons of men in other generations as it has now been revealed to his holy Apostles and prophets by the Spirit. This mystery is that the Gentiles are fellow heirs, members of the same body, and partakers of the promise in Christ Jesus through the gospel.

The word of the Lord.
Thanks be to God.

ACCLAMATION BEFORE THE GOSPEL *Matthew 2:2*

**Alleluia, alleluia.
We saw his star when it rose
and have come to worship the Lord.
Alleluia.**

GOSPEL *Matthew 2:1–12*

The Lord be with you.
And with your spirit.

A reading from the holy Gospel according to Matthew.
Glory to you, O Lord.

'We have come from the east to worship the king.'

Now after Jesus was born in Bethlehem of Judea in the days of Herod the king, behold, wise men from the east came to Jerusalem, saying, 'Where is he who has been born king of the Jews? For we saw his star when it rose and have come to worship him.' When Herod the king heard this, he was troubled, and all Jerusalem with him; and assembling all the chief priests and scribes of the people, he enquired of them where the Christ was to be born. They told him, 'In Bethlehem of Judea, for so it is written by the prophet:

"And you, O Bethlehem, in the land of Judah, are by no means least among the rulers of Judah; for from you shall come a ruler who will shepherd my people Israel."'

Then Herod summoned the wise men secretly and ascertained from them what time the star had appeared. And he sent them to Bethlehem, saying, 'Go and search diligently for the child, and when you have found him, bring me word, that I too may come and worship him.' After listening to the king, they went on their way. And behold, the star that they had seen when it rose went before them until it came to rest over the place where the child was. When they saw the star, they rejoiced exceedingly with great joy. And going into the house, they saw the child with Mary his mother, and they fell down and worshipped him. Then, opening their treasures, they offered him gifts, gold and frankincense and myrrh. And being warned in a dream not to return to Herod, they departed to their own country by another way.

The Gospel of the Lord.
Praise to you, Lord Jesus Christ.

▷ *page 11*

CHRISTMAS

PROCLAMATION OF MOVEABLE FEASTS

Where it is the practice, if appropriate, the moveable Feasts of the current year may be proclaimed after the Gospel.

PRAYER OVER THE OFFERINGS

Look with favour, Lord, we pray,
on these gifts of your Church,
in which are offered now not gold or frankincense or myrrh,
but he who by them is proclaimed,
sacrificed and received, Jesus Christ.
Who lives and reigns for ever and ever. **Amen.**

▷ *page 15*

Preface of the Epiphany of the Lord, p 67.

COMMUNION ANTIPHON *cf Matthew 2:2*

We have seen his star in the East,
and have come with gifts to adore the Lord.

▷ *page 58*

PRAYER AFTER COMMUNION

Go before us with heavenly light, O Lord,
always and everywhere,
that we may perceive with clear sight
and revere with true affection
the mystery in which you have willed us to participate.
Through Christ our Lord. **Amen.**

▷ page 59

A solemn blessing or prayer over the people may be used.

BAPTISM OF THE LORD

SUNDAY AFTER 6 JANUARY

When the Solemnity of the Epiphany is transferred to Sunday, if this Sunday occurs on 7 or 8 January, the Feast of the Baptism of the Lord is celebrated on the following Monday with only one reading before the Gospel.

ENTRANCE ANTIPHON *cf Matthew 3:16–17*

After the Lord was baptized, the heavens were opened,
and the Spirit descended upon him like a dove,
and the voice of the Father thundered:
This is my beloved Son, with whom I am well pleased.

▷ page 7

COLLECT

Almighty ever-living God,
who, when Christ had been baptized in the River Jordan
and as the Holy Spirit descended upon him,
solemnly declared him your beloved Son,
grant that your children by adoption,
reborn of water and the Holy Spirit,
may always be well pleasing to you.
Through our Lord Jesus Christ, your Son,
who lives and reigns with you in the unity of the Holy Spirit,
God, for ever and ever. **Amen.**

or

O God, whose Only Begotten Son
has appeared in our very flesh,
grant, we pray, that we may be inwardly transformed
through him whom we recognize as outwardly like ourselves.
Who lives and reigns with you in the unity of the Holy Spirit,
God, for ever and ever. **Amen.**

There are two options for the readings before the Gospel, either of which may be used. The first option follows. The alternative readings are found on page 120.

First Option

FIRST READING *Isaiah 42:1–4, 6–7*

'Behold my servant, in whom my soul delights.'

A reading from the Prophet Isaiah.

Thus says the LORD: Behold my servant, whom I uphold, my chosen, in whom my soul delights; I have put my Spirit upon him; he will bring forth justice to the nations. He will not cry aloud or lift up his voice, or make it heard in the street; a bruised reed he will not break, and a faintly burning wick he will not quench; he will faithfully bring forth justice. He will not grow faint or be discouraged till he has established justice in the earth; and the coastlands wait for his law.

'I am the LORD; I have called you in righteousness; I will take you by the hand and keep you; I will give you as a covenant for the people, a light for the nations, to open the eyes that are blind, to bring out the prisoners from the dungeon, from the prison those who sit in darkness.'

The word of the Lord.
Thanks be to God.

CHRISTMAS

RESPONSORIAL PSALM *Psalm 29(28):1-2. 3ac-4. 3b, 9b-10. R.11b*

R. The LORD will bless his people with peace.

1 Ascribe to the LORD, you heavenly powers,
ascribe to the LORD glory and strength.
Ascribe to the LORD the glory of his name;
bow down before the LORD, majestic in holiness. R.

2 The voice of the LORD upon the waters,
the LORD on the immensity of waters;
the voice of the LORD full of power;
the voice of the LORD full of splendour. R.

3 The God of glory thunders;
in his temple they all cry, 'Glory!'
The LORD sits enthroned above the flood;
the LORD sits as king for ever. R.

SECOND READING *Acts 10:34–38*

'God anointed Jesus with the Holy Spirit.'

A reading from the Acts of the Apostles.

In those days: Peter opened his mouth and said: 'Truly I understand that God shows no partiality, but in every nation anyone who fears him and does what is right is acceptable to him. As for the word that he sent to Israel, preaching good news of peace through Jesus Christ—he is Lord of all— you yourselves know what happened throughout all Judea, beginning from Galilee after the baptism that John proclaimed: how God anointed Jesus of Nazareth with the Holy Spirit and with power. He went about doing good and healing all who were oppressed by the devil, for God was with him.'

The word of the Lord.
Thanks be to God.

Alternative readings for use *ad libitum* in Year C

FIRST READING *Isaiah 40:1–5, 9–11*

'The glory of the Lord shall be revealed, and all flesh shall see it together.'

A reading from the Prophet Isaiah.

Comfort, comfort my people, says your God. Speak tenderly to Jerusalem, and cry to her that her warfare is ended, that her iniquity is pardoned, that she has received from the LORD's hand double for all her sins.

A voice cries: 'In the wilderness prepare the way of the LORD; make straight in the desert a highway for our God. Every valley shall be lifted up, and every mountain and hill be made low; the uneven ground shall become level, and the rough places a plain. And the glory of the LORD shall be revealed, and all flesh shall see it together, for the mouth of the LORD has spoken.'

Go on up to a high mountain, O Sion, herald of good news; lift up your voice with strength, O Jerusalem, herald of good news; lift it up, fear not; say to the cities of Judah, 'Behold your God!' Behold, the Lord GOD comes with might, and his arm rules for him; behold, his reward is with him, and his recompense before him. He will tend his flock like a shepherd; he will gather the lambs in his arms; he will carry them in his bosom, and gently lead those that are with young.

The word of the Lord.
Thanks be to God.

RESPONSORIAL PSALM *Psalm 104(103):1b-2. 3-4. 24-25. 27-28. 29-30. R.1*

R. **Bless the LORD, O my soul!**
My God, how great you are!

1 O LORD my God, how great you are,
clothed in majesty and honour,
wrapped in light as with a robe!
You stretch out the heavens like a tent. R.

2 On the waters you lay the foundation for your dwelling.
You make the clouds your chariot;
you ride on the wings of the wind.
You make the winds your messengers,
flame and fire your servants. R.

3 How many are your works, O LORD!
In wisdom you have made them all.
The earth is full of your creatures.
Vast and wide is the span of the sea,
with its creeping things past counting,
living things great and small. R.

4 All of these look to you
to give them their food in due season.
You give it, they gather it up;
you open wide your hand, they are well filled. R.

5 You hide your face, they are dismayed;
you take away their breath, they die,
returning to the dust from which they came.
You send forth your spirit, and they are created,
and you renew the face of the earth. R.

SECOND READING *Titus 2:11–14; 3:4–7*

'He saved us by the washing of regeneration and renewal of the Holy Spirit.'

A reading from the letter of Saint Paul to Titus.

Beloved: The grace of God has appeared, bringing salvation for all people, training us to renounce ungodliness and worldly passions, and to live self-controlled, upright, and godly lives in the present age, waiting for our blessed hope, the appearing of the glory of our great God and Saviour Jesus Christ, who gave himself for us to redeem us from all lawlessness, and to purify for himself a people for his own possession who are zealous for good works.

But when the goodness and loving kindness of God our Saviour appeared, he saved us, not because of works done by us in righteousness, but according to his own mercy, by the washing of regeneration and renewal of the Holy Spirit, whom he poured out on us richly through Jesus Christ our Saviour, so that being justified by his grace we might become heirs according to the hope of eternal life.

The word of the Lord.
Thanks be to God.

ACCLAMATION BEFORE THE GOSPEL *cf Mark 9:7*

Alleluia, alleluia.
The heavens were opened and the voice of the Father thundered:
'This is my beloved Son; listen to him'.
Alleluia.

or *cf Luke 3:16*

Alleluia, alleluia.
He who is mightier than I is coming, said John.
He will baptise you with the Holy Spirit and fire.
Alleluia.

GOSPEL *Luke 3:15–16, 21–22*

The Lord be with you.
And with your spirit.

A reading from the holy Gospel according to Luke.
Glory to you, O Lord.

'When Jesus had been baptised and was praying, the heavens were opened.'

At that time: As the people were filled with expectation, and all were questioning in their hearts concerning John, whether he might be the Christ, John answered them all, saying, 'I baptise you with water, but he who is mightier than I is coming, the strap of whose sandals I am not worthy to untie. He will baptise you with the Holy Spirit and fire.'

CHRISTMAS

Now when all the people were baptised by John the Baptist and when Jesus also had been baptised and was praying, the heavens were opened, and the Holy Spirit descended on him in bodily form, like a dove; and a voice came from heaven, 'You are my beloved Son; with you I am well pleased.'

The Gospel of the Lord.

Praise to you, Lord Jesus Christ.

▷ page 11

PRAYER OVER THE OFFERINGS

Accept, O Lord, the offerings
we have brought to honour the revealing of your beloved Son,
so that the oblation of your faithful
may be transformed into the sacrifice of him
who willed in his compassion
to wash away the sins of the world.
Who lives and reigns for ever and ever. **Amen.**

▷ page 15

Preface of the Baptism of the Lord, p 68.

COMMUNION ANTIPHON *John 1:32, 34*

Behold the One of whom John said:
I have seen and testified that this is the Son of God.

▷ page 58

PRAYER AFTER COMMUNION

Nourished with these sacred gifts,
we humbly entreat your mercy, O Lord,
that, faithfully listening to your Only Begotten Son,
we may be your children in name and in truth.
Through Christ our Lord. **Amen.**

▷ page 59

A solemn blessing or prayer over the people may be used.

ORDINARY TIME

ABOUT THE SEASON

Besides the times of year that have their own distinctive character, there remain in the yearly cycle thirty-three or thirty-four weeks in which no particular aspect of the mystery of Christ is celebrated, but rather the mystery of Christ itself is honoured in its fullness, especially on Sundays. This period is known as Ordinary Time.

Universal Norms on the Liturgical Year and the Calendar n 43

ABOUT THE READINGS

On the Second Sunday of Ordinary Time the gospel continues to centre on the manifestation of the Lord, which Epiphany celebrates through the traditional passage about the wedding feast at Cana and two other passages from John.

Beginning with the Third Sunday, there is a semi-continuous reading of the Synoptic Gospels. This reading is arranged in such a way that as the Lord's life and preaching unfold the teaching proper to each of these Gospels is presented.

This distribution also provides a certain co-ordination between the meaning of each Gospel and the progress of the liturgical year. Thus after Epiphany the readings are on the beginning of the Lord's preaching and they fit in well with Christ's baptism and the first events in which he manifests himself. The liturgical year leads quite naturally to a termination in the eschatological theme proper to the last Sundays, since the chapters of the Synoptics that precede the account of the passion treat this eschatological theme rather extensively.

In the semicontinuous reading of Luke for Year C, the introduction of this Gospel has been prefixed to the first text (that is, on the Third Sunday). This passage expresses the author's intention very beautifully and there seemed to be no better place for it.

Introduction to the Lectionary n 105

COMMON RESPONSORIAL PSALMS FOR ORDINARY TIME

COMMON RESPONSES

WITH A PSALM OF PRAISE

R. O give thanks to the Lord for he is good.

or

R. We praise you, Lord, for the wonder of your works.

or

R. O sing a new song to the Lord.

WITH A PSALM OF PETITION

R. The Lord is close to all who call him.

or

R. Hear us, Lord, and save us.

or

R. The Lord is compassionate and gracious.

COMMON PSALM 1 *Psalm 19(18):8. 9. 10. 11. R.John 6:68c or John 6:63c*

R. O Lord, you have the words of eternal life.
or **R. Your words, O Lord, are spirit and life.**

1 The law of the Lord is perfect;
it revives the soul.
The decrees of the Lord are steadfast;
they give wisdom to the simple. R.

2 The precepts of the Lord are right;
they gladden the heart.
The command of the Lord is clear;
it gives light to the eyes.

3 The fear of the Lord is pure,
abiding for ever.
The judgements of the Lord are true;
they are, all of them, just. R.

4 They are more to be desired than gold,
than quantities of gold.
and sweeter are they than honey,
than honey flowing from the comb. R.

COMMON PSALM 2 *Psalm 27(26):1. 4. 13-14. R.1a*

R. The Lord is my light and my salvation.

1 The Lord is my light and my salvation;
whom shall I fear?
The Lord is the stronghold of my life;
whom should I dread? R.

2 There is one thing I ask of the Lord,
only this do I seek:
to live in the house of the Lord
all the days of my life,
to gaze on the beauty of the Lord,
to enquire at his Temple. R.

3 I believe I shall see the Lord's goodness
in the land of the living.
Wait for the Lord; be strong;
be stout-hearted, and wait for the Lord! R.

COMMON PSALM 3 *Psalm 34(33):2-3. 4-5. 6-7. 8-9. R.2a or 9a*

R. I will bless the Lord at all times. *or* **Taste and see that the Lord is good.**

1 I will bless the Lord at all times,
praise of him is always in my mouth.
In the Lord my soul shall make its boast;
the humble shall hear and be glad. R.

2 Glorify the Lord with me;
together let us praise his name.
I sought the Lord, and he answered me;
from all my terrors he set me free. R.

3 Look towards him and be radiant;
let your faces not be abashed.
This lowly one called; the Lord heard,
and rescued him from all his distress. R.

4 The angel of the Lord is encamped
around those who fear him, to rescue them.
Taste and see that the Lord is good.
Blessed the man who seeks refuge in him. R.

COMMON PSALM 4 *Psalm 63(62):2. 3-4. 5-6. 8-9. R.2b*

R. For you my soul is thirsting, O Lord, my God.

1 O God, you are my God; at dawn I seek you;
for you my soul is thirsting.
For you my flesh is pining,
like a dry, weary land without water. R.

2 I have come before you in the sanctuary,
to behold your strength and your glory.
Your loving mercy is better than life;
my lips will speak your praise. R.

3 I will bless you all my life;
in your name I will lift up my hands.
My soul shall be filled as with a banquet;
with joyful lips, my mouth shall praise you. R.

4 For you have been my strength;
in the shadow of your wings I rejoice.
My soul clings fast to you;
your right hand upholds me. R.

COMMON PSALM 5 *Psalm 95(94):1-2. 6-7ab. 7c-9. R.7c, 8a*

**R. O that today you would listen to his voice!
'Harden not your hearts.'**

1 Come, let us ring out our joy to the LORD;
hail the rock who saves us.
Let us come into his presence, giving thanks;
let us hail him with a song of praise. R.

2 O come; let us bow and bend low.
Let us kneel before the LORD who made us,
for he is our God, and we the people,
the people of his pasture, the flock of his hand. R.

3 O that today you would listen to his voice!
'Harden not your hearts as at Meribah,
as on that day at Massah in the desert
when your forebears put me to the test;
when they tried me, though they saw my work.'

COMMON PSALM 6 *Psalm 100(99):1-2. 3. 5. R.3c*

R. We are his people, the sheep of his flock.

1 Cry out with joy to the LORD, all the earth.
Serve the LORD with gladness.
Come before him, singing for joy. R.

2 Know that he, the LORD, is God.
He made us, we belong to him,
we are his people, the sheep of his flock. R.

3 Indeed, how good is the LORD,
eternal his merciful love.
He is faithful from age to age. R.

COMMON PSALM 7 *Psalm 103(102):1-2. 3-4. 8, 10. 12-13. R.8a*

R. The LORD is compassionate and gracious.

1 Bless the LORD, O my soul,
and all within me, his holy name.
Bless the LORD, O my soul,
and never forget all his benefits. R.

2 It is the Lord who forgives all your sins,
who heals every one of your ills,
who redeems your life from the grave,
who crowns you with mercy and compassion. R.

3 The LORD is compassionate and gracious,
slow to anger and rich in mercy.
He does not treat us according to our sins,
nor repay us according to our faults. R.

4 As far as the east is from the west,
so far from us does he remove our transgressions.
As a father has compassion on his children,
the LORD's compassion is on those who fear him. R.

COMMON PSALM 8 *Psalm 145(144):1-2. 8-9. 10-11. 13cd-14. R.cf. 1*

R. I will bless your name for ever, my God and king.

1 I will extol you, my God and king,
and bless your name for ever and ever.
I will bless you day after day,
and praise your name for ever and ever. R.

2 The LORD is kind and full of compassion,
slow to anger, abounding in mercy.
How good is the LORD to all,
compassionate to all his creatures. R.

3 All your works shall thank you, O LORD,
and all your faithful ones bless you.
They shall speak of the glory of your reign,
and declare your mighty deeds. R.

4 The LORD is faithful in all his words,
and holy in all his deeds.
The LORD supports all who fall,
and raises up all who are bowed down. R.

SECOND SUNDAY IN ORDINARY TIME

ENTRANCE ANTIPHON *Psalm 65:4*

All the earth shall bow down before you, O God,
and shall sing to you,
shall sing to your name, O Most High!

▷ page 7

COLLECT

Almighty ever-living God,
who govern all things,
both in heaven and on earth,
mercifully hear the pleading of your people
and bestow your peace on our times.
Through our Lord Jesus Christ, your Son,
who lives and reigns with you in the unity of the Holy Spirit,
God, for ever and ever. **Amen.**

FIRST READING *Isaiah 62:1–5*

'The bridegroom rejoices over the bride.'

A reading from the Prophet Isaiah.

For Sion's sake I will not keep silent, and for Jerusalem's sake I will not be quiet, until her righteousness goes forth as brightness, and her salvation as a burning torch. The nations shall see your righteousness, and all the kings your glory, and you shall be called by a new name that the mouth of the LORD will give. You shall be a crown of beauty in the hand of the LORD, and a royal diadem in the hand of your God. You shall no more be termed Forsaken, and your land shall no more be termed Desolate, but you shall be called My Delight Is in Her, and your land Married; for the LORD delights in you, and your land shall be married. For as a young man marries a young woman, so shall your sons marry you, and as the bridegroom rejoices over the bride, so shall your God rejoice over you.

The word of the Lord.
Thanks be to God.

RESPONSORIAL PSALM *Psalm 96 (95):1–2a. 2b-3. 7–8a. 9-10ac. R.3*

R. **Proclaim the wonders of the Lord**
among all the peoples.

1 O sing a new song to the LORD;
sing to the LORD, all the earth.
O sing to the LORD; bless his name. R.

2 Proclaim his salvation day by day.
Tell among the nations his glory,
and his wonders among all the peoples. R.

3 Ascribe to the LORD, you families of peoples,
ascribe to the LORD glory and power;
ascribe to the LORD the glory of his name. R.

continued...

R. Proclaim the wonders of the Lord among all the peoples.

4 Worship the LORD in holy splendour.
O tremble before him, all the earth.
Say to the nations, 'The LORD is king.'
He will judge the peoples in fairness. R.

SECOND READING *1 Corinthians 12:4–11*

'The one and the same Spirit, who apportions to each one individually as he wills.'

A reading from the First Letter of Saint Paul to the Corinthians.

Brothers and sisters: There are varieties of gifts, but the same Spirit; and there are varieties of service, but the same Lord; and there are varieties of activities, but it is the same God who empowers them all in everyone. To each is given the manifestation of the Spirit for the common good. For to one is given through the Spirit the utterance of wisdom, and to another the utterance of knowledge according to the same Spirit, to another faith by the same Spirit, to another gifts of healing by the one Spirit, to another the working of miracles, to another prophecy, to another the ability to distinguish between spirits, to another various kinds of tongues, to another the interpretation of tongues. All these are empowered by one and the same Spirit, who apportions to each one individually as he wills.

The word of the Lord.
Thanks be to God.

ACCLAMATION BEFORE THE GOSPEL *cf 2 Thessalonians 2:14*

Alleluia, alleluia.
God called us through the gospel,
so that we may obtain the glory of our Lord Jesus Christ.
Alleluia.

GOSPEL *John 2:1–11*

The Lord be with you.
And with your spirit.

A reading from the holy Gospel according to John.

Glory to you, O Lord.

'This, the first of his signs, Jesus did at Cana in Galilee.'

At that time: There was a wedding at Cana in Galilee, and the mother of Jesus was there. Jesus also was invited to the wedding with his disciples. When the wine ran out, the mother of Jesus said to him, 'They have no wine.' And Jesus said to her, 'Woman, what does this have to do with me? My hour has not yet come.' His mother said to the servants, 'Do whatever he tells you.' Now there were six stone water jars there for the Jewish rites of purification, each holding seventy or one hundred litres. Jesus said to the servants, 'Fill the jars with water.' And they filled them up to the brim. And he said to them, 'Now draw some out and take it to the master of the feast.' So they took it. When the master of the feast tasted the water now become wine, and did not know where it came from (though the servants who had drawn the water knew), the master of the feast called the bridegroom and said to him, 'Everyone serves the good wine first, and when people have drunk freely, then the poor wine. But you have kept the good wine until now.' This, the first of his signs, Jesus did at Cana in Galilee, and manifested his glory. And his disciples believed in him.

The Gospel of the Lord.
Praise to you, Lord Jesus Christ.

▷ *page 11*

PRAYER OVER THE OFFERINGS

Grant us, O Lord, we pray,
that we may participate worthily in these mysteries,
for whenever the memorial of this sacrifice is celebrated
the work of our redemption is accomplished.
Through Christ our Lord. **Amen.**

▷ *page 15*

COMMUNION ANTIPHON *cf Psalm 22:5*

You have prepared a table before me,
and how precious is the chalice that quenches my thirst.

or *1 John 4:16*

We have come to know and to believe
in the love that God has for us.

▷ *page 58*

PRAYER AFTER COMMUNION

Pour on us, O Lord, the Spirit of your love,
and in your kindness
make those you have nourished
by this one heavenly Bread
one in mind and heart.
Through Christ our Lord. **Amen.**

▷ *page 59*

THIRD SUNDAY IN ORDINARY TIME

ENTRANCE ANTIPHON *cf Psalm 95:1, 6*

O sing a new song to the Lord;
sing to the Lord, all the earth.
In his presence are majesty and splendour,
strength and honour in his holy place.

▷ *page 7*

COLLECT

Almighty ever-living God,
direct our actions according to your good pleasure,
that in the name of your beloved Son
we may abound in good works.
Through our Lord Jesus Christ, your Son,
who lives and reigns with you in the unity of the Holy Spirit,
God, for ever and ever. **Amen.**

FIRST READING *Nehemiah 8:2–6, 8–10*

'They read from the book of the Law, and gave the meaning.'

A reading from the book of Nehemiah.

In those days: Ezra the priest brought the Law before the assembly, both men and women and all who could understand what they heard, on the first day of the seventh month. And he read from it facing the square before the Water Gate from early morning until midday, in the presence of the men and the women and those who could understand. And the ears of all the people were attentive to the Book of the Law.

And Ezra the scribe stood on a wooden platform that they had made for the purpose. And Ezra opened the book in the sight of all the people, for he was above all the people, and as he opened it, all the people stood. And Ezra blessed the LORD, the great God, and all the people answered, 'Amen, Amen,' lifting up their hands. And they bowed their heads and worshipped the LORD with their faces to the ground. Ezra and the Levites read from the book, from the Law of God, clearly, and they gave the meaning, so that the people understood the reading.

And Nehemiah, who was the governor, and Ezra the priest and scribe, and the Levites who taught the people said to all the people, 'This day is holy to the LORD your God; do not mourn or weep.' For all the people wept as they heard the words of the Law. Then he said to them, 'Go on your way. Eat the fat and drink sweet wine and send portions to anyone who has nothing ready, for this day is holy to our Lord. And do not be grieved, for the joy of the LORD is your strength.'

The word of the Lord.
Thanks be to God.

RESPONSORIAL PSALM *Psalm 18:8–10, 15 response John 6:63*

R. Your words, O Lord, are spirit and life.

1 The law of the LORD is perfect;
it revives the soul.
The decrees of the LORD are steadfast;
they give wisdom to the simple. R.

2 The precepts of the LORD are right;
they gladden the heart.
The command of the LORD is clear;
it gives light to the eyes. R.

3 The fear of the LORD is pure,
abiding for ever.
The judgements of the LORD are true;
they are, all of them, just. R.

4 May the spoken words of my mouth,
the thoughts of my heart,
win favour in your sight, O LORD,
my rock and my redeemer! R.

SECOND READING *1 Corinthians 12:12–30 Shorter form: 1 Corinthians 12:12–14, 27 (read text with side line only).*

'You are the body of Christ and individually members of it.'

A reading from the First Letter of Saint Paul to the Corinthians.

Brothers and sisters: Just as the body is one and has many members, and all the members of the body, though many, are one body, so it is with Christ. For in one Spirit we were all baptised into one body—Jews or Greeks, slaves or free—and all were made to drink of one Spirit.

For the body does not consist of one member but of many. | If the foot should say, 'Because I am not a hand, I do not belong to the body', that would not make it any less a part of the body. And if the ear should say, 'Because I am not an eye, I do not belong to the body', that would not make it any less a part of the body. If the whole body were an eye, where would be the sense of hearing? If the whole body were an ear, where would be the sense of smell? But as it is, God arranged the members in the body, each one of them, as he chose. If all were a single member, where would the body be? As it is, there are many parts, yet one body. The eye cannot say to the hand, 'I have no need of you', nor again the head to the feet, 'I have no need of you.' On the contrary, the parts of the body that seem to be weaker are indispensable, and on those parts of the body that we think less honourable we bestow the greater honour, and our unpresentable parts are treated with greater modesty, which our more presentable parts do not require. But God has so composed the body, giving greater honour to the part that lacked it, that there may be no division in the body, but that the members may have the same care for one another. If one member suffers, all suffer together; if one member is honoured, all rejoice together.

Now you are the body of Christ and individually members of it. And God has appointed in the Church first Apostles, second prophets, third teachers, then miracles, then gifts of healing, helping, administrating, and various kinds of tongues. Are all apostles? Are all prophets? Are all teachers? Do all work miracles? Do all possess gifts of healing? Do all speak with tongues? Do all interpret?

The word of the Lord.
Thanks be to God.

ORDINARY

ACCLAMATION BEFORE THE GOSPEL *Luke 4:18*

Alleluia, alleluia.
The Lord has sent me to proclaim good news to the poor;
to proclaim liberty to the captives.
Alleluia.

GOSPEL *Luke 1:1–4; 4:14–21*

The Lord be with you.
And with your spirit.

A reading from the holy Gospel according to Luke.
Glory to you, O Lord.

'Today this Scripture has been fulfilled.'

Inasmuch as many have undertaken to compile a narrative of the things that have been accomplished among us, just as those who from the beginning were eyewitnesses and ministers of the word have delivered them to us, it seemed good to me also, having followed all things closely for some time past, to write an orderly account for you, most excellent Theophilus, that you may have certainty concerning the things you have been taught.

At that time: Jesus returned in the power of the Spirit to Galilee, and a report

about him went out through all the surrounding country. And he taught in their synagogues, being glorified by all.
And he came to Nazareth, where he had been brought up. And as was his custom, he went to the synagogue on the Sabbath day, and he stood up to read. And the scroll of the prophet Isaiah was given to him. He unrolled the scroll, and found the place where it was written, 'The Spirit of the Lord is upon me, because he has anointed me to proclaim good news to the poor. He has sent me to proclaim liberty to the captives and recovering of sight to the blind, to set at liberty those who are oppressed, to proclaim the year of the Lord's favour.'
And he rolled up the scroll, and gave it back to the attendant, and sat down. And the eyes of all in the synagogue were fixed on him. And he began to say to them, 'Today this Scripture has been fulfilled in your hearing.'
The Gospel of the Lord.
Praise to you, Lord Jesus Christ.

▷ *page 11*

PRAYER OVER THE OFFERINGS
Accept our offerings, O Lord, we pray,
and in sanctifying them
grant that they may profit us for salvation.
Through Christ our Lord. **Amen.**

▷ *page 15*

COMMUNION ANTIPHON *cf Psalm 33:6*
Look toward the Lord and be radiant;
let your faces not be abashed.

or *John 8:12*

I am the light of the world, says the Lord;
whoever follows me will not walk in darkness,
but will have the light of life.

▷ *page 58*

PRAYER AFTER COMMUNION
Grant, we pray, almighty God,
that, receiving the grace
by which you bring us to new life,
we may always glory in your gift.
Through Christ our Lord. **Amen.**

▷ *page 59*

FOURTH SUNDAY IN ORDINARY TIME

ENTRANCE ANTIPHON *Psalm 105:47*
Save us, O Lord our God!
And gather us from the nations,
to give thanks to your holy name,
and make it our glory to praise you.

▷ *page 7*

COLLECT

Grant us, Lord our God,
that we may honour you with all our mind,
and love everyone in truth of heart.
Through our Lord Jesus Christ, your Son,
who lives and reigns with you in the unity of the Holy Spirit,
God, for ever and ever. **Amen.**

FIRST READING *Jeremiah 1:4–5, 17–19*

'I appointed you a prophet to the nations.'

A reading from the Prophet Jeremiah.

In the days of King Josiah: The word of the LORD came to me, saying, 'Before I formed you in the womb I knew you, and before you were born I consecrated you; I appointed you a prophet to the nations.

'Dress yourself for work; arise, and say to them everything that I command you. Do not be dismayed by them, lest I dismay you before them. And I, behold, I make you this day a fortified city, an iron pillar, and bronze walls, against the whole land, against the kings of Judah, its officials, its priests, and the people of the land. They will fight against you, but they shall not prevail against you, for I am with you, declares the LORD, to deliver you.'

The word of the Lord.

Thanks be to God.

RESPONSORIAL PSALM *Psalm 71(70):1-2. 3-4a. 5-6b. 15ab, 17. R. cf. 15ab*

R. My mouth will tell of your salvation, O Lord.

1 In you, O LORD, I take refuge;
let me never be put to shame.
In your uprightness, rescue me, free me;
incline your ear to me and save me. R.

2 Be my rock, my constant refuge,
a mighty stronghold to save me,
for you are my rock, my stronghold.
My God, free me from the hand of
the wicked. R.

3 It is you, O Lord, who are my hope,
my trust, O LORD, from my youth.
On you I have leaned from my birth;
from my mother's womb, you have drawn me forth. R.

4 My mouth will tell of your justice,
and all the day long of your salvation.
O God, you have taught me from my youth,
and I proclaim your wonders still. R.

SECOND READING *1 Corinthians 12:31–13:13 Shorter form: 1 Corinthians 13:4–13 (read text with side line only).*

'Faith, hope, and love abide; but the greatest is love.'

A reading from the First Letter of Saint Paul to the Corinthians.

| Brothers and sisters: | Earnestly desire the higher gifts. And I will show you a still more excellent way. If I speak in the tongues of men and of angels, but have not love, I am a noisy gong or a clanging cymbal. And if I have prophetic powers, and understand all mysteries and all knowledge, and if I have all faith, so as to remove mountains, but have not love, I am nothing. If I give away all I have, and if I deliver up my body to be burned, but have not love, I gain nothing.

Love is patient and kind; love does not envy or boast; it is not arrogant or rude. It does not insist on its own way; it is not irritable or resentful; it does not rejoice at wrongdoing, but rejoices with the truth. Love bears all things, believes all things, hopes all things, endures all things.

Love never ends. As for prophecies, they will pass away; as for tongues, they will cease; as for knowledge, it will pass away.

For we know in part and we prophesy in part, but when the perfect comes, the partial will pass away. When I was a child, I spoke like a child, I thought like a child, I reasoned like a child. When I became a man, I gave up childish ways. For now we see in a mirror dimly, but then face to face. Now I know in part; then I shall know fully, even as I have been fully known. So now faith, hope, and love abide, these three; but the greatest of these is love.

The word of the Lord.
Thanks be to God.

ACCLAMATION BEFORE THE GOSPEL *Luke 4:18*

Alleluia, alleluia.
The Lord has sent me to bring proclaim good news to the poor,
to proclaim liberty to captives.
Alleluia.

GOSPEL *Luke 4:21–30*

The Lord be with you.
And with your spirit.

A reading from the holy Gospel according to Luke.
Glory to you, O Lord.

Jesus, like Elijah and Elisha, was not sent only to the Jews.

At that time: Jesus began to say in the synagogue, 'Today this Scripture has been fulfilled in your hearing.' And all spoke well of him and marvelled at the gracious words that were coming from his mouth. And they said, 'Is not this Joseph's son?' And he said to them, 'Doubtless you will quote to me this proverb, "'Physician, heal yourself.' What we have heard you did at Capernaum, do here in your home town as well."' And he said, 'Truly, I say to you, no prophet is acceptable in his home town. But in truth, I tell you, there were many widows in Israel in the days of Elijah, when the heavens were shut up three years and six months, and a great famine came over all the land, and Elijah was sent to none of them but only to Zarephath, in the land of Sidon, to a woman who was a widow. And there were many lepers in Israel in the time of the prophet Elisha, and none of them was cleansed, but only Naaman the Syrian.'

When they heard these things, all in the synagogue were filled with wrath. And they rose up, and drove him out of the town, and brought him to the brow of the hill on which their town was built, so that they could throw him down the cliff. But passing through their midst, he went away.

The Gospel of the Lord.
Praise to you, Lord Jesus Christ.

▷ page 11

PRAYER OVER THE OFFERINGS

O Lord, we bring to your altar
these offerings of our service:
be pleased to receive them, we pray,
and transform them
into the Sacrament of our redemption.
Through Christ our Lord. **Amen.**

▷ page 15

COMMUNION ANTIPHON *cf Psalm 30:17–18*

Let your face shine on your servant.
Save me in your merciful love.
O Lord, let me never be put to shame,
for I call on you.

or *Matthew 5:3–4*

Blessed are the poor in spirit,
for theirs is the Kingdom of Heaven.
Blessed are the meek, for they shall possess the land.

▷ page 58

PRAYER AFTER COMMUNION

Nourished by these redeeming gifts,
we pray, O Lord,
that through this help to eternal salvation
true faith may ever increase.
Through Christ our Lord. **Amen.**

▷ page 59

FIFTH SUNDAY IN ORDINARY TIME

ENTRANCE ANTIPHON *Psalm 94:6–7*

O come, let us worship God
and bow low before the God who made us,
for he is the Lord our God.

▷ page 7

COLLECT

Keep your family safe, O Lord, with unfailing care,
that, relying solely on the hope of heavenly grace,
they may be defended always by your protection.
Through our Lord Jesus Christ, your Son,
who lives and reigns with you in the unity of the Holy Spirit,
God, for ever and ever. **Amen.**

FIRST READING *Isaiah 6:1-2a, 3-8*

'Here I am! Send me.'

A reading from the Prophet Isaiah.

In the year that King Uzziah died, I saw the Lord sitting upon a throne, high and lifted up; and the train of his robe filled the Temple. Above him stood the seraphim. Each had six wings. And one called to another and said: 'Holy, holy, holy is the LORD of hosts; the whole earth is full of his glory!' And the foundations of the thresholds shook at the voice of him who called, and the house was filled with smoke.

And I said: 'Woe is me! For I am lost; for I am a man of unclean lips, and I dwell in the midst of a people of unclean lips; for my eyes have seen the King, the LORD of hosts!'

Then one of the seraphim flew to me, having in his hand a burning coal that he had taken with tongs from the altar. And he touched my mouth and said: 'Behold, this has touched your lips; your guilt is taken away, and your sin atoned for.'

And I heard the voice of the Lord saying, 'Whom shall I send, and who will go for us?' Then I said, 'Here I am! Send me.'

The word of the Lord.
Thanks be to God.

RESPONSORIAL PSALM *Psalm 138(137):1-2a. 2bc, 3. 4-5. 7c-8. R.1c*

R. In the presence of the angels I praise you, O Lord.

1 I thank you, LORD, with all my heart;
you have heard the words of my mouth.
In the presence of the angels I praise you.
I bow down towards your holy Temple. R.

2 I give thanks to your name
for your merciful love and your faithfulness.
On the day I called, you answered me;
you increased the strength of my soul. R.

3 All earth's kings shall thank you, O LORD,
when they hear the words of your mouth.
They shall sing of the ways of the LORD,
'How great is the glory of the LORD!' R.

4 With your right hand you save me;
the LORD will accomplish this for me.
O LORD, your merciful love is eternal;
discard not the work of your hands. R.

SECOND READING *1 Corinthians 15:1–11 | Shorter form: 1 Corinthians 15:3–8, 11 (read text with side line only).*

'So we preach and so you believed.'

A reading from the First Letter of Saint Paul to the Corinthians.

I would remind you, brothers and sisters, of the gospel I preached to you, which you received, in which you stand, and by which you are being saved, if you hold fast to the word I preached to you—unless you believed in vain.

For I delivered to you as of first importance what I also received: that Christ died for our sins in accordance with the Scriptures, that he was buried, that he was raised on the third day in accordance with the Scriptures, and that he appeared to Cephas, then to the Twelve. Then he appeared to more than five hundred brothers and sisters at one time, most of whom are still alive, though some have fallen asleep.

Then he appeared to James, then to all the Apostles. Last of all, as to one untimely born, he appeared also to me.

For I am the least of the Apostles, unworthy to be called an Apostle, because I persecuted the Church of God. But by the grace of God I am what I am, and his grace towards me was not in vain. On the contrary, I worked harder than any of them, though it was not I, but the grace of God that is with me.

Whether then it was I or they, so we preach and so you believed.

The word of the Lord.
Thanks be to God.

ORDINARY

ACCLAMATION BEFORE THE GOSPEL *Matthew 4:19*

Alleluia, alleluia
Follow me, says the Lord,
and I will make you fishers of men.
Alleluia

GOSPEL *Luke 5:1–11*

The Lord be with you.
And with your spirit.

A reading from the holy Gospel according to Luke.
Glory to you, O Lord.

'They left everything and followed him.'

At that time: The crowd was pressing in on Jesus to hear the word of God. He was standing by the lake of Gennesaret, and he saw two boats by the lake, but the fishermen had gone out of them and were washing their nets. Getting into one of the boats, which was Simon's, he asked him to put out a little from the land. And he sat down and taught the people from the boat. And when he had finished speaking, he said to Simon, 'Put out into the deep and let down your nets for a catch.' And Simon answered, 'Master, we toiled all night and took nothing! But at your word I will let down the nets.' And when they had done this, they enclosed a large number of fish, and their nets were breaking. They signalled to their partners in the other boat to come and help them. And they came and filled both the boats, so that they began to sink. But when

Simon Peter saw it, he fell down at Jesus' knees, saying, 'Depart from me, for I am a sinful man, O Lord.' For he and all who were with him were astonished at the catch of fish that they had taken, and so also were James and John, sons of Zebedee, who were partners with Simon. And Jesus said to Simon, 'Do not be afraid; from now on you will be catching men.' And when they had brought their boats to land, they left everything and followed him.

The Gospel of the Lord.
Praise to you, Lord Jesus Christ.

▷ page 11

PRAYER OVER THE OFFERINGS

O Lord, our God,
who once established these created things
to sustain us in our frailty,
grant, we pray,
that they may become for us now
the Sacrament of eternal life.
Through Christ our Lord. **Amen.**

▷ page 15

COMMUNION ANTIPHON *cf Psalm 106:8–9*

Let them thank the Lord for his mercy,
his wonders for the children of men,
for he satisfies the thirsty soul,
and the hungry he fills with good things.

or *Matthew 5:5–6*

Blessed are those who mourn, for they shall be consoled.
Blessed are those who hunger and thirst for righteousness,
for they shall have their fill.

▷ page 58

PRAYER AFTER COMMUNION

O God, who have willed that we be partakers
in the one Bread and the one Chalice,
grant us, we pray, so to live
that, made one in Christ,
we may joyfully bear fruit
for the salvation of the world.
Through Christ our Lord. **Amen.**

▷ page 59

SIXTH SUNDAY IN ORDINARY TIME

ENTRANCE ANTIPHON *cf Psalm 30:3–4*

Be my protector, O God,
a mighty stronghold to save me.
For you are my rock, my stronghold!
Lead me, guide me, for the sake of your name.

▷ *page 7*

COLLECT

O God, who teach us that you abide
in hearts that are just and true,
grant that we may be so fashioned by your grace
as to become a dwelling pleasing to you.
Through our Lord Jesus Christ, your Son,
who lives and reigns with you in the unity of the Holy Spirit,
God, for ever and ever. **Amen.**

FIRST READING *Jeremiah 17:5–8*

'Cursed is the man who trusts in man; blessed is the man who trusts in the Lord.'

A reading from the Prophet Jeremiah.

Thus says the Lord: 'Cursed is the man who trusts in man and makes flesh his strength, whose heart turns away from the Lord. He is like a shrub in the desert, and shall not see any good come. He shall dwell in the parched places of the wilderness, in an uninhabited salt land.

'Blessed is the man who trusts in the Lord, whose trust is the Lord. He is like a tree planted by water, that sends out its roots by the stream, and does not fear when heat comes, for its leaves remain green, and is not anxious in the year of drought, for it does not cease to bear fruit.'

The word of the Lord.
Thanks be to God.

RESPONSORIAL PSALM *Psalm 1:1-2. 3. 4, 6. R. Psalm 40 (39):5a*

R. Blessed the man who has placed his trust in the Lord.

1 Blessed indeed is the man
who follows not the counsel of the wicked,
nor stands in the path with sinners,
nor abides in the company of scorners,
but whose delight is the law of the Lord,
and who ponders his law day and night. R.

2 He is like a tree that is planted
beside the flowing waters,
that yields its fruit in due season,
and whose leaves shall never fade;
and all that he does shall prosper. R.

continued...

R. Blessed the man who has placed his trust in the Lord.

3 Not so are the wicked, not so!
For they, like winnowed chaff,
shall be driven away by the wind.
For the Lord knows the way of the righteous,
but the way of the wicked will perish. R.

SECOND READING *1 Corinthians 15:12, 16–20*

'If Christ has not been raised, your faith is futile.'

A reading from the First Letter of Saint Paul to the Corinthians.

Brothers and sisters: If Christ is proclaimed as raised from the dead, how can some of you say that there is no resurrection of the dead? For if the dead are not raised, not even Christ has been raised. And if Christ has not been raised, your faith is futile and you are still in your sins. Then those also who have fallen asleep in Christ have perished. If in Christ we have hope in this life only, we are of all people most to be pitied. But in fact Christ has been raised from the dead, the first fruits of those who have fallen asleep.

The word of the Lord.
Thanks be to God.

ACCLAMATION BEFORE THE GOSPEL *Luke 6:23ab*

Alleluia, alleluia.
Rejoice and leap for joy, says the Lord,
for behold, your reward is great in heaven.
Alleluia.

GOSPEL *Luke 6:17, 20–26*

The Lord be with you.
And with your spirit.

A reading from the holy Gospel according to Luke.
Glory to you, O Lord.

'Blessed are you who are poor. Woe to you who are rich.'

At that time: Jesus came down with the Twelve and stood on a level place, with a great crowd of his disciples and a great multitude of people from all Judea and Jerusalem and the sea coast of Tyre and Sidon. And he lifted up his eyes on his disciples, and said: 'Blessed are you who are poor, for yours is the kingdom of God. Blessed are you who are hungry now, for you shall be satisfied. Blessed are you who weep now, for you shall laugh. Blessed are you when people hate you, and when they exclude you, and revile you, and spurn your name as evil on account of the Son of Man! Rejoice in that day, and leap for joy, for behold, your reward is great in heaven; for so their fathers did to the prophets. But woe to you who are rich, for you have received your consolation. Woe to you who are full now, for you shall be hungry. Woe to you who laugh now, for you shall mourn and weep. Woe to you, when all people speak well of you, for so their fathers did to the false prophets.'

The Gospel of the Lord.
Praise to you, Lord Jesus Christ.

▷ page 11

PRAYER OVER THE OFFERINGS

May this oblation, O Lord, we pray,
cleanse and renew us
and may it become for those who do your will
the source of eternal reward.
Through Christ our Lord. **Amen.**

▷ *page 15*

COMMUNION ANTIPHON *cf Psalm 77:29–30*

They ate and had their fill,
and what they craved the Lord gave them;
they were not disappointed in what they craved.

or *John 3:16*

God so loved the world
that he gave his Only Begotten Son,
so that all who believe in him may not perish,
but may have eternal life.

▷ *page 58*

PRAYER AFTER COMMUNION

Having fed upon these heavenly delights,
we pray, O Lord,
that we may always long
for that food by which we truly live.
Through Christ our Lord. **Amen.**

▷ *page 59*

SEVENTH SUNDAY IN ORDINARY TIME

ENTRANCE ANTIPHON *Psalm 12:6*

O Lord, I trust in your merciful love.
My heart will rejoice in your salvation.
I will sing to the Lord who has been bountiful with me.

▷ *page 7*

COLLECT

Grant, we pray, almighty God,
that, always pondering spiritual things,
we may carry out in both word and deed
that which is pleasing to you.
Through our Lord Jesus Christ, your Son,
who lives and reigns with you in the unity of the Holy Spirit,
God, for ever and ever. **Amen.**

FIRST READING *1 Samuel 26:2, 7–9, 12–13, 22–23*

'The Lord gave you into my hand today, and I would not put out my hand against the Lord's anointed.'

A reading from the First Book of Samuel.

In those days: Saul arose and went down to the wilderness of Ziph with three thousand chosen men of Israel to seek David in the wilderness of Ziph.
David and Abishai went to the army by night. And there lay Saul sleeping within the encampment, with his spear stuck in the ground at his head, and Abner and the army lay round him. Then Abishai said to David, 'God has given your enemy into your hand this day. Now please let me pin him to the earth with one stroke of the spear, and I will not strike him twice.' But David said to Abishai, 'Do not destroy him, for who can put out his hand against the Lord's anointed and be guiltless?' So David took the spear and the jar of water from Saul's head, and they went away. No man saw it or knew it, nor did any awake, for they were all asleep, because a deep sleep from the Lord had fallen upon them.
Then David went over to the other side and stood far off on the top of the hill, with a great space between them. David said, 'Here is the spear, O king! Let one of the young men come over and take it. The Lord rewards every man for his righteousness and his faithfulness, for the Lord gave you into my hand today, and I would not put out my hand against the Lord's anointed.'

The word of the Lord.
Thanks be to God.

RESPONSORIAL PSALM *Psalm 103(102):1-2. 3-4. 8, 10. 12-13. R.8a*

R. The Lord is compassionate and gracious.

1 Bless the Lord, O my soul,
and all within me, his holy name.
Bless the Lord, O my soul,
and never forget all his benefits. R.

2 It is the Lord who forgives all your sins,
who heals every one of your ills,
who redeems your life from the grave,
who crowns you with mercy and compassion. R.

3 The Lord is compassionate and gracious,
slow to anger and rich in mercy.
He does not treat us according to our sins,
nor repay us according to our faults. R.

4 As far as the east is from the west,
so far from us does he remove our transgressions.
As a father has compassion on his children,
the Lord's compassion is on those who fear him. R.

SECOND READING *1 Corinthians 15:45–49*

'Just as we have borne the image of the man of dust, we shall also bear the image of the man of heaven.'

A reading from the First Letter of Saint Paul to the Corinthians.

Brothers and sisters: 'The first man Adam became a living being'; the last Adam became a life-giving spirit. But it is not the spiritual that is first but the natural, and then the spiritual. The first man was from the earth, a man of dust; the second man is from heaven. As was the man of dust, so also are those who are of the dust, and as is the man of heaven, so also are those who are of heaven. Just as we have borne the image of the man of dust, we shall also bear the image of the man of heaven.

The word of the Lord.
Thanks be to God.

ACCLAMATION BEFORE THE GOSPEL *John 13:34*

Alleluia, alleluia.
A new commandment I give to you, says the Lord,
that you love one another, just as I have loved you.
Alleluia.

GOSPEL *Luke 6:27–38*

The Lord be with you.
And with your spirit.

A reading from the holy Gospel according to Luke.
Glory to you, O Lord.

'Be merciful, even as your Father is merciful.'

At that time: Jesus said to his disciples, 'I say to you who hear: Love your enemies, do good to those who hate you, bless those who curse you, pray for those who abuse you. To one who strikes you on the cheek, offer the other also; and from one who takes away your cloak do not withhold your tunic either. Give to everyone who begs from you; and from one who takes away your goods, do not demand them back. And as you wish that others would do to you, do so to them.

'If you love those who love you, what benefit is that to you? For even sinners love those who love them. And if you do good to those who do good to you, what benefit is that to you? For even sinners do the same. And if you lend to those from whom you expect to receive, what credit is that to you? Even sinners lend to sinners, to get back the same amount. But love your enemies, and do good, and lend, expecting nothing in return, and your reward will be great, and you will be sons of the Most High, for he is kind to the ungrateful and the evil.

'Be merciful, even as your Father is merciful. Judge not, and you will not be judged; condemn not, and you will not be condemned; forgive, and you will be forgiven. Give, and it will be given to you; good measure, pressed down, shaken together, running over, will be put into your lap. For with the measure you use it will be measured back to you.'

The Gospel of the Lord.
Praise to you, Lord Jesus Christ.

▷ page 11

PRAYER OVER THE OFFERINGS

As we celebrate your mysteries, O Lord,
with the observance that is your due,
we humbly ask you,
that what we offer to the honour of your majesty
may profit us for salvation.
Through Christ our Lord. **Amen.**

▷ *page 15*

COMMUNION ANTIPHON *Psalm 9:2–3*

I will recount all your wonders,
I will rejoice in you and be glad,
and sing psalms to your name, O Most High.

or *John 11:27*

Lord, I have come to believe that you are the Christ,
the Son of the living God, who is coming into this world.

▷ *page 58*

PRAYER AFTER COMMUNION

Grant, we pray, almighty God,
that we may experience the effects of the salvation
which is pledged to us by these mysteries.
Through Christ our Lord. **Amen.**

▷ *page 59*

EIGHTH SUNDAY IN ORDINARY TIME

ENTRANCE ANTIPHON *cf Psalm 17:19–20*

The Lord became my protector.
He brought me out to a place of freedom;
he saved me because he delighted in me.

▷ *page 7*

COLLECT

Grant us, O Lord, we pray,
that the course of our world
may be directed by your peaceful rule
and that your Church may rejoice,
untroubled in her devotion.
Through our Lord Jesus Christ, your Son,
who lives and reigns with you in the unity of the Holy Spirit,
God, for ever and ever. **Amen.**

FIRST READING *Sirach 27:4–7*[4]

'Do not praise a man before you hear him reason.'

A reading from the Book of Sirach.

When a sieve is shaken, the refuse appears; so a person's filth in his thoughts. The kiln tests the potter's vessels; likewise the test of a person is in his reasoning. The fruit discloses the cultivation of a tree; so the expression of a thought discloses the cultivation of a person's mind.

Do not praise a man before you hear him reason, for this is the test of people.

The word of the Lord.
Thanks be to God.

RESPONSORIAL PSALM *Psalm 92(91):2-3. 13-14. 15-16. R. cf. 2a*

R. It is good to give thanks to you, O LORD.

1 It is good to give thanks to the LORD,
to make music to your name, O Most High,
to proclaim your loving mercy in the morning,
and your truth in the watches of the night. R.

2 The just one will flourish like the palm tree,
and grow like a Lebanon cedar.
Planted in the house of the LORD,
they will flourish in the courts of our God. R.

3 Still bearing fruit when they are old,
still full of sap, still green,
to proclaim that the LORD is upright.
In him, my rock, there is no wrong. R.

SECOND READING *1 Corinthians 15:54–58*

'He gives us the victory through Jesus Christ.'

A reading from the First Letter of Saint Paul to the Corinthians.

Brothers and sisters: When the perishable puts on the imperishable, and the mortal puts on immortality, then shall come to pass the saying that is written: 'Death is swallowed up in victory.' 'O death, where is your victory? O death, where is your sting?' The sting of death is sin, and the power of sin is the law. But thanks be to God, who gives us the victory through our Lord Jesus Christ. Therefore, my beloved brothers and sisters, be steadfast, immovable, always abounding in the work of the Lord, knowing that in the Lord your labour is not in vain.

The word of the Lord.
Thanks be to God.

ACCLAMATION BEFORE THE GOSPEL *Philippians 2:15d, 16a*

Alleluia, alleluia.
Shine as lights in the world,
holding fast to the word of life.
Alleluia.

---

4 *Sirach 27:5-8*

ORDINARY

GOSPEL *Luke 6:39–45*

The Lord be with you.
And with your spirit.

A reading from the holy Gospel according to Luke.
Glory to you, O Lord.

'Out of the abundance of the heart the mouth speaks.'

At that time: Jesus told his disciples a parable: 'Can a blind man lead a blind man? Will they not both fall into a pit? A disciple is not above his teacher, but everyone when he is fully trained will be like his teacher. Why do you see the speck that is in your brother's eye, but do not notice the log that is in your own eye? How can you say to your brother, "Brother, let me take out the speck that is in your eye", when you yourself do not see the log that is in your own eye? You hypocrite! First take the log out of your own eye, and then you will see clearly to take out the speck that is in your brother's eye.

'For no good tree bears bad fruit, nor again does a bad tree bear good fruit, for each tree is known by its own fruit. For figs are not gathered from thorn bushes, nor are grapes picked from a bramble bush. The good person out of the good treasure of his heart produces good, and the evil person out of his evil treasure produces evil, for out of the abundance of the heart his mouth speaks.'

The Gospel of the Lord.
Praise to you, Lord Jesus Christ.

▷ page 11

PRAYER OVER THE OFFERINGS

O God, who provide gifts to be offered to your name
and count our oblations as signs
of our desire to serve you with devotion,
we ask of your mercy
that what you grant as the source of merit
may also help us to attain merit's reward.
Through Christ our Lord. **Amen.**

▷ page 15

COMMUNION ANTIPHON *cf Psalm 12:6*

I will sing to the Lord who has been bountiful with me,
sing psalms to the name of the Lord Most High.

or Matthew 28:20

Behold, I am with you always,
even to the end of the age, says the Lord.

▷ page 58

PRAYER AFTER COMMUNION

Nourished by your saving gifts,
we beseech your mercy, Lord,
that by this same Sacrament
with which you feed us in the present age,
you may make us partakers of life eternal.
Through Christ our Lord. **Amen.**

▷ page 59

LENT

ABOUT THE SEASON

The annual observance of Lent is the special season for the ascent to the holy mountain of Easter. Through its twofold theme of repentance and baptism, the season of Lent disposes both the catechumens and the faithful to celebrate the paschal mystery. Catechumens are led to the sacraments of initiation by means of the rite of election, the scrutinies, and catechesis. The faithful, listening more intently to the word of God and devoting themselves to prayer, are prepared through a spirit of repentance to renew their baptismal promises.

Ceremonial of Bishops n 249

ABOUT THE READINGS

The gospel readings are arranged as follows:

The first and second Sundays retain the accounts of the Lord's temptations and transfiguration, with readings, however, from all three Synoptics.

On the next three Sundays, the gospels about the Samaritan woman, the man born blind, and the raising of Lazarus have been restored in Year A. Because these gospels are of major importance in regard to Christian initiation, they may also be read in Year B and Year C, especially in places where there are catechumens.

Other texts, however, are provided for Year B and Year C: for Year B, a text from John about Christ's coming glorification through his cross and resurrection and for Year C, a text from Luke about conversion.

On Passion Sunday (Palm Sunday) the texts for the procession are selections from the Synoptic Gospels concerning the Lord's triumphal entrance into Jerusalem. For the Mass the reading is the account of the Lord's passion.

The Old Testament readings are about the history of salvation, which is one of the themes proper to the catechesis of Lent. The series of texts for each Year presents the main elements of salvation history from its beginning until the promise of the New Covenant.

The readings from the letters of the apostles have been selected to fit the gospel and the Old Testament readings and, to the extent possible, to provide a connection between them.

Introduction to the Lectionary n 97

COMMON RESPONSORIAL PSALMS FOR LENT

COMMON RESPONSE

Remember, O Lord, your faithfulness and love.

COMMON PSALM 1 *Psalm 51(50):3-4. 5-6b. 12-13. 14, 17. R. cf. 3a*

R. Have mercy on us, O Lord, for we have sinned.

1 Have mercy on me, O God,
according to your merciful love;
according to your great compassion,
blot out my transgressions.
Wash me completely from my iniquity,
and cleanse me from my sin. R.

2 My transgressions, truly I know them;
my sin is always before me.
Against you, you alone, have I sinned;
what is evil in your sight I have done. R.

3 Create a pure heart for me, O God;
renew a steadfast spirit within me.
Do not cast me away from your presence;
take not your holy spirit from me. R.

4 Restore in me the joy of your salvation;
sustain in me a willing spirit.
O Lord, open my lips
and my mouth shall proclaim your praise. R.

COMMON PSALM 2 *Psalm 91(90):1-2. 10-11. 12-13. 14-15. R. cf. 15b*

R. Be with me, O Lord, in my distress.

1 He who dwells in the shelter of the Most High,
and abides in the shade of the Almighty,
says to the LORD, 'My refuge,
my stronghold, my God in whom I trust!' R.

2 Upon you no evil shall fall,
no plague approach your tent.
For you has he commanded his angels
to keep you in all your ways. R.

3 They shall bear you upon their hands,
lest you strike your foot against a stone.
On the lion and the viper you will tread,
and trample the young lion and the serpent. R.

4 Since he clings to me in love, I will free him,
protect him, for he knows my name.
When he calls on me, I will answer him;
I will be with him in distress;
I will deliver him, and give him glory. R.

COMMON PSALM 3 *Psalm 130 (129):1-2. 3-4. 5-6b. 6c-8. R. 7bc*

**R. With the LORD there is mercy,
in him is plentiful redemption.**

1 Out of the depths I cry to you, O LORD;
Lord, hear my voice!
O let your ears be attentive
to the sound of my pleadings. R.

2 If you, O LORD, should mark iniquities,
Lord, who could stand?
But with you is found forgiveness,
that you may be revered. R.

3 I long for you, O LORD,
my soul longs for his word.
My soul awaits the Lord
more than watchmen for daybreak. R.

4 More than watchmen for daybreak,
let Israel hope for the LORD.
For with the LORD there is mercy,
in him is plentiful redemption.
It is he who will redeem Israel
from all its iniquities. R.

GOSPEL ACCLAMATIONS DURING LENT

During Lent, one of the following acclamations is used instead of *Alleluia* as a response to the verse before the Gospel.

Glory and praise to you, O Christ.
Glory to you, O Christ, Wisdom of God the Father.
Glory to you, O Christ, you are the Word of God.
Glory to you, O Christ, Son of the living God.
Praise and honour to you, Lord Jesus.
Praise to you, O Christ, King of eternal glory.
Great and wonderful are your works, O Lord.
Salvation, glory, and power belong to the Lord Jesus Christ.

In the text which follows an acclamation has been given for each week of Lent. This may be replaced by one of the other acclamations.

ASH WEDNESDAY

In the course of today's Mass, ashes are blessed and distributed.
These are made from the olive branches or branches of other trees that were blessed the previous year.

THE PENITENTIAL ACT IS OMITTED

ENTRANCE ANTIPHON *Wisdom 11:24, 25, 27*

You are merciful to all, O Lord,
and despise nothing that you have made.
You overlook people's sins, to bring them to repentance,
and you spare them, for you are the Lord our God.

The Penitential Act and Gloria are omitted, and the Distribution of Ashes takes its place after the homily.

COLLECT

Grant, O Lord, that we may begin with holy fasting
this campaign of Christian service,
so that, as we take up battle against spiritual evils,
we may be armed with weapons of self-restraint.
Through our Lord Jesus Christ, your Son,
who lives and reigns with you in the unity of the Holy Spirit,
God, for ever and ever.

FIRST READING *Joel 2:12–18*

'Rend your hearts and not your garments.'

A reading from the Prophet Joel.

Thus says the LORD: 'Return to me with all your heart, with fasting, with weeping, and with mourning; and rend your hearts and not your garments.' Return to the LORD your God, for he is gracious and merciful, slow to anger, and abounding in steadfast love; and he relents over disaster. Who knows whether he will not turn and relent, and leave a blessing behind him, a grain offering and a drink offering for the LORD your God? Blow the trumpet in Sion; consecrate a fast; call a solemn assembly; gather the people. Consecrate the congregation; assemble the elders; gather the children, even nursing infants. Let the bridegroom leave his room, and the bride her chamber. Between the vestibule and the altar let the priests, the ministers of the LORD, weep and say, 'Spare your people, O

LORD, and make not your heritage a reproach, a byword among the nations. Why should they say among the peoples, "Where is their God?"'

Then the LORD became jealous for his land and had pity on his people.

The word of the Lord.

Thanks be to God.

RESPONSORIAL PSALM *Psalm 51(50):3-4. 5-6b. 12-13. 14, 17. R. cf. 3a*

R. **Have mercy on us, O Lord, for we have sinned.**

1 Have mercy on me, O God,
according to your merciful love;
according to your great compassion,
blot out my transgressions.
Wash me completely from my iniquity,
and cleanse me from my sin. R.

2 My transgressions, truly I know them;
my sin is always before me.
Against you, you alone, have I sinned;
what is evil in your sight I have done. R.

3 Create a pure heart for me, O God;
renew a steadfast spirit within me.
Do not cast me away from your presence;
take not your holy spirit from me. R.

4 Restore in me the joy of your salvation;
sustain in me a willing spirit.
O Lord, open my lips
and my mouth shall proclaim your praise. R.

SECOND READING *2 Corinthians 5:20–6:2*

'Be reconciled to God. Behold, now is the favourable time.'

A reading from the Second Letter of Saint Paul to the Corinthians.

Brothers and sisters: We are ambassadors for Christ; God making his appeal through us. We implore you on behalf of Christ: be reconciled to God. For our sake he made him to be sin who knew no sin, so that in him we might become the righteousness of God. Working together with him, then, we appeal to you not to receive the grace of God in vain. For he says, 'In a favourable time I listened to you, and in a day of salvation I have helped you.' Behold, now is the favourable time; behold, now is the day of salvation.

The word of the Lord.

Thanks be to God.

ACCLAMATION BEFORE THE GOSPEL *cf. Psalm 95(94):8a, 7c*

Glory and praise to you, O Christ.
Harden not your hearts today,
but listen to the voice of the LORD.
Glory and praise to you, O Christ.

GOSPEL *Matthew 6:1–6, 16–18*

The Lord be with you.
And with your spirit.

A reading from the holy Gospel according to Matthew.
Glory to you, O Lord.

'Your Father who sees in secret will reward you.'

At that time: Jesus said to his disciples: 'Beware of practising your righteousness before other people in order to be seen by them, for then you will have no reward from your Father who is in heaven.

'Thus, when you give to the needy, sound no trumpet before you, as the hypocrites do in the synagogues and in the streets, that they may be praised by others. Truly, I say to you, they have received their reward. But when you give to the needy, do not let your left hand know what your right hand is doing, so that your giving may be in secret. And your Father who sees in secret will reward you.

'And when you pray, you must not be like the hypocrites. For they love to stand and pray in the synagogues and at the street corners, that they may be seen by others. Truly, I say to you, they have received their reward. But when you pray, go into your room and shut the door and pray to your Father who is in secret. And your Father who sees in secret will reward you.

'And when you fast, do not look gloomy like the hypocrites, for they disfigure their faces that their fasting may be seen by others. Truly, I say to you, they have received their reward. But when you fast, anoint your head and wash your face, that your fasting may not be seen by others but by your Father who is in secret. And your Father who sees in secret will reward you.'

The Gospel of the Lord.
Praise to you, Lord Jesus Christ.

HOMILY

BLESSING AND DISTRIBUTION OF ASHES

After the Homily, the Priest says:

Dear brethren (brothers and sisters), let us humbly ask God our Father
that he be pleased to bless with the abundance of his grace
these ashes, which we will put on our heads in penitence.

After a brief prayer in silence he continues:

O God, who are moved by acts of humility
and respond with forgiveness to works of penance,
lend your merciful ear to our prayers
and in your kindness pour out the grace of your ✠ blessing
on your servants who are marked with these ashes,
that, as they follow the Lenten observances,
they may be worthy to come with minds made pure
to celebrate the Paschal Mystery of your Son.
Through Christ our Lord. **Amen.**

An alternative prayer is given overleaf.

or

O God, who desire not the death of sinners,
but their conversion,
mercifully hear our prayers
and in your kindness be pleased to bless ✠ these ashes,
which we intend to receive upon our heads,
that we, who acknowledge we are but ashes
and shall return to dust,
may, through a steadfast observance of Lent,
gain pardon for sins and newness of life
after the likeness of your Risen Son.
Who lives and reigns for ever and ever. **Amen.**

He sprinkles the ashes with holy water.

All who wish to receive ashes then come forward. As the Priest places ashes on the head each person, he says:

Repent, and believe in the Gospel.

or

Remember that you are dust, and to dust you shall return.

Meanwhile, the following, or other appropriate chant(s) are sung:

ANTIPHON 1
Let us change our garments to sackcloth and ashes,
let us fast and weep before the Lord,
that our God, rich in mercy, might forgive us our sins.

ANTIPHON 2 *cf Joel 2:17; Esther 4:17*
Let the priests, the ministers of the Lord,
stand between the porch and the altar and weep and cry out:
Spare, O Lord, spare your people;
do not close the mouths of those who sing your praise, O Lord.

ANTIPHON 3 *Psalm 50:3*
Blot out my transgressions, O Lord.
This may be repeated after each verse of Psalm 50 (Have mercy on me, O God).

RESPONSORY *cf Baruch 3:2; Psalm 78:9*

R Let us correct our faults which we have committed in ignorance, let us not be taken unawares by the day of our death, looking in vain for leisure to repent. * Hear us, O Lord, and show us your mercy, for we have sinned against you.

V Help us, O God our Saviour; for the sake of your name, O Lord, set us free. * Hear us, O Lord...

The Profession of Faith is not said and the Mass continues with the Prayer of the Faithful. ▷ *page 13*

PRAYER OVER THE OFFERINGS

As we solemnly offer
the annual sacrifice for the beginning of Lent,
we entreat you, O Lord,
that, through works of penance and charity,
we may turn away from harmful pleasures
and, cleansed from our sins, may become worthy
to celebrate devoutly the Passion of your Son.
Who lives and reigns for ever and ever. **Amen.**

▷ *page 15*

Preface III or IV of Lent, p 71.

COMMUNION ANTIPHON *cf Psalm 1:2–3*

He who ponders the law of the Lord day and night
will yield fruit in due season.

▷ page 58

PRAYER AFTER COMMUNION

May the Sacrament we have received sustain us, O Lord,
that our Lenten fast may be pleasing to you
and be for us a healing remedy.
Through Christ our Lord. **Amen.**

▷ page 59

PRAYER OVER THE PEOPLE

For the dismissal, the Priest stands facing the people and, extending his hands over them, says this prayer:

Pour out a spirit of compunction, O God,
on those who bow before your majesty,
and by your mercy may they merit the rewards you promise
to those who do penance.
Through Christ our Lord. **Amen.**

FIRST SUNDAY OF LENT

ENTRANCE ANTIPHON *cf Psalm 90:15–16*

When he calls on me, I will answer him;
I will deliver him and give him glory,
I will grant him length of days.

▷ page 7

The Gloria is omitted.

COLLECT

Grant, almighty God,
through the yearly observances of holy Lent,
that we may grow in understanding
of the riches hidden in Christ
and by worthy conduct pursue their effects.
Through our Lord Jesus Christ, your Son,
who lives and reigns with you in the unity of the Holy Spirit,
God, for ever and ever. **Amen.**

FIRST READING *Deuteronomy 26:4–10*

The confession of faith of the chosen people.

A reading from the Book of Deuteronomy.

Moses spoke to the people: 'The priest shall take the basket from your hand and set it down before the altar of the LORD your God. And you shall make response before the LORD your God, "A wandering Aramean was my father. And he went down into Egypt and sojourned there, few in number, and there he became a nation, great, mighty, and populous. And the Egyptians treated us harshly and humiliated us and laid on us hard labour.

Then we cried to the LORD, the God of our fathers, and the LORD heard our voice and saw our affliction, our toil, and our oppression. And the LORD brought us out of Egypt with a mighty hand and an outstretched arm, with great deeds of terror, with signs and wonders. And he brought us into this place and gave us this land, a land flowing with milk and honey. And behold, now I bring the first of the fruit of the ground, which you, O LORD, have given me." And you shall set it down before the LORD your God and worship before the LORD your God.'

The word of the Lord.
Thanks be to God.

RESPONSORIAL PSALM *Psalm 91 (90):1-2. 10-11. 12-13. 14-15. R. cf 15b*

R. Be with me, O Lord, in my distress.

1 He who dwells in the shelter of the Most High,
and abides in the shade of the Almighty,
says to the LORD, 'My refuge,
my stronghold, my God in whom I trust!' R.

2 Upon you no evil shall fall,
no plague approach your tent.
For you has he commanded his angels
to keep you in all your ways. R.

3 They shall bear you upon their hands,
lest you strike your foot against a stone.
On the lion and the viper you will tread,
and trample the young lion and the serpent. R.

4 Since he clings to me in love, I will free him,
protect him, for he knows my name.
When he calls on me, I will answer him;
I will be with him in distress;
I will deliver him, and give him glory. R.

SECOND READING *Romans 10:8–13*

The confession of faith of believers in Christ.

A reading from the Letter of Saint Paul to the Romans.

Brothers and sisters: What does Scripture say? 'The word is near you, in your mouth and in your heart' (that is, the word of faith that we proclaim); because, if you confess with your mouth that Jesus is Lord and believe in your heart that God raised him from the dead, you will be saved. For with the heart one believes and is justified, and with the mouth one confesses and is saved. For the Scripture says, 'Everyone who believes in him will not be put to shame.' For there is no distinction between Jew and Greek; for the same Lord is Lord of all, bestowing his riches on all who call on him. For, 'everyone who calls on the name of the Lord will be saved.'

The word of the Lord.
Thanks be to God.

ACCLAMATION BEFORE THE GOSPEL *Matthew 4:4b*

Glory and praise to you, O Christ.
One does not live on bread alone,
but by every word that comes forth from the mouth of God.
Glory and praise to you, O Christ.

GOSPEL *Luke 4:1–13*

The Lord be with you.
And with your spirit.

A reading from the holy Gospel according to Luke.
Glory to you, O Lord.

'Jesus was led by the Spirit in the wilderness and tempted by the devil'

At that time: Jesus, full of the Holy Spirit, returned from the Jordan and was led by the Spirit in the wilderness for forty days, being tempted by the devil. And he ate nothing during those days. And when they were over, he was hungry.

The devil said to him, 'If you are the Son of God, command this stone to become bread.' And Jesus answered him, 'It is written, "Man shall not live by bread alone."'

And the devil took him up and showed him all the kingdoms of the world in a moment of time, and said to him, 'To you I will give all this authority and their glory, for it has been delivered to me, and I give it to whom I will. If you, then, will worship me, it will all be yours.' And Jesus answered him, 'It is written, "You shall worship the Lord your God, and him only shall you serve."'

And he took him to Jerusalem and set him on the pinnacle of the temple and said to him, 'If you are the Son of God, throw yourself down from here, for it is written, "He will command his angels concerning you, to guard you", and "On their hands they will bear you up, lest you strike your foot against a stone."' And Jesus answered him, 'It is said, "You shall not put the Lord your God to the test."'

And when the devil had ended every temptation, he departed from him until an opportune time.

The Gospel of the Lord.
Praise to you, Lord Jesus Christ.

▷ *page 11*

PRAYER OVER THE OFFERINGS

Give us the right dispositions, O Lord, we pray,
to make these offerings,
for with them we celebrate the beginning
of this venerable and sacred time.
Through Christ our Lord. **Amen.**

▷ *page 15*

Preface: The Temptation of the Lord, p 71.

COMMUNION ANTIPHON *Matthew 4:4*

One does not live by bread alone,
but by every word that comes forth from the mouth of God.

or *cf Psalm 90:4*

The Lord will conceal you with his pinions,
and under his wings you will trust.

▷ page 58

PRAYER AFTER COMMUNION

Renewed now with heavenly bread,
by which faith is nourished, hope increased,
and charity strengthened,
we pray, O Lord,
that we may learn to hunger for Christ,
the true and living Bread,
and strive to live by every word
which proceeds from your mouth.
Through Christ our Lord. **Amen.**

▷ page 59

PRAYER OVER THE PEOPLE

May bountiful blessing, O Lord, we pray,
come down upon your people,
that hope may grow in tribulation,
virtue be strengthened in temptation,
and eternal redemption be assured.
Through Christ our Lord. **Amen.**

SECOND SUNDAY OF LENT

ENTRANCE ANTIPHON *cf Psalm 26:8–9*

Of you my heart has spoken: Seek his face.
It is your face, O Lord, that I seek;
hide not your face from me.

or *cf Psalm 24:6, 2, 22*

Remember your compassion, O Lord,
and your merciful love, for they are from of old.
Let not our enemies exult over us.
Redeem us, O God of Israel, from all our distress.

▷ page 7

The Gloria is omitted.

COLLECT

O God, who have commanded us
to listen to your beloved Son,
be pleased, we pray,
to nourish us inwardly by your word,
that, with spiritual sight made pure,
we may rejoice to behold your glory.
Through our Lord Jesus Christ, your Son,
who lives and reigns with you in the unity of the Holy Spirit,
God, for ever and ever. **Amen.**

FIRST READING *Genesis 15:5–12, 17–18*

God enters into a covenant with Abram, the man of faith.

A reading from the Book of Genesis.

In those days: God brought Abram outside and said, 'Look towards heaven, and number the stars, if you are able to number them.' Then he said to him, 'So shall your offspring be.' And he believed the LORD, and he counted it to him as righteousness.

And he said to him 'I am the LORD who brought you out from Ur of the Chaldeans to give you this land to possess.' But he said, 'O Lord GOD, how am I to know that I shall possess it?' He said to him, 'Bring me a heifer three years old, a female goat three years old, a ram three years old, a turtle-dove, and a young pigeon.' And he brought him all these, cut them in half, and laid each half over against the other. But he did not cut the birds in half. And when birds of prey came down on the carcasses, Abram drove them away.

As the sun was going down, a deep sleep fell on Abram. And behold, dreadful and great darkness fell upon him. When the sun had gone down and it was dark, behold, a smoking firepot and a flaming torch passed between these pieces. On that day the LORD made a covenant with Abram, saying, 'To your offspring I give this land, from the river of Egypt to the great river, the river Euphrates.'

The word of the Lord.
Thanks be to God.

LENT

RESPONSORIAL PSALM *Psalm 27(26):1. 7-8b. 8c-9c. 13-14. R.1a*

R. The LORD is my light and my salvation.

1 The LORD is my light and my salvation;
whom shall I fear?
The LORD is the stronghold of my life;
whom should I dread? R.

2 O LORD, hear my voice when I call;
have mercy and answer me.
Of you my heart has spoken,
'Seek his face.' R.

3 It is your face, O LORD, that I seek;
hide not your face from me.
Dismiss not your servant in anger;
you have been my help. R.

continued...

R. The Lord is my light and my salvation.

4 I believe I shall see the Lord's goodness
in the land of the living.
Wait for the Lord; be strong;
be stout-hearted, and wait for the Lord! R.

SECOND READING *Philippians 3:17–4:1 Shorter form: Philippians 3:20–4:1 (only read text with side line next to it).*

Christ will configure us to his glorious body.

A reading from the Letter of Saint Paul to the Philippians.

Brothers and sisters, | join in imitating me, and keep your eyes on those who walk according to the example you have in us. For many, of whom I have often told you and now tell you even with tears, walk as enemies of the cross of Christ. Their end is destruction, their god is their belly, and they glory in their shame, with minds set on earthly things. But | our citizenship is in heaven, and from it we await a Saviour, the Lord Jesus Christ, who will transform our lowly body to be like his glorious body, by the power that enables him even to subject all things to himself. Therefore, my brothers and sisters, whom I love and long for, my joy and crown, stand firm thus in the Lord, my beloved.

The word of the Lord.
Thanks be to God.

ACCLAMATION BEFORE THE GOSPEL *Matthew 17:5*

Glory to you, O Christ, Wisdom of God the Father.
From a bright cloud, the Father's voice was heard:
'This is my beloved Son, listen to him'.
Glory to you, O Christ, Wisdom of God the Father.

GOSPEL *Luke 9:28b–36*

The Lord be with you.
And with your spirit.

A reading from the holy Gospel according to Luke.
Glory to you, O Lord.

'As Jesus was praying, the appearance of his face was altered.'

At that time: Jesus took with him Peter and John and James and went up on the mountain to pray. And as he was praying, the appearance of his face was altered, and his clothing became dazzling white. And behold, two men were talking with him, Moses and Elijah, who appeared in glory and spoke of his departure, which he was about to accomplish at Jerusalem. Now Peter and those who were with him were heavy with sleep, but when they became fully awake they saw his glory and the two men who stood with him. And as the men were parting from him, Peter said to Jesus, 'Master, it is good that we are here. Let us make three tents, one for you and one for Moses and one for

Elijah'— not knowing what he said. As he was saying these things, a cloud came and overshadowed them, and they were afraid as they entered the cloud. And a voice came out of the cloud, saying, 'This is my Son, my Chosen One; listen to him!' And when the voice had spoken, Jesus was found alone. And they kept silent and told no one in those days anything of what they had seen.

The Gospel of the Lord.
Praise to you, Lord Jesus Christ.

▷ *page 11*

PRAYER OVER THE OFFERINGS

May this sacrifice, O Lord, we pray,
cleanse us of our faults
and sanctify your faithful in body and mind
for the celebration of the paschal festivities.
Through Christ our Lord. **Amen.**

▷ *page 15*

Preface: The Transfiguration of the Lord, p 72.

COMMUNION ANTIPHON *Matthew 17:5*

This is my beloved Son, with whom I am well pleased;
listen to him.

▷ *page 58*

PRAYER AFTER COMMUNION

As we receive these glorious mysteries,
we make thanksgiving to you, O Lord,
for allowing us while still on earth
to be partakers even now of the things of heaven.
Through Christ our Lord. **Amen.**

▷ *page 59*

PRAYER OVER THE PEOPLE

Bless your faithful, we pray, O Lord,
with a blessing that endures for ever,
and keep them faithful
to the Gospel of your Only Begotten Son,
so that they may always desire and at last attain
that glory whose beauty he showed in his own Body,
to the amazement of his Apostles.
Through Christ our Lord. **Amen.**

THIRD SUNDAY OF LENT (YEAR C)

This Mass is used when the First Scrutiny is not being celebrated.
Readings for Year A may be used with this Mass as an alternative (see p 164).

If the First Scrutiny is being celebrated today
the Ritual Mass for the Celebration of the First Scrutiny, with the readings for Year A is used (see p 163).

ENTRANCE ANTIPHON *cf Psalm 24:15–16*

My eyes are always on the Lord,
for he rescues my feet from the snare.
Turn to me and have mercy on me,
for I am alone and poor.

or *cf Ezechiel 36:23–26*

When I prove my holiness among you,
I will gather you from all the foreign lands;
and I will pour clean water upon you
and cleanse you from all your impurities,
and I will give you a new spirit, says the Lord.

▷ page 7

The Gloria is omitted.

COLLECT

O God, author of every mercy and of all goodness,
who in fasting, prayer and almsgiving
have shown us a remedy for sin,
look graciously on this confession of our lowliness,
that we, who are bowed down by our conscience,
may always be lifted up by your mercy.
Through our Lord Jesus Christ, your Son,
who lives and reigns with you in the unity of the Holy Spirit,
God, for ever and ever. **Amen.**

The Readings for Year A may be used as an alternative *(see page 164).*

FIRST READING *Exodus 3:1–8a, 13–15*

'"I Am" has sent me to you.

A reading from the Book of Exodus. In those days: Moses was keeping the flock of his father-in-law, Jethro, the priest of Midian, and he led his flock to the west side of the wilderness and came to Horeb, the mountain of God. And the angel of the Lord appeared to him in a flame of fire out of the midst of a bush. He looked, and behold, the bush was burning, yet it was not consumed. And Moses said, 'I will turn aside to see this great sight, why the bush is not burned.' When the Lord saw that he turned aside to see, God called to him out of the bush, 'Moses, Moses!' And he said, 'Here I am.' Then he said, 'Do not come near; take your sandals off your feet, for the place on which you are standing is holy ground.' And he said, 'I am the God of your father, the God of Abraham, the God of Isaac, and the God of Jacob.' And Moses hid his face, for he was afraid to look at God.

Then the Lord said, 'I have surely seen the affliction of my people who are in Egypt and have heard their cry because of their taskmasters. I know their sufferings, and I have come down to deliver them out of the hand of the Egyptians and to bring them up out of that land to a good and broad land, a land flowing with milk and honey.'

Then Moses said to God, 'If I come to the people of Israel and say to them, "The God of your fathers has sent me to you", and they ask me, "What is his name?" what shall I say to them?' God said to Moses, 'I AM WHO I AM.' And he said, 'Say this to the people of Israel: "I AM has sent me to you."' God also said to Moses, 'Say this to the people of Israel: "The LORD, the God of your fathers, the God of Abraham, the God of Isaac, and the God of Jacob, has sent me to you." This is my name for ever, and thus I am to be remembered throughout all generations.'

The word of the Lord.
Thanks be to God.

RESPONSORIAL PSALM *Psalm 103 (102):1-2. 3-4. 6-7. 8, 11. R.8a*

R. The LORD is compassionate and gracious.

1 Bless the LORD, O my soul,
and all within me, his holy name.
Bless the LORD, O my soul,
and never forget all his benefits. R.

2 It is the Lord who forgives all your sins,
who heals every one of your ills,
who redeems your life from the grave,
who crowns you with mercy and compassion. R.

3 The LORD does deeds of justice,
gives full justice to all who are oppressed.
He made known his ways to Moses,
and his deeds to the children of Israel. R.

4 The LORD is compassionate and gracious,
slow to anger and rich in mercy.
For as the heavens are high above the earth,
so strong his mercy for those who fear him. R.

SECOND READING *1 Corinthians 10:1–6, 10–12*

The way of life of the people with Moses in the desert was written down for our instruction.

A reading from the First Letter of Saint Paul to the Corinthians.

I do not want you to be unaware, brothers and sisters, that our fathers were all under the cloud, and all passed through the sea, and all were baptised into Moses in the cloud and in the sea, and all ate the same spiritual food, and all drank the same spiritual drink. For they drank from the spiritual Rock that followed them, and the Rock was Christ. Nevertheless, with most of them God was not pleased, for they were overthrown in the wilderness.

Now these things took place as examples for us, that we might not desire evil as they did, nor grumble, as some of them did and were destroyed by the Destroyer.

Now these things happened to them as an example, but they were written down for our instruction, on whom the end of the ages has come. Therefore let anyone who thinks that he stands take heed lest he fall.

The word of the Lord.
Thanks be to God.

ACCLAMATION BEFORE THE GOSPEL *Matthew 4:17*

Glory to you, O Christ, you are the Word of God.
Repent, says the Lord,
for the kingdom of heaven is at hand.
Glory to you, O Christ, you are the Word of God.

GOSPEL *Luke 13:1–9*

The Lord be with you.
And with your spirit.

A reading from the holy Gospel according to Luke.
Glory to you, O Lord.

'Unless you repent, you will all likewise perish.'

There were some present at that very time who told Jesus about the Galileans whose blood Pilate had mingled with their sacrifices. And he answered them, 'Do you think that these Galileans were worse sinners than all the other Galileans because they suffered in this way? No, I tell you; but unless you repent, you will all likewise perish. Or those eighteen on whom the tower in Siloam fell and killed them: do you think that they were worse offenders than all the others who lived in Jerusalem? No, I tell you; but unless you repent, you will all likewise perish.'

And he told this parable: 'A man had a fig tree planted in his vineyard, and he came seeking fruit on it and found none. And he said to the vine dresser, "Look, for three years now I have come seeking fruit on this fig tree, and I find none. Cut it down. Why should it use up the ground?" And he answered him, "Sir, let it alone this year also, until I dig round it and put on manure. Then if it should bear fruit next year, well and good; but if not, you can cut it down."'

The Gospel of the Lord.
Praise to you, Lord Jesus Christ.

▷ *page 11*

PRAYER OVER THE OFFERINGS

Be pleased, O Lord, with these sacrificial offerings,
and grant that we who beseech pardon for our own sins,
may take care to forgive our neighbour.
Through Christ our Lord. **Amen.**

▷ *page 15*

When Year C readings are used, Preface I or II of Lent is used, p 70.
When Year A readings are used, Preface: The Samaritan Woman is used, p 72.

COMMUNION ANTIPHON *for Year C readings cf Psalm 83:4–5*

The sparrow finds a home,
and the swallow a nest for her young:
by your altars, O Lord of hosts, my King and my God.
Blessed are they who dwell in your house,
for ever singing your praise.

or *for Year A readings: John 4:13–14*

For anyone who drinks it, says the Lord,
the water I shall give will become in him
a spring welling up to eternal life.

▷ *page 58*

PRAYER AFTER COMMUNION

As we receive the pledge
of things yet hidden in heaven
and are nourished while still on earth
with the Bread that comes from on high,
we humbly entreat you, O Lord,
that what is being brought about in us in mystery
may come to true completion.
Through Christ our Lord. **Amen.**

▷ *page 59*

PRAYER OVER THE PEOPLE

Direct, O Lord, we pray, the hearts of your faithful,
and in your kindness grant your servants this grace:
that, abiding in the love of you and their neighbour,
they may fulfil the whole of your commands.
Through Christ our Lord. **Amen.**

THIRD SUNDAY OF LENT (YEAR A) AND FIRST SCRUTINY

RITUAL MASS FOR THE CELEBRATION OF THE SCRUTINIES: FIRST SCRUTINY

This Mass is used when the First Scrutiny is being celebrated today.

ENTRANCE ANTIPHON *Ezekiel 36:23–26*

When I prove my holiness among you,
I will gather you from all the foreign lands
and I will pour clean water upon you
and cleanse you from all your impurities,
and I will give you a new spirit, says the Lord.

or *cf Isaiah 55:1*

Come to the waters, you who are thirsty, says the Lord;
you who have no money, come and drink joyfully.

▷ *page 7*

The Gloria is omitted.

COLLECT

Grant, we pray, O Lord,
that these chosen ones may come worthily and wisely
to the confession of your praise,
so that in accordance with that first dignity
which they lost by original sin
they may be fashioned anew through your glory.
Through our Lord Jesus Christ, your Son,
who lives and reigns with you in the unity of the Holy Spirit,
God, for ever and ever. **Amen.**

These readings may be used in any year.

If the First Scrutiny is not celebrated today, the Mass prayers of the Third Sunday of Lent (Year C) are used, page 160.

FIRST READING *Exodus 17:3–7*[5]

'Give us water to drink.'[1]

A reading from the Book of Exodus.

In those days: The people thirsted for water, and the people grumbled against Moses and said, 'Why did you bring us up out of Egypt, to kill us and our children and our livestock with thirst?' So Moses cried to the LORD, 'What shall I do with this people? They are almost ready to stone me.' And the LORD said to Moses, 'Pass on before the people, taking with you some of the elders of Israel, and take in your hand the staff with which you struck the Nile, and go. Behold, I will stand before you there on the rock at Horeb, and you shall strike the rock, and water shall come out of it, and the people will drink.' And Moses did so, in the sight of the elders of Israel. And he called the name of the place Massah and Meribah, because of the quarrelling of the people of Israel, and because they tested the LORD by saying, 'Is the LORD among us or not?'

The word of the Lord.
Thanks be to God.

RESPONSIVE PSALM *Psalm 95 (94):1-2. 6-7b. 7c-9. R.7c, 8a*

**R. O that today you would listen to his voice!
'Harden not your hearts.'**

1 Come, let us ring out our joy to the LORD;
hail the rock who saves us.
Let us come into his presence, giving thanks;
let us hail him with a song of praise. R.

2 O come; let us bow and bend low.
Let us kneel before the LORD who made us,
for he is our God, and we the people,
the people of his pasture, the flock of his hand. R.

3 O that today you would listen to his voice!
'Harden not your hearts as at Meribah,
as on that day at Massah in the desert
when your forebears put me to the test;
when they tried me, though they saw my work.' R.

---

5 *Exodus 17:2*

SECOND READING *Romans 5:1–2, 5–8*

Love has been poured into our hearts through the Spirit who has been given to us.

A reading from the Letter of Saint Paul to the Romans.

Brothers and sisters: Since we have been justified by faith, we have peace with God through our Lord Jesus Christ. Through him we have also obtained access by faith into this grace in which we stand, and we rejoice in hope of the glory of God, and hope does not put us to shame, because God's love has been poured into our hearts through the Holy Spirit who has been given to us.

For while we were still weak, at the right time Christ died for the ungodly. For one will scarcely die for a righteous person—though perhaps for a good person one would dare even to die—but God shows his love for us in that while we were still sinners, Christ died for us.

The word of the Lord.
Thanks be to God.

ACCLAMATION BEFORE THE GOSPEL *cf John 4:42, 15*

Glory to you, O Christ, you are the Word of God.
Lord, you are indeed the Saviour of the world;
give me living water, so that I will not be thirsty.
Glory to you, O Christ, you are the Word of God.

GOSPEL *John 4:5–42 Shorter form: John 4:5-15, 19b-26, 39a, 40-42 (only read text with side line next to it).*

The Lord be with you.
And with your spirit.

A reading from the holy Gospel according to John.
Glory to you, O Lord.

'A spring of water welling up to eternal life.'

At that time: Jesus came to a town of Samaria called Sychar, near the field that Jacob had given to his son Joseph. Jacob's well was there; so Jesus, wearied as he was from his journey, was sitting beside the well. It was about the sixth hour.

A woman from Samaria came to draw water. Jesus said to her, 'Give me a drink.' (For his disciples had gone away into the city to buy food.) The Samaritan woman said to him, 'How is it that you, a Jew, ask for a drink from me, a woman of Samaria?' (For Jews have no dealings with Samaritans.) Jesus answered her, 'If you knew the gift of God, and who it is that is saying to you, "Give me a drink", you would have asked him, and he would have given you living water.' The woman said to him, 'Sir, you have nothing to draw water with, and the well is deep. Where do you get that living water? Are you greater than our father Jacob? He gave us the well and drank from it himself, as did his sons and his livestock.' Jesus said to her, 'Everyone who drinks of this water will be thirsty again, but whoever drinks of the water that I will give him will never be thirsty again. The water that I will give him will become in him a spring of water welling up to eternal life.' The woman said to him, 'Sir, give me this water, so that I will not be thirsty or have to come here to draw water.'

Jesus said to her, 'Go, call your husband, and come here.' The woman answered him, 'I have no husband.' Jesus said to her, 'You are right in saying, "I have no husband"; for you have had five husbands, and the one you now have is not your husband. What you have said is true.' The woman said to him,

'Sir, I perceive that you are a prophet. Our fathers worshipped on this mountain, but you say that in Jerusalem is the place where people ought to worship.' Jesus said to her, 'Woman, believe me, the hour is coming when neither on this mountain nor in Jerusalem will you worship the Father. You worship what you do not know; we worship what we know, for salvation is from the Jews. But the hour is coming, and is now here, when the true worshippers will worship the Father in spirit and truth, for the Father is seeking such people to worship him. God is spirit, and those who worship him must worship in spirit and truth.' The woman said to him, 'I know that Messiah is coming—he who is called Christ. When he comes, he will tell us all things.' Jesus said to her, 'I who speak to you am he.'

Just then his disciples came back. They marvelled that he was talking with a woman, but no one said, 'What do you seek?' or, 'Why are you talking with her?' So the woman left her water jar and went away into town and said to the people, 'Come, see a man who told me all that I ever did. Can this be the Christ?' They went out of the town and were coming to him.

Meanwhile the disciples were urging him, saying, 'Rabbi, eat.' But he said to them, 'I have food to eat that you do not know about.' So the disciples said to one another, 'Has anyone brought him something to eat?'

Jesus said to them, 'My food is to do the will of him who sent me and to accomplish his work. Do you not say, "There are yet four months, then comes the harvest"? Look, I tell you, lift up your eyes, and see that the fields are white for harvest. Already the one who reaps is receiving wages and gathering fruit for eternal life, so that sower and reaper may rejoice together. For here the saying holds true, "One sows and another reaps." I sent you to reap that for which you did not labour. Others have laboured, and you have entered into their labour.'

Many Samaritans from that town believed in him because of the woman's testimony, 'He told me all that I ever did.' So when the Samaritans came to him, they asked him to stay with them, and he stayed there two days. And many more believed because of his word. They said to the woman, 'It is no longer because of what you said that we believe, for we have heard for ourselves, and we know that this is indeed the Saviour of the world.'

The Gospel of the Lord.
Praise to you, Lord Jesus Christ.

HOMILY

After the readings, and guided by them, the minister explains the meaning of the First Scrutiny in the light of the Lenten liturgy and of the spiritual journey of the elect.

FIRST SCRUTINY

The First Scrutiny of those seeking Baptism takes place after the Homily.

PRAYER OF THE FAITHFUL AND PROFESSION OF FAITH

Intercessory prayer is resumed with the usual Prayer of the Faithful for the needs of the Church and the whole world; then, if required, the Profession of Faith is said. But for pastoral reasons, the Prayer of the Faithful and the Profession of Faith may be omitted.

▷ *page 13*

PRAYER OVER THE OFFERINGS

May your merciful grace prepare your servants, O Lord,
for the worthy celebration of these mysteries,
and lead them to it by a devout way of life.
Through Christ our Lord. **Amen.**

▷ *page 15*

EUCHARISTIC PRAYER

Preface: The Samaritan Woman is used, p 72.
In Eucharistic Prayers I, II and III, proper forms of certain sections are used:

EUCHARISTIC PRAYER I

Memento, Domine
(Remember, Lord, your servants):
Remember, Lord, your servants
who are to present your chosen ones
for the holy grace of your Baptism,
Here the names of the godparents are read out
and all gathered here,
whose faith and devotion are known to you…

Hanc igitur (Therefore, Lord, we pray):
Therefore, Lord, we pray:
graciously accept this oblation
which we make to you for your servants,
whom you have been pleased
to enrol, choose and call for eternal life
and for the blessed gift of your grace.
(Through Christ our Lord. Amen.)

EUCHARISTIC PRAYER II

After the words 'and all the clergy,' the following is added:
Remember also, Lord, your servants
who are to present these chosen ones
at the font of rebirth.

EUCHARISTIC PRAYER III

After the words 'the entire people you have gained for your own', the following is added:
Assist your servants with your grace,
O Lord, we pray,
that they may lead these chosen ones by word and example
to new life in Christ, our Lord.

COMMUNION ANTIPHON *cf John 4:13–14*

For anyone who drinks it, says the Lord,
the water I shall give will become in him a spring
welling up to eternal life.

▷ *page 58*

PRAYER AFTER COMMUNION

Give help, O Lord, we pray,
by the grace of your redemption
and be pleased to protect and prepare
those you are to initiate
through the Sacraments of eternal life.
Through Christ our Lord. **Amen.**

▷ *page 59*

FOURTH SUNDAY OF LENT (YEAR C)

This Mass is used when the Second Scrutiny is not being celebrated.
Readings for Year A may be used with this Mass as an alternative (see p 172).

If the Second Scrutiny is being celebrated today
the Ritual Mass for the Celebration of the Second Scrutiny, with the readings for Year A is used (see p 172).

ENTRANCE ANTIPHON *cf Isaiah 66:10–11*

Rejoice, Jerusalem, and all who love her.
Be joyful, all who were in mourning;
exult and be satisfied at her consoling breast.

▷ page 7

The Gloria is omitted.

COLLECT

O God, who through your Word
reconcile the human race to yourself in a wonderful way,
grant, we pray,
that with prompt devotion and eager faith
the Christian people may hasten
toward the solemn celebrations to come.
Through our Lord Jesus Christ, your Son,
who lives and reigns with you in the unity of the Holy Spirit,
God, for ever and ever. **Amen.**

The Readings for Year A may be used as an alternative *(see page 172).*

FIRST READING *Joshua 5:9a–12*

The people of God entered the promised land and there kept the Passover.

A reading from the Book of Joshua.

In those days: The LORD said to Joshua, 'Today I have rolled away the reproach of Egypt from you.' While the people of Israel were encamped at Gilgal, they kept the Passover on the fourteenth day of the month in the evening on the plains of Jericho. And the day after the Passover, on that very day, they ate of the produce of the land, unleavened cakes and parched grain. And the manna ceased the day after they ate of the produce of the land. And there was no longer manna for the people of Israel, but they ate of the fruit of the land of Canaan that year.

The word of the Lord.
Thanks be to God.

RESPONSORIAL PSALM *Psalm 34(33):2-3. 4-5. 6-7. R.9a*

R. Taste and see that the Lord is good.

1 I will bless the Lord at all times,
praise of him is always in my mouth.
In the Lord my soul shall make its boast;
the humble shall hear and be glad. R.

2 Glorify the Lord with me;
together let us praise his name.
I sought the Lord, and he answered me;
from all my terrors he set me free. R.

3 Look towards him and be radiant;
let your faces not be abashed.
This lowly one called; the Lord heard,
and rescued him from all his distress. R.

SECOND READING *2 Corinthians 5:17–21*

'God who through Christ reconciled us to himself.'

A reading from the Second Letter of Saint Paul to the Corinthians.

Brothers and sisters: If anyone is in Christ, he is a new creation. The old has passed away; behold, the new has come. All this is from God, who through Christ reconciled us to himself and gave us the ministry of reconciliation; that is, in Christ God was reconciling the world to himself, not counting their trespasses against them, and entrusting to us the message of reconciliation. Therefore, we are ambassadors for Christ; God making his appeal through us. We implore you on behalf of Christ: be reconciled to God. For our sake he made him to be sin who knew no sin, so that in him we might become the righteousness of God.

The word of the Lord.

Thanks be to God.

ACCLAMATION BEFORE THE GOSPEL *Luke 15:18*

Praise and honour to you, Lord Jesus.
I will arise and go to my father, and I will say to him,
'Father, I have sinned against heaven and before you'.
Praise and honour to you, Lord Jesus.

GOSPEL *Luke 15:1–3, 11–32*

The Lord be with you.
And with your spirit.

A reading from the holy Gospel according to Luke.
Glory to you, O Lord.

'Your brother was dead, and is alive.'

At that time: The tax collectors and sinners were all drawing near to hear Jesus. And the Pharisees and the scribes grumbled, saying, 'This man receives sinners and eats with them.'
So he told them this parable: 'There was a man who had two sons. And the younger of them said to his father, "Father, give me the share of property that is coming to me." And he divided his property between them. Not many days later, the younger son gathered all he had and took a journey into a far country, and there he squandered his property in reckless living. And when he had spent everything, a severe famine arose in that country, and he began to be in need. So he went and hired himself out to one of the citizens of that country, who sent him into his fields to feed pigs. And he was longing to be fed with the pods that the pigs ate, and no one gave him anything.

'But when he came to himself, he said, "How many of my father's hired servants have more than enough bread, but I perish here with hunger! I will arise and go to my father, and I will say to him, 'Father, I have sinned against heaven and before you. I am no longer worthy to be called your son. Treat me as one of your hired servants.'" '

And he arose and came to his father. But while he was still a long way off, his father saw him and felt compassion, and ran and embraced him and kissed him. And the son said to him, "Father, I have sinned against heaven and before you. I am no longer worthy to be called your son." But the father said to his servants, "Bring quickly the best robe, and put it on him, and put a ring on his hand, and shoes on his feet. And bring the fattened calf and kill it, and let us eat and celebrate. For this my son was dead, and is alive again; he was lost, and is found." And they began to celebrate.
'Now his older son was in the field, and as he came and drew near to the house, he heard music and dancing. And he called one of the servants and asked what these things meant. And he said to him, "Your brother has come, and your father has killed the fattened calf, because he has received him back safe and sound." But he was angry and refused to go in. His father came out and entreated him, but he answered his father, "Look, these many years I have served you, and I never disobeyed your command, yet you never gave me a young goat, that I might celebrate with my friends. But when this son of yours came, who has devoured your property with prostitutes, you killed the fattened calf for him!" And he said to him, "Son, you are always with me, and all that is mine is yours. It was fitting to celebrate and be glad, for this your brother was dead, and is alive; he was lost, and is found."'

The Gospel of the Lord.
Praise to you, Lord Jesus Christ.

▷ *page 11*

PRAYER OVER THE OFFERINGS

We place before you with joy these offerings,
which bring eternal remedy, O Lord,
praying that we may both faithfully revere them
and present them to you, as is fitting,
for the salvation of all the world.
Through Christ our Lord. **Amen.**

▷ page 15

When Year C readings are used, Preface I or II of Lent is used, p 70.
When Year A readings are used, Preface: The Man Born Blind is used, p 72.

COMMUNION ANTIPHON *Year C readings Luke 15:32*

You must rejoice, my son,
for your brother was dead and has come to life;
he was lost and is found.

or for Year A readings cf John 9:11, 38

The Lord anointed my eyes: I went, I washed,
I saw and I believed in God.

▷ page 58

PRAYER AFTER COMMUNION

O God, who enlighten everyone who comes into this world,
illuminate our hearts, we pray,
with the splendour of your grace,
that we may always ponder
what is worthy and pleasing to your majesty
and love you in all sincerity.
Through Christ our Lord. **Amen.**

▷ page 59

PRAYER OVER THE PEOPLE

Look upon those who call to you, O Lord,
and sustain the weak;
give life by your unfailing light
to those who walk in the shadow of death,
and bring those rescued by your mercy from every evil
to reach the highest good.
Through Christ our Lord.

FOURTH SUNDAY OF LENT (YEAR A) AND SECOND SCRUTINY

RITUAL MASS FOR THE CELEBRATION OF THE SCRUTINIES: SECOND SCRUTINY

This Mass is used when the Second Scrutiny is being celebrated today.

ENTRANCE ANTIPHON *cf Psalm 24:15–16*

My eyes are always on the Lord, for he rescues my feet from the snare.
Turn to me and have mercy on me, for I am alone and poor.

▷ page 7

The Gloria is omitted.

COLLECT

Almighty ever-living God,
give to your Church an increase in spiritual joy,
so that those once born of earth
may be reborn as citizens of heaven.
Through our Lord Jesus Christ, your Son,
who lives and reigns with you in the unity of the Holy Spirit,
God, for ever and ever. **Amen.**

These readings may be used in any year.

If the Second Scrutiny is not celebrated today, the Mass prayers of the Fourth Sunday of Lent (Year C) are used, page 168.

FIRST READING *1 Samuel 16:1b, 6-7, 10-13a*

David is anointed king of Israel.

A reading from the First Book of Samuel.

In those days: The LORD said to Samuel, 'Fill your horn with oil, and go. I will send you to Jesse the Bethlehemite, for I have provided for myself a king among his sons.'

When they came, he looked on Eliab and thought, 'Surely the LORD's anointed is before him.' But the LORD said to Samuel, 'Do not look on his appearance or on the height of his stature, because I have rejected him. For the LORD sees not as man sees: man looks on the outward appearance, but the LORD looks on the heart.' And Jesse made seven of his sons pass before Samuel. And Samuel said to Jesse, 'The LORD has not chosen these.' Then Samuel said to Jesse, 'Are all your sons here?' And he said, 'There remains yet the youngest, but behold, he is keeping the sheep.' And Samuel said to Jesse, 'Send and get him, for we will not sit down till he comes here.' And he sent and brought him in. Now he was ruddy and had beautiful eyes and was handsome. And the LORD said, 'Arise, anoint him, for this is he.' Then Samuel took the horn of oil and anointed him in the midst of his brothers. And the Spirit of the LORD rushed upon David from that day forward.

The word of the Lord.
Thanks be to God.

RESPONSORIAL PSALM *Psalm 23(22):1-3a. 3b-4. 5. 6. R.1*

R. The Lord is my shepherd;
there is nothing I shall want.

1 The Lord is my shepherd;
there is nothing I shall want.
Fresh and green are the pastures
where he gives me repose.
Near restful waters he leads me;
he revives my soul. R.

2 He guides me along the right path,
for the sake of his name.
Though I should walk in the valley of the shadow of death,
no evil would I fear, for you are with me.
Your crook and your staff will give me comfort. R.

3 You have prepared a table before me
in the sight of my foes.
My head you have anointed with oil;
my cup is overflowing. R.

4 Surely goodness and mercy shall follow me
all the days of my life.
In the Lord's own house shall I dwell
for length of days unending. R.

SECOND READING *Ephesians 5:8–14*

'Arise from the dead, and Christ will shine on you.'

A reading from the Letter of Saint Paul to the Ephesians.

Brothers and sisters: At one time you were darkness, but now you are light in the Lord. Walk as children of light, for the fruit of light is found in all that is good and right and true, and try to discern what is pleasing to the Lord. Take no part in the unfruitful works of darkness, but instead expose them. For it is shameful even to speak of the things that they do in secret. But when anything is exposed by the light, it becomes visible, for anything that becomes visible is light. Therefore it says, 'Awake, O sleeper, and arise from the dead, and Christ will shine on you.'

The word of the Lord.
Thanks be to God.

ACCLAMATION BEFORE THE GOSPEL *John 8:12*

Praise and honour to you, Lord Jesus.
I am the light of the world, says the Lord;
whoever follows me will have the light of life.
Praise and honour to you, Lord Jesus.

GOSPEL *John 9:1–41 Shorter form: John 9:1, 6–9, 13–17, 34–38 (only read text with side line next to it).*

The Lord be with you.
And with your spirit.

A reading from the holy Gospel according to John.
Glory to you, O Lord.

'He went and washed and received his sight.'

At that time: As Jesus passed by, he saw a man blind from birth. | And his disciples asked him, 'Rabbi, who sinned, this man or his parents, that he was born blind?' Jesus answered, 'It was not that this man sinned, or his parents, but that the works of God might be displayed in him. We must work the works of him who sent me while it is day; night is coming, when no one can work. As long as I am in the world, I am the light of the world.' Having said these things, he spat on the ground and made mud with the saliva. Then he anointed the man's eyes with the mud and said to him, 'Go, wash in the pool of Siloam' (which means Sent). So he went and washed and came back seeing.

The neighbours and those who had seen him before as a beggar were saying, 'Is this not the man who used to sit and beg?' Some said, 'It is he.' Others said, 'No, but he is like him.' He kept saying, 'I am the man.' | So they said to him, 'Then how were your eyes opened?' He answered, 'The man called Jesus made mud and anointed my eyes and said to me, "Go to Siloam and wash." So I went and washed and received my sight.' They said to him, 'Where is he?' He said, 'I do not know.'

They brought to the Pharisees the man who had formerly been blind. Now it was a Sabbath day when Jesus made the mud and opened his eyes. So the Pharisees again asked him how he had received his sight. And he said to them, 'He put mud on my eyes, and I washed, and I see.' Some of the Pharisees said, 'This man is not from God, for he does not keep the Sabbath.' But others said, 'How can a man who is a sinner do such signs?' And there was a division among them. So they said again to the blind man, 'What do you say about him, since he has opened your eyes?' He said, 'He is a prophet.'

The Jews did not believe that he had been blind and had received his sight, until they called the parents of the man who had received his sight and asked them, 'Is this your son, who you say was born blind? How then does he now see?' His parents answered, 'We know that this is our son and that he was born blind. But how he now sees we do not know, nor do we know who opened his eyes. Ask him; he is of age. He will speak for himself.' His parents said these things because they feared the Jews, for the Jews had already agreed that if anyone should confess Jesus to be Christ, he was to be put out of the synagogue. Therefore his parents said, 'He is of age; ask him.'

So for the second time they called the man who had been blind and said to him, 'Give glory to God. We know that this man is a sinner.' He answered, 'Whether he is a sinner I do not know. One thing I do know, that though I was blind, now I see.' They said to him, 'What did he do to you? How did he open your eyes?' He answered them, 'I have told you already, and you would not listen. Why do you want to hear it again? Do you also want to become his disciples?' And they reviled him, saying, 'You are his disciple, but we are disciples of Moses. We know that God has spoken to Moses, but as for this man, we do not know where he comes from.' The man answered, 'Why, this is an amazing thing! You do not know where he comes from, and yet he opened my eyes. We know that God does not listen to sinners, but if anyone is a worshipper of God and does his will, God listens to him. Never since the world began has it been heard that anyone opened the eyes of a man born blind. If this man were not from God, he could do nothing.' They answered him, 'You were born in utter sin, and would you teach us?' And they cast him out.

Jesus heard that they had cast him out, and having found him he said, 'Do you believe in the Son of Man?' He answered, 'And who is he, sir, that I may believe in him?' Jesus said to him, 'You have seen him, and it is he who is speaking to you.' He said, 'Lord, I believe', and he worshipped him. Jesus said, 'For judgement I came into this world, that those who do not see may see, and those who see may become blind.' Some of the Pharisees near him heard these things, and said to him, 'Are we also blind?' Jesus said to them, 'If you were blind, you would have no guilt; but now that you say, "We see", your guilt remains.'

The Gospel of the Lord.
Praise to you, Lord Jesus Christ.

HOMILY

After the readings, and guided by them, the minister explains the meaning of the Second Scrutiny in the light of the Lenten liturgy and of the spiritual journey of the elect.

SECOND SCRUTINY

The Second Scrutiny of those seeking Baptism takes place after the Homily.

PRAYER OF THE FAITHFUL AND PROFESSION OF FAITH

Intercessory prayer is resumed with the usual Prayer of the Faithful for the needs of the Church and the whole world; then, if required, the Profession of Faith is said. But for pastoral reasons, the Prayer of the Faithful and the Profession of Faith may be omitted.

▷ *page 13*

PRAYER OVER THE OFFERINGS

We place before you with joy these offerings,
which bring eternal remedy, O Lord,
praying that we may both faithfully revere them
and present them to you, as is fitting,
for those who seek salvation.
Through Christ our Lord. **Amen.**

▷ *page 15*

EUCHARISTIC PRAYER

Preface: The Man Born Blind is used, p 72.
In Eucharistic Prayers I, II and III, proper forms of certain sections are used, see p 168.

COMMUNION ANTIPHON *cf John 9:11, 38*

The Lord anointed my eyes; I went, I washed,
I saw and I believed in God.

▷ page 58

PRAYER AFTER COMMUNION

Sustain your family always in your kindness,
O Lord, we pray,
correct them, set them in order,
graciously protect them under your rule,
and in your unfailing goodness
direct them along the way of salvation.
Through Christ our Lord. **Amen.**

▷ page 59

FIFTH SUNDAY OF LENT (YEAR C)

This Mass is used when the Third Scrutiny is not being celebrated.
Readings for Year A may be used with this Mass as an alternative (see p 180).

If the Third Scrutiny is being celebrated today
the Ritual Mass for the Celebration of the Third Scrutiny, with the readings for Year A is used (see p 179).

ENTRANCE ANTIPHON *cf Psalm 42:1–2*

Give me justice, O God,
and plead my cause against a nation that is faithless.
From the deceitful and cunning rescue me,
for you, O God, are my strength.

▷ page 7

The Gloria is omitted.

COLLECT

By your help, we beseech you, Lord our God,
may we walk eagerly in that same charity
with which, out of love for the world,
your Son handed himself over to death.
Through our Lord Jesus Christ, your Son,
who lives and reigns with you in the unity of the Holy Spirit,
God, for ever and ever. **Amen.**

The Readings for Year A may be used as an alternative *(see below, page 180).*

FIRST READING *Isaiah 43:16–21*

'Behold, I am doing a new thing and I will give drink to my chosen people.'

A reading from the Prophet Isaiah.

Thus says the LORD, who makes a way in the sea, a path in the mighty waters, who brings forth chariot and horse, army and warrior; they lie down, they cannot rise, they are extinguished, quenched like a wick: 'Remember not the former things, nor consider the things of old. Behold, I am doing a new thing; now it springs forth, do you not perceive it? I will make a way in the wilderness and rivers in the desert. The wild beasts will honour me, the jackals and the ostriches, for I give water in the wilderness, rivers in the desert, to give drink to my chosen people, the people whom I formed for myself that they might declare my praise.'

The word of the Lord.
Thanks be to God.

RESPONSORIAL PSALM *Psalm 126(125):1-2b. 2c-3. 4-5. 6. R.3*

R. **What great deeds the LORD worked for us!**
Indeed, we were glad.

1 When the LORD brought back the exiles of Sion,
we thought we were dreaming.
Then was our mouth filled with laughter;
on our tongues, songs of joy. R.

2 Then they said among the nations,
'What great deeds the LORD worked for them!'
What great deeds the LORD worked for us!
Indeed, we were glad. R.

3 Bring back our exiles, O LORD,
as streams in the Negeb.
Those who are sowing in tears
will sing when they reap. R.

4 They go out, they go out, full of tears,
bearing seed for the sowing;
they come back, they come back with a song,
bearing their sheaves. R.

SECOND READING *Philippians 3:8–14*

'For the sake of Christ I have suffered the loss of all things, becoming like him in his death.'

A reading from the Letter of Saint Paul to the Philippians.

Brothers and sisters: I count everything as loss because of the surpassing worth of knowing Christ Jesus my Lord. For his sake I have suffered the loss of all things and count them as rubbish, in order that I may gain Christ and be found in him, not having a righteousness of my own that comes from the law, but that which comes through faith in Christ, the righteousness from God that depends on faith— that I may know him and the power of his resurrection, and may share his sufferings, becoming like him in his death, that by any means possible I may attain the resurrection from the dead.

Not that I have already obtained this or am already perfect, but I press on to make it my own, because Christ Jesus has made me his own. Brothers and sisters, I do not consider that I have made it my own. But one thing I do: forgetting what lies behind and straining forward to what lies ahead, I press on towards the goal for the prize of the upward call of God in Christ Jesus.

The word of the Lord.
Thanks be to God.

ACCLAMATION BEFORE THE GOSPEL *Joel 2:12–13*

Glory to you, O Christ, Son of the living God.
Even now, says the LORD,
return to me with all your heart,
for I am gracious and merciful.
Glory to you, O Christ, Son of the living God.

GOSPEL *John 8:1–11*

The Lord be with you.
And with your spirit.

A reading from the holy Gospel according to John.
Glory to you, O Lord.

'Let him who is without sin among you be the first to throw a stone at her.'

At that time: Jesus went to the Mount of Olives. Early in the morning he came again to the temple. All the people came to him, and he sat down and taught them. The scribes and the Pharisees brought a woman who had been caught in adultery, and placing her in the midst they said to him, 'Teacher, this woman has been caught in the act of adultery. Now in the Law, Moses commanded us to stone such women. So what do you say?' This they said to test him, that they might have some charge to bring against him. Jesus bent down and wrote with his finger on the ground. And as they continued to ask him, he stood up and said to them, 'Let him who is without sin among you be the first to throw a stone at her.' And once more he bent down and wrote on the ground. But when they heard it, they went away one by one, beginning with the older ones, and Jesus was left alone with the woman standing before him. Jesus stood up and said to her, 'Woman, where are they? Has no one condemned you?' She said, 'No one, Lord.' And Jesus said, 'Neither do I condemn you; go, and from now on sin no more.'

The Gospel of the Lord.
Praise to you, Lord Jesus Christ.

▷ page 11

PRAYER OVER THE OFFERINGS

Hear us, almighty God,
and, having instilled in your servants
the teachings of the Christian faith,
graciously purify them
by the working of this sacrifice.
Through Christ our Lord. **Amen.**

▷ page 15

When Year C readings are used, Preface I or II of Lent is used, p 70.
When Year A readings are used, Preface: Lazarus is used, p 72.

COMMUNION ANTIPHON *for Year C readings John 8:10–11*

Has no one condemned you, woman? No one, Lord.
Neither shall I condemn you. From now on, sin no more.

or *for Year A readings: cf John 11:26*

Everyone who lives and believes in me
will not die for ever, says the Lord.

▷ page 58

PRAYER AFTER COMMUNION

We pray, almighty God,
that we may always be counted among the members of Christ,
in whose Body and Blood we have communion.
Who lives and reigns for ever and ever.

▷ page 59

PRAYER OVER THE PEOPLE

Bless, O Lord, your people,
who long for the gift of your mercy,
and grant that what, at your prompting, they desire
they may receive by your generous gift.
Through Christ our Lord.

FIFTH SUNDAY OF LENT (YEAR A) AND THIRD SCRUTINY

RITUAL MASS FOR THE CELEBRATION OF THE SCRUTINIES: THIRD SCRUTINY
This Mass is used when the Third Scrutiny is being celebrated today.

ENTRANCE ANTIPHON *cf Psalm 17:5–7*

The waves of death rose about me;
the pains of the nether world surrounded me.
In my anguish I called to the Lord;
and from his holy temple he heard my voice.

▷ page 7

The Gloria is omitted.

COLLECT

Grant, O Lord, to these chosen ones
that, instructed in the holy mysteries,
they may receive new life at the font of Baptism
and be numbered among the members of your Church.
Through our Lord Jesus Christ, your Son,
who lives and reigns with you in the unity of the Holy Spirit,
God, for ever and ever. **Amen.**

These readings may be used in any year.

If the Third Scrutiny is not celebrated today, the Mass prayers of the Fifth Sunday of Lent (Year C) are used, page 176.

FIRST READING *Ezekiel 37:12–14*

'I will put my spirit within you, and you shall live.'

A reading from the Prophet Ezekiel.

Thus says the Lord GOD: Behold, I will open your graves and raise you from your graves, O my people. And I will bring you into the land of Israel. And you shall know that I am the LORD, when I open your graves, and raise you from your graves, O my people. And I will put my Spirit within you, and you shall live, and I will place you in your own land. Then you shall know that I am the LORD; I have spoken, and I will do it, declares the LORD.

The word of the Lord.
Thanks be to God.

RESPONSORIAL PSALM *Psalm 130 (129):1-2. 3-4. 5-6b. 6c-8. R.7bc*

**R. With the LORD there is mercy,
in him is plentiful redemption.**

1 Out of the depths I cry to you, O LORD;
Lord, hear my voice!
O let your ears be attentive
to the sound of my pleadings. R.

2 If you, O LORD, should mark iniquities,
Lord, who could stand?
But with you is found forgiveness,
that you may be revered. R.

3 I long for you, O LORD,
my soul longs for his word.
My soul awaits the Lord
more than watchmen for
daybreak. R.

4 More than watchmen for daybreak,
let Israel hope for the LORD.
For with the LORD there is mercy,
in him is plentiful redemption.
It is he who will redeem Israel
from all its iniquities. R.

SECOND READING *Romans 8:8–11*

'The Spirit of him who raised Jesus from the dead dwells in you.'

A reading from the Letter of Saint Paul to the Romans.

Brothers and sisters: Those who are in the flesh cannot please God. You, however, are not in the flesh but in the Spirit, if in fact the Spirit of God dwells in you. Anyone who does not have the Spirit of Christ does not belong to him. But if Christ is in you, although the body is dead because of sin, the Spirit is life because of righteousness. If the Spirit of him who raised Jesus from the dead dwells in you, he who raised Christ Jesus from the dead will also give life to your mortal bodies through his Spirit who dwells in you.

The word of the Lord.
Thanks be to God.

ACCLAMATION BEFORE THE GOSPEL *John 11:25a, 26*

Glory to you, O Christ, Son of the living God.
I am the resurrection and the life, says the Lord.
Everyone who believes in me shall never die.
Glory to you, O Christ, Son of the living God.

GOSPEL *John 11:1–45 Shorter form: John 11:3–7, 17, 20–27, 33b–45 (only read text with underlines / side line next to it).*

The Lord be with you.
And with your spirit.

A reading from the holy Gospel according to John.
Glory to you, O Lord.

'I am the resurrection and the life.'

At that time: A certain man was ill, Lazarus of Bethany, the village of Mary and her sister Martha. It was Mary, who anointed the Lord with ointment and wiped his feet with her hair, whose brother Lazarus was ill. So the sisters sent to him, saying, | The sisters of Lazarus sent to Jesus, saying, 'Lord, he whom you love is ill.' But when Jesus heard it he said, 'This illness does not lead to death. It is for the glory of God, so that the Son of God may be glorified through it.'

Now Jesus loved Martha and her sister and Lazarus. So, when he heard that Lazarus was ill, he stayed two days longer in the place where he was. Then after this he said to the disciples, 'Let us go to Judea again.' | The disciples said to him, 'Rabbi, the Jews were just now seeking to stone you, and are you going there again?' Jesus answered, 'Are there not twelve hours in the day? If anyone walks in the day, he does not stumble, because he sees the light of this world. But if anyone walks in the night, he stumbles, because the light is not in him.' After saying these things, he said to them, 'Our friend Lazarus has fallen asleep, but I go to awaken him.' The disciples said to him, 'Lord, if he has fallen asleep, he will recover.' Now Jesus had spoken of his death, but they thought that he meant taking rest in sleep. Then Jesus told them plainly, 'Lazarus has died, and for your sake I am glad that I was not there, so that you may believe. But let us go to him.' So Thomas, called the Twin, said to his fellow disciples, 'Let us also go, that we may die with him.'

Now when Jesus came, he found that Lazarus had already been in the tomb four days. | Bethany was near Jerusalem, about two miles off, and many of the Jews had come to Martha and Mary to console them concerning their brother. | So when Martha heard that Jesus was coming, she went and met him, but Mary remained seated in the house. Martha said to Jesus, 'Lord, if you had been here, my brother would not have died. But even now I know that whatever you ask from God, God will give you.' Jesus said to her, 'Your brother will rise again.' Martha said to him, 'I know that he will rise again in the resurrection on the last day.' Jesus said to her, 'I am the resurrection and the life. Whoever believes in me, though he die, yet shall he live, and everyone who lives and believes in me shall never die. Do you believe this?' She said to him, 'Yes, Lord; I believe that you are the Christ, the Son of God, who is coming into the world.'

When she had said this, she went and called her sister Mary, saying in private, 'The Teacher is here and is calling for you.' And when she heard it, she rose quickly and went to him. Now Jesus had not yet come into the village, but was still in the place where Martha had met him. When the Jews who were with her in the house, consoling her, saw Mary rise quickly and go out, they followed her, supposing that she was going to the tomb to weep there. Now when Mary came to where Jesus was and saw him, she fell at his feet, saying to him, 'Lord, if you had been here, my brother would not have died.' When Jesus saw her weeping, and the Jews who had come with her also weeping, he | Jesus was deeply moved in his spirit and greatly troubled. And he said, 'Where have you laid him?' They said to him, 'Lord, come and see.' Jesus wept. So the Jews said, 'See how he loved him!' But some of them said, 'Could not he who opened the eyes of the blind man also have kept this man from dying?'

Then Jesus, deeply moved again, came to the tomb. It was a cave, and a stone lay against it. Jesus said, 'Take away the stone.' Martha, the sister of the dead man, said to him, 'Lord, by this time there will be a smell, for he has been dead four days.' Jesus said to her, 'Did I not tell you that if you believed you would see the glory of God?' So they took away the stone. And Jesus lifted up his eyes and said, 'Father, I thank you that you have heard me. I knew that you always hear me, but I said this on account of the people standing around, that they may believe that you sent me.' When he had said these things, he cried out with a loud voice, 'Lazarus, come out.' The man who had died came out, his hands and feet bound with linen strips, and his face wrapped with a cloth. Jesus said to them, 'Unbind him, and let him go.'

Many of the Jews therefore, who had come with Mary and had seen what he did, believed in him.

The Gospel of the Lord.
Praise to you, Lord Jesus Christ.

HOMILY

After the readings, and guided by them, the minister explains the meaning of the Third Scrutiny in the light of the Lenten liturgy and of the spiritual journey of the elect.

THIRD SCRUTINY

The Third Scrutiny of those seeking Baptism takes place after the Homily.

PRAYER OF THE FAITHFUL AND PROFESSION OF FAITH

Intercessory prayer is resumed with the usual Prayer of the Faithful for the needs of the Church and the whole world; then, if required, the Profession of Faith is said. But for pastoral reasons, the Prayer of the Faithful and the Profession of Faith may be omitted.

▷ page 13

PRAYER OVER THE OFFERINGS

Hear us, almighty God,
and, having instilled in your servants
the first fruits of the Christian faith,
graciously purify them by the working of this sacrifice.
Through Christ our Lord. **Amen.**

▷ page 15

EUCHARISTIC PRAYER

Preface: Lazarus is used, p 72.
In Eucharistic Prayers I, II and III, proper forms of certain sections are used, see p 168.

COMMUNION ANTIPHON *cf John 11:26*

Everyone who lives and believes in me
will not die for ever, says the Lord.

▷ *page 58*

PRAYER AFTER COMMUNION

May your people be at one, O Lord, we pray,
and in wholehearted submission to you
may they obtain this grace:
that, safe from all distress,
they may readily live out their joy at being saved
and remember in loving prayer those to be reborn.
Through Christ our Lord. **Amen.**

▷ *page 59*

PALM SUNDAY OF THE PASSION OF THE LORD

On this day the Church recalls the entrance of Christ the Lord into Jerusalem to accomplish his Paschal Mystery. Accordingly, the memorial of this entrance of the Lord takes place at all Masses.

There are three forms of commemoration of the Lord's entrance into Jerusalem:

1 Procession	page 184 (below)
2 Solemn Entrance	page 189
3 Simple Entrance	page 190

At the principal Mass of the day, one of the first two forms is used.
At other Masses, either the Second or Third Form is used.

If either of the first two forms is used, the Penitential Act is omitted and the Mass continues with the Collect.

COMMEMORATION OF THE LORD'S ENTRANCE INTO JERUSALEM
FIRST FORM: PROCESSION

The people gather outside the Church or a building other than the Church.
As the Priest an other ministers arrive the following antiphon or other appropriate chant is sung.

ANTIPHON *Matthew 21:9*

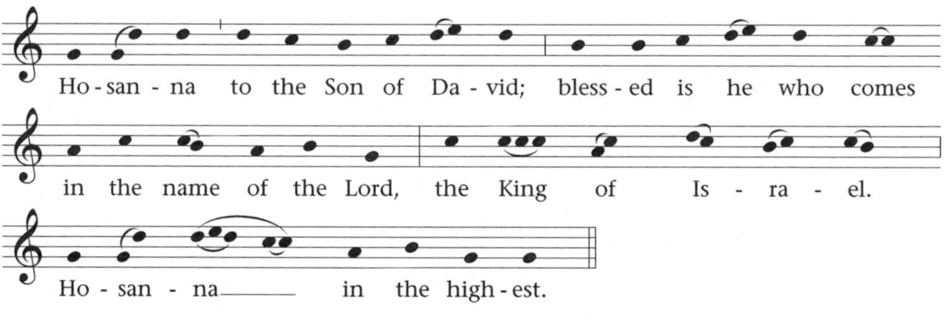
Ho-san-na to the Son of Da-vid; bless-ed is he who comes
in the name of the Lord, the King of Is-ra-el.
Ho-san-na in the high-est.

SIGN OF THE CROSS

All make the Sign of the Cross as the Priest says.

Priest: In the name of the Father, and of the Son, and of the Holy Spirit.
People: **Amen.**

GREETING

Priest: The grace of our Lord Jesus Christ,
and the love of God,
and the communion of the Holy Spirit
be with you all.

or

Priest: Grace to you and peace from God our Father
and the Lord Jesus Christ.

or

Priest: The Lord be with you.
People: **And with your spirit.**

A brief address is given, in which the faithful are invited to participate actively and consciously in the celebration of this day, in these or similar words:

Dear brethren (brothers and sisters),
since the beginning of Lent until now
we have prepared our hearts by penance and charitable works.
Today we gather together to herald with the whole Church
the beginning of the celebration
of our Lord's Paschal Mystery,
that is to say, of his Passion and Resurrection.
For it was to accomplish this mystery
that he entered his own city of Jerusalem.
Therefore, with all faith and devotion,
let us commemorate
the Lord's entry into the city for our salvation,
following in his footsteps,
so that, being made by his grace partakers of the Cross,
we may have a share also in his Resurrection and in his life.

After the address, the Priest says one of the following prayers with hands extended.

Let us pray.
Almighty ever-living God,
sanctify ✠ these branches with your blessing,
that we, who follow Christ the King in exultation,
may reach the eternal Jerusalem through him.
Who lives and reigns for ever and ever. **Amen.**

or

Increase the faith of those who place their hope in you, O God,
and graciously hear the prayers of those who call on you,
that we, who today hold high these branches
to hail Christ in his triumph,
may bear fruit for you by good works accomplished in him.
Who lives and reigns for ever and ever. **Amen.**

He sprinkles the branches with holy water without saying anything.

Then a Deacon or, if there is no Deacon, a Priest, proclaims the Gospel concerning the Lord's entrance. The Deacon or Priest may use a different translation.

GOSPEL *Luke 19:28–40*

The Lord be with you.
And with your spirit.

A reading from the holy Gospel according to Luke.
Glory to you, O Lord.

'Blessed is he who comes in the name of the Lord!'

At that time: Jesus went on ahead, going up to Jerusalem. When he drew near to Bethphage and Bethany, at the mount that is called Olivet, he sent two of the disciples, saying, 'Go into the village in front of you, where on entering you will find a colt tied, on which no one has ever yet sat. Untie it and bring it here. If anyone asks you, "Why are you untying it?" you shall say this: "The Lord has need of it."'

So those who were sent went away and found it just as he had told them. And as they were untying the colt, its owners said to them, 'Why are you untying the colt?' And they said, 'The Lord has need of it.' And they brought it to Jesus, and throwing their cloaks on the colt, they set Jesus on it. And as he rode along, they spread their cloaks on the road. As he was drawing near—already on the way down the Mount of Olives—the whole multitude of his disciples began to rejoice and praise God with a loud voice for all the mighty works that they had seen, saying, 'Blessed is the King who comes in the name of the Lord! Peace in heaven and glory in the highest!' And some of the Pharisees in the crowd said to him, 'Teacher, rebuke your disciples.' He answered, 'I tell you, if these were silent, the very stones would cry out.'

The Gospel of the Lord.
Praise to you, Lord Jesus Christ.

HOMILY

A brief homily may be given.

PROCESSION

To begin the Procession, an invitation may be given by a Priest or a Deacon or a lay minister, in these or similar words:

Dear brethren (brothers and sisters),
like the crowds who acclaimed Jesus in Jerusalem,
let us go forth in peace.

or

Priest or Deacon:

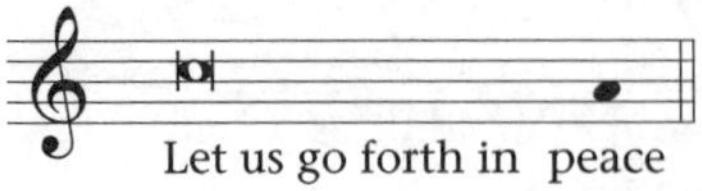
Let us go forth in peace

People:

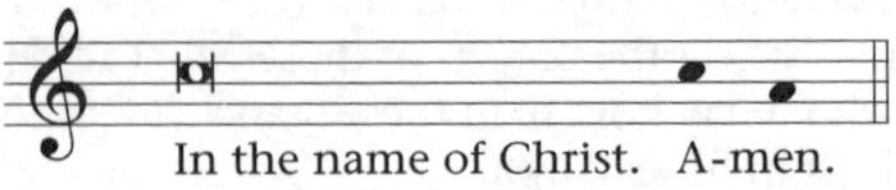
In the name of Christ. A-men.

As the Procession moves forward, the following or other suitable chants in honour of Christ the King are sung by the choir and people (see over).

Antiphon 1

The children of the Hebrews, carrying olive branches,
went to meet the Lord, crying out and saying:
Hosanna in the highest.

If appropriate, this antiphon is repeated between the strophes of the following Psalm.

Psalm 23

1 The LORD'S is the earth and its fullness, *
the world, and those who dwell in it.
It is he who set it on the seas; *
on the rivers he made it firm.

The children of the Hebrews, carrying olive branches...

2 Who shall climb the mountain of the LORD? *
The clean of hands and pure of heart,
whose soul is not set on vain things, †
who has not sworn deceitful words. *

3 Blessings from the LORD shall he receive, *
and right reward from the God who saves him.
Such are the people who seek him, *
who seek the face of the God of Jacob.

4 O gates, lift high your heads, †
grow higher, ancient doors. *
Let him enter, the king of glory!
Who is this king of glory? *
The LORD, the mighty, the valiant;
the LORD, the valiant in war.

5 O gates, lift high your heads; †
grow higher, ancient doors. *
Let him enter, the king of glory!
Who is this king of glory? *
He, the LORD of hosts,
he is the king of glory.

Antiphon 2

The children of the Hebrews spread their garments on the road,
crying out and saying: Hosanna to the Son of David;
blessed is he who comes in the name of the Lord.

If appropriate, this antiphon is repeated between the strophes of the following Psalm.

Psalm 46

1 All peoples, clap your hands. *
Cry to God with shouts of joy!
For the LORD, the Most high, is awesome, *
the great king over all the earth.

The children of the Hebrews spread their garments...

2 He humbles peoples under us *
and nations under our feet.
Our heritage he chose for us, *
the pride of Jacob whom he loves.
God goes up with shouts of joy. *
The LORD goes up with trumpet blast.

3 Sing praise for God; sing praise! *
Sing praise to our king; sing praise!
God is king of all earth. *
Sing praise with all your skill.

4 God reigns over the nations. *
God sits upon his holy throne.
The princes of the peoples are assembled
with the people of the God of Abraham. †
The rulers of the earth belong to God, *
who is greatly exalted.

Hymn to Christ the King

**Glory and honour and praise be to you, Christ, King and Redeemer,
to whom young children cried out loving Hosannas with joy.**

Israel's King are you, King David's magnificent offspring;
you are the ruler who come blest in the name of the Lord.

Heavenly hosts on high unite in singing your praises;
men and women on earth and all creation join in.

Bearing branches of palm, Hebrews came crowding to greet you;
see how with prayers and hymns we come to pay you our vows.

They offered gifts of praise to you, so near to your Passion;
see how we sing this song now to you reigning on high.

Those you were pleased to accept; now accept our gifts of devotion,
good and merciful King, lover of all that is good.

The following is a popular version of this hymn

**All glory, laud and honour,
To thee, Redeemer King,
To whom the lips of children
Made sweet hosannas ring.**

1 Thou art the King of Israel,
Thou David's royal Son,
Who in the Lord's name comest,
The King and blessed one.

2 The company of angels
Are praising thee on high,
And mortal folk and all things
Created make reply.

3 The people of the Hebrews
With palms before thee went:
Our praise and prayer and anthems
Before thee we present.

4 To thee before thy passion
They sang their hymns of praise;
To thee now high exalted
Our melody we raise.

5 Thou didst accept their praises,
Accept the prayers we bring,
Who in all good delightest,
Thou good and gracious king.

As the procession enters the church, the following responsory or another chant about the Lord's triumphal entry into Jerusalem is sung.

RESPONSORY

R As the Lord entered the holy city, the children of the Hebrews proclaimed the resurrection of life.
* Waving their branches of palm, they cried: Hosanna in the Highest.

V When the people heard that Jesus was coming to Jerusalem, they went out to meet him.
* Waving their branches...

The Mass continues with the Collect (see page 190).

SECOND FORM: SOLEMN ENTRANCE

When a procession outside the church cannot take place, the entrance of the Lord is celebrated inside the church by means of a Solemn Entrance before the principal Mass.

Holding branches in their hands, the faithful gather either outside, in front of the church door, or inside the church itself. The Priest and ministers and a representative group of the faithful go to a suitable place in the church outside the sanctuary, where at least the greater part of the faithful can see the rite.

As the Priest and other ministers arrive the following antiphon or other appropriate chant is sung.

ANTIPHON *Matthew 21:9*

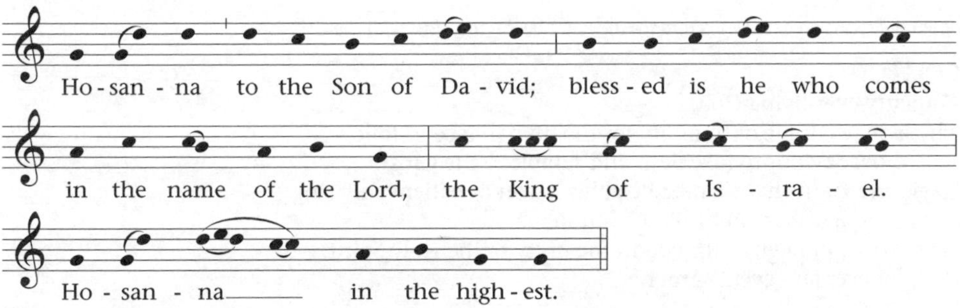
Ho - san - na to the Son of Da - vid; bless - ed is he who comes
in the name of the Lord, the King of Is - ra - el.
Ho - san - na in the high - est.

Then the blessing of branches and the proclamation of the Gospel of the Lord's entrance into Jerusalem take place as above (p 185).

After the Gospel, the Priest processes solemnly with the ministers and the representative group of the faithful through the church to the sanctuary, while the responsory 'As the Lord entered' (see above) or another appropriate chant is sung.

The Mass continues with the Collect (see page 190).

THIRD FORM: SIMPLE ENTRANCE

If the Simple Entrance is used, Mass begins in the usual way.

ENTRANCE ANTIPHON *cf John 12:1, 12–13; Psalm 23:9–10*

Six days before the Passover,
when the Lord came into the city of Jerusalem,
the children ran to meet him;
in their hands they carried palm branches
and with a loud voice cried out:
* Hosanna in the highest!
Blessed are you, who have come in your abundant mercy!

O gates, lift high your heads;
grow higher, ancient doors.
Let him enter, the king of glory!
Who is this king of glory?
He, the Lord of hosts, he is the king of glory.
* Hosanna in the highest!
Blessed are you, who have come in your abundant mercy!

The Gloria is omitted.

▷ page 7

AT THE MASS

After the Procession or Solemn Entrance the Priest begins the Mass with the Collect.

COLLECT

Almighty ever-living God,
who as an example of humility for the human race to follow
caused our Saviour to take flesh and submit to the Cross,
graciously grant that we may heed his lesson of patient suffering
and so merit a share in his Resurrection.
Who lives and reigns with you in the unity of the Holy Spirit,
God, for ever and ever. **Amen.**

FIRST READING *Isaiah 50:4–7*

'I hid not my face from disgrace, and I know that I shall not be put to shame.' [6]

A reading from the Prophet Isaiah.

The Lord GOD has given me the tongue of those who are taught, that I may know how to sustain with a word him who is weary. Morning by morning he awakens; he awakens my ear to hear as those who are taught. The Lord GOD has opened my ear, and I was not rebellious; I turned not backwards. I gave my back to those who strike, and my cheeks to those who pull out the beard; I hid not my face from disgrace and spitting. But the Lord GOD helps me; therefore I have not been disgraced; therefore I have set my face like a flint, and I know that I shall not be put to shame.

The word of the Lord.
Thanks be to God.

6 *Third Song of the Servant of the Lord*

RESPONSORIAL PSALM *Psalm 22(21):8-9. 17-18a. 19-20. 23-24. R.2a*

R. My God, my God, why have you forsaken me?

1 All who see me deride me;
they curl their lips, they toss their heads:
'He trusted in the LORD, let him save him;
let him release him, for in him he delights.' R.

2 For dogs have surrounded me;
a band of the wicked besets me.
They tear holes in my hands and my feet;
I can count every one of my bones. R.

3 They divide my clothing among them,
they cast lots for my robe.
But you, O LORD, do not stay afar off;
my strength, make haste to help me! R.

4 I will tell of your name to my kin,
and praise you in the midst of the assembly;
'You who fear the LORD, give him praise;
all descendants of Jacob, give him glory;
revere him, all you descendants of Israel.' R.

SECOND READING *Philippians 2:6–11*

'He humbled himself, therefore God has highly exalted him.'

A reading from the Letter of Saint Paul to the Philippians.

Christ Jesus, though he was in the form of God, did not count equality with God a thing to be grasped, but emptied himself, by taking the form of a servant, being born in the likeness of men. And being found in human form, he humbled himself by becoming obedient to the point of death, even death on a cross. Therefore God has highly exalted him and bestowed on him the name that is above every name, so that at the name of Jesus every knee should bow, in heaven and on earth and under the earth, and every tongue confess that Jesus Christ is Lord, to the glory of God the Father.

The word of the Lord.
Thanks be to God.

ACCLAMATION BEFORE THE GOSPEL *Philippians 2:8–9*

Praise to you, O Christ, King of eternal glory.
Christ became for us obedient to the point of death,
even death on a cross.
Therefore God has highly exalted him
and bestowed on him the name that is above every name.
Praise to you, O Christ, King of eternal glory.

GOSPEL *Luke 22:14–23:56*

The Passion of our Lord Jesus Christ.

The narrative of the Lord's Passion is read without candles and without incense, with no greeting or signing of the book. It is read by a Deacon or, if there is no Deacon, by a Priest. It may also be read by readers, with the part of Christ, if possible, reserved to a Priest. Deacons, but not others, ask for the blessing of the Priest before singing the Passion, as at other times before the Gospel.

In the following Passion narrative: N = narrator; + = Christ; S = speakers other than Christ.

The Passion of our Lord Jesus Christ according to Luke.

N When the hour came, Jesus reclined at table, and the Apostles with him. And he said to them,

\+ I have earnestly desired to eat this Passover with you before I suffer. For I tell you I will not eat it until it is fulfilled in the kingdom of God.

N And he took a cup, and when he had given thanks he said,

\+ Take this, and divide it among yourselves. For I tell you that from now on I will not drink of the fruit of the vine until the kingdom of God comes.

N And he took bread, and when he had given thanks, he broke it and gave it to them, saying,

\+ This is my body, which is given for you. Do this in remembrance of me.

N And likewise the cup after they had eaten, saying,

\+ This cup that is poured out for you is the new covenant in my blood. But behold, the hand of him who betrays me is with me on the table. For the Son of Man goes as it has been determined, but woe to that man by whom he is betrayed!

N And they began to question one another, which of them it could be who was going to do this.

A dispute also arose among them, as to which of them was to be regarded as the greatest. And he said to them,

\+ The kings of the Gentiles exercise lordship over them, and those in authority over them are called benefactors. But not so with you. Rather, let the greatest among you become as the youngest, and the leader as one who serves. For who is the greater, one who reclines at table or one who serves? Is it not the one who reclines at table? But I am among you as the one who serves. You are those who have stayed with me in my trials, and I assign to you, as my Father assigned to me, a kingdom, that you may eat and drink at my table in my kingdom and sit on thrones judging the twelve tribes of Israel. Simon, Simon, behold, Satan demanded to have you, that he might sift you like wheat, but I have prayed for you that your faith may not fail. And when you have turned again, strengthen your brothers.

N Peter said to him,

S Lord, I am ready to go with you both to prison and to death.

N Jesus said,

\+ I tell you, Peter, the cock will not crow this day, until you deny three times that you know me.

N And he said to them,

\+ When I sent you out with no money bag or knapsack or sandals, did you lack anything?

N They said,

S Nothing.

N He said to them,

\+ But now let the one who has a money bag take it, and likewise a knapsack. And let the one who has no sword sell his cloak and buy one. For I tell you that this Scripture must be fulfilled in me: 'And he was numbered with the transgressors.' For what is written about me has its fulfilment.

N And they said,

S Look, Lord, here are two swords.

N And he said to them,

\+ It is enough.

N And he came out and went, as was his custom, to the Mount of Olives, and the disciples followed him. And when he came to the place, he said to them,

\+ Pray that you may not enter into temptation.

N And he withdrew from them about a stone's throw, and knelt down and prayed, saying,

\+ Father, if you are willing, remove this cup from me. Nevertheless, not my will, but yours, be done.

N And there appeared to him an angel from heaven, strengthening him. And being in agony he prayed more earnestly; and his sweat became like great drops of blood falling down to the ground. And when he rose from prayer, he came to the disciples and found them sleeping for sorrow, and he said to them,

\+ Why are you sleeping? Rise and pray that you may not enter into temptation.

N While he was still speaking, there came a crowd, and the man called Judas, one of the Twelve, was leading them. He drew near to Jesus to kiss him, but Jesus said to him,

\+ Judas, would you betray the Son of Man with a kiss?

N And when those who were around him saw what would follow, they said,

S Lord, shall we strike with the sword?

N And one of them struck the servant of the high priest and cut off his right ear. But Jesus said,

\+ No more of this!

N And he touched his ear and healed him. Then Jesus said to the chief priests and officers of the temple and elders, who had come out against him,

\+ Have you come out as against a robber, with swords and clubs? When I was with you day after day in the temple, you did not lay hands on me. But this is your hour, and the power of darkness.

N Then they seized him and led him away, bringing him into the high priest's house, and Peter was following at a distance. And when they had kindled a fire in the middle of the courtyard and sat down together, Peter sat down among them. Then a servant girl, seeing him as he sat in the light and looking closely at him, said,

S This man also was with him.

N But he denied it, saying,

S Woman, I do not know him.

N And a little later someone else saw him and said,

S You also are one of them.

N But Peter said,

S Man, I am not.

N And after an interval of about an hour still another insisted, saying,

S Certainly this man also was with him, for he too is a Galilean.

N But Peter said,

S Man, I do not know what you are talking about.

N And immediately, while he was still speaking, the cock crowed. And the Lord turned and looked at Peter. And Peter remembered the saying of the Lord, how he had said to him, 'Before the cock crows today, you will deny me three times.' And he went out and wept bitterly.

Now the men who were holding Jesus in custody were mocking him as they beat him. They also blindfolded him and kept asking him,

S Prophesy! Who is it that struck you?

N And they said many other things against him, blaspheming him.

When day came, the assembly of the elders of the people gathered together, both chief priests and scribes. And they led him away to their council, and they said,

S If you are the Christ, tell us.

N But he said to them,

\+ If I tell you, you will not believe, and if I ask you, you will not answer. But from now on the Son of Man shall be seated at the right hand of the power of God.

N So they all said,

S Are you the Son of God, then?

N And he said to them,

\+ You say that I am.

N Then they said,

S What further testimony do we need? We have heard it ourselves from his own lips.

N Then the whole company of them arose and brought him before Pilate. And they began to accuse him, saying,

---

The shorter version of this reading begins:

At that time: The whole company of the elders of the people, both chief priests and scribes, arose and brought Jesus before Pilate. And they began to accuse him, saying,

---

S We found this man misleading our nation and forbidding us to give tribute to Caesar, and saying that he himself is Christ, a king.

N And Pilate asked him,

S Are you the King of the Jews?

N And he answered him,

\+ You have said so.

N Then Pilate said to the chief priests and the crowds,

S I find no guilt in this man.

N But they were urgent, saying,

S He stirs up the people, teaching throughout all Judea, from Galilee even to this place.

N When Pilate heard this, he asked whether the man was a Galilean. And when he learned that he belonged to Herod's jurisdiction, he sent him over to Herod, who was himself in Jerusalem at that time. When Herod saw Jesus, he was very glad, for he had long desired to see him, because he had heard about him, and he was hoping to see some sign done by him. So he questioned him at some length, but he made no answer. The chief priests and the scribes stood by, vehemently accusing him. And Herod with his soldiers treated him with contempt and mocked him. Then, arraying him in splendid clothing, he sent him back to Pilate. And Herod and Pilate became friends with each other that very day, for before this they had been at enmity with each other.

Pilate then called together the chief priests and the rulers and the people, and said to them,

S You brought me this man as one who was misleading the people. And after examining him before you, behold, I did not find this man guilty of any of your charges against him. Neither did Herod, for he sent him back to us. Look, nothing deserving death has been done by him. I will therefore punish and release him.

N But they all cried out together,

S Away with this man, and release to us Barabbas.

N A man who had been thrown into prison for an insurrection started in the city and for murder. Pilate addressed them once more, desiring to release Jesus, but they kept shouting,

S Crucify, crucify him!

N A third time he said to them,

S Why? What evil has he done? I have found in him no guilt deserving death. I will therefore punish and release him.

N But they were urgent, demanding with loud cries that he should be crucified. And their voices prevailed. So Pilate decided that their demand should be granted. He released the man who had been thrown into prison for insurrection and murder, for whom they asked, but he delivered Jesus over to their will.

And as they led him away, they seized one Simon of Cyrene, who was coming in from the country, and laid on him the cross, to carry it behind Jesus. And there followed him a great multitude of the people and of women who were mourning and lamenting for him. But turning to them Jesus said,

\+ Daughters of Jerusalem, do not weep for me, but weep for yourselves and for your children. For behold, the days are coming when they will say, 'Blessed are the barren and the wombs that never bore and the breasts that never nursed!' Then they will begin to say to the mountains, 'Fall on us', and to the hills, 'Cover us.' For if they do these things when the wood is green, what will happen when it is dry?

N Two others, who were criminals, were led away to be put to death with him. And when they came to the place that is called The Skull, there they crucified him, and the criminals, one on his right and one on his left. And Jesus said,

\+ Father, forgive them, for they know not what they do.

N And they cast lots to divide his garments. And the people stood by, watching, but the rulers scoffed at him, saying,

S He saved others; let him save himself, if he is the Christ of God, his Chosen One!

N The soldiers also mocked him, coming up and offering him sour wine and saying,

S If you are the King of the Jews, save yourself!

N There was also an inscription over him, 'This is the King of the Jews.' One of the criminals who were hanged there railed at Jesus, saying,

S Are you not the Christ? Save yourself and us!

N But the other rebuked him, saying,

S Do you not fear God, since you are under the same sentence of condemnation? And we indeed justly, for we are receiving the due reward of our deeds; but this man has done nothing wrong.

N And he said,

S Jesus, remember me when you come into your kingdom.

N And he said to him,

\+ Truly, I say to you, today you will be with me in paradise.

N It was now about the sixth hour, and there was darkness over the whole land until the ninth hour, while the sun's light failed. And the curtain of the temple was torn in two. Then Jesus, calling out with a loud voice, said,

\+ Father, into your hands I commit my spirit!

N And having said this he breathed his last.

All kneel for a period of silence.

N Now when the centurion saw what had taken place, he praised God, saying,

S Certainly this man was innocent!

N And all the crowds that had assembled for this spectacle, when they saw what had taken place, returned home beating their breasts. And all his acquaintances and the women who had followed him from Galilee stood at a distance watching these things.

Now there was a man named Joseph, from the Jewish town of Arimathea. He was a member of the council, a good and righteous man, who had not consented to their decision and action; and he was looking for the kingdom of God. This man went to Pilate and asked for the body of Jesus. Then he took it down, and wrapped it in a linen shroud, and laid him in a tomb cut in stone, where no one had ever yet been laid. It was the day of Preparation, and the Sabbath was beginning. The women who had come with him from Galilee followed and saw the tomb and how his body was laid. Then they returned and prepared spices and ointments. On the Sabbath they rested according to the commandment.

The Gospel of the Lord.
Praise to you, Lord Jesus Christ.

HOMILY

After the narrative of the Passion, a brief homily should take place, if appropriate.
A period of silence may also be observed.

▷ page 11

PRAYER OVER THE OFFERINGS

Through the Passion of your Only Begotten Son, O Lord,
may our reconciliation with you be near at hand,
so that, though we do not merit it by our own deeds,
yet by this sacrifice made once for all,
we may feel already the effects of your mercy.
Through Christ our Lord. **Amen.**

▷ page 15

Preface: The Passion of the Lord, see page 73.

COMMUNION ANTIPHON *Matthew 26:42*

Father, if this chalice cannot pass without my drinking it,
your will be done.

▷ page 58

PRAYER AFTER COMMUNION

Nourished with these sacred gifts,
we humbly beseech you, O Lord,
that, just as through the death of your Son
you have brought us to hope for what we believe,
so by his Resurrection
you may lead us to where you call.
Through Christ our Lord. **Amen.**

▷ page 59

PRAYER OVER THE PEOPLE

Look, we pray, O Lord, on this your family,
for whom our Lord Jesus Christ
did not hesitate to be delivered into the hands of the wicked
and submit to the agony of the Cross.
Who lives and reigns for ever and ever. **Amen.**

SACRED PASCHAL TRIDUUM

ABOUT THE SEASON

Since Christ accomplished his work of human redemption and of the perfect glorification of God principally through his Paschal Mystery, in which by dying he has destroyed our death, and by rising restored our life, the sacred Paschal Triduum of the Passion and Resurrection of the Lord shines forth as the high point of the entire liturgical year. Therefore the pre-eminence that Sunday has in the week, the Solemnity of Easter has in the liturgical year.

The Paschal Triduum of the Passion and Resurrection of the Lord begins with the evening Mass of the Lord's Supper, has its centre in the Easter Vigil, and closes with Vespers (Evening Prayer) of the Sunday of the Resurrection.

On Friday of the Passion of the Lord and, if appropriate, also on Holy Saturday until the Easter Vigil, the sacred Paschal Fast is everywhere observed.

The Easter Vigil, in the holy night when the Lord rose again, is considered the 'mother of all holy Vigils', in which the Church, keeping watch, awaits the Resurrection of Christ and celebrates it in the Sacraments. Therefore, the entire celebration of this sacred Vigil must take place at night, so that it both begins after nightfall and ends before the dawn on the Sunday.

Universal Norms on the Liturgical Year and the Calendar nn 18–21

ABOUT THE READINGS

On Holy Thursday at the evening Mass the remembrance of the supper preceding Christ's departure casts its own special light because of the Lord's example in washing the feet of his disciples and Paul's account of the institution of the Christian Passover in the eucharist.

On Good Friday the liturgical service has as its centre John's narrative of the passion of him who was portrayed in Isaiah as the Servant of the LORD and who became the one High Priest by offering himself to the Father.

On the holy night of the Easter Vigil there are seven Old Testament readings, recalling the wonderful works of God in the history of salvation. There are two New Testament readings, the announcement of the resurrection according to one of the Synoptic Gospels and a reading from St. Paul on Christian baptism as the sacrament of Christ's resurrection.

Introduction to the Lectionary n 99

MAUNDY THURSDAY

MASS OF THE LORD'S SUPPER

ENTRANCE ANTIPHON *cf Galatians 6:14*

We should glory in the Cross of our Lord Jesus Christ,
in whom is our salvation, life and resurrection,
through whom we are saved and delivered.

▷ *page 7*

The Gloria is sung during which bells are rung.
When it is finished, they remain silent until the Gloria of the Easter Vigil.

COLLECT

O God, who have called us to participate
in this most sacred Supper,
in which your Only Begotten Son,
when about to hand himself over to death,
entrusted to the Church a sacrifice new for all eternity,
the banquet of his love,
grant, we pray,
that we may draw from so great a mystery,
the fullness of charity and of life.
Through our Lord Jesus Christ, your Son,
who lives and reigns with you in the unity of the Holy Spirit,
God, for ever and ever. **Amen.**

FIRST READING *Exodus 12:1–8, 11–14*

Ordinances for the Passover meal.

A reading from the Book of Exodus.

In those days: The LORD said to Moses and Aaron in the land of Egypt, 'This month shall be for you the beginning of months. It shall be the first month of the year for you. Tell all the congregation of Israel that on the tenth day of this month every man shall take a lamb according to their fathers' houses, a lamb for a household. And if the household is too small for a lamb, then he and his nearest neighbour shall take according to the number of persons; according to what each can eat you shall make your count for the lamb. Your lamb shall be without blemish, a male, a year old. You may take it from the sheep or from the goats, and you shall keep it until the fourteenth day of this month, when the whole assembly of the congregation of Israel shall kill their lambs at twilight.

'Then they shall take some of the blood and put it on the two doorposts and the lintel of the houses in which they eat it. They shall eat the flesh that night, roasted on the fire; with unleavened bread and bitter herbs they shall eat it.

'In this manner you shall eat it: with your belt fastened, your sandals on your feet, and your staff in your hand. And you shall eat it in haste. It is the LORD's Passover. For I will pass through the land of Egypt that night, and I will strike all the firstborn in the land of Egypt, both man and beast; and on all the gods of Egypt I will execute judgements: I am the LORD. The blood shall be a sign for you, on the houses where you are. And when I see the blood, I will pass over you, and no plague will befall you to destroy you, when I strike the land of Egypt.

'This day shall be for you a memorial day, and you shall keep it as a feast to the LORD; throughout your generations, as a statute for ever, you shall keep it as a feast.'

The word of the Lord.
Thanks be to God.

RESPONSORIAL PSALM *Psalm 116(115):12-13. 15, 16bc. 17-18. R. cf. 1 Corinthians 10:16*

R. The cup of blessing is a communion in the blood of Christ.

1 How can I repay the LORD
for all his goodness to me?
The cup of salvation I will raise;
I will call on the name of the LORD. R.

2 How precious in the eyes of the LORD
is the death of his faithful.
Your servant am I, the son of your handmaid;
you have loosened my bonds. R.

3 I will offer a thanksgiving sacrifice;
I will call on the name of the LORD.
My vows to the LORD I will fulfil
before all his people. R.

SECOND READING *1 Corinthians 11:23–26*

'For as often as you eat and drink, you proclaim the Lord's death.'

A reading from the First Letter of Saint Paul to the Corinthians.

Brothers and sisters: I received from the Lord what I also delivered to you; that the Lord Jesus on the night when he was betrayed took bread, and when he had given thanks, he broke it, and said, 'This is my body, which is for you. Do this in remembrance of me.' In the same way also he took the cup, after supper, saying, 'This cup is the new covenant in my blood. Do this, as often as you drink it, in remembrance of me.' For as often as you eat this bread and drink the cup, you proclaim the Lord's death until he comes.

The word of the Lord.
Thanks be to God.

ACCLAMATION BEFORE THE GOSPEL *John 13:34*

Praise to you, O Christ, King of eternal glory.
A new commandment I give to you, says the Lord, that you love one another, just as I have loved you.
Praise to you, O Christ, King of eternal glory.

GOSPEL *John 13:1–15*

The Lord be with you.
And with your spirit.

A reading from the holy Gospel according to John.
Glory to you, O Lord.

'He loved them to the end.'

Before the Feast of the Passover, when Jesus knew that his hour had come to depart out of this world to the Father, having loved his own who were in the world, he loved them to the end. During supper, when the devil had already put it into the heart of Judas Iscariot, Simon's son, to betray him, Jesus, knowing that the Father had given all things into his hands, and that he had come from God and was going back to God, rose from supper. He laid aside his outer garments, and taking a towel, tied it round his waist. Then he poured water into a basin and began to wash the disciples' feet and to wipe them with the towel that was wrapped round him. He came to Simon Peter, who said to him, 'Lord, do you wash my feet?' Jesus answered him, 'What I am doing you do not understand now, but afterwards you will understand.' Peter said to him, 'You shall never wash my feet.' Jesus answered him, 'If I do not wash you, you have no share with me.' Simon Peter said to him, 'Lord, not my feet only but also my hands and my head!' Jesus said to him, 'The one who has bathed does not need to wash, except for his feet, but is completely clean. And you are clean, but not every one of you.' For he knew who was to betray him; that was why he said, 'Not all of you are clean.'

When he had washed their feet and put on his outer garments and resumed his place, he said to them, 'Do you understand what I have done to you? You call me Teacher and Lord, and you are right, for so I am. If I then, your Lord and Teacher, have washed your feet, you also ought to wash one another's feet. For I have given you an example, that you also should do just as I have done to you.'

The Gospel of the Lord.
Praise to you, Lord Jesus Christ.

HOMILY

WASHING OF FEET

During the Washing of the Feet some of the following antiphons or other appropriate chants are sung.

ANTIPHON 1 *cf John 13:4, 5, 15*

After the Lord had risen from supper,
he poured water into a basin
and began to wash the feet of his disciples:
he left them this example.

ANTIPHON 2 *cf John 13:12, 13, 15*

The Lord Jesus, after eating supper with his disciples,
washed their feet and said to them:
Do you know what I, your Lord and Master, have done for you?
I have given you an example, that you should do likewise.

ANTIPHON 3 *John 13:6, 7, 8*

* Lord, are you to wash my feet? Jesus said to him in answer:
If I do not wash your feet, you will have no share with me.

V So he came to Simon Peter and Peter said to him:
* Lord...

V What I am doing, you do not know for now,
but later you will come to know.
* Lord...

TRIDUUM

ANTIPHON 4 *cf John 13:14*
If I, your Lord and Master, have washed your feet,
how much more should you wash each other's feet?

ANTIPHON 5 *John 13:35*
* This is how all will know that you are my disciples:
if you have love for one another.

V Jesus said to his disciples:
* This is how...

ANTIPHON 6 *John 13:34*
I give you a new commandment,
that you love one another
as I have loved you, says the Lord.

ANTIPHON 7 *1 Corinthians 13:13*
* Let faith, hope and charity, these three, remain among you,
but the greatest of these is charity.

V Now faith, hope and charity, these three, remain;
but the greatest of these is charity.
* Let faith...

The Profession of Faith is not said. The Mass continues with the Prayer of the Faithful.

▷ *page 13*

PREPARATION OF THE GIFTS

At the beginning of the Liturgy of the Eucharist, there may be a procession of the faithful in which gifts for the poor may be presented with the bread and wine.

Meanwhile the following, or another appropriate chant, is sung.

Ant Where true charity is dwelling, God is present there.

V By the love of Christ we have been brought together:
V let us find in him our gladness and our pleasure;
V may we love him and revere him, God the living,
V and in love respect each other with sincere hearts.

Ant Where true charity is dwelling, God is present there.
V So when we as one are gathered all together,
V let us strive to keep our minds free of division;
V may there be an end to malice, strife and quarrels,
V and let Christ our God be dwelling here among us.

Ant Where true charity is dwelling, God is present there.
V May your face thus be our vision, bright in glory,
V Christ our God, with all the blessed Saints in heaven:
V such delight is pure and faultless, joy unbounded,
V which endures through countless ages world without end Amen.

PRAYER OVER THE OFFERINGS

Grant us, O Lord, we pray,
that we may participate worthily in these mysteries,
for whenever the memorial of this sacrifice is celebrated
the work of our redemption is accomplished.
Through Christ our Lord. **Amen.**

▷ page 15

EUCHARISTIC PRAYER

Eucharistic Prayer I, II, or III may be used with Preface I of the Most Holy Eucharist, p 73.

When the Roman Canon (Eucharistic Prayer I) is used, the proper forms of the Communicantes (In communion with those), Hanc igitur (Therefore, Lord, we pray), and Qui pridie (On the day before he was to suffer) are said, pp 19–21.

COMMUNION ANTIPHON *1 Corinthians 11:24–25*

This is the Body that will be given up for you;
this is the Chalice of the new covenant in my Blood, says the Lord;
do this, whenever you receive it, in memory of me.

▷ page 58

After the distribution of Communion, a ciborium with hosts for Communion on the following day is left on the altar.

PRAYER AFTER COMMUNION

Grant, almighty God,
that, just as we are renewed
by the Supper of your Son in this present age,
so we may enjoy his banquet for all eternity.
Who lives and reigns for ever and ever. **Amen.**

THE TRANSFER OF THE MOST BLESSED SACRAMENT

After the Prayer after Communion, the Priest incenses the Blessed Sacrament. After this, a procession is formed in which the Blessed Sacrament, accompanied by torches and incense, is carried through the church to a place of repose.

Meanwhile a suitable eucharistic chant is sung. If the hymn Pange, lingua, gloriosi (Of the glorious body telling) is sung, the last two stanzas are reserved until the procession reaches the place of repose.

When the procession reaches the place of repose, the Priest, kneeling, incenses the Blessed Sacrament, while Tantum ergo Sacramentum (Therefore, we before him bending) or another eucharistic chant is sung.

After a period of adoration in silence, the Priest and ministers genuflect and return to the sacristy.

The faithful are invited to continue adoration before the Blessed Sacrament for a suitable length of time during the night, according to local circumstances, but after midnight the adoration should take place without solemnity.

GOOD FRIDAY

CELEBRATION OF THE PASSION OF THE LORD

The celebration of the Lord's Passion consists of three parts

Liturgy of the Word

Adoration of the Cross

Holy Communion

The altar is bare: without a cross, without candles and without cloths.

The Priest and the Deacon, if a Deacon is present, go to the altar in silence and, after making a reverence to the altar, prostrate themselves or, if appropriate, kneel and pray in silence for a while.

All others kneel.

Then the Priest says one of the following prayers, omitting the invitation 'Let us pray'.

PRAYER

Remember your mercies, O Lord,
and with your eternal protection sanctify your servants,
for whom Christ your Son,
by the shedding of his Blood,
established the Paschal Mystery.
Who lives and reigns for ever and ever. **Amen.**
or

O God, who by the Passion of Christ your Son, our Lord,
abolished the death inherited from ancient sin
by every succeeding generation,
grant that just as, being conformed to him,
we have borne by the law of nature
the image of the man of earth,
so by the sanctification of grace
we may bear the image of the Man of heaven.
Through Christ our Lord. **Amen.**

FIRST PART: LITURGY OF THE WORD

FIRST READING *Isaiah 52:13–53:12*

'He was pierced for our transgressions.' [6]

A reading from the Prophet Isaiah.

Behold, my servant shall act wisely; he shall be high and lifted up, and shall be exalted. As many were astonished at you—his appearance was so marred, beyond human semblance, and his form beyond that of the children of mankind—so shall he sprinkle many nations. Kings shall shut their mouths because of him, for that which has not been told them they see, and that which they have not heard they understand.

Who has believed what he has heard from us? And to whom has the arm of the LORD been revealed? For he grew up before him like a young plant, and like a root out of dry ground; he had no form

6 *Fourth Song of the Servant of the Lord*

or majesty that we should look at him, and no beauty that we should desire him. He was despised and rejected by men, a man of sorrows and acquainted with grief; and as one from whom men hide their faces he was despised, and we esteemed him not. Surely he has borne our griefs and carried our sorrows; yet we esteemed him stricken, smitten by God, and afflicted. But he was pierced for our transgressions; he was crushed for our iniquities; upon him was the chastisement that brought us peace, and with his wounds we are healed. All we like sheep have gone astray; we have turned—every one—to his own way; and the LORD has laid on him the iniquity of us all. He was oppressed, and he was afflicted, yet he opened not his mouth; like a lamb that is led to the slaughter, and like a sheep that before its shearers is silent, so he opened not his mouth. By oppression and judgement he was taken away; and as for his generation, who considered that he was cut off out of the land of the living, stricken for the transgression of my people? And they made his grave with the wicked and with a rich man in his death, although he had done no violence, and there was no deceit in his mouth.

Yet it was the will of the LORD to crush him; he has put him to grief; when his soul makes an offering for guilt, he shall see his offspring; he shall prolong his days; the will of the LORD shall prosper in his hand. Out of the anguish of his soul he shall see and be satisfied; by his knowledge shall the righteous one, my servant, make many to be accounted righteous, and he shall bear their iniquities. Therefore I will divide him a portion with the many, and he shall divide the spoil with the strong, because he poured out his soul to death and was numbered with the transgressors; yet he bore the sin of many, and makes intercession for the transgressors.

The word of the Lord.
Thanks be to God.

RESPONSORIAL PSALM *Psalm 31(30):2, 6. 12a-d. 12e-13. 15-16. 17, 25. R. Luke 23:46*

R. Father, into your hands I commend my spirit.

1 In you, O LORD, I take refuge.
Let me never be put to shame.
In your justice, set me free.
Into your hands I commend my spirit.
You will redeem me, O LORD, O faithful God. R.

2 Because of all my foes
I have become a reproach,
an object of scorn to my neighbours
and of fear to my friends. R.

3 Those who see me in the street,
they flee from me.
I am forgotten, like someone dead,
and have become like a broken vessel. R.

4 But as for me, I trust in you, O LORD;
I say, 'You are my God.
There in your hands is my lot,
from the hands of my enemies deliver me
and from those who pursue me.' R.

5 'Let your face shine on your servant.
Save me in your merciful love.'
Be strong, let your heart take courage,
all who hope in the LORD. R.

SECOND READING *Hebrews 4:14–16; 5:7–9*

'He learned obedience and became the source of salvation to all who obey him.'

A reading from the Letter to the Hebrews.

Brothers and sisters: We have a great high priest who has passed through the heavens, Jesus, the Son of God; let us hold fast our confession. For we do not have a high priest who is unable to sympathise with our weaknesses, but one who in every respect has been tempted as we are, yet without sin. Let us then with confidence draw near to the throne of grace, that we may receive mercy and find grace to help in time of need.

In the days of his flesh, Jesus offered up prayers and supplications, with loud cries and tears, to him who was able to save him from death, and he was heard because of his reverence. Although he was a son, he learned obedience through what he suffered. And being made perfect, he became the source of eternal salvation to all who obey him.

The word of the Lord.
Thanks be to God.

ACCLAMATION BEFORE THE GOSPEL *Philippians 2:8–9*

Praise to you, O Christ, King of eternal glory.
Christ became for us obedient to the point of death,
even death on a cross.
Therefore God has highly exalted him
and bestowed on him the name that is above every name.
Praise to you, O Christ, King of eternal glory.

GOSPEL *John 18:1–19:42*

The narrative of the Lord's Passion is read without candles and without incense, with no greeting or signing of the book. It is read by a Deacon or, if there is no Deacon, by a Priest. It may also be read by readers, with the part of Christ, if possible, reserved to a Priest.

Deacons, but not others, ask for the blessing of the Priest before singing the Passion, as at other times before the Gospel.

In the following Passion narrative: N = narrator, + = Christ, S = speakers other than Christ.

The Passion of our Lord Jesus Christ according to John.

N At that time: Jesus went out with his disciples across the brook Kidron, where there was a garden, which he and his disciples entered. Now Judas, who betrayed him, also knew the place, for Jesus often met there with his disciples. So Judas, having procured a band of soldiers and some officers from the chief priests and the Pharisees, went there with lanterns and torches and weapons. Then Jesus, knowing all that would happen to him, came forward and said to them,

\+ Whom do you seek?

N They answered him,

S Jesus of Nazareth.

N Jesus said to them,

\+ I am he.

N Judas, who betrayed him, was standing with them. When Jesus said to them, 'I am he', they drew back and fell to the ground. So he asked them again,

\+ Whom do you seek?

N And they said,

S Jesus of Nazareth.

N Jesus answered,

\+ I told you that I am he. So, if you seek me, let these men go.

N This was to fulfil the word that he had spoken: 'Of those whom you gave me I have lost not one.' Then Simon Peter, having a sword, drew it and struck the high priest's servant and cut off his right ear. The servant's name was Malchus. So Jesus said to Peter,

\+ Put your sword into its sheath; shall I not drink the cup that the Father has given me?

N So the band of soldiers and their captain and the officers of the Jews arrested Jesus and bound him. First they led him to Annas, for he was the father-in-law of Caiaphas, who was high priest that year. It was Caiaphas who had advised the Jews that it would be expedient that one man should die for the people.

Simon Peter followed Jesus, and so did another disciple. Since that disciple was known to the high priest, he entered with Jesus into the courtyard of the high priest, but Peter stood outside at the door. So the other disciple, who was known to the high priest, went out and spoke to the servant girl who kept watch at the door, and brought Peter in. The servant girl at the door said to Peter,

S You also are not one of this man's disciples, are you?

N He said,

S I am not.

N Now the servants and officers had made a charcoal fire, because it was cold, and they were standing and warming themselves. Peter also was with them, standing and warming himself.

The high priest then questioned Jesus about his disciples and his teaching. Jesus answered him,

\+ I have spoken openly to the world. I have always taught in synagogues and in the temple, where all Jews come together. I have said nothing in secret. Why do you ask me? Ask those who have heard me what I said to them; they know what I said.

N When he had said these things, one of the officers standing by struck Jesus with his hand, saying,

S Is that how you answer the high priest?

N Jesus answered him,

\+ If what I said is wrong, bear witness about the wrong; but if what I said is right, why do you strike me?

N Annas then sent him bound to Caiaphas the high priest.

Now Simon Peter was standing and warming himself. So they said to him,

S You also are not one of his disciples, are you?

N He denied it and said,

S I am not.

N One of the servants of the high priest, a relative of the man whose ear Peter had cut off, asked,

S Did I not see you in the garden with him?

N Peter again denied it, and at once a cock crowed.

Then they led Jesus from the house of Caiaphas to the governor's headquarters. It was early morning. They themselves did not enter the governor's headquarters, so that they would not be defiled, but could eat the Passover. So Pilate went outside to them and said,

S What accusation do you bring against this man?

N They answered him,

S If this man were not doing evil,

we would not have delivered him over to you.

N Pilate said to them,

S Take him yourselves and judge him by your own law.

N The Jews said to him,

S It is not lawful for us to put anyone to death.

N This was to fulfil the word that Jesus had spoken to show by what kind of death he was going to die.

So Pilate entered his headquarters again and called Jesus and said to him,

S Are you the King of the Jews?

N Jesus answered,

+ Do you say this of your own accord, or did others say it to you about me?

N Pilate answered,

S Am I a Jew? Your own nation and the chief priests have delivered you up to me. What have you done?

N Jesus answered,

+ My kingdom is not of this world. If my kingdom were of this world, my servants would have been fighting, that I might not be delivered over to the Jews. But my kingdom is not from the world.

N Then Pilate said to him,

S So you are a king?

N Jesus answered,

+ You say that I am a king. For this purpose I was born and for this purpose I have come into the world—to bear witness to the truth. Everyone who is of the truth listens to my voice.

N Pilate said to him,

S What is truth?

N After he had said this, he went back outside to the Jews and told them,

S I find no guilt in him. But you have a custom that I should release one man for you at the Passover. So do you want me to release to you the King of the Jews?

N They cried out again,

S Not this man, but Barabbas!

N Now Barabbas was a robber.

Then Pilate took Jesus and flogged him. And the soldiers twisted together a crown of thorns and put it on his head and arrayed him in a purple robe. They came up to him, saying,

S Hail, King of the Jews!

N and struck him with their hands. Pilate went out again and said to them,

S See, I am bringing him out to you that you may know that I find no guilt in him.

N So Jesus came out, wearing the crown of thorns and the purple robe. Pilate said to them,

S Behold the man!

N When the chief priests and the officers saw him, they cried out,

S Crucify him, crucify him!

N Pilate said to them,

S Take him yourselves and crucify him, for I find no guilt in him.

N The Jews answered him,

S We have a law, and according to that law he ought to die because he has made himself the Son of God.

N When Pilate heard this statement, he was even more afraid. He entered his headquarters again and said to Jesus,

S Where are you from?

N But Jesus gave him no answer. So Pilate said to him,

S You will not speak to me?

Do you not know that I have authority to release you and authority to crucify you?

N Jesus answered him,

\+ You would have no authority over me at all unless it had been given you from above. Therefore he who delivered me over to you has the greater sin.

N From then on Pilate sought to release him, but the Jews cried out,

S If you release this man, you are not Caesar's friend. Everyone who makes himself a king opposes Caesar.

N So when Pilate heard these words, he brought Jesus out and sat down on the judgement seat at a place called The Stone Pavement, and in Aramaic Gabbatha. Now it was the day of Preparation of the Passover. It was about the sixth hour. He said to the Jews,

S Behold your King!

N They cried out,

S Away with him, away with him, crucify him!

N Pilate said to them,

S Shall I crucify your King?

N The chief priests answered,

S We have no king but Caesar.

N So he delivered him over to them to be crucified. So they took Jesus, and he went out, bearing his own cross, to the place called The Place of the Skull, which in Aramaic is called Golgotha. There they crucified him, and with him two others, one on either side, and Jesus between them. Pilate also wrote an inscription and put it on the cross. It read, 'Jesus of Nazareth, the King of the Jews.' Many of the Jews read this inscription, for the place where Jesus was crucified was near the city, and it was written in Aramaic, in Latin, and in Greek. So the chief priests of the Jews said to Pilate,

S Do not write, 'The King of the Jews', but rather, 'This man said, I am King of the Jews.'

N Pilate answered,

S What I have written I have written.

N When the soldiers had crucified Jesus, they took his garments and divided them into four parts, one part for each soldier; also his tunic. But the tunic was seamless, woven in one piece from top to bottom, so they said to one another,

S Let us not tear it, but cast lots for it to see whose it shall be.

N This was to fulfil the Scripture which says, 'They divided my garments among them, and for my clothing they cast lots.' So the soldiers did these things, but standing by the cross of Jesus were his mother and his mother's sister, Mary the wife of Clopas, and Mary Magdalene. When Jesus saw his mother and the disciple whom he loved standing nearby, he said to his mother,

\+ Woman, behold, your son!

N Then he said to the disciple,

\+ Behold, your mother!

N And from that hour the disciple took her to his own home.

After this, Jesus, knowing that all was now finished, said (to fulfil the Scripture),

\+ I thirst.

N A jar full of sour wine stood there, so they put a sponge full of the sour wine on a hyssop branch and held it to his mouth. When Jesus had received the sour wine, he said,

\+ It is finished,

N and he bowed his head and gave up his spirit.

All kneel for a period of silence.

N Since it was the day of Preparation, and so that the bodies would not remain on the cross on the Sabbath (for that Sabbath was a high day), the Jews asked Pilate that their legs might be broken and that they might be taken away. So the soldiers came and broke the legs of the first, and of the other who had been crucified with him. But when they came to Jesus and saw that he was already dead, they did not break his legs. But one of the soldiers pierced his side with a spear, and at once there came out blood and water. He who saw it has borne witness—his testimony is true, and he knows that he is telling the truth—that you also may believe. For these things took place that the Scripture might be fulfilled: 'Not one of his bones will be broken.' And again another Scripture says, 'They will look on him whom they have pierced.'

After these things Joseph of Arimathea, who was a disciple of Jesus, but secretly for fear of the Jews, asked Pilate that he might take away the body of Jesus, and Pilate gave him permission. So he came and took away his body. Nicodemus also, who earlier had come to Jesus by night, came bringing a mixture of myrrh and aloes, about thirty-five kilograms in weight. So they took the body of Jesus and bound it in linen cloths with the spices, as is the burial custom of the Jews. Now in the place where he was crucified there was a garden, and in the garden a new tomb in which no one had yet been laid. So because of the Jewish day of Preparation, since the tomb was close at hand, they laid Jesus there.

The Gospel of the Lord.
Praise to you, Lord Jesus Christ.

HOMILY

THE SOLEMN INTERCESSIONS

A Deacon or lay reader says or sings each invitation to pray.
All pray in silence for a while, then the Priest says or sings the prayer for that intention.

I For Holy Church

Let us pray, dearly beloved, for the holy Church of God,
that our God and Lord be pleased to give her peace,
to guard her and to unite her throughout the whole world
and grant that, leading our life in tranquillity and quiet,
we may glorify God the Father almighty.

Prayer in silence. Then the Priest says:

Almighty ever-living God,
who in Christ revealed your glory to all the nations,
watch over the works of your mercy,
that your Church, spread throughout all the world,
may persevere with steadfast faith in confessing your name.
Through Christ our Lord. **Amen.**

II For the Pope

Let us pray also for our most Holy Father Pope N.,
that our God and Lord,
who chose him for the Order of Bishops,
may keep him safe and unharmed for the Lord's holy Church,
to govern the holy People of God.

Prayer in silence. Then the Priest says:

Almighty ever-living God,
by whose decree all things are founded,
look with favour on our prayers
and in your kindness protect the Pope chosen for us,
that, under him, the Christian people,
governed by you their maker,
may grow in merit by reason of their faith.
Through Christ our Lord. **Amen.**

III For all orders and degrees of the faithful

Let us pray also for our Bishop N.[1],
for all Bishops, Priests, and Deacons of the Church
and for the whole of the faithful people.

Prayer in silence. Then the Priest says:

Almighty ever-living God,
by whose Spirit the whole body of the Church
is sanctified and governed,
hear our humble prayer for your ministers,
that, by the gift of your grace,
all may serve you faithfully.
Through Christ our Lord. **Amen.**

IV For catechumens

Let us pray also for (our) catechumens,
that our God and Lord
may open wide the ears of their inmost hearts
and unlock the gates of his mercy,
that, having received forgiveness of all their sins
through the waters of rebirth,
they, too, may be one with Christ Jesus our Lord.

Prayer in silence. Then the Priest says:

Almighty ever-living God,
who make your Church ever fruitful with new offspring,
increase the faith and understanding of (our) catechumens,
that, reborn in the font of Baptism,
they may be added to the number of your adopted children.
Through Christ our Lord. **Amen.**

1 Mention may be made here of the Coadjutor Bishop, or Auxiliary Bishops.

V For the unity of Christians

Let us pray also for all our brothers and sisters who believe in Christ,
that our God and Lord may be pleased,
as they live the truth,
to gather them together and keep them in his one Church.

Prayer in silence. Then the Priest says:

Almighty ever-living God,
who gather what is scattered
and keep together what you have gathered,
look kindly on the flock of your Son,
that those whom one Baptism has consecrated
may be joined together by integrity of faith
and united in the bond of charity.
Through Christ our Lord. **Amen.**

VI For the Jewish people

Let us pray also for the Jewish people,
to whom the Lord our God spoke first,
that he may grant them to advance in love of his name
and in faithfulness to his covenant.

Prayer in silence. Then the Priest says:

Almighty ever-living God,
who bestowed your promises on Abraham and his descendants,
graciously hear the prayers of your Church,
that the people you first made your own
may attain the fullness of redemption.
Through Christ our Lord. **Amen.**

VII For those who do not believe in Christ

Let us pray also for those who do not believe in Christ,
that, enlightened by the Holy Spirit,
they, too, may enter on the way of salvation.

Prayer in silence. Then the Priest says:

Almighty ever-living God,
grant to those who do not confess Christ
that, by walking before you with a sincere heart,
they may find the truth
and that we ourselves, being constant in mutual love
and striving to understand more fully the mystery of your life,
may be made more perfect witnesses to your love in the world.
Through Christ our Lord. **Amen.**

VIII For those who do not believe in God

Let us pray also for those who do not acknowledge God,
that, following what is right in sincerity of heart,
they may find the way to God himself.

Prayer in silence.

Then the Priest says:

Almighty ever-living God,
who created all people
to seek you always by desiring you
and, by finding you, come to rest,
grant, we pray,
that, despite every harmful obstacle,
all may recognize the signs of your fatherly love
and the witness of the good works
done by those who believe in you,
and so in gladness confess you,
the one true God and Father of our human race.
Through Christ our Lord. **Amen.**

IX For those in public office

Let us pray also for those in public office,
that our God and Lord
may direct their minds and hearts according to his will
for the true peace and freedom of all.

Prayer in silence. Then the Priest says:

Almighty ever-living God,
in whose hand lies every human heart
and the rights of peoples,
look with favour, we pray,
on those who govern with authority over us,
that throughout the whole world,
the prosperity of peoples,
the assurance of peace,
and freedom of religion
may through your gift be made secure.
Through Christ our Lord. **Amen.**

X For those in tribulation

Let us pray, dearly beloved,
to God the Father almighty,
that he may cleanse the world of all errors,
banish disease, drive out hunger,
unlock prisons, loosen fetters,
granting to travellers safety, to pilgrims return,
health to the sick, and salvation to the dying.

Prayer in silence. Then the Priest says:

Almighty ever-living God,
comfort of mourners, strength of all who toil,
may the prayers of those who cry out in any tribulation
come before you,
that all may rejoice,
because in their hour of need
your mercy was at hand.
Through Christ our Lord. **Amen.**

SECOND PART: ADORATION OF THE HOLY CROSS

The Holy Cross is shown three times to the assembly. This is done either by a progressive unveiling of the Cross at the front of the church, or by a procession through the church to the sanctuary.

After each showing, the Priest (assisted, if need be, by the Deacon or the choir) sings or says:

Priest / Deacon / Choir:

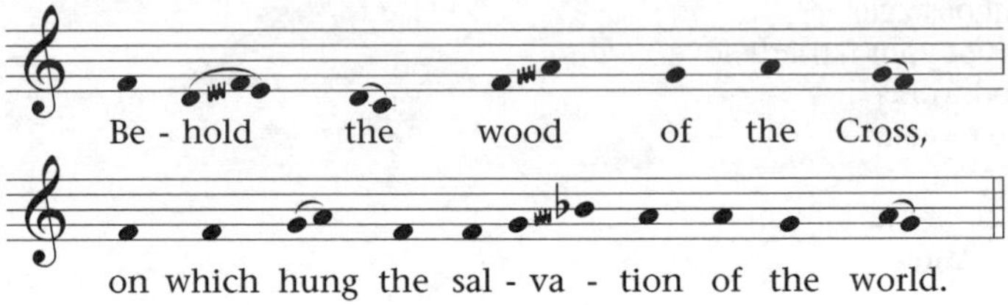

People:

or

Priest / Deacon / Choir:

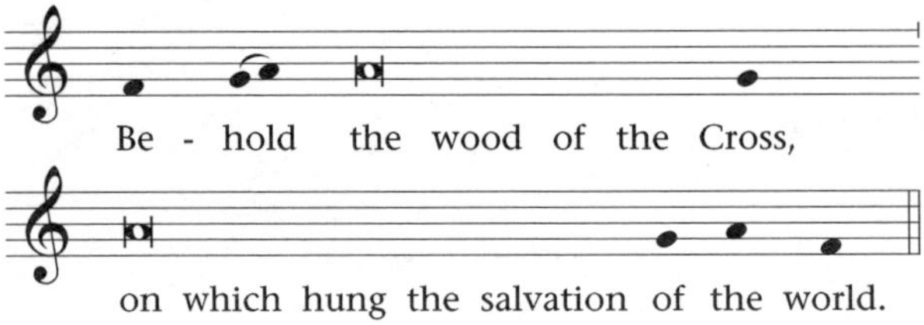

People:

At the end of the singing, all kneel and for a brief moment adore in silence, while the Priest stands and holds the Cross raised.

THE ADORATION OF THE HOLY CROSS

The Cross is placed or held at the entrance to the sanctuary (or another suitable place), with candles placed on either side.

After the Priest Celebrant has venerated the Cross, other clergy, lay ministers, and the assembly approach in procession. They show reverence to the Cross by a simple genuflection or by some other appropriate sign, for example, by kissing the Cross.

If, because of the large number of people, it is not possible for all to approach individually, the Priest, after some of the clergy and faithful have adored, takes the Cross and, standing in the middle before the altar, invites the people in a few words to adore the Holy Cross and afterwards holds the Cross elevated higher for a brief time, for the faithful to adore it in silence.

SINGING DURING THE ADORATION OF THE HOLY CROSS

While the adoration of the Holy Cross is taking place, the following, or other suitable chants, are sung. During the singing, all who have already adored the Cross remain seated.

Ant. We adore your Cross, O Lord,
we praise and glorify your holy Resurrection,
for behold, because of the wood of a tree
joy has come to the whole world.

May God have mercy on us and bless us; *cf Psalm 66:2*
may he let his face shed its light upon us
and have mercy on us.

We adore your Cross...

Reproaches

– I –

Parts assigned to one of the two choirs separately are indicated by the numbers 1 (first choir) and 2 (second choir); parts sung by both choirs together are marked: 1 and 2. Some of the verses may also be sung by two cantors.

1 and 2 My people, what have I done to you?
Or how have I grieved you? Answer me!
1 Because I led you out of the land of Egypt,
you have prepared a Cross for your Saviour.

1 Hagios o Theos,
2 Holy is God,
1 Hagios Ischyros,
2 Holy and Mighty,
1 Hagios Athanatos, eleison himas.
2 Holy and Immortal One, have mercy on us.

1 and 2 Because I led you out through the desert forty years
and fed you with manna and brought you into a land of plenty,
you have prepared a Cross for your Saviour.
1 Hagios o Theos,
2 Holy is God,
1 Hagios Ischyros,
2 Holy and Mighty,
1 Hagios Athanatos, eleison himas.
2 Holy and Immortal One, have mercy on us.

1 and 2 What more should I have done for you and have not done?
Indeed, I planted you as my most beautiful chosen vine
and you have turned very bitter for me,
for in my thirst you gave me vinegar to drink
and with a lance you pierced your Saviour's side.

1 Hagios o Theos,
2 Holy is God,
1 Hagios Ischyros,
2 Holy and Mighty,
1 Hagios Athanatos, eleison himas.
2 Holy and Immortal One, have mercy on us.

– II –

Cantors: I scourged Egypt for your sake with its firstborn sons,
and you scourged me and handed me over.

1 and 2 repeat: My people, what have I done to you?
Or how have I grieved you? Answer me!

Cantors: I led you out from Egypt as Pharoah lay sunk in the Red Sea,
and you handed me over to the chief priests.

1 and 2 repeat: My people...

Cantors: I opened up the sea before you,
and you opened my side with a lance.

1 and 2 repeat: My people...

Cantors: I went before you in a pillar of cloud,
and you led me into Pilate's palace.

1 and 2 repeat: My people...

Cantors: I fed you with manna in the desert,
and on me you rained blows and lashes.

1 and 2 repeat: My people...

Cantors: I gave you saving water from the rock to drink,
and for drink you gave me gall and vinegar.

1 and 2 repeat: My people...

Cantors: I struck down for you the kings of the Canaanites,
and you struck my head with a reed.

1 and 2 repeat: My people...

Cantors: I put in your hand a royal sceptre,
and you put on my head a crown of thorns.

1 and 2 repeat: My people...

Cantors: I exalted you with great power,
and you hung me on the scaffold of the Cross.

1 and 2 repeat: My people...

Hymn

All:
Faithful Cross the Saints rely on,
Noble tree beyond compare!
Never was there such a scion,
Never leaf or flower so rare.
Sweet the timber, sweet the iron,
Sweet the burden that they bear!

Cantors:
Sing, my tongue, in exultation
Of our banner and device!
Make a solemn proclamation
Of a triumph and its price:
How the Saviour of creation
Conquered by his sacrifice!

All:
Faithful Cross the Saints rely on,
Noble tree beyond compare!
Never was there such a scion,
Never leaf or flower so rare.

Cantors:
For, when Adam first offended,
Eating that forbidden fruit,
Not all hopes of glory ended
With the serpent at the root:
Broken nature would be mended
By a second tree and shoot.

All:
Sweet the timber, sweet the iron,
Sweet the burden that they bear!

Cantors:
Thus the tempter was outwitted
By a wisdom deeper still:
Remedy and ailment fitted,
Means to cure and means to kill;
That the world might be acquitted,
Christ would do his Father's will.

All:
Faithful Cross the Saints rely on,
Noble tree beyond compare!
Never was there such a scion,
Never leaf or flower so rare.

Cantors:
So the Father, out of pity
For our self-inflicted doom,
Sent him from the heavenly city
When the holy time had come:
He, the Son and the Almighty,
Took our flesh in Mary's womb.

All:
Sweet the timber, sweet the iron,
Sweet the burden that they bear!

Cantors:
Hear a tiny baby crying,
Founder of the seas and strands;
See his virgin Mother tying
Cloth around his feet and hands;
Find him in a manger lying
Tightly wrapped in swaddling-bands!

All:
Faithful Cross the Saints rely on,
Noble tree beyond compare!
Never was there such a scion,
Never leaf or flower so rare.

Cantors:
So he came, the long-expected,
Not in glory, not to reign;
Only born to be rejected,
Choosing hunger, toil and pain,
Till the scaffold was erected
And the Paschal Lamb was slain.

All:
Sweet the timber, sweet the iron,
Sweet the burden that they bear!

Cantors:
No disgrace was too abhorrent:
Nailed and mocked and parched he died;
Blood and water, double warrant,
Issue from his wounded side,
Washing in a mighty torrent
Earth and stars and oceantide.

All:
Faithful Cross the Saints rely on,
Noble tree beyond compare!
Never was there such a scion,
Never leaf or flower so rare.

Cantors:
Lofty timber, smooth your roughness,
Flex your boughs for blossoming;
Let your fibres lose their toughness,
Gently let your tendrils cling;
Lay aside your native gruffness,
Clasp the body of your King!

All:
Sweet the timber, sweet the iron,
Sweet the burden that they bear!

Cantors:
Noblest tree of all created,
Richly jewelled and embossed:
Post by Lamb's blood consecrated;
Spar that saves the tempest-tossed;
Scaffold-beam which, elevated,
Carries what the world has cost!

All:
Faithful Cross the Saints rely on,
Noble tree beyond compare!
Never was there such a scion,
Never leaf or flower so rare.

The following conclusion is never to be omitted:

All:
Wisdom, power, and adoration
To the blessed Trinity
For redemption and salvation
Through the Paschal Mystery,
Now, in every generation,
And for all eternity. Amen.

THIRD PART: HOLY COMMUNION

The Altar is prepared.
As the Blessed Sacrament is brought to the Altar, all stand in silence. **ALL STAND**

LORD'S PRAYER

Priest: At the Saviour's command
and formed by divine teaching,
we dare to say:

All: **Our Father, who art in heaven,**
hallowed be thy name;
thy kingdom come,
thy will be done
on earth as it is in heaven.
Give us this day our daily bread,
and forgive us our trespasses,
as we forgive those who trespass against us;
and lead us not into temptation,
but deliver us from evil.

Priest: Deliver us, Lord, we pray, from every evil,
graciously grant peace in our days,
that, by the help of your mercy,
we may be always free from sin
and safe from all distress,
as we await the blessed hope
and the coming of our Saviour, Jesus Christ.

People: **For the kingdom,**
the power and the glory are yours
now and for ever.

INVITATION TO COMMUNION

ALL KNEEL

The Priest then genuflects, takes a particle, and, holding it slightly raised over the ciborium, while facing the people, says aloud:

Priest: Behold the Lamb of God,
behold him who takes away the sins of the world.
Blessed are those called to the supper of the Lamb.

All: **Lord, I am not worthy**
that you should enter under my roof,
but only say the word
and my soul shall be healed.

COMMUNION

During Communion, Psalm 21 or another appropriate chant may be sung.

PRAYER AFTER COMMUNION

Almighty ever-living God,
who have restored us to life
by the blessed Death and Resurrection of your Christ,
preserve in us the work of your mercy,
that, by partaking of this mystery,
we may have a life unceasingly devoted to you.
Through Christ our Lord. **Amen.**

PRAYER OVER THE PEOPLE:

May abundant blessing, O Lord, we pray,
descend upon your people,
who have honoured the Death of your Son
in the hope of their resurrection:
may pardon come,
comfort be given,
holy faith increase,
and everlasting redemption be made secure.
Through Christ our Lord. **Amen.**

HOLY SATURDAY

On Holy Saturday the Church waits at the Lord's tomb in prayer and fasting, meditating on his Passion and Death and on his Descent into Hell, and awaiting his Resurrection.

The Church abstains from the Sacrifice of the Mass, with the sacred table left bare, until after the solemn Vigil, that is, the anticipation by night of the Resurrection, when the time comes for paschal joys, the abundance of which overflows to occupy fifty days.

Some or all of the Preparation Rites for Baptism may be celebrated in a liturgy during the day:
Recitation of the Creed, Ephphetha Rite, Choosing a Baptismal Name, Anointing with the Oil of Catechumens.
(Rite of Christian Initiation of Adults nn 172–197)

EASTER TIME

ABOUT THE SEASON

The Easter Vigil, in the holy night when the Lord rose again, is considered the 'mother of all holy Vigils', in which the Church, keeping watch, awaits the Resurrection of Christ and celebrates it in the Sacraments. Therefore, the entire celebration of this sacred Vigil must take place at night, so that it both begins after nightfall and ends before the dawn on the Sunday.

The fifty days from the Sunday of the Resurrection to Pentecost Sunday are celebrated in joy and exultation as one feast day, indeed as one 'great Sunday'.

These are the days above all others in which the *Alleluia* is sung.

The Sundays of this time of year are considered to be Sundays of Easter and are called, after Easter Sunday itself, the Second, Third, Fourth, Fifth, Sixth, and Seventh Sundays of Easter. This sacred period of fifty days concludes with Pentecost Sunday.

The first eight days of Easter Time constitute the Octave of Easter and are celebrated as Solemnities of the Lord.

On the fortieth day after Easter the Ascension of the Lord is celebrated, except where, not being observed as a Holyday of Obligation, it has been assigned to the Seventh Sunday of Easter.

The weekdays from the Ascension up to and including the Saturday before Pentecost prepare for the coming of the Holy Spirit, the Paraclete.

Universal Norms on the Liturgical Year and the Calendar nn 21–26

ABOUT THE READINGS

On the holy night of the Easter Vigil there are seven Old Testament readings, recalling the wonderful works of God in the history of salvation. There are two New Testament readings, the announcement of the resurrection according to one of the Synoptic Gospels and a reading from St. Paul on Christian baptism as the sacrament of Christ's resurrection.

The gospel reading for the Mass on Easter day is from John on the finding of the empty tomb. There is also, however, the option to use the gospel texts from the Easter Vigil or, when there is an evening Mass on Easter Sunday, to use the account in Luke of the Lord's appearance to the disciples on the road to Emmaus. The first reading is from Acts, which throughout the Easter season replaces the Old Testament reading. The reading from St. Paul concerns the living out of the paschal mystery in the Church.

The gospel readings for the first three Sundays recount the appearances of the risen Christ. The readings about the Good Shepherd are assigned to the Fourth Sunday. On the Fifth, Sixth, and Seventh Sundays, there are excerpts from the Lord's discourse and prayer at the last supper.

The first reading is from Acts, in a three-year cycle of parallel and progressive selections: material is presented on the life oft he primitive Church, its witness, and its growth.

For the reading from the apostles… Revelation [is used in] Year C… These are the texts that seem to fit in especially well with the spirit of joyous faith and sure hope proper to this season.

Introduction to the Lectionary nn 99–100

COMMON RESPONSORIAL PSALMS FOR EASTER TIME

COMMON RESPONSE

Alleluia. *(Repeated two or three times)*

EASTER VIGIL — COMMON PSALM 1 *Psalm 136(135):1-3. 4-6. 7-9. 24-26.*

In the two Common Psalms for the Easter Vigil, the response is sung after every line.

R. For his mercy endures for ever.

1 O give thanks to the Lord for he is good.
For his mercy endures for ever.
Give thanks to the God of gods,
For his mercy endures for ever.
Give thanks to the Lord of lords,
For his mercy endures for ever.

2 Who alone has wrought marvellous works.
who in wisdom made the heavens,
who spread the earth on the waters,

3 It was he who made the great lights,
the sun to rule in the day,
the moon and the stars in the night,

4 And he snatched us away from our foes,
He gives bread to all mortal flesh,
To the God of heaven give thanks,

EASTER VIGIL — COMMON PSALM 2 *Psalm 136(135):1, 3, 16. 21-23. 24-26.*

R. For his mercy endures for ever. *(Sung after every line.)*

1 O give thanks to the Lord for he is good,
For his mercy endures for ever.
Give thanks to the Lord of lords,
For his mercy endures for ever.
Through the desert his people he led.
For his mercy endures for ever.

2 He gave their land as a heritage,
A heritage for Israel, his servant,
He remembered us in our distress.

3 And he snatched us away from our foes,
He gives bread to all mortal flesh,
To the God of heaven give thanks,

EASTER SEASON — COMMON PSALM 1 *Psalm 118 (117):1-2. 16-17. 22-23. R.24*

R. This is the day the Lord has made;
let us rejoice in it and be glad.

or **Alleluia.** *(Repeated two or three times)*

1 Give praise to the Lord, for he is good;
his mercy endures for ever.
Let the house of Israel say,
'His mercy endures for ever.' R.

2 The Lord's right hand is exalted.
The Lord's right hand has done
mighty deeds.
I shall not die, I shall live
and recount the deeds of the Lord. R.

3 The stone that the builders rejected
has become the cornerstone.
By the Lord has this been done,
a marvel in our eyes. R.

EASTER SEASON — COMMON PSALM 2 *Psalm 66 (65):1-3a. 4-5. 6-7a. 16, 20. R.1*

R. Cry out with joy to God, all the earth. Alleluia.

1 Cry out with joy to God, all the earth;
O sing to the glory of his name.
O render him glorious praise.
Say to God, 'How wondrous your deeds!' R.

continued...

R. Cry out with joy to God, all the earth. Alleluia.

2 'Before you all the earth shall bow down,
shall sing to you, sing to your name!'
Come and see the works of God:
his wondrous deeds among the children of Adam. R.

3 He turned the sea into dry land;
they passed through the river on foot.
Let our joy, then, be in him;
he rules for ever by his might. R.

4 Come and hear, all who fear God;
I will tell what he did for my soul.
Blest be God, who did not reject my prayer,
nor withhold from me his merciful love. R.

COMMON PSALM — ASCENSION *Psalm 47 (46):2-3. 6-7. 8-9. R.6a*

R. God has gone up with shouts of joy.

1 All peoples, clap your hands.
Cry to God with shouts of joy!
For the LORD, the Most High, to be feared,
the great king over all the earth. R.

2 God has gone up with shouts of joy.
The LORD goes up with trumpet blast.
Sing praise for God; sing praise!
Sing praise to our king; sing praise! R.

3 For God is king of all the earth.
Sing praise with a hymn.
God is reigning over nations.
God sits upon his holy throne. R.

COMMON PSALM — PENTECOST SUNDAY *Psalm 104 (103):1ab, 24ac. 29b-30. 31, 34. R.cf. 30*

**R. Send forth your Spirit, O Lord,
and renew the face of the earth.**

1 Bless the LORD, O my soul!
O LORD my God, how great you are!
How many are your works, O LORD!
The earth is full of your creatures. R.

2 You take away their breath, they die,
returning to the dust from which they came.
You send forth your spirit, and they are created,
and you renew the face of the earth. R.

3 May the glory of the LORD last for ever!
May the LORD rejoice in his works!
May my thoughts be pleasing to him.
I will rejoice in the LORD. R.

EASTER SUNDAY OF THE RESURRECTION OF THE LORD

Easter Sunday forms both the pinnacle of the Season of Triduum
and the fifty days of paschal rejoicing of Easter Time.

EASTER VIGIL IN THE HOLY NIGHT

The celebration of the Easter Vigil takes place after dark. The lights of the church are extinguished and candles prepared for all who participate.
The Vigil consists of four parts:

Solemn Beginning of the Vigil or Lucernarium

Liturgy of the Word

Baptismal Liturgy

Liturgy of the Eucharist

FIRST PART: LUCERNARIUM

THE BLESSING OF THE FIRE AND PREPARATION OF THE CANDLE

A blazing fire is prepared outside the church. If circumstances require, a smaller fire is prepared inside the church entrance. When the people are gathered there, the Priest approaches with the ministers, one of whom carries the paschal candle.

All make the Sign of the Cross as the Priest says.

Priest: In the name of the Father, and of the Son, and of the Holy Spirit.
People: **Amen.**

The Priest greets the people in the usual way and then instructs them in these or similar words.

Dear brethren (brothers and sisters),
on this most sacred night,
in which our Lord Jesus Christ
passed over from death to life,
the Church calls upon her sons and daughters,
scattered throughout the world,
to come together to watch and pray.
If we keep the memorial
of the Lord's paschal solemnity in this way,
listening to his word and celebrating his mysteries,
then we shall have the sure hope
of sharing his triumph over death
and living with him in God.

The Priest blesses the fire:

Let us pray.
O God, who through your Son
bestowed upon the faithful the fire of your glory,
sanctify ✠ this new fire, we pray,
and grant that,
by these paschal celebrations,
we may be so inflamed with heavenly desires,
that with minds made pure
we may attain festivities of unending splendour.
Through Christ our Lord. Amen.

After the blessing of the new fire, one of the ministers brings the paschal candle to the Priest, who cuts a cross into the candle with a stylus. Then he makes the Greek letter Alpha above the cross, the letter Omega below, and the four numerals of the current year between the arms of the cross, saying meanwhile:

Christ yesterday and today
the Beginning and the End
the Alpha
and the Omega
All time belongs to him
and all the ages
To him be glory and power
through every age and for ever. Amen

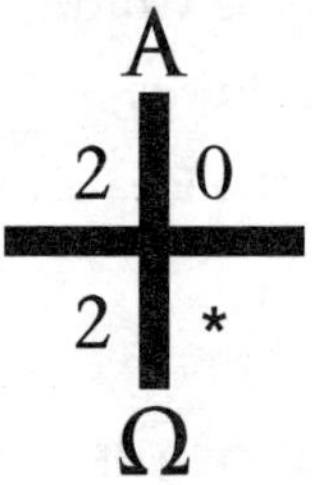

When the cutting of the cross and of the other signs has been completed, the Priest may insert five grains of incense into the candle in the form of a cross, meanwhile saying:

1 By his holy
2 and glorious wounds,
3 may Christ the Lord
4 guard us
5 and protect us. Amen.

1
4 2 5
3

The Priest lights the paschal candle from the new fire, saying:

May the light of Christ rising in glory
dispel the darkness of our hearts and minds.

PROCESSION

When the candle has been lit, the thurible is lit from the fire. Then the Deacon, standing at the door of the church, raises the candle and sings:

Deacon:

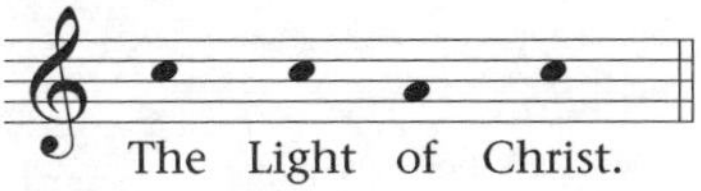

All:

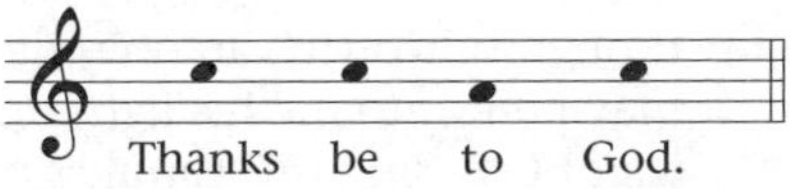

or

Deacon:

All:

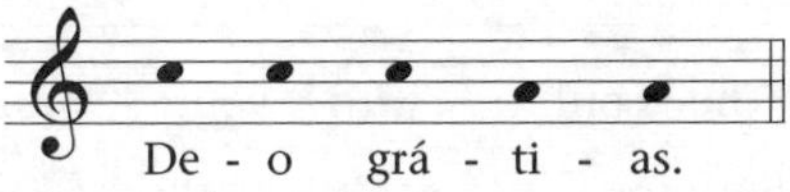

The Priest lights his candle from the flame of the paschal candle.

Then the Deacon moves forward to the middle of the church and, standing and raising up the candle, sings a second time:

Deacon: The Light of Christ.
All: **Thanks be to God.**

or

Deacon: Lumen Christi.
All: **Deo grátias.**

All light their candles from the flame of the paschal candle and continue in procession.

When the Deacon arrives before the altar, he stands facing the people, raises up the candle and sings a third time:

Deacon: The Light of Christ.
All: **Thanks be to God.**

or

Deacon: Lumen Christi.
All: **Deo grátias.**

Then the Deacon places the paschal candle on a large candlestand prepared next to the ambo or in the middle of the sanctuary.

And lights are lit throughout the church, except for the altar candles.

THE EASTER PROCLAMATION (EXSULTET)

If the Exsultet is sung by a lay cantor, the words in brackets are omitted.

(A shorter version of the Exsultet may be sung.)

Exult, let them exult, the hosts of heaven,
exult, let Angel ministers of God exult,
let the trumpet of salvation
sound aloud our mighty King's triumph!
Be glad, let earth be glad, as glory floods her,
ablaze with light from her eternal King,
let all corners of the earth be glad,
knowing an end to gloom and darkness.
Rejoice, let Mother Church also rejoice,
arrayed with the lightning of his glory,
let this holy building shake with joy,
filled with the mighty voices of the peoples.

(Therefore, dearest friends,
standing in the awesome glory of this holy light,
invoke with me, I ask you,
the mercy of God almighty,
that he, who has been pleased to number me,
though unworthy, among the Levites,
may pour into me his light unshadowed,
that I may sing this candle's perfect praises).

Deacon: All:

(The Lord be with you. And with your spir - it.)

Deacon/cantor: All:

Lift up your hearts. We lift them up to the Lord.

Deacon/cantor: All:

Let us give thanks to the Lord our God. It is right and just.

It is truly right and just,
with ardent love of mind and heart
and with devoted service of our voice,
to acclaim our God invisible, the almighty Father,
and Jesus Christ, our Lord, his Son, his Only Begotten.

Who for our sake paid Adam's debt to the eternal Father,
and, pouring out his own dear Blood,
wiped clean the record of our ancient sinfulness.

These then are the feasts of Passover,
in which is slain the Lamb, the one true Lamb,
whose Blood anoints the doorposts of believers.

This is the night,
when once you led our forebears, Israel's children,
from slavery in Egypt
and made them pass dry-shod through the Red Sea.

This is the night
that with a pillar of fire
banished the darkness of sin.

This is the night
that even now, throughout the world,
sets Christian believers apart from worldly vices

and from the gloom of sin,
leading them to grace
and joining them to his holy ones.

This is the night,
when Christ broke the prison-bars of death
and rose victorious from the underworld.

Our birth would have been no gain,
had we not been redeemed.
O wonder of your humble care for us!
O love, O charity beyond all telling,
to ransom a slave you gave away your Son!

O truly necessary sin of Adam,
destroyed completely by the Death of Christ!

O happy fault
that earned so great, so glorious a Redeemer!

O truly blessed night,
worthy alone to know the time and hour
when Christ rose from the underworld!

This is the night
of which it is written:
The night shall be as bright as day,
dazzling is the night for me,
and full of gladness.

The sanctifying power of this night
dispels wickedness, washes faults away,
restores innocence to the fallen, and joy to mourners,
drives out hatred, fosters concord, and brings down the mighty.

On this, your night of grace, O holy Father,
accept this candle, a solemn offering,
the work of bees and of your servants' hands,
an evening sacrifice of praise,
this gift from your most holy Church.

But now we know the praises of this pillar,
which glowing fire ignites for God's honour,
a fire into many flames divided,
yet never dimmed by sharing of its light,
for it is fed by melting wax,
drawn out by mother bees
to build a torch so precious.

O truly blessed night,
when things of heaven are wed to those of earth,
and divine to the human.

Therefore, O Lord,
we pray you that this candle,
hallowed to the honour of your name,
may persevere undimmed,
to overcome the darkness of this night.
Receive it as a pleasing fragrance,
and let it mingle with the lights of heaven.
May this flame be found still burning
by the Morning Star:
the one Morning Star who never sets,
Christ your Son,
who, coming back from death's domain,
has shed his peaceful light on humanity,
and lives and reigns for ever and ever.

All: **Amen.**

SECOND PART: LITURGY OF THE WORD

Wherever possible all the readings are read. However, in serious pastoral circumstances, a selection may be made of at least Old Testament readings, one of which must be the reading from Exodus 14.

After each reading, a Responsorial Psalm is sung, or this may be replaced by a sacred silence.

All set aside their candles, and sit. **ALL SIT**

The Priest introduces the Liturgy of the Word in these or similar words:

Dear brethren (brothers and sisters),
now that we have begun our solemn Vigil,
let us listen with quiet hearts to the Word of God.
Let us meditate on how God in times past saved his people
and in these, the last days, has sent us his Son as our Redeemer.
Let us pray that our God may complete this paschal work of salvation
by the fullness of redemption.

FIRST READING *Genesis 1:1–2:2 Shorter form: 1:1, 26–31a (only read text with side line next to it).*

'God saw everything that he had made and it was very good.'

A reading from the Book of Genesis.

In the beginning, God created the heavens and the earth. | The earth was without form and void, and darkness was over the face of the deep. And the Spirit of God was hovering over the face of the waters.

And God said, 'Let there be light', and there was light. And God saw that the light was good. And God separated the light from the darkness. God called the light Day, and the darkness he called Night. And there was evening and there was morning, the first day.

And God said, 'Let there be a firmament in the midst of the waters, and let it separate the waters from the waters.'

And God made the firmament and separated the waters that were under the firmament from the waters that were above the firmament. And it was so. And God called the firmament Heaven. And there was evening and there was morning, the second day.

And God said, 'Let the waters under the heavens be gathered together into one place, and let the dry land appear.' And it was so. God called the dry land

Earth, and the waters that were gathered together he called Seas. And God saw that it was good.

And God said, 'Let the earth sprout vegetation, plants yielding seed, and fruit trees bearing fruit in which is their seed, each according to its kind, on the earth.' And it was so. The earth brought forth vegetation, plants yielding seed according to their own kinds, and trees bearing fruit in which is their seed, each according to its kind. And God saw that it was good. And there was evening and there was morning, the third day.

And God said, 'Let there be lights in the firmament of the heavens to separate the day from the night. And let them be for signs and for seasons, and for days and years, and let them be lights in the firmament of the heavens to give light upon the earth.' And it was so. And God made the two great lights— the greater light to rule the day and the lesser light to rule the night— and the stars. And God set them in the firmament of the heavens to give light on the earth, to rule over the day and over the night, and to separate the light from the darkness. And God saw that it was good. And there was evening and there was morning, the fourth day.

And God said, 'Let the waters swarm with swarms of living creatures, and let birds fly above the earth across the firmament of the heavens.' So God created the great sea creatures and every living creature that moves, with which the waters swarm, according to their kinds, and every winged bird according to its kind. And God saw that it was good. And God blessed them, saying, 'Be fruitful and multiply and fill the waters in the seas, and let birds multiply on the earth.' And there was evening and there was morning, the fifth day.

And God said, 'Let the earth bring forth living creatures according to their kinds—livestock and creeping things and beasts of the earth according to their kinds.' And it was so. And God made the beasts of the earth according to their kinds and the livestock according to their kinds, and everything that creeps on the ground according to its kind. And God saw that it was good.

Then God said, 'Let us make man in our image, after our likeness. And let them have dominion over the fish of the sea, and over the birds of the heavens and over the livestock, and over all the earth and over every creeping thing that creeps on the earth.' So God created man in his own image, in the image of God he created him; male and female he created them. And God blessed them. And God said to them, 'Be fruitful and multiply and fill the earth and subdue it, and have dominion over the fish of the sea, and over the birds of the heavens, and over every living thing that moves on the earth.' And God said, 'Behold, I have given you every plant yielding seed that is on the face of all the earth, and every tree with seed in its fruit. You shall have them for food. And to every beast of the earth, and to every bird of the heavens, and to everything that creeps on the earth, everything that has the breath of life, I have given every green plant for food.' And it was so. And God saw everything that he had made, and behold, it was very good. | And there was evening and there was morning, the sixth day.

Thus the heavens and the earth were finished, and all the host of them. And on the seventh day God finished his work that he had done, and he rested on the seventh day from all his work that he had done.

The word of the Lord.
Thanks be to God.

RESPONSORIAL PSALM *Psalm 104(103):1-2a. 5-6. 10, 12. 13-14. 24, 35c R.cf.30*

R. Send forth your Spirit, O Lord, and renew the face of the earth.

1 Bless the LORD, O my soul!
O LORD my God, how great you are,
clothed in majesty and honour,
wrapped in light as with a robe! R.

2 You set the earth on its foundation,
immovable from age to age.
You wrapped it with the depths like a cloak;
the waters stood higher than the mountains. R.

3 You make springs gush forth in the valleys;
they flow in between the hills.
There the birds of heaven build their nests;
from the branches they sing their song. R.

4 From your dwelling you water the mountains;
by your works the earth has its fill.
You make the grass grow for the cattle
and plants to serve mankind's need,
that he may bring forth bread from the earth. R.

5 How many are your works, O LORD!
In wisdom you have made them all.
The earth is full of your creatures.
Bless the LORD, O my soul. R.

or ALTERNATIVE RESPONSORIAL PSALM *Psalm 33(32):4-5. 6-7. 12-13. 20, 22. R.5b*

R. The merciful love of the LORD fills the earth.

1 The word of the LORD is upright,
and all his works to be trusted.
The LORD loves justice and right,
and his merciful love fills the earth. R.

2 By the word of the LORD the heavens were made,
by the breath of his mouth all their host.
As in a flask, he collects the waves of the ocean;
he stores up the depths of the sea. R.

3 Blessed the nation whose God is the LORD,
the people he has chosen as his heritage.
From the heavens the Lord looks forth;
he sees the whole human race. R.

4 Our soul is waiting for the LORD.
He is our help and our shield.
May your merciful love be upon us,
as we hope in you, O LORD. R.

PRAYER

ALL STAND

Let us pray.

Almighty ever-living God,
who are wonderful in the ordering of all your works,
may those you have redeemed understand
that there exists nothing more marvellous
than the world's creation in the beginning
except that, at the end of the ages,
Christ our Passover has been sacrificed.
Who lives and reigns for ever and ever. **Amen.**

or

On the creation of man:

O God, who wonderfully created human nature
and still more wonderfully redeemed it,
grant us, we pray,
to set our minds against the enticements of sin,
that we may merit to attain eternal joys.
Through Christ our Lord. **Amen.**

ALL SIT

SECOND READING *Genesis 22:1–18 Shorter form: 22:1–2, 9a, 10-13, 15–18 (only read text with side line next to it).*

'The sacrifice of Abraham, our father in faith.'

| A reading from the Book of Genesis.

| In those days: God tested Abraham and said to him, 'Abraham!' And he said, 'Here I am.' He said, 'Take your son, your only son Isaac, whom you love, and go to the land of Moriah, and offer him there as a burnt offering on one of the mountains of which I shall tell you.'

So Abraham rose early in the morning, saddled his donkey, and took two of his young men with him, and his son Isaac. And he cut the wood for the burnt offering and arose and went to the place of which God had told him. On the third day Abraham lifted up his eyes and saw the place from afar. Then Abraham said to his young men, 'Stay here with the donkey; I and the boy will go over there and worship and come again to you.' And Abraham took the wood of the burnt offering and laid it on Isaac his son. And he took in his hand the fire and the knife. So they went both of them together. And Isaac said to his father Abraham, 'My father!' And he said, 'Here I am, my son.' He said, 'Behold, the fire and the wood, but where is the lamb for a burnt offering?' Abraham said, 'God will provide for himself the lamb for a burnt offering, my son.' So they went both of them together.

| When they came to the place of which God had told him, | Abraham built the altar there and laid the wood in order and bound Isaac his son and laid him on the altar, on top of the wood. Then | Abraham reached out his hand and took the knife to slaughter his son. But the angel of the Lord called to him from heaven and said, 'Abraham, Abraham!' And he said, 'Here I am.' He said, 'Do not lay your hand on the boy or do anything to him, for now I know that you fear God, seeing you have not withheld your son, your only son, from me.' And Abraham lifted up his eyes and looked, and behold, behind him was a ram, caught in a thicket by his horns. And Abraham went and took the ram and offered it up as a burnt offering instead of his son. | So Abraham called the name of that place, 'The Lord will

provide'; as it is said to this day, 'On the mount of the LORD it shall be provided.' And the angel of the LORD called to Abraham a second time from heaven and said, 'By myself I have sworn, declares the LORD, because you have done this and have not withheld your son, your only son, I will surely bless you, and I will surely multiply your offspring as the stars of heaven and as the sand that is on the seashore. And your offspring shall possess the gate of his enemies, and in your offspring shall all the nations of the earth be blessed, because you have obeyed my voice.'

The word of the Lord.
Thanks be to God.

RESPONSORIAL PSALM *Psalm 16(15):5, 8. 9-10. 11. R.1*

R. Preserve me, O God, for in you I take refuge.

1 O LORD, it is you who are my portion and cup;
you yourself who secure my lot.
I keep the LORD before me always;
with him at my right hand, I shall not be moved. R.

2 And so, my heart rejoices, my soul is glad;
even my flesh shall rest in hope.
For you will not abandon my soul to Sheol,
nor let your holy one see corruption. R.

3 You will show me the path of life,
the fullness of joy in your presence,
at your right hand, bliss for ever. R.

PRAYER

ALL STAND

Let us pray.

O God, supreme Father of the faithful,
who increase the children of your promise
by pouring out the grace of adoption
throughout the whole world
and who through the Paschal Mystery
make your servant Abraham father of nations,
as once you swore,
grant, we pray,
that your peoples may enter worthily
into the grace to which you call them.
Through Christ our Lord. **Amen.**

ALL SIT

THIRD READING *Exodus 14:15–15:1*

'The people of Israel went into the midst of the sea on dry ground.'

A reading from the Book of Exodus. In those days: The LORD said to Moses, 'Why do you cry to me? Tell the people of Israel to go forward. Lift up your staff, and stretch out your hand over the sea and divide it, that the people of Israel may go through the sea on dry ground. And I will harden the hearts of the Egyptians so that they shall go in after them, and I will get glory over Pharaoh and all his host, his chariots, and his horsemen. And the Egyptians shall know that I am the LORD, when I have gained glory over Pharaoh, his chariots, and his horsemen.'

Then the angel of God who was going before the host of Israel moved and went behind them, and the pillar of cloud moved from before them and stood behind them, coming between the host of Egypt and the host of Israel. And there was the cloud and the darkness. And it lit up the night without one coming near the other all night.

Then Moses stretched out his hand over the sea, and the LORD drove the sea back by a strong east wind all night and made the sea dry land, and the waters were divided. And the people of Israel went into the midst of the sea on dry ground, the waters being a wall to them on their right hand and on their left. The Egyptians pursued and went in after them into the midst of the sea, all Pharaoh's horses, his chariots, and his horsemen. And in the morning watch the LORD in the pillar of fire and of cloud looked down on the Egyptian forces and threw the Egyptian forces into a panic, clogging their chariot wheels so that they drove heavily. And the Egyptians said, 'Let us flee from before Israel, for the LORD fights for them against the Egyptians.'

Then the LORD said to Moses, 'Stretch out your hand over the sea, that the water may come back upon the Egyptians, upon their chariots, and upon their horsemen.' So Moses stretched out his hand over the sea, and the sea returned to its normal course when the morning appeared And as the Egyptians fled into it, the LORD threw the Egyptians into the midst of the sea. The waters returned and covered the chariots and the horsemen; of all the host of Pharaoh that had followed them into the sea, not one of them remained. But the people of Israel walked on dry ground through the sea, the waters being a wall to them on their right hand and on their left.

Thus the LORD saved Israel that day from the hand of the Egyptians, and Israel saw the Egyptians dead on the seashore. Israel saw the great power that the LORD used against the Egyptians, so the people feared the LORD, and they believed in the LORD and in his servant Moses.

Then Moses and the people of Israel sang this song to the LORD.

The canticle is sung immediately after the reading. The usual conclusion to the reading, 'The word of the Lord', is omitted.

RESPONSORIAL PSALM *Exodus 15:1-2. 3-4. 5-6. 17-18. R.1a*

R. Let us sing to the LORD, glorious his triumph.

1 Let us sing to the LORD who has gloriously triumphed;
horse and rider he has hurled into the sea.
The LORD is my strength and might;
he has become my salvation.
This is my God, and I will praise him,
my father's God, and I will exalt him. R.

2 The LORD is a warrior;
the LORD is his name.
The chariots of Pharaoh and his army
he has cast into the sea. R.

3 The waters of the flood covered over them;
they went down to the depths like a stone.
Your right hand, O LORD, majestic in power;
your right hand, O LORD, shatters the enemy. R.

continued...

4 You will bring them in and plant them
upon the mount of your inheritance:
the place which you, O LORD, have made your dwelling,
the holy place, O LORD, that your hands have established.
The LORD will reign for ever and ever. R.

PRAYER

ALL STAND

Let us pray.

O God, whose ancient wonders
remain undimmed in splendour even in our day,
for what you once bestowed on a single people,
freeing them from Pharaoh's persecution
by the power of your right hand
now you bring about as the salvation of the nations
through the waters of rebirth,
grant, we pray, that the whole world
may become children of Abraham
and inherit the dignity of Israel's birthright.
Through Christ our Lord. **Amen.**

or

O God, who by the light of the New Testament
have unlocked the meaning
of wonders worked in former times,
so that the Red Sea prefigures the sacred font
and the nation delivered from slavery
foreshadows the Christian people,
grant, we pray, that all nations,
obtaining the privilege of Israel by merit of faith,
may be reborn by partaking of your Spirit.
Through Christ our Lord. **Amen.**

ALL SIT

FOURTH READING *Isaiah 54:5–14*

'With everlasting love the Lord, your Redeemer, will have compassion on you.'

A reading from the Prophet Isaiah.

'Your Maker is your husband, the LORD of hosts is his name; and the Holy One of Israel is your Redeemer, the God of the whole earth he is called. For the LORD has called you like a wife deserted and grieved in spirit, like a wife of youth when she is cast off, says your God. For a brief moment I deserted you, but with great compassion I will gather you. In overflowing anger for a moment I hid my face from you, but with everlasting love I will have compassion on you,' says the LORD, your Redeemer.

'This is like the days of Noah to me: as I swore that the waters of Noah should no more go over the earth, so I have sworn that I will not be angry with you, and will not rebuke you. For the mountains may depart and the hills be removed, but my steadfast love shall not depart from you, and my covenant of peace shall not be removed,' says the LORD, who has compassion on you.

'O afflicted one, storm-tossed and not comforted, behold, I will set your stones in antimony, and lay your foundations with sapphires.

I will make your pinnacles of agate, your gates of carbuncles, and all your wall of precious stones.

All your children shall be taught by the LORD, and great shall be the peace of your children. In righteousness you shall be established; you shall be far from oppression, for you shall not fear; and from terror, for it shall not come near you.'

The word of the Lord.

Thanks be to God.

RESPONSORIAL PSALM *Psalm 30(29):2, 4. 5-6. 11, 12a, 13b. R.2a*

R. I will extol you, LORD, for you have raised me up.

1 I will extol you, LORD, for you have raised me up,
and have not let my enemies rejoice over me.
O LORD, you have lifted up my soul from Sheol,
restored me to life from those who sink into the pit. R.

2 Sing psalms to the LORD, you faithful ones;
give thanks to his holy name.
His anger lasts a moment; his favour all through life.
At night come tears, but dawn brings joy. R.

3 Hear, O LORD, and have mercy on me;
be my helper, O LORD.
You have changed my mourning into dancing.
O LORD my God, I will thank you for ever. R.

PRAYER

ALL STAND

Let us pray.

Almighty ever-living God,
surpass, for the honour of your name,
what you pledged to the Patriarchs by reason of their faith,
and through sacred adoption increase the children of your promise,
so that what the Saints of old never doubted would come to pass
your Church may now see in great part fulfilled.
Through Christ our Lord. **Amen.**

ALL SIT

Alternatively, other prayers may be used from among those which follow the readings that have been omitted.

FIFTH READING *Isaiah 55:1–11*

'Come to me, that your soul may live, and I will make with you an everlasting covenant.'

A reading from the Prophet Isaiah.

Thus says the LORD: 'Come, everyone who thirsts, come to the waters; and he who has no money, come, buy and eat! Come, buy wine and milk without money and without price. Why do you spend your money for that which is not bread, and your labour for that which does not satisfy? Listen diligently to me, and eat what is good, and delight yourselves in rich food. Incline your ear, and come to me; hear, that your soul may live; and I will make with you an everlasting covenant, my steadfast, sure love for David. Behold, I made him a witness to the peoples, a leader and

commander for the peoples. Behold, you shall call a nation that you do not know, and a nation that did not know you shall run to you, because of the LORD your God, and of the Holy One of Israel, for he has glorified you.
'Seek the LORD while he may be found; call upon him while he is near; let the wicked forsake his way, and the unrighteous man his thoughts; let him return to the LORD, that he may have compassion on him, and to our God, for he will abundantly pardon. For my thoughts are not your thoughts, neither are your ways my ways, declares the LORD. For as the heavens are higher than the earth, so are my ways higher than your ways and my thoughts than your thoughts.
'For as the rain and the snow come down from heaven and do not return there but water the earth, making it bring forth and sprout, giving seed to the sower and bread to the eater, so shall my word be that goes out from my mouth; it shall not return to me empty, but it shall accomplish that which I purpose, and shall succeed in the thing for which I sent it.'

The word of the Lord.
Thanks be to God.

RESPONSORIAL PSALM *Isaiah 12: 2-3. 4bcd. 5-6 R.3*

R. With joy will you draw water from the springs of salvation.

1 Behold, God is my salvation!
I will trust, and will not be afraid,
for the LORD is my strength and my praise,
and he has been my salvation.
With joy will you draw water
from the springs of salvation. R.

2 Give thanks to the LORD, invoke his name;
make known among the peoples his deeds;
proclaim that his name is exalted. R.

3 Sing to the LORD for he has wrought wonders;
let this be known through all the earth.
Shout aloud and sing praise, you who dwell in Sion,
for great in your midst is the Holy One of Israel. R.

PRAYER

ALL STAND

Let us pray.
Almighty ever-living God,
sole hope of the world,
who by the preaching of your Prophets
unveiled the mysteries of this present age,
graciously increase the longing of your people,
for only at the prompting of your grace
do the faithful progress in any kind of virtue.
Through Christ our Lord. **Amen.**

ALL SIT

SIXTH READING *Baruch 3:9-15, 32-4:4*

'Walk towards the shining light of the Lord.'

A reading from the Prophet Baruch.

Hear the commandments of life, O Israel; give ear and learn wisdom! Why is it, O Israel, why is it that you are in the land of your enemies, that you are growing old in a foreign country, that you are defiled with the dead, that you are counted among those in Hades? You have forsaken the fountain of wisdom. If you had walked in the way of God, you would be dwelling in peace for ever. Learn where there is wisdom, where there is strength, where there is understanding, that you may at the same time discern where there is length of days and life, where there is light for the eyes and peace. Who has found her place? And who has entered her storehouses? But he who knows all things knows her, he found her by his understanding. He who prepared the earth for all time filled it with four-footed creatures; he who sends forth the light, and it goes, called it, and it obeyed him in fear; the stars shone in their watches and were glad; he called them, and they said, 'Here we are!' They shone with gladness for him who made them. This is our God; no other can be compared to him! He found the whole way to knowledge and gave her to Jacob his servant and to Israel whom he loved. Afterwards she appeared upon earth and lived among humans.

This is the book of the commandments of God and the law that endures for ever. All who hold her fast will live, and those who forsake her will die. Turn, O Jacob, and take her; walk towards the shining of her light. Do not give your glory to another or your advantages to an alien people. Happy are we, O Israel, for we know what is pleasing to God.

The word of the Lord.
Thanks be to God.

RESPONSORIAL PSALM *Psalm 19(18):8. 9. 10. 11. R. John 6:68c*

R. O Lord, you have the words of eternal life.

1 The law of the Lord is perfect;
it revives the soul.
The decrees of the Lord are steadfast;
they give wisdom to the simple. R.

2 The precepts of the Lord are right;
they gladden the heart.
The command of the Lord is clear;
it gives light to the eyes. R.

3 The fear of the Lord is pure,
abiding for ever.
The judgements of the Lord are true;
they are, all of them, just. R.

4 They are more to be desired than gold,
than quantities of gold.
And sweeter are they than honey,
than honey flowing from the comb. R.

PRAYER

ALL STAND

Let us pray.
O God, who constantly increase your Church
by your call to the nations,
graciously grant
to those you wash clean in the waters of Baptism
the assurance of your unfailing protection.
Through Christ our Lord. **Amen.**

ALL SIT

SEVENTH READING *Ezekiel 36:16-17a, 18-28*

'I will sprinkle clean water on you and I will give you a new heart.'

A reading from the Prophet Ezekiel.

The word of the LORD came to me: 'Son of man, when the house of Israel lived in their own land, they defiled it by their ways and their deeds. So I poured out my wrath upon them for the blood that they had shed in the land, for the idols with which they had defiled it. I scattered them among the nations, and they were dispersed through the countries. In accordance with their ways and their deeds I judged them. But when they came to the nations, wherever they came, they profaned my holy name, in that people said of them, "These are the people of the Lord, and yet they had to go out of his land." But I had concern for my holy name, which the house of Israel had profaned among the nations to which they came.

'Therefore say to the house of Israel, Thus says the Lord GOD: It is not for your sake, O house of Israel, that I am about to act, but for the sake of my holy name, which you have profaned among the nations to which you came. And I will vindicate the holiness of my great name, which has been profaned among the nations, and which you have profaned among them. And the nations will know that I am the LORD, declares the Lord GOD, when through you I vindicate my holiness before their eyes. I will take you from the nations and gather you from all the countries, and bring you into your own land. I will sprinkle clean water on you, and you shall be clean from all your uncleannesses, and from all your idols I will cleanse you. And I will give you a new heart, and a new spirit I will put within you. And I will remove the heart of stone from your flesh and give you a heart of flesh. And I will put my Spirit within you, and cause you to walk in my statutes and be careful to obey my rules. You shall dwell in the land that I gave to your fathers, and you shall be my people, and I will be your God.

The word of the Lord.
Thanks be to God.

RESPONSORIAL PSALM *Psalms 42(41):3. 5b-d. Psalm 43(42):3. 4. R.42(41):2*

If a baptism takes place the Responsorial Psalm which follows the Fifth Reading is used, or Psalm 50 (see below)

R. Like the deer that yearns for running streams,
so my soul is yearning for you, my God.

1 My soul is thirsting for God,
the living God;
when can I enter and appear
before the face of God? R.

2 For I would go to the place
of your wondrous tent,
all the way to the house of God,
amid cries of gladness and thanksgiving. R.

3 O send forth your light and your truth;
they will guide me on.
They will bring me to your holy mountain,
to the place where you dwell. R.

4 And I will come to the altar of God,
to God, my joy and gladness.
To you will I give thanks on the harp,
O God, my God. R.

When Baptism is celebrated, the Responsorial Psalm after the Fifth Reading (Isaiah 12), as above, may be used; or the following:

OR: *Psalm 51(50):12-13. 14-15. 18-19. R.12a*

R. Create a pure heart for me, O God.

1 Create a pure heart for me, O God;
renew a steadfast spirit within me.
Do not cast me away from your presence;
take not your holy spirit from me. R.

2 Restore in me the joy of your salvation;
sustain in me a willing spirit.
I will teach transgressors your ways,
that sinners may return to you. R.

3 For in sacrifice you take no delight;
burnt offering from me would not please you.
My sacrifice to God, a broken spirit:
a broken and humbled heart,
you will not spurn, O God. R.

PRAYER

ALL STAND

Let us pray.

O God of unchanging power and eternal light,
look with favour on the wondrous mystery of the whole Church
and serenely accomplish the work of human salvation,
which you planned from all eternity;
may the whole world know and see
that what was cast down is raised up,
what had become old is made new,
and all things are restored to integrity through Christ,
just as by him they came into being.
Who lives and reigns for ever and ever. **Amen.**

or

O God, who by the pages of both Testaments
instruct and prepare us to celebrate the Paschal Mystery,
grant that we may comprehend your mercy,
so that the gifts we receive from you this night
may confirm our hope of the gifts to come.
Through Christ our Lord. **Amen.**

GLORIA

▷ *Music p 316*

After the last reading from the Old Testament with its Responsorial Psalm and its prayer, the altar candles are lit, and the Priest intones the hymn Gloria in excelsis Deo (Glory to God in the highest), which is taken up by all, while bells are rung, according to local custom.

COLLECT

Let us pray.

O God, who make this most sacred night radiant
with the glory of the Lord's Resurrection,
stir up in your Church a spirit of adoption,
so that, renewed in body and mind,
we may render you undivided service.
Through our Lord Jesus Christ, your Son,
who lives and reigns with you in the unity of the Holy Spirit,
God, for ever and ever. **Amen.**

ALL SIT

EPISTLE *Romans 6:3–11*

'Christ, being raised from the dead, will never die again.'

A reading from the Letter of Saint Paul to the Romans.

Brothers and sisters: Do you not know that all of us who have been baptised into Christ Jesus were baptised into his death? We were buried, therefore, with him by baptism into death in order that, just as Christ was raised from the dead by the glory of the Father, we too might walk in newness of life.

For if we have been united with him in a death like his, we shall certainly be united with him in a resurrection like his. We know that our old self was crucified with him in order that the body of sin might be brought to nothing, so that we would no longer be enslaved to sin. For one who has died has been set free from sin. Now if we have died with Christ, we believe that we will also live with him. We know that Christ, being raised from the dead, will never die again; death no longer has dominion over him. For the death he died he died to sin, once for all, but the life he lives he lives to God. So you also must consider yourselves dead to sin and alive to God in Christ Jesus.

The word of the Lord.
Thanks be to God.

After the Epistle has been read, all rise, then the Priest solemnly intones the 'Alleluia' three times, raising his voice by a step each time, with all repeating it. If necessary, the psalmist intones the Alleluia.

ALL STAND

RESPONSORIAL PSALM AND GOSPEL ACCLAMATION *Psalm 118(117):1-2. 16-17. 22-23.*

R. Alleluia. Alleluia. Alleluia.

1 Give praise to the LORD, for he is good;
his mercy endures for ever.
Let the house of Israel say,
'His mercy endures for ever.' R.

2 The LORD's right hand is exalted.
The LORD's right hand has done mighty deeds.
I shall not die, I shall live
and recount the deeds of the LORD. R.

3 The stone that the builders rejected
has become the cornerstone.
By the LORD has this been done,
a marvel in our eyes. R.

GOSPEL *Luke 24:1–12*

The Lord be with you.
And with your spirit.

A reading from the holy Gospel according to Luke.
Glory to you, O Lord.

'Why do you seek the living among the dead?'

On the first day of the week, at early dawn, the women went to the tomb, taking the spices they had prepared. And they found the stone rolled away from the tomb, but when they went in they did not find the body of the Lord Jesus. While they were perplexed about this, behold, two men stood by them in dazzling apparel. And as they were frightened and bowed their faces to the ground, the men said to them, 'Why do you seek the living among the dead? He is not here, but has risen. Remember how he told you, while he was still in Galilee, that the Son of Man must be delivered into the hands of sinful men and be crucified and on the third day rise.' And they remembered his words, and returning from the tomb they told all these things to the Eleven and to all the rest. Now it was Mary Magdalene and Joanna and Mary the mother of James and the other women with them who told these things to the Apostles, but these words seemed to them an idle tale, and they did not believe them. But Peter rose and ran to the tomb; stooping and looking in, he saw the linen cloths by themselves; and he went home marvelling at what had happened.

The Gospel of the Lord.
Praise to you, Lord Jesus Christ.

HOMILY

THE BAPTISMAL LITURGY

37 *After the Homily the Baptismal Liturgy begins. The Priest goes with the ministers to the baptismal font, if this can be seen by the faithful. Otherwise a vessel with water is placed in the sanctuary.*

38 *Catechumens, if there are any, are called forward and presented by their godparents in front of the assembled Church or, if they are small children, are carried by their parents and godparents.*

39 *Then, if there is to be a procession to the baptistery or to the font, it forms immediately.*
A minister with the paschal candle leads off, and those to be baptized follow him with their godparents, then the ministers, the Deacon, and the Priest.
During the procession, the Litany (n 43) is sung.

▷ *page 243*

When the Litany is completed, the Priest gives the address (n 40).

40 *If, however, the Baptismal Liturgy takes place in the sanctuary, the Priest immediately makes an introductory statement in these or similar words.*

INTRODUCTORY STATEMENT

If there are candidates to be baptized:
Dearly beloved,
with one heart and one soul, let us by our prayers
come to the aid of these our brothers and sisters in their blessed hope,
so that, as they approach the font of rebirth,
the almighty Father may bestow on them
all his merciful help.

If the font is to be blessed, but no one is to be baptized:
Dearly beloved,
let us humbly invoke upon this font
the grace of God the almighty Father,
that those who from it are born anew
may be numbered among the children of adoption in Christ.

LITANY OF SAINTS

41 *The Litany is sung by two cantors, with all standing (because it is Easter Time) and responding. If, however, there is to be a procession of some length to the baptistery, the Litany is sung during the procession; in this case, those to be baptized are called forward before the procession begins, and the procession takes place led by the paschal candle, followed by the catechumens with their godparents, then the ministers, the Deacon, and the Priest. The address should occur before the Blessing of Water.*

42 *If no one is to be baptized and the font is not to be blessed, the Litany is omitted, and the Blessing of Water (n 54) takes place at once.*

▷ *page 246*

43 *In the Litany the names of some Saints may be added, especially the Titular Saint of the church and the Patron Saints of the place and of those to be baptized.*

Cantors: All:

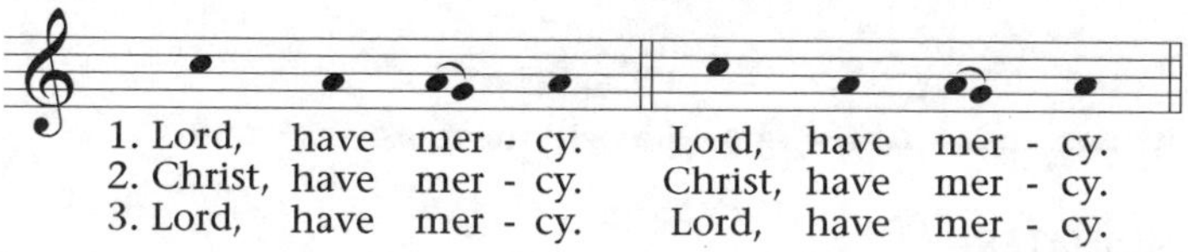
1. Lord, have mer - cy. Lord, have mer - cy.
2. Christ, have mer - cy. Christ, have mer - cy.
3. Lord, have mer - cy. Lord, have mer - cy.

Cantors: All:

1. Holy Mary, Mother of God, pray for us.
2. Saint Mich - ael, pray for us.

Other verses follow, with the same response.

Cantors: All:

Lord, be mer - ci - ful, Lord, de - li - ver us we pray.

From all evil	**Lord, deliver us, we pray.**
From every sin	**Lord, deliver us, we pray.**
From everlasting death	**Lord, deliver us, we pray.**
By your Incarnation	**Lord, deliver us, we pray.**
By your Death and Resurrection	**Lord, deliver us, we pray.**
By the outpouring of the Holy Spirit	**Lord, deliver us, we pray.**

Cantors: All:

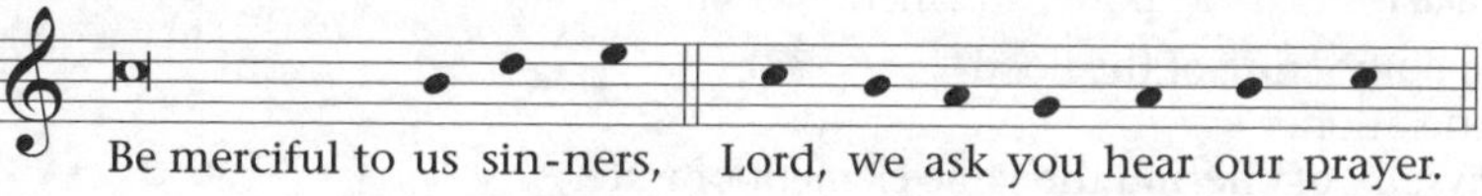
Be merciful to us sin-ners, Lord, we ask you hear our prayer.

If there are candidates to be baptized:
Bring these chosen ones to new birth
through the grace of baptism, **Lord, we ask you, hear our prayer.**

or

If there is no one to be baptized:
Makes this font holy by your grace
for the new birth of your children, **Lord, we ask you, hear our prayer.**

Jesus, Son of the living God, **Lord, we ask you, hear our prayer.**

Cantors: All:

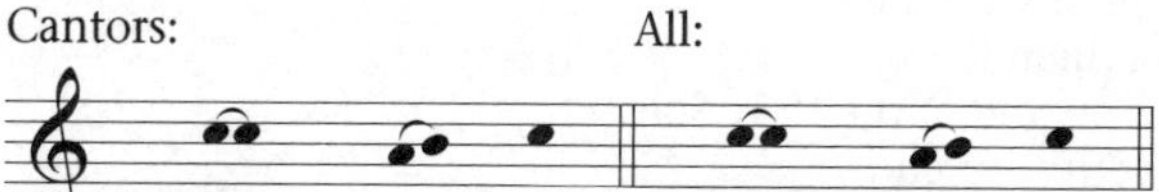
Christ, hear us. Christ, hear us.

Cantors: All:

Christ, gra - cious - ly hear us.
Christ, gra - cious - ly hear us.

PRAYER OVER THE CANDIDATES

If there are candidates to be baptized, the Priest, with hands extended, says the following prayer:

Almighty ever-living God,
be present by the mysteries of your great love
and send forth the spirit of adoption
to create the new peoples
brought to birth for you in the font of Baptism,
so that what is to be carried out by our humble service
may be brought to fulfilment by your mighty power.
Through Christ our Lord. **Amen.**

BLESSING OF BAPTISMAL WATER

46 *The Priest then blesses the baptismal water, saying the following prayer:*

O God, who by invisible power
accomplish a wondrous effect
through sacramental signs
and who in many ways have prepared water, your creation,
to show forth the grace of Baptism;

O God, whose Spirit
in the first moments of the world's creation
hovered over the waters,
so that the very substance of water
would even then take to itself the power to sanctify;

O God, who by the outpouring of the flood
foreshadowed regeneration,
so that from the mystery of one and the same element of water
would come an end to vice and a beginning of virtue;

O God, who caused the children of Abraham
to pass dry-shod through the Red Sea,
so that the chosen people,
set free from slavery to Pharaoh,
would prefigure the people of the baptized;

O God, whose Son,
baptized by John in the waters of the Jordan,
was anointed with the Holy Spirit,
and, as he hung upon the Cross,
gave forth water from his side along with blood,
and after his Resurrection, commanded his disciples:
'Go forth, teach all nations, baptizing them
in the name of the Father and of the Son and of the Holy Spirit',
look now, we pray, upon the face of your Church
and graciously unseal for her the fountain of Baptism.

May this water receive by the Holy Spirit
the grace of your Only Begotten Son,
so that human nature, created in your image
and washed clean through the Sacrament of Baptism
from all the squalor of the life of old,
may be found worthy to rise to the life of newborn children
through water and the Holy Spirit.

And, if appropriate, lowering the paschal candle into the water either once or three times, he continues:

May the power of the Holy Spirit,
O Lord, we pray,
come down through your Son
into the fullness of this font,

and, holding the candle in the water, he continues:

so that all who have been buried with Christ
by Baptism into death
may rise again to life with him.
Who lives and reigns with you in the unity of the Holy Spirit,
God, for ever and ever. **Amen.**

47 *Then the candle is lifted out of the water, as the people acclaim:*

All:

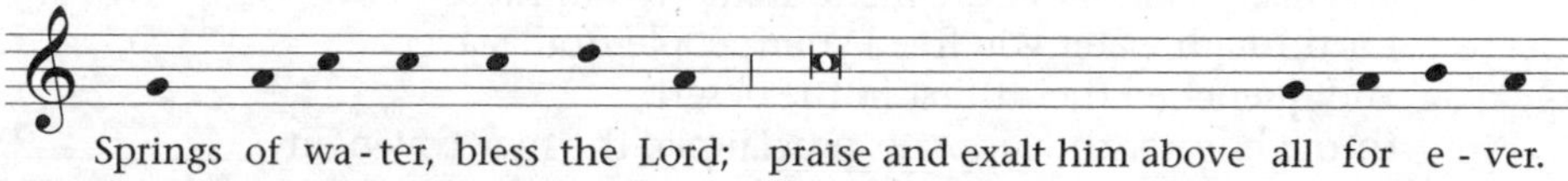

Springs of wa - ter, bless the Lord; praise and exalt him above all for e - ver.

RENUNCIATION OF SIN BY BAPTISMAL CANDIDATES

48 *After the blessing of baptismal water and the acclamation of the people, the Priest, standing, puts the prescribed questions to the adults and the parents or godparents of the children, as is set out in the respective Rites of the Roman Ritual, in order for them to make the required renunciation.*

49 *Where many are to be baptized on this night, it is possible to arrange the rite so that, immediately after the response of those to be baptized and of the godparents and the parents, the Celebrant asks for and receives the renewal of baptismal promises of all present.*
In this case, the profession of faith on page 247 is used ▷ *page 247*

50 *When the interrogation is concluded, the Priest baptizes the elect.*

51 *After the Baptism a white garment is given. Then the Priest or Deacon receives the paschal candle and the candles of the newly baptized are lighted.*

52 *Afterwards, unless the baptismal washing and other explanatory rites have occurred in the sanctuary, a procession returns to the sanctuary, formed as before, with the newly baptized carrying lighted candles. During this procession, the baptismal canticle Vidi Aquam (I saw water) or other appropriate chant is sung (no.56).*

53 *If adults have been baptized, the Bishop or, in his absence, the Priest who has conferred Baptism, should at once administer the Sacrament of Confirmation to them in the sanctuary.*

BLESSING OF WATER

54 *If no one present is to be baptized and the font is not to be blessed, the Priest introduces the faithful to the blessing of water, saying:*

Priest: Dear brothers and sisters,
let us humbly beseech the Lord our God
to bless this water he has created,
which will be sprinkled upon us
as a memorial of our Baptism.
May he graciously renew us,
that we may remain faithful to the Spirit
whom we have received.

And after a brief pause in silence, he proclaims the following prayer:

Priest: Lord our God,
in your mercy be present to your people
who keep vigil on this most sacred night,
and, for us who recall the wondrous work of our creation
and the still greater work of our redemption,
graciously bless this water.
For you created water to make the fields fruitful
and to refresh and cleanse our bodies.
You also made water the instrument of your mercy:
for through water you freed your people from slavery
and quenched their thirst in the desert;
through water the Prophets proclaimed the new covenant
you were to enter upon with the human race;
and last of all,
through water, which Christ made holy in the Jordan,
you have renewed our corrupted nature
in the bath of regeneration.
Therefore, may this water be for us
a memorial of the Baptism we have received,
and grant that we may share
in the gladness of our brothers and sisters,
who at Easter have received their Baptism.
Through Christ our Lord.

All: **Amen.**

RENEWAL OF BAPTISMAL PROMISES

55 *When the Rite of Baptism (and Confirmation) has been completed or, if this has not taken place, after the blessing of water, all stand, holding lighted candles in their hands, and renew the promise of baptismal faith, unless this has already been done together with those to be baptized (cf no* **49***).*

The Priest addresses the faithful in these or similar words:

Priest: Dear brethren (brothers and sisters), through the Paschal Mystery
we have been buried with Christ in Baptism,
so that we may walk with him in newness of life.
And so, now that our Lenten observance is concluded,
let us renew the promises of Holy Baptism,
by which we once renounced Satan and his works
and promised to serve God in the holy Catholic Church.
And so I ask you:

Priest: Do you renounce Satan?
All: **I do.**

Priest: And all his works?
All: **I do.**

Priest: And all his empty show?
All: **I do.**

Priest: Do you renounce sin,
so as to live in the freedom of the children of God?
All: **I do.**

Priest: Do you renounce the lure of evil,
so that sin may have no mastery over you?
All: **I do.**

Priest: Do you renounce Satan,
the author and prince of sin?
All: **I do.**

If the situation warrants, this second formula may be adapted by Conferences of Bishops according to local needs.

Then the Priest continues:

Priest: Do you believe in God,
the Father almighty,
Creator of heaven and earth?
All: **I do.**

Priest: Do you believe in Jesus Christ, his only Son, our Lord,
who was born of the Virgin Mary,
suffered death and was buried,
rose again from the dead
and is seated at the right hand of the Father?
All: **I do.**

Priest: Do you believe in the Holy Spirit,
the holy Catholic Church,
the communion of saints,
the forgiveness of sins,
the resurrection of the body,
and life everlasting?
All: **I do.**

And the Priest concludes:

Priest: And may almighty God, the Father of our Lord Jesus Christ,
who has given us new birth by water and the Holy Spirit
and bestowed on us forgiveness of our sins,
keep us by his grace,
in Christ Jesus our Lord,
for eternal life.
All: **Amen.**

SPRINKLING WITH BAPTISMAL WATER

56 *The Priest sprinkles the people with the blessed water, while all sing the following antiphon, or another chant that is baptismal in character.*

Antiphon
I saw water flowing from the Temple,
from its right-hand side, alleluia;
and all to whom this water came were saved
and shall say: Alleluia, alleluia.

PRAYER OF THE FAITHFUL

The Priest returns to the chair.

The Profession of Faith is omitted and the Prayer of the Faithful begins immediately in which the newly baptized participate for the first time.

▷ *page 13*

FOURTH PART: LITURGY OF THE EUCHARIST

The Priest goes to the altar and begins the Liturgy of the Eucharist in the usual way.

It is desirable that the bread and wine be brought forward by the newly baptized or, if they are children, by their parents or godparents.

▷ *page 14*

PRAYER OVER THE OFFERINGS

Accept, we ask, O Lord,
the prayers of your people
with the sacrificial offerings,
that what has begun in the paschal mysteries
may, by the working of your power,
bring us to the healing of eternity.
Through Christ our Lord. **Amen.**

EUCHARISTIC PRAYER

Preface I of Easter: The Paschal Mystery (...on this night above all...), p 74.

When the Roman Canon is used, the proper form of the Hanc igitur (Therefore, Lord, we pray) is said, p 20.
If there has been a baptism, proper forms of certain sections are used in Eucharistic Prayers I, II and III.

EUCHARISTIC PRAYER I

Memento, Domine
(Remember, Lord, your servants):

Remember, Lord, your servants
who have presented your chosen ones
for the holy grace of your Baptism,

Here the names of the godparents are read out.

and all gathered here,
whose faith and devotion are known to you...

EUCHARISTIC PRAYER II

After the words 'and all the clergy,' the following is added:

Remember also, Lord, the newly baptized
who, through Baptism (and Confirmation),
have today been joined to your family,
that they may follow Christ, your Son,
with a generous heart and a willing spirit.
Remember also our brothers and sisters...

EUCHARISTIC PRAYER III

After the words 'whom you have summoned before you', the following is added:

Strengthen, we pray, in their holy purpose
your servants who by the cleansing waters of rebirth
(and the bestowing of the Holy Spirit)
have today been joined to your people
and grant that they may always walk in newness of life.
In your compassion, O merciful Father,
gather to yourself all your children
scattered throughout the earth.
To our departed brothers and sisters...

COMMUNION RITE

Before the 'Ecce Agnus Dei' ('Behold the Lamb of God'), the Priest may briefly address the newly baptized about receiving their first Communion and about the excellence of this great mystery, which is the climax of Initiation and the centre of the whole of Christian life.

It is desirable that the newly baptized receive Holy Communion under both kinds, together with their godfathers, godmothers, and Catholic parents and spouses, as well as their lay catechists.

Communion Antiphon *1 Corinthians 5:7–8*

Christ our Passover has been sacrificed;
therefore let us keep the feast
with the unleavened bread of purity and truth, alleluia. ▷ page 58

Psalm 117 may appropriately be sung.

Prayer after Communion

Pour out on us, O Lord, the Spirit of your love,
and in your kindness make those you have nourished
by this paschal Sacrament
one in mind and heart.
Through Christ our Lord. **Amen.**

CONCLUDING RITES

SOLEMN BLESSING

Priest: May almighty God bless you
through today's Easter Solemnity
and, in his compassion,
defend you from every assault of sin.

All: **Amen.**

Priest: And may he, who restores you to eternal life
in the Resurrection of his Only Begotten Son,
endow you with the prize of immortality.

All: **Amen.**

Priest: Now that the days of the Lord's Passion have drawn to a close,
may you who celebrate the gladness of the Paschal Feast
come with Christ's help, and exulting in spirit,
to those feasts that are celebrated in eternal joy.

All: **Amen.**

Priest: And may the blessing of almighty God,
the Father, and the Son, ✠ and the Holy Spirit,
come down on you and remain with you for ever.

All: **Amen.**

The final blessing formula from the Rite of Baptism of Adults or of Children may also be used, according to circumstances.

DISMISSAL

The following dismissal is used on Easter Sunday, the Octave of Easter, and in the Mass during the day on Pentecost Sunday.

Deacon/Priest:

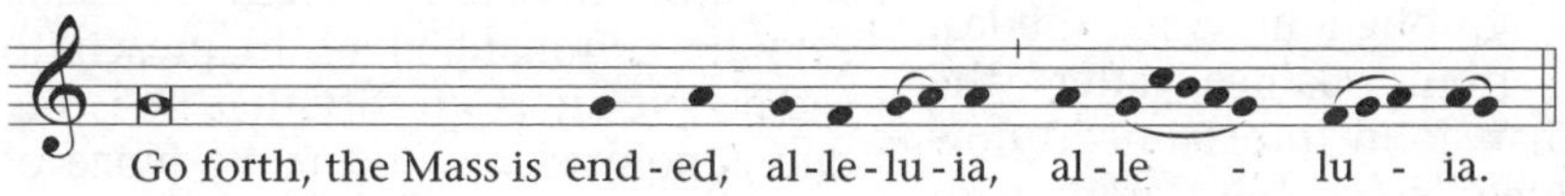
Go forth, the Mass is end - ed, al - le - lu - ia, al - le - lu - ia.

or

Deacon/Priest:

Go in peace, al - le - lu - ia, al - le - lu - ia.

All:

Thanks be to God, al - le - lu - ia, al - le - lu - ia.

EASTER SUNDAY — MASS DURING THE DAY

ENTRANCE ANTIPHON *cf Psalm 138:18, 5–6*

I have risen, and I am with you still, alleluia.
You have laid your hand upon me, alleluia.
Too wonderful for me, this knowledge, alleluia, alleluia.

or *Luke 24:34; cf Revelation 1:6*

The Lord is truly risen, alleluia.
To him be glory and power
for all the ages of eternity, alleluia, alleluia.

▷ *page 7*

COLLECT

O God, who on this day,
through your Only Begotten Son,
have conquered death
and unlocked for us the path to eternity,
grant, we pray, that we who keep
the solemnity of the Lord's Resurrection
may, through the renewal brought by your Spirit,
rise up in the light of life.
Through our Lord Jesus Christ, your Son,
who lives and reigns with you in the unity of the Holy Spirit,
God, for ever and ever. **Amen.**

FIRST READING *Acts 10:34a, 37-43*

'We ate and drank with him after he rose from the dead.'

A reading from the Acts of the Apostles.

In those days: Peter opened his mouth and said: 'You yourselves know what happened throughout all Judea, beginning from Galilee after the baptism that John proclaimed: how God anointed Jesus of Nazareth with the Holy Spirit and with power. He went about doing good and healing all who were oppressed by the devil, for God was with him. And we are witnesses of all that he did both in the country of the Jews and in Jerusalem. They put him to death by hanging him on a tree, but God raised him on the third day and caused him to appear, not to all the people but to us who had been chosen by God as witnesses, who ate and drank with him after he rose from the dead. And he commanded us to preach to the people and to testify that he is the one appointed by God to be judge of the living and the dead. To him all the prophets bear witness that everyone who believes in him receives forgiveness of sins through his name.'

The word of the Lord.
Thanks be to God.

RESPONSORIAL PSALM *Psalm 118(117):1-2. 16-17. 22-23. R.24*

R. **This is the day the Lord has made;**
let us rejoice in it and be glad. *or* **Alleluia.**

1 Give praise to the **Lord**, for he is good;
his mercy endures for ever.
Let the house of Israel say,
'His mercy endures for ever.' R.

2 The **Lord**'s right hand is exalted.
The **Lord**'s right hand has done
mighty deeds.
I shall not die, I shall live
and recount the deeds of the **Lord**. R.

3 The stone that the builders rejected
has become the cornerstone.
By the **Lord** has this been done,
a marvel in our eyes. R.

SECOND READING *Colossians 3:1–4*

'Seek the things that are above, where Christ is.'

A reading from the Letter of Saint Paul to the Colossians.

Brothers and sisters: If you have been raised with Christ, seek the things that are above, where Christ is, seated at the right hand of God Set your minds on things that are above, not on things that are on earth. For you have died, and your life is hidden with Christ in God. When Christ who is your life appears, then you also will appear with him in glory.

The word of the Lord.
Thanks be to God.

ALTERNATIVE SECOND READING

1 Corinthians 5:6b–8

'Cleanse out the old leaven that you may be a new lump.'

A reading from the First Letter of Saint Paul to the Corinthians.

Brothers and sisters: Do you not know that a little leaven leavens the whole lump? Cleanse out the old leaven that you may be a new lump, as you really are unleavened. For Christ, our Passover lamb, has been sacrificed. Let us therefore celebrate the festival, not with the old leaven, the leaven of malice and evil, but with the unleavened bread of sincerity and truth.

The word of the Lord.
Thanks be to God.

SEQUENCE

The Sequence is said or sung at all Masses.

Christians, to the Paschal Victim offer sacrifice and praise.
The sheep are ransomed by the Lamb;
and Christ, the undefiled,
hath sinners to his Father reconciled.
Death with life contended: combat strangely ended!
Life's own Champion, slain, yet lives to reign.
Tell us, Mary: say what thou didst see upon the way.
The tomb the Living did enclose;
I saw Christ's glory as he rose!
The angels there attesting;
shroud with grave-clothes resting.
Christ, my hope, has risen: he goes before you into Galilee.
That Christ is truly risen from the dead we know.
Victorious king, thy mercy show!

ACCLAMATION BEFORE THE GOSPEL *1 Corinthians 5:7b-8a*

Alleluia, alleluia.
Christ, our Passover lamb, has been sacrificed;
let us therefore celebrate the festival in the Lord.
Alleluia.

Alternative Gospel Readings

As an alternative to the Gospel reading below, the Gospel of the Mass of the Easter Vigil may be read, p 241.
At an evening Mass, Luke 24:13–35 may be used as an alternative, see below.

GOSPEL *John 20:1–9*

The Lord be with you.
And with your spirit.

A reading from the holy Gospel according to John.
Glory to you, O Lord.

'He must rise from the dead.'

On the first day of the week Mary Magdalene came to the tomb early, while it was still dark, and saw that the stone had been taken away from the tomb. So she ran and went to Simon Peter and the other disciple, the one whom Jesus loved, and said to them, 'They have taken the Lord out of the tomb, and we do not know where they have laid him.' So Peter went out with the other disciple, and they were going towards the tomb. Both of them were running together, but the other disciple outran Peter and reached the tomb first. And stooping to look in, he saw the linen cloths lying there, but he did not go in. Then Simon Peter came, following him, and went into the tomb. He saw the linen cloths lying there, and the face cloth, which had been on the head of Jesus, not lying with the linen cloths but folded up in a place by itself. Then the other disciple, who had reached the tomb first, also went in, and he saw and believed; for as yet they did not understand the Scripture, that he must rise from the dead.

The Gospel of the Lord.
Praise to you, Lord Jesus Christ.

ALTERNATIVE GOSPEL FOR EVENING MASS *Luke 24:13–35*

The Lord be with you.
And with your spirit.

A reading from the holy Gospel according to Luke.
Glory to you, O Lord.

'He was known to them in the breaking of the bread.'

On the first day of the week, two of the disciples of Jesus were going to a village named Emmaus, about seven miles from Jerusalem, and they were talking with each other about all these things that had happened. While they were talking and discussing together, Jesus himself drew near and went with them. But their eyes were kept from recognising him. And he said to them, 'What is this conversation that you are holding with each other as you walk?' And they stood still, looking sad. Then one of them, named Cleopas, answered him, 'Are you the only visitor to Jerusalem who does not know the things that have happened there in these days?' And he said to them, 'What things?' And they said to him, 'Concerning Jesus of Nazareth, a man who was a prophet mighty in deed and word before God and all the people, and how our chief priests and rulers delivered him up to be condemned to death, and crucified him. But we had hoped that he was the one to redeem Israel. Yes, and besides all this, it is now the third day since these things happened. Moreover, some women of our company amazed us. They were at the tomb early in the morning, and when they did not find his body, they came back saying that they had even seen a vision of angels, who said that he was alive. Some of those who were with us went to the tomb and found it just as the women had said, but him they did not see.' And he said to them, 'O foolish ones, and slow of heart to believe all that the prophets have spoken! Was it not necessary that the Christ should suffer these things and enter into his glory?' And beginning with Moses and all the Prophets, he interpreted to them in all the Scriptures the things concerning himself.

So they drew near to the village to which they were going. He acted as if he were going farther, but they urged him strongly, saying, 'Stay with us, for it is towards evening and the day is now far spent.' So he went in to stay with them. When he was at table with them, he took the bread, and blessed, and broke it, and gave it to them. And their eyes were opened, and they recognised him. And he vanished from their sight. They said to each other, 'Did not our hearts burn within us while he talked to us on the road, while he opened to us the Scriptures?' And they rose that same hour and returned to Jerusalem. And they found the Eleven and those who were with them gathered together, saying, 'The Lord has risen indeed, and has appeared to Simon!' Then they told what had happened on the road, and how he was known to them in the breaking of the bread.

The Gospel of the Lord.
Praise to you, Lord Jesus Christ.

▷ *page 11*

The Profession of Faith is said. However, in Easter Sunday Masses which are celebrated with a congregation, the rite of renewal of baptismal promises may take place after the homily, according to the text used at the Easter Vigil (p 251). In that case the Profession of Faith is omitted.

PRAYER OVER THE OFFERINGS

Exultant with paschal gladness, O Lord,
we offer the sacrifice
by which your Church
is wondrously reborn and nourished.
Through Christ our Lord. **Amen.**

▷ *page 15*

Preface I of Easter, The Paschal Mystery, p 74. When the Roman Canon is used, the proper forms of the 'Communicantes '(In communion with those) and 'Hanc igitur' (Therefore, Lord, we pray) are said, p 20.

COMMUNION ANTIPHON *1 Corinthians 5:7–8*

Christ our Passover has been sacrificed, alleluia;
therefore let us keep the feast with the unleavened bread
of purity and truth, alleluia, alleluia.

▷ page 58

PRAYER AFTER COMMUNION

Look upon your Church, O God,
with unfailing love and favour,
so that, renewed by the paschal mysteries,
she may come to the glory of the resurrection.
Through Christ our Lord. **Amen.**

A solemn blessing may be used.

▷ page 59

DISMISSAL

▷ Music p 251

Deacon or Priest: Go forth, the Mass is ended, alleluia, alleluia.
or
Deacon or Priest: Go in peace, alleluia, alleluia.
All: **Thanks be to God, alleluia, alleluia.**

SECOND SUNDAY OF EASTER

(OR OF DIVINE MERCY)

ENTRANCE ANTIPHON *1 Peter 2:2*

Like newborn infants, you must long for the pure, spiritual milk,
that in him you may grow to salvation, alleluia.

Or *4 Esdras 2:36-37*

Receive the joy of your glory, giving thanks to God,
who has called you into the heavenly kingdom, alleluia.

▷ page 7

COLLECT

God of everlasting mercy,
who, in the very recurrence of the paschal feast
kindle the faith of the people you have made your own,
increase, we pray, the grace you have bestowed,
that all may grasp and rightly understand
in what font they have been washed,
by whose Spirit they have been reborn,
by whose Blood they have been redeemed.
Through our Lord Jesus Christ, your Son,
who lives and reigns with you in the unity of the Holy Spirit,
God, for ever and ever. **Amen.**

FIRST READING *Acts 5:12–6*

'More than ever believers were added to the Lord, multitudes of both men and women.'

A reading from the Acts of the Apostles.

Many signs and wonders were regularly done among the people by the hands of the Apostles. And they were all together in Solomon's Portico. None of the rest dared join them, but the people held them in high esteem. And more than ever believers were added to the Lord, multitudes of both men and women, so that they even carried out the sick into the streets and laid them on cots and mats, that as Peter came by at least his shadow might fall on some of them. The people also gathered from the towns round Jerusalem, bringing the sick and those afflicted with unclean spirits, and they were all healed.

The word of the Lord.

Thanks be to God.

RESPONSORIAL PSALM *Psalm 118 (117):2-4. 22-24. 25-27a. R.1*

R. Give praise to the LORD for he is good,
his mercy endures for ever.

or: **Alleluia.**

1 Let the house of Israel say,
'His mercy endures for ever.'
Let the house of Aaron say,
'His mercy endures for ever.'
Let those who fear the LORD say,
'His mercy endures for ever.' R.

2 The stone that the builders rejected
has become the cornerstone.
By the LORD has this been done,
a marvel in our eyes.
This is the day the LORD has made;
let us rejoice in it and be glad. R.

3 We beseech you, O LORD, grant salvation;
we beseech you, O LORD, grant success.
Blest is he who comes
in the name of the LORD.
We bless you from the house of the LORD;
the LORD is God, and has given us light. R.

EASTER

SECOND READING

Revelation 1:9-11a, 12-13, 17-19

'I died, and behold I am alive for evermore.'

A reading from the Book of Revelation.

I, John, your brother and partner in the tribulation and the kingdom and the patient endurance that are in Jesus, was on the island called Patmos on account of the word of God and the testimony of Jesus. I was in the Spirit on the Lord's day, and I heard behind me a loud voice like a trumpet saying, 'Write what you see in a book and send it to the seven churches.'

Then I turned to see the voice that was speaking to me, and on turning I saw

seven golden lampstands, and in the midst of the lampstands one like a son of man, clothed with a long robe and with a golden sash round his chest.
When I saw him, I fell at his feet as though dead. But he laid his right hand on me, saying, 'Fear not, I am the first and the last, and the living one. I died, and behold I am alive for evermore, and I have the keys of Death and Hades. Write therefore the things that you have seen, those that are and those that are to take place after this.'

The word of the Lord.
Thanks be to God.

ACCLAMATION BEFORE THE GOSPEL *John 20:29*

Alleluia, alleluia.
You believed, Thomas, because you have seen me, says the Lord.
Blessed are those who have not seen and yet have believed.
Alleluia.

GOSPEL *John 20:19–31*

The Lord be with you.
And with your spirit.

A reading from the holy Gospel according to John.
Glory to you, O Lord.

'Eight days later, Jesus came.'

On the evening of that day, the first day of the week, the doors being locked where the disciples were for fear of the Jews, Jesus came and stood among them and said to them, 'Peace be with you.' When he had said this, he showed them his hands and his side. Then the disciples were glad when they saw the Lord. Jesus said to them again, 'Peace be with you. As the Father has sent me, even so I am sending you.' And when he had said this, he breathed on them and said to them, 'Receive the Holy Spirit. If you forgive the sins of any, they are forgiven them; if you withhold forgiveness from any, it is withheld.'

Now Thomas, one of the Twelve, called the Twin, was not with them when Jesus came. So the other disciples told him, 'We have seen the Lord'. But he said to them, 'Unless I see in his hands the mark of the nails, and place my finger into the mark of the nails, and place my hand into his side, I will never believe.'

Eight days later, his disciples were inside again, and Thomas was with them. Although the doors were locked, Jesus came and stood among them and said, 'Peace be with you.' Then he said to Thomas, 'Put your finger here, and see my hands; and put out your hand, and place it in my side. Do not disbelieve, but believe.' Thomas answered him, 'My Lord and my God!' Jesus said to him, 'Have you believed because you have seen me? Blessed are those who have not seen and yet have believed.'

Now Jesus did many other signs in the presence of the disciples, which are not written in this book; but these are written so that you may believe that Jesus is the Christ, the Son of God, and that by believing you may have life in his name.

The Gospel of the Lord.
Praise to you, Lord Jesus Christ.

▷ *page 11*

PRAYER OVER THE OFFERINGS

Accept, O Lord, we pray,
the oblations of your people
(and of those you have brought to new birth),
that, renewed by confession of your name and by Baptism,
they may attain unending happiness.
Through Christ our Lord. **Amen.**

▷ page 15

Preface I of Easter (…on this day above all), p 74. When the Roman Canon is used, the proper forms of the Communicantes (In communion with those) and Hanc igitur (Therefore, Lord, we pray) are said, p 20.

COMMUNION ANTIPHON *Cf John 20:27*

Bring your hand and feel the place of the nails,
and do not be unbelieving but believing, alleluia.

▷ page 58

PRAYER AFTER COMMUNION

Grant, we pray, almighty God,
that our reception of this paschal Sacrament
may have a continuing effect
in our minds and hearts.
Through Christ our Lord. **Amen.**

▷ page 59

A solemn blessing may be used.

DISMISSAL

▷ Music p 251

Deacon or Priest: Go forth, the Mass is ended, alleluia, alleluia.
or
Deacon or Priest: Go in peace, alleluia, alleluia.
All: **Thanks be to God, alleluia, alleluia.**

THIRD SUNDAY OF EASTER

ENTRANCE ANTIPHON *cf Psalm 65:1–2*

Cry out with joy to God, all the earth;
O sing to the glory of his name.
O render him glorious praise, alleluia.

▷ page 7

COLLECT

May your people exult for ever, O God,
in renewed youthfulness of spirit,
so that, rejoicing now in the restored glory of our adoption,
we may look forward in confident hope
to the rejoicing of the day of resurrection.
Through our Lord Jesus Christ, your Son,
who lives and reigns with you in the unity of the Holy Spirit,
God, for ever and ever. **Amen.**

FIRST READING *Acts 5:27b-32, 40b-41*

'We are witnesses to these things, and so is the Holy Spirit.'

A reading from the Acts of the Apostles.

In those days: The high priest questioned the Apostles, saying, 'We strictly charged you not to teach in this name, yet here you have filled Jerusalem with your teaching, and you intend to bring this man's blood upon us.' But Peter and the Apostles answered, 'We must obey God rather than men. The God of our fathers raised Jesus, whom you killed by hanging him on a tree. God exalted him at his right hand as Leader and Saviour, to give repentance to Israel and forgiveness of sins. And we are witnesses to these things, and so is the Holy Spirit, whom God has given to those who obey him.'

Having called in the Apostles, the council beat them and charged them not to speak in the name of Jesus, and let them go. Then they left the presence of the council, rejoicing that they were counted worthy to suffer dishonour for the name.

The word of the Lord.
Thanks be to God.

RESPONSORIAL PSALM *Psalm 30(29):2, 4. 5-6. 11, 12a, 13b. R.2a*

R. I will extol you, LORD, for you have raised me up.

1 I will extol you, LORD, for you have raised me up,
and have not let my enemies rejoice over me.
O LORD, you have lifted up my soul from Sheol,
restored me to life from those who sink into the pit. R.

2 Sing psalms to the LORD, you faithful ones;
give thanks to his holy name.
His anger lasts a moment; his favour all through life.
At night come tears, but dawn brings joy. R.

3 Hear, O LORD, and have mercy on me;
be my helper, O LORD.
You have changed my mourning into dancing.
O LORD my God, I will thank you for ever. R.

SECOND READING *Revelation 5:11-14*

'Worthy is the Lamb who was slain, to receive power and wealth.'

A reading from the Book of Revelation.

I, John looked, and I heard around the throne and the living creatures and the elders the voice of many angels, numbering myriads of myriads and thousands of thousands, saying with a loud voice, 'Worthy is the Lamb who was slain, to receive power and wealth and wisdom and might and honour and glory and blessing!' And I heard every creature in heaven and on earth and under the earth and in the sea, and all that is in them, saying, 'To him who sits on the throne and to the Lamb be blessing and honour and glory and might for ever and ever!' And the four living creatures said, 'Amen!' and the elders fell down and worshipped.

The word of the Lord.
Thanks be to God.

ACCLAMATION BEFORE THE GOSPEL *cf Luke 24:32*

Alleluia, alleluia.
Christ is risen, who created all things
and has shown compassion on the human race.
Alleluia.

GOSPEL *John 21:1–19 Shorter form: John 21:1–14 (only read text with side line next to it).*

The Lord be with you.
And with your spirit.

A reading from the holy Gospel according to John.
Glory to you, O Lord.

'Jesus came and took the bread and gave it to them, and so with the fish.'

At that time: Jesus revealed himself again to the disciples by the Sea of Tiberias, and he revealed himself in this way. Simon Peter, Thomas (called the Twin), Nathanael of Cana in Galilee, the sons of Zebedee, and two others of his disciples were together. Simon Peter said to them, 'I am going fishing.' They said to him, 'We will go with you.' They went out and got into the boat, but that night they caught nothing.

Just as day was breaking, Jesus stood on the shore; yet the disciples did not know that it was Jesus. Jesus said to them, 'Children, do you have any fish?' They answered him, 'No.' He said to them, 'Cast the net on the right side of the boat, and you will find some.' So they cast it, and now they were not able to haul it in, because of the quantity of fish. That disciple whom Jesus loved therefore said to Peter, 'It is the Lord!' When Simon Peter heard that it was the Lord, he put on his outer garment, for he was stripped for work, and threw himself into the sea. The other disciples came in the boat, dragging the net full of fish, for they were not far from the land, but about a hundred metres off.

When they got out on land, they saw a charcoal fire in place, with fish laid out on it, and bread. Jesus said to them, 'Bring some of the fish that you have just caught.' So Simon Peter went aboard and hauled the net ashore, full of large fish, one hundred and fifty-three of them. And although there were so many, the net was not torn. Jesus said to them, 'Come and have breakfast.' Now none of the disciples dared ask him, 'Who are you?' They knew it was the Lord. Jesus came and took the bread and gave it to them, and so with the fish. This was now the third time that Jesus was revealed to the disciples after he was raised from the dead.

When they had finished breakfast, Jesus said to Simon Peter, 'Simon, son of John, do you love me more than these?' He said to him, 'Yes, Lord; you know that I love you.' He said to him, 'Feed my lambs.' He said to him a second time, 'Simon, son of John, do you love me?' He said to him, 'Yes, Lord; you know that I love you.' He said to him, 'Tend my sheep.' He said to him the third time, 'Simon, son of John, do you love me?' Peter was grieved because he said to him the third time, 'Do you love me?' and he said to him, 'Lord, you know everything; you know that I love you.'

Jesus said to him, 'Feed my sheep. Truly, truly, I say to you, when you were young, you used to dress yourself and walk wherever you wanted, but when you are old, you will stretch out your hands, and another will dress you and carry you where you do not want to go.' (This he said to show by what kind of death he was to glorify God.) And after saying this he said to him, 'Follow me.'

The Gospel of the Lord.
Praise to you, Lord Jesus Christ.

▷ page 11

PRAYER OVER THE OFFERINGS

Receive, O Lord, we pray,
these offerings of your exultant Church,
and, as you have given her cause for such great gladness,
grant also that the gifts we bring
may bear fruit in perpetual happiness.
Through Christ our Lord. **Amen.**

▷ page 15

Preface of Easter, pp 74–75.

COMMUNION ANTIPHON *Luke 24:35*

The disciples recognized the Lord Jesus
in the breaking of the bread, alleluia.

Optional for Year C: *Cf John 21:12–13*
Jesus said to his disciples: Come and eat.
And he took bread and gave it to them, alleluia.

▷ page 58

PRAYER AFTER COMMUNION

Look with kindness upon your people, O Lord,
and grant, we pray,
that those you were pleased to renew by eternal mysteries
may attain in their flesh
the incorruptible glory of the resurrection.
Through Christ our Lord. **Amen.**

A solemn blessing may be used.

▷ page 59

FOURTH SUNDAY OF EASTER

ENTRANCE ANTIPHON *cf Psalm 32:5–6*

The merciful love of the Lord fills the earth;
by the word of the Lord the heavens were made, alleluia.

▷ page 7

COLLECT

Almighty ever-living God,
lead us to a share in the joys of heaven,
so that the humble flock may reach
where the brave Shepherd has gone before.
Who lives and reigns with you in the unity of the Holy Spirit,
God, for ever and ever. **Amen.**

FIRST READING *Acts 13:14, 43b-52*

'Behold, we are turning to the Gentiles.'

A reading from the Acts of the Apostles.

In those days: Paul and Barnabas went on from Perga and came to Antioch in Pisidia. And on the Sabbath day they went into the synagogue and sat down. Many Jews and devout converts to Judaism followed Paul and Barnabas, who, as they spoke with them, urged them to continue in the grace of God.

The next Sabbath almost the whole city gathered to hear the word of the Lord. But when the Jews saw the crowds, they were filled with jealousy and began to contradict what was spoken by Paul, reviling him. And Paul and Barnabas spoke out boldly, saying, 'It was necessary that the word of God be spoken first to you. Since you thrust it aside and judge yourselves unworthy of eternal life, behold, we are turning to the Gentiles. For so the Lord has commanded us, saying, "I have made you a light for the Gentiles, that you may bring salvation to the ends of the earth."' And when the Gentiles heard this, they began rejoicing and glorifying the word of the Lord, and as many as were appointed to eternal life believed. And the word of the Lord was spreading throughout the whole region. But the Jews incited the devout women of high standing and the leading men of the city, stirred up persecution against Paul and Barnabas, and drove them out of their district. But they shook off the dust from their feet against them and went to Iconium. And the disciples were filled with joy and with the Holy Spirit.

The word of the Lord.
Thanks be to God.

RESPONSORIAL PSALM *Psalm 100 (99):1-2. 3. 5. R.3c*

R. **We are his people, the sheep of his flock.**
or **Alleluia.**

1 Cry out with joy to the LORD, all the earth
Serve the LORD with gladness.
Come before him, singing for joy. R.

2 Know that he, the LORD, is God.
He made us; we belong to him.
We are his people, the sheep of his flock. R.

3 Indeed, how good is the LORD,
eternal his merciful love.
He is faithful from age to age. R.

EASTER

SECOND READING *Revelation 7:9, 13a, 14b-17*

'The Lamb will be their shepherd and will lead them to springs of living water.'

A reading from the Book of Revelation.

I, John, looked, and behold, a great multitude that no one could number, from every nation, from all tribes and peoples and languages, standing before the throne and before the Lamb, clothed in white robes, with palm branches in their hands.

Then one of the elders addressed me, saying, 'These are the ones coming out of the great tribulation. They have washed their robes and made them white in the blood of the Lamb. Therefore they are before the throne of God, and serve him day and night in his temple; and he who sits on the throne will shelter them with his presence. They shall hunger no more, neither thirst any more; the sun shall not strike them, nor any scorching heat. For the Lamb in the midst of the throne will be their shepherd, and he will guide them to springs of living water, and God will wipe away every tear from their eyes.'

The word of the Lord.
Thanks be to God.

ACCLAMATION BEFORE THE GOSPEL *John 10:14*

Alleluia, alleluia.
I am the good shepherd, says the Lord.
I know my own sheep and my own know me.
Alleluia.

GOSPEL *John 10:27–30*

The Lord be with you.
And with your spirit.

A reading from the holy Gospel according to John.
Glory to you, O Lord.

'I give eternal life to my sheep.'

A reading from the holy Gospel according to John.

At that time: Jesus said, 'My sheep hear my voice, and I know them, and they follow me. I give them eternal life, and they will never perish, and no one will snatch them out of my hand. My Father, who has given them to me, is greater than all, and no one is able to snatch them out of the Father's hand. I and the Father are one.'

The Gospel of the Lord.
Praise to you, Lord Jesus Christ.

▷ *page 11*

PRAYER OVER THE OFFERINGS

Grant, we pray, O Lord,
that we may always find delight in these paschal mysteries,
so that the renewal constantly at work within us
may be the cause of our unending joy.
Through Christ our Lord. **Amen.**

▷ *page 15*

Preface of Easter, pp 74–75.

COMMUNION ANTIPHON

The Good Shepherd has risen,
who laid down his life for his sheep
and willingly died for his flock, alleluia.

▷ *page 58*

PRAYER AFTER COMMUNION

Look upon your flock, kind Shepherd,
and be pleased to settle in eternal pastures
the sheep you have redeemed
by the Precious Blood of your Son.
Who lives and reigns for ever and ever. **Amen.**

▷ page 59

A solemn blessing may be used.

FIFTH SUNDAY OF EASTER

ENTRANCE ANTIPHON *cf Psalm 97:1–2*

O sing a new song to the Lord,
for he has worked wonders;
in the sight of the nations
he has shown his deliverance, alleluia.

▷ page 7

COLLECT

Almighty ever-living God,
constantly accomplish the Paschal Mystery within us,
that those you were pleased to make new in Holy Baptism
may, under your protective care, bear much fruit
and come to the joys of life eternal.
Through our Lord Jesus Christ, your Son,
who lives and reigns with you in the unity of the Holy Spirit,
God, for ever and ever. **Amen.**

FIRST READING *Acts 14:21b-27*

'They declared to the Church all that God had done with them.'

A reading from the Acts of the Apostles.

In those days: Paul and Barnabas returned to Lystra and to Iconium and to Antioch, strengthening the souls of the disciples, encouraging them to continue in the faith, and saying that through many tribulations we must enter the kingdom of God. And when they had appointed elders for them in every church, with prayer and fasting they committed them to the Lord in whom they had believed. Then they passed through Pisidia and came to Pamphylia. And when they had spoken the word in Perga, they went down to Attalia, and from there they sailed to Antioch, where they had been commended to the grace of God for the work that they had fulfilled. And when they arrived and gathered the church together, they declared all that God had done with them, and how he had opened a door of faith to the Gentiles.

The word of the Lord.
Thanks be to God.

RESPONSORIAL PSALM *Psalm 145 (144):8-9. 10-11. 12-13b. R. cf. 1*

R. I will bless your name for ever, my God and king.
or **Alleluia.**

1 The LORD is kind and full of compassion,
slow to anger, abounding in mercy.
How good is the LORD to all,
compassionate to all his creatures. R.

2 All your works shall thank you, O LORD,
and all your faithful ones bless you.
They shall speak of the glory of your reign,
and declare your mighty deeds. R.

3 To make known your might to the whole human race,
and the glorious splendour of your reign.
Your kingdom is an everlasting kingdom;
your rule endures for all generations. R.

SECOND READING *Apocalypse 21:1–5a*

'God will wipe away every tear from their eyes.'

A reading from the Book of Revelation.

I, John, saw a new heaven and a new earth, for the first heaven and the first earth had passed away, and the sea was no more. And I saw the holy city, new Jerusalem, coming down out of heaven from God, prepared as a bride adorned for her husband. And I heard a loud voice from the throne saying, 'Behold, the dwelling place of God is with man. He will dwell with them, and they will be his people, and God himself will be with them as their God. He will wipe away every tear from their eyes, and death shall be no more, neither shall there be mourning, nor crying, nor pain any more, for the former things have passed away.'

And he who was seated on the throne said, 'Behold, I am making all things new.'

The word of the Lord.
Thanks be to God.

ACCLAMATION BEFORE THE GOSPEL *John 13:34*

Alleluia, alleluia.
A new commandment I give to you, says the Lord,
that you love one another, just as I have loved you.
Alleluia.

GOSPEL *John 13:31-33a, 34-35*

The Lord be with you.
And with your spirit.

A reading from the holy Gospel according to John.
Glory to you, O Lord.

'A new commandment I give to you, that you love one another.'

When Judas had gone out from the upper room, Jesus said, 'Now is the Son of Man glorified, and God is glorified in him. If God is glorified in him, God will also glorify him in himself, and glorify him at once. Little children, yet a little while I am with you.

'A new commandment I give to you, that you love one another: just as I have loved you, you also are to love one another. By this all people will know that you are my disciples, if you have love for one another.'

The Gospel of the Lord.
Praise to you, Lord Jesus Christ.

▷ page 11

PRAYER OVER THE OFFERINGS

O God, who by the wonderful exchange effected in this sacrifice
have made us partakers of the one supreme Godhead,
grant, we pray,
that, as we have come to know your truth,
we may make it ours by a worthy way of life.
Through Christ our Lord. **Amen.**

▷ page 15

Preface of Easter, pp 74–75.

COMMUNION ANTIPHON *cf John 15:1, 5*

I am the true vine and you are the branches, says the Lord.
Whoever remains in me, and I in him, bears fruit in plenty, alleluia.

▷ page 58

PRAYER AFTER COMMUNION

Graciously be present to your people, we pray, O Lord,
and lead those you have imbued with heavenly mysteries
to pass from former ways to newness of life.
Through Christ our Lord. **Amen.**

▷ page 59

A solemn blessing may be used.

SIXTH SUNDAY OF EASTER

ENTRANCE ANTIPHON *cf Isaiah 48:20*

Proclaim a joyful sound and let it be heard;
proclaim to the ends of the earth:
The Lord has freed his people, alleluia.

COLLECT

Grant, almighty God,
that we may celebrate with heartfelt devotion these days of joy,
which we keep in honour of the risen Lord,
and that what we relive in remembrance
we may always hold to in what we do.
Through our Lord Jesus Christ, your Son,
who lives and reigns with you in the unity of the Holy Spirit,
God, for ever and ever. **Amen.**

FIRST READING *Acts 15:1–2, 22–29*

'It has seemed good to the Holy Spirit and to us to lay on you no greater burden than these requirements.'

A reading from the Acts of the Apostles.

In those days: Some men came down from Judea and were teaching the brothers, 'Unless you are circumcised according to the custom of Moses, you cannot be saved.' And after Paul and Barnabas had no small dissension and debate with them, Paul and Barnabas and some of the others were appointed to go up to Jerusalem to the Apostles and the elders about this question.

Then it seemed good to the Apostles and the elders, with the whole Church, to choose men from among them and send them to Antioch with Paul and Barnabas. They sent Judas called Barsabbas, and Silas, leading men among the brothers and sisters, with the following letter: 'The brothers, both the Apostles and the elders, to the brothers and sisters who are of the Gentiles in Antioch and Syria and Cilicia, greetings. Since we have heard that some persons have gone out from us and troubled you with words, unsettling your minds, although we gave them no instructions, it has seemed good to us, having come to one accord, to choose men and send them to you with our beloved Barnabas and Paul, men who have risked their lives for the name of our Lord Jesus Christ. We have therefore sent Judas and Silas, who themselves will tell you the same things by word of mouth. For it has seemed good to the Holy Spirit and to us to lay on you no greater burden than these requirements: that you abstain from what has been sacrificed to idols, and from blood, and from what has been strangled, and from sexual immorality. If you keep yourselves from these, you will do well. Farewell.'

The word of the Lord.
Thanks be to God.

RESPONSORIAL PSALM *Psalm 67(66):2-3. 5. 6, 8. R.4*

R. **Let the peoples praise you, O God;
let all the peoples praise you.** *or* **Alleluia.**

1 May God be gracious and bless us
and let his face shed its light upon us.
So will your ways be known upon earth
and all nations learn your salvation. R.

2 Let the nations be glad and shout for joy,
with uprightness you rule the peoples;
you guide the nations on earth. R.

3 Let the peoples praise you, O God;
let all the peoples praise you.
May God still give us his blessing
that all the ends of the earth may
revere him. R.

SECOND READING *Revelation 21:10–14, 22–23*

'He showed me the holy city coming down out of heaven.'

A reading from the Book of Revelation.

The angel carried me away in the Spirit to a great, high mountain, and showed me the holy city Jerusalem coming down out of heaven from God, having the glory of God, its radiance like a most rare jewel, like a jasper, clear as crystal. It had a great, high wall, with twelve gates, and at the gates twelve angels, and on the gates the names of the twelve tribes of the sons of Israel were inscribed—on the east three gates, on the north three gates, on the south three gates, and on the west three gates. And the wall of the city had twelve foundations, and on them were the twelve names of the twelve Apostles of the Lamb.

And I saw no temple in the city, for its temple is the Lord God the Almighty and the Lamb. And the city has no need of sun or moon to shine on it, for the glory of God gives it light, and its lamp is the Lamb.

The word of the Lord.
Thanks be to God.

ACCLAMATION BEFORE THE GOSPEL *John 14:23*

Alleluia, alleluia.
If anyone loves me, he will keep my word, says the Lord,
and my Father will love him, and we will come to him.
Alleluia.

GOSPEL *John 14:23–29*

The Lord be with you.
And with your spirit.

A reading from the holy Gospel according to John.
Glory to you, O Lord.

'The Holy Spirit will bring to your remembrance all that I have said to you.'

At that time: Jesus said to his disciples, 'If anyone loves me, he will keep my word, and my Father will love him, and we will come to him and make our home with him. Whoever does not love me does not keep my words. And the word that you hear is not mine but the Father's who sent me.

'These things I have spoken to you while I am still with you. But the Helper, the Holy Spirit, whom the Father will send in my name, he will teach you all things and bring to your remembrance all that I have said to you. Peace I leave with you; my peace I give to you. Not as the world gives do I give to you. Let not your hearts be troubled, neither let them be afraid. You heard me say to you, "I am going away, and I will come to you." If you loved me, you would have rejoiced, because I am going to the Father, for the Father is greater than I. And now I have told you before it takes place, so that when it does take place you may believe.'

The Gospel of the Lord.
Praise to you, Lord Jesus Christ.

▷ *page 11*

PRAYER OVER THE OFFERINGS

May our prayers rise up to you, O Lord,
together with the sacrificial offerings,
so that, purified by your graciousness,
we may be conformed to the mysteries of your mighty love.
Through Christ our Lord. **Amen.**

▷ page 15

Preface of Easter, pp 74–75.

COMMUNION ANTIPHON *John 14:15–16*

If you love me, keep my commandments, says the Lord,
and I will ask the Father and he will send you another Paraclete,
to abide with you for ever, alleluia.

▷ page 58

PRAYER AFTER COMMUNION

Almighty ever-living God,
who restore us to eternal life in the Resurrection of Christ,
increase in us, we pray, the fruits of this paschal Sacrament
and pour into our hearts the strength of this saving food.
Through Christ our Lord. **Amen.**

A solemn blessing may be used.

▷ page 59

ASCENSION OF THE LORD — VIGIL MASS

THURSDAY AFTER THE SIXTH SUNDAY OF EASTER
OR (if not a Holyday of Obligation) SEVENTH SUNDAY OF EASTER

This Mass is used on the evening of the day before the Solemnity.

ENTRANCE ANTIPHON *Psalm 67:33, 35*

You kingdoms of the earth, sing to God;
praise the Lord, who ascends above the highest heavens;
his majesty and might are in the skies, alleluia.

▷ page 7

COLLECT

O God, whose Son today ascended to the heavens
as the Apostles looked on,
grant, we pray, that, in accordance with his promise,
we may be worthy for him to live with us always on earth,
and we with him in heaven.
Who lives and reigns with you in the unity of the Holy Spirit,
God, for ever and ever. **Amen.**

LITURGY OF THE WORD

The readings are as for the Mass During the Day. See page 272.

PRAYER OVER THE OFFERINGS

O God, whose Only Begotten Son, our High Priest,
is seated ever-living at your right hand to intercede for us,
grant that we may approach with confidence the throne of grace
and there obtain your mercy.
Through Christ our Lord. **Amen.**

▷ page 15

Preface I or II of the Ascension, p 75.
When the Roman Canon is used, the proper form of the Communicantes (In communion with those) is said, p 20.

COMMUNION ANTIPHON *cf Hebrews 10:12*

Christ, offering a single sacrifice for sins,
is seated for ever at God's right hand, alleluia.

▷ page 58

PRAYER AFTER COMMUNION

May the gifts we have received from your altar, Lord,
kindle in our hearts a longing for the heavenly homeland
and cause us to press forward, following in the Saviour's footsteps,
to the place where for our sake he entered before us.
Who lives and reigns for ever and ever. **Amen.**

▷ page 59

A solemn blessing may be used.

ASCENSION OF THE LORD — MASS DURING THE DAY

THURSDAY AFTER THE SIXTH SUNDAY OF EASTER
OR (IF NOT A HOLYDAY OF OBLIGATION) SEVENTH SUNDAY OF EASTER

ENTRANCE ANTIPHON *Acts 1:11*

Men of Galilee, why gaze in wonder at the heavens?
This Jesus whom you saw ascending into heaven
will return as you saw him go, alleluia.

▷ page 7

COLLECT

Gladden us with holy joys, almighty God,
and make us rejoice with devout thanksgiving,
for the Ascension of Christ your Son
is our exaltation,
and, where the Head has gone before in glory,
the Body is called to follow in hope.
Through our Lord Jesus Christ, your Son,
who lives and reigns with you in the unity of the Holy Spirit,
God, for ever and ever. **Amen.**

An alternative Collect is found overleaf.

ALTERNATIVE COLLECT

Grant, we pray, almighty God,
that we, who believe that your Only Begotten Son, our Redeemer,
ascended this day to the heavens,
may in spirit dwell already in heavenly realms.
Who lives and reigns with you in the unity of the Holy Spirit,
God, for ever and ever. **Amen.**

FIRST READING *Acts 1:1–11*

'As they were looking on, he was lifted up.'

A reading from the Acts of the Apostles.

In the first book, O Theophilus, I have dealt with all that Jesus began to do and teach, until the day when he was taken up, after he had given commands through the Holy Spirit to the Apostles whom he had chosen. He presented himself alive to them after his suffering by many proofs, appearing to them during forty days and speaking about the kingdom of God.

And while staying with them he ordered them not to depart from Jerusalem, but to wait for the promise of the Father, which, he said, 'You heard from me; for John baptised with water, but you will be baptised with the Holy Spirit not many days from now.'

So when they had come together, they asked him, 'Lord, will you at this time restore the kingdom to Israel?' He said to them, 'It is not for you to know times or seasons that the Father has fixed by his own authority. But you will receive power when the Holy Spirit has come upon you, and you will be my witnesses in Jerusalem and in all Judea and Samaria, and to the end of the earth.' And when he had said these things, as they were looking on, he was lifted up, and a cloud took him out of their sight. And while they were gazing into heaven as he went, behold, two men stood by them in white robes, and said, 'Men of Galilee, why do you stand looking into heaven? This Jesus, who was taken up from you into heaven, will come in the same way as you saw him go into heaven.'

The word of the Lord.
Thanks be to God.

RESPONSORIAL PSALM *Psalm 47(46):2-3. 6-7. 8-9. R.6*

R. God has gone up with shouts of joy.
The LORD goes up with trumpet blast.

or **Alleluia.**

1 All peoples, clap your hands.
Cry to God with shouts of joy!
For the LORD, the Most High, to be feared,
the great king over all the earth. R.

2 God has gone up with shouts of joy.
The LORD goes up with trumpet blast.
Sing praise for God; sing praise!
Sing praise to our king; sing praise! R.

3 For God is king of all the earth.
Sing praise with a hymn.
God is reigning over nations.
God sits upon his holy throne. R.

An alternative Second Reading is found below.

SECOND READING *Ephesians 1:16–23*

'God seated him at his right hand in the heavenly places.'

A reading from the Letter of Saint Paul to the Ephesians.

Brothers and sisters: I do not cease to give thanks for you, remembering you in my prayers, that the God of our Lord Jesus Christ, the Father of glory, may give you the Spirit of wisdom and of revelation in the knowledge of him, having the eyes of your hearts enlightened, that you may know what is the hope to which he has called you, what are the riches of his glorious inheritance in the saints, and what is the immeasurable greatness of his power towards us who believe, according to the working of his great might that he worked in Christ when he raised him from the dead and seated him at his right hand in the heavenly places, far above all rule and authority and power and dominion, and above every name that is named, not only in this age but also in the one to come. And he put all things under his feet and gave him as head over all things to the Church, which is his body, the fullness of him who fills all in all.

The word of the Lord.
Thanks be to God.

ALTERNATIVE SECOND READING *Hebrews 9:24–28; 10:19–23*

'Christ has entered into heaven itself.'

A reading from the Letter to the Hebrews.

Christ has entered, not into holy places made with hands, which are copies of the true things, but into heaven itself, now to appear in the presence of God on our behalf. Nor was it to offer himself repeatedly, as the high priest enters the holy places every year with blood not his own, for then he would have had to suffer repeatedly since the foundation of the world. But as it is, he has appeared once for all at the end of the ages to put away sin by the sacrifice of himself. And just as it is appointed for man to die once, and after that comes judgement, so Christ, having been offered once to bear the sins of many, will appear a second time, not to deal with sin but to save those who are eagerly waiting for him.

Therefore, brothers and sisters, since we have confidence to enter the holy places by the blood of Jesus, by the new and living way that he opened for us through the curtain, that is, through his flesh, and since we have a great priest over the house of God, let us draw near with a true heart in full assurance of faith, with our hearts sprinkled clean from an evil conscience and our bodies washed with pure water. Let us hold fast the confession of our hope without wavering, for he who promised is faithful.

The word of the Lord.
Thanks be to God.

ACCLAMATION BEFORE THE GOSPEL *Matthew 28:19a, 20b*

Alleluia, alleluia.
Go, therefore, and make disciples of all nations, says the Lord.
I am with you always, to the end of the age.
Alleluia.

GOSPEL *Luke 24:46–53*

The Lord be with you.
And with your spirit.

The conclusion of the holy Gospel according to Luke.
Glory to you, O Lord.

'While he blessed them, he was carried up into heaven.'

At that time: Jesus said to his disciples, 'Thus it is written, that the Christ should suffer and on the third day rise from the dead, and that repentance for the forgiveness of sins should be proclaimed in his name to all nations, beginning from Jerusalem. You are witnesses of these things. And behold, I am sending the promise of my Father upon you. But stay in the city until you are clothed with power from on high.' And he led them out as far as Bethany, and lifting up his hands he blessed them. While he blessed them, he parted from them and was carried up into heaven. And they worshipped him and returned to Jerusalem with great joy, and were continually in the Temple blessing God.

The Gospel of the Lord.
Praise to you, Lord Jesus Christ.

▷ *page 11*

PRAYER OVER THE OFFERINGS

We offer sacrifice now in supplication, O Lord,
to honour the wondrous Ascension of your Son:
grant, we pray,
that through this most holy exchange
we, too, may rise up to the heavenly realms.
Through Christ our Lord. **Amen.**

▷ *page 15*

Preface I or II of the Ascension, p 75.
When the Roman Canon is used, the proper form of the Communicantes (In communion with those) is said, p 20.

COMMUNION ANTIPHON *Matthew 28:20*

Behold, I am with you always,
even to the end of the age, alleluia.

▷ *page 58*

PRAYER AFTER COMMUNION

Almighty ever-living God,
who allow those on earth to celebrate divine mysteries,
grant, we pray,
that Christian hope may draw us onward
to where our nature is united with you.
Through Christ our Lord. **Amen.**

▷ *page 59*

A solemn blessing may be used.

SEVENTH SUNDAY OF EASTER

Where the Solemnity of the Ascension is not to be observed as a Holyday of Obligation, it replaces the Seventh Sunday of Easter.

ENTRANCE ANTIPHON *cf Psalm 26:7–9*

O Lord, hear my voice, for I have called to you;
of you my heart has spoken: Seek his face;
hide not your face from me, alleluia.

▷ *page 7*

COLLECT

Graciously hear our supplications, O Lord,
so that we, who believe that the Saviour of the human race
is with you in your glory,
may experience, as he promised,
until the end of the world,
his abiding presence among us.
Who lives and reigns with you in the unity of the Holy Spirit,
God, for ever and ever. **Amen.**

FIRST READING *Acts 7:55–60*

'I can see the Son of Man standing at the right hand of God.'

A reading from the Acts of Apostles.

In those days: Stephen, full of the Holy Spirit, gazed into heaven and saw the glory of God, and Jesus standing at the right hand of God. And he said, 'Behold, I see the heavens opened, and the Son of Man standing at the right hand of God.' But they cried out with a loud voice and stopped their ears and rushed together at him. Then they cast him out of the city and stoned him. And the witnesses laid down their garments at the feet of a young man named Saul.

And as they were stoning Stephen, he called out, 'Lord Jesus, receive my spirit.' And falling to his knees he cried out with a loud voice, 'Lord, do not hold this sin against them.' And when he had said this, he fell asleep.

The word of the Lord.
Thanks be to God.

RESPONSORIAL PSALM *Psalm 97(96):1, 2b. 6, 7c. 9. R.1a, 9b*

R. The Lord is king, most high above all the earth.

or **Alleluia.**

1 The Lord is king, let earth rejoice;
let the many islands be glad.
Justice and right are the foundation
of his throne. R.

2 The skies proclaim his justice;
all peoples see his glory.
All you angels, worship him. R.

3 For you indeed are the Lord,
most high above all the earth,
exalted far above all gods. R.

SECOND READING *Revelation 22:12-14, 16-17, 20*

'Come, Lord Jesus!'

A reading from the Book of Revelation.

I, John, heard a voice saying to me, 'Behold, I am coming soon, bringing my recompense with me, to repay each one for what he has done. I am the Alpha and the Omega, the first and the last, the beginning and the end.' Blessed are those who wash their robes, so that they may have the right to the tree of life and that they may enter the city by the gates.

'I, Jesus, have sent my angel to testify to you about these things for the churches. I am the root and the descendant of David, the bright morning star.'

The Spirit and the Bride say, 'Come.' And let the one who hears say, 'Come.' And let the one who is thirsty come; let the one who desires take the water of life without price.

He who testifies to these things says, 'Surely I am coming soon.' Amen. Come, Lord Jesus!

The word of the Lord.
Thanks be to God.

ACCLAMATION BEFORE THE GOSPEL *cf John 14:18*

Alleluia, alleluia.
I will not leave you as orphans, says the Lord.
I am going away and I will come to you, and your hearts will rejoice.
Alleluia.

GOSPEL *John 17:20–26*

The Lord be with you.
And with your spirit.

A reading from the holy Gospel according to John.
Glory to you, O Lord.

'May they become perfectly one.'

At that time: Jesus lifted up his eyes to heaven, and praying said, 'Holy Father, I do not ask for these only, but also for those who will believe in me through their word, that they may all be one, just as you, Father, are in me, and I in you, that they also may be in us, so that the world may believe that you have sent me. The glory that you have given me I have given to them, that they may be one even as we are one, I in them and you in me, that they may become perfectly one, so that the world may know that you sent me and loved them even as you loved me. Father, I desire that they also, whom you have given me, may be with me where I am, to see my glory that you have given me because you loved me before the foundation of the world. O righteous Father, even though the world does not know you, I know you, and these know that you have sent me. I made known to them your name, and I will continue to make it known, that the love with which you have loved me may be in them, and I in them.'

The Gospel of the Lord.
Praise to you, Lord Jesus Christ.

▷ page 11

PRAYER OVER THE OFFERINGS

Accept, O Lord, the prayers of your faithful
with the sacrificial offerings,
that through these acts of devotedness
we may pass over to the glory of heaven.
Through Christ our Lord. **Amen.**

▷ page 15

Preface of Easter, or of the Ascension, pp 74–75.

COMMUNION ANTIPHON *John 17:22*

Father, I pray that they may be one
as we also are one, alleluia.

▷ page 58

PRAYER AFTER COMMUNION

Hear us, O God our Saviour,
and grant us confidence,
that through these sacred mysteries
there will be accomplished in the body of the whole Church
what has already come to pass in Christ her Head.
Who lives and reigns for ever and ever. **Amen.**

▷ page 59

A solemn blessing may be used

Pentecost Sunday is found overleaf.

PENTECOST SUNDAY — VIGIL MASS

The Vigil Mass may be celebrated in either an extended form (with or without the celebration of Evening Prayer I) or a simple form.

EXTENDED FORM

ENTRANCE ANTIPHON *Romans 5:5; cf 8:11*

The love of God has been poured into our hearts
through the Spirit of God dwelling within us, alleluia.

The Mass begins in the usual way. ▷ page 7
After the Kyrie (Lord, have mercy) the Priest says the following prayer

PRAYER

Grant, we pray, almighty God,
that the splendour of your glory
may shine forth upon us
and that, by the bright rays of the Holy Spirit,
the light of your light may confirm the hearts
of those born again by your grace.
Through our Lord Jesus Christ, your Son,
who lives and reigns with you in the unity of the Holy Spirit,
God, for ever and ever. **Amen.**

LITURGY OF THE WORD

Then the Priest may address the people in these or similar words:
Dear brethren (brothers and sisters),
we have now begun our Pentecost Vigil,
after the example of the Apostles and disciples,
who with Mary, the Mother of Jesus, persevered in prayer,
awaiting the Spirit promised by the Lord;
like them, let us, too, listen with quiet hearts to the Word of God.
Let us meditate on how many great deeds
God in times past did for his people
and let us pray that the Holy Spirit,
whom the Father sent as the first fruits for those who believe,
may bring to perfection his work in the world.

After each reading, a Responsorial Psalm is sung, or this may be replaced by a sacred silence.

FIRST READING *Genesis 11:1–9*

'It was called Babel, because there the language of all the earth was confused.'

A reading from the Book of Genesis.

The whole earth had one language and the same words. And as people migrated from the east, they found a plain in the land of Shinar and settled there. And they said to one another, 'Come, let us make bricks, and burn them thoroughly.' And they had brick for stone, and bitumen for mortar. Then they said, 'Come, let us build ourselves a city and a tower with its top in the heavens, and let us make a name for ourselves, lest we be dispersed over the face of the whole earth.' And the LORD came down to see the city and the tower, which the children of man had built. And the LORD said, 'Behold, they are one people, and they have all one language, and this is only the beginning of what they will do. And nothing that they propose to do will now be impossible for them. Come, let us go down and there confuse their language, so that they may not understand one another's speech.' So the LORD dispersed them from there over the face of all the earth, and they left off building the city. Therefore its name was called Babel, because there the LORD confused the language of all the earth. And from there the LORD dispersed them over the face of all the earth.

The word of the Lord.
Thanks be to God.

RESPONSORIAL PSALM *Psalm 33(32):10-11. 12-13. 14-15. R.12b*

R. Blessed the people the LORD has chosen as his heritage.

1 The LORD frustrates the designs of the nations;
he defeats the plans of the peoples.
The designs of the LORD stand for ever,
the plans of his heart from age to age. R.

2 Blessed the nation whose God is the LORD,
the people he has chosen as his heritage.
From the heavens the LORD looks forth;
he sees the whole human race. R.

3 From the place where he dwells he gazes
on all the dwellers on the earth,
he who shapes the hearts of them all,
and considers all their deeds. R.

PRAYER

Let us pray.
Grant, we pray, almighty God,
that your Church may always remain that holy people,
formed as one by the unity of Father, Son and Holy Spirit,
which manifests to the world
the Sacrament of your holiness and unity
and leads it to the perfection of your charity.
Through Christ our Lord. **Amen.**

SECOND READING *Exodus 19:3-8a, 16-20b*

'The Lord will come down on Mount Sinai in the sight of all the people.'

A reading from the Book of Exodus.

In those days: Moses went up to God. The LORD called to him out of the mountain, saying, 'Thus you shall say to the house of Jacob, and tell the people of Israel: "You yourselves have seen what I did to the Egyptians, and how I bore you on eagles' wings and brought you to myself. Now therefore, if you will indeed obey my voice and keep my covenant, you shall be my treasured possession among all peoples, for all the earth is mine; and you shall be to me a kingdom of priests and a holy nation." These are the words that you shall speak to the people of Israel.'

So Moses came and called the elders of the people and set before them all these words that the LORD had commanded him. All the people answered together and said, 'All that the LORD has spoken we will do.'

On the morning of the third day there was thunder and lightning and a thick cloud on the mountain and a very loud trumpet blast, so that all the people in the camp trembled. Then Moses brought the people out of the camp to meet God, and they took their stand at the foot of the mountain. Now Mount Sinai was wrapped in smoke because the LORD had descended on it in fire. The smoke of it went up like the smoke of a kiln, and the whole mountain trembled greatly. And as the sound of the trumpet grew louder and louder, Moses spoke, and God answered him in thunder. The LORD came down on Mount Sinai, to the top of the mountain. And the LORD called Moses to the top of the mountain.

The word of the Lord.
Thanks be to God.

An alternative Responsorial Psalm is found overleaf.

RESPONSORIAL PSALM *Daniel: 3:52. 53. 54. 55. 56. R.52b*

The response is sung after every line.
R. To be praised and highly exalted for ever!

1 Blessed are you, O Lord, the God of our ancestors.
R. To be praised and highly exalted for ever!
Blessed is your glorious and holy name,
R. To be praised and highly exalted for ever!

2 Blessed are you in the temple of your holy glory,
R. To be praised and highly exalted for ever!
Blessed are you on the throne of your kingdom,
R. To be praised and highly exalted for ever!

3 Blessed are you who look into the depths, seated upon the cherubim,
R. To be praised and highly exalted for ever!
Blessed are you in the firmament of heaven.
R. To be praised and highly exalted for ever!

ALTERNATIVE RESPONSORIAL PSALM *Psalm 19(18):8. 9. 10. 11. R. John 6:68c*

R. O Lord, you have the words of eternal life.

1 The law of the Lord is perfect;
it revives the soul.
The decrees of the Lord are steadfast;
they give wisdom to the simple. R.

2 The precepts of the Lord are right;
they gladden the heart.
The command of the Lord is clear;
it gives light to the eyes. R.

3 The fear of the Lord is pure,
abiding for ever.
The judgements of the Lord are true;
they are, all of them, just. R.

4 They are more to be desired than gold,
than quantities of gold.
And sweeter are they than honey,
than honey flowing from the comb. R.

PRAYER

Let us pray.
O God, who in fire and lightning
gave the ancient Law to Moses on Mount Sinai
and on this day manifested the new covenant
in the fire of the Spirit,
grant, we pray,
that we may always be aflame with that same Spirit
whom you wondrously poured out on your Apostles,
and that the new Israel,
gathered from every people,
may receive with rejoicing
the eternal commandment of your love.
Through Christ our Lord. **Amen.**

THIRD READING *Ezekiel 37:1–14*

'Dry bones, I will cause breath to enter you, and you shall live.'

A reading from the Prophet Ezekiel.

In those days: The hand of the Lord was upon me, and he brought me out in the Spirit of the Lord and set me down in the middle of the valley; it was full of bones. And he led me around among them, and behold, there were very many on the surface of the valley, and behold, they were very dry. And he said to me, 'Son of man, can these bones live?' And I answered, 'O Lord God, you know.' Then he said to me, 'Prophesy over these bones, and say to them, O dry bones, hear the word of the Lord. Thus says the Lord God to these bones: Behold, I will cause breath to enter you, and you shall live. And I will lay sinews upon you, and will cause flesh to come upon you, and cover you with skin, and put breath in you, and you shall live, and you shall know that I am the Lord.'

So I prophesied as I was commanded. And as I prophesied, there was a sound, and behold, a rattling, and the bones came together, bone to its bone. And I looked, and behold, there were sinews on them, and flesh had come upon them, and skin had covered them. But there was no breath in them. Then he said to me, 'Prophesy to the breath; prophesy, son of man, and say to the breath, Thus says the Lord God: Come from the four winds, O breath, and breathe on these slain, that they may live.' So I prophesied as he commanded me, and the breath came into them, and they lived and stood on their feet, an exceedingly great army.

Then he said to me, 'Son of man, these bones are the whole house of Israel. Behold, they say, "Our bones are dried up, and our hope is lost; we are indeed cut off." Therefore prophesy, and say to them, Thus says the Lord GOD: Behold, I will open your graves and raise you from your graves, O my people. And I will bring you into the land of Israel. And you shall know that I am the LORD, when I open your graves, and raise you from your graves, O my people. And I will put my Spirit within you, and you shall live, and I will place you in your own land. Then you shall know that I am the LORD; I have spoken, and I will do it, declares the LORD.'

The word of the Lord.
Thanks be to God.

RESPONSORIAL PSALM *Psalm 107(106):2-3. 4-5. 6-7. 8-9. R. cf. 1*

R. O give thanks to the LORD, for his mercy endures for ever.

or **Alleluia.**

1 Let the redeemed of the LORD say this,
those he redeemed from the hand of the foe,
and gathered from far-off lands,
from east and west, north and south. R.

2 They wandered in a barren desert,
finding no way to a city they could dwell in.
Hungry they were and thirsty;
their soul was fainting within them. R.

3 Then they cried to the LORD in their need,
and he rescued them from their distress,
and he guided them along a straight path,
to reach a city they could dwell in. R.

4 Let them thank the LORD for his mercy,
his wonders for the whole human race;
for he satisfies the thirsty soul,
and the hungry he fills with good things. R.

PRAYER

Alternative prayers are to be found overleaf

Let us pray.
Lord, God of power,
who restore what has fallen
and preserve what you have restored,
increase, we pray, the peoples
to be renewed by the sanctification of your name,
that all who are washed clean by holy Baptism
may always be directed by your prompting.
Through Christ our Lord. **Amen.**

ALTERNATIVE PRAYERS

O God, who have brought us to rebirth by the word of life,
pour out upon us your Holy Spirit,
that walking in oneness of faith,
we may attain in our flesh
the incorruptible glory of the resurrection.
Through Christ our Lord. **Amen.**

or

May your people exult for ever, O God,
in renewed youthfulness of spirit,
so that, rejoicing now in the restored glory of our adoption,
we may look forward in confident hope
to the rejoicing of the day of resurrection.
Through Christ Our Lord. **Amen.**

FOURTH READING *Joel 2:28-32*[7]

'On the male and female servants I shall pour out my Spirit.'

A reading from the Prophet Joel.

Thus says the Lord: 'I will pour out my Spirit on all flesh; your sons and your daughters shall prophesy, your old men shall dream dreams, and your young men shall see visions. Even on the male and female servants in those days I will pour out my Spirit.

'And I will show wonders in the heavens and on the earth, blood and fire and columns of smoke. The sun shall be turned to darkness, and the moon to blood, before the great and awesome day of the LORD comes. And it shall come to pass that everyone who calls on the name of the LORD shall be saved. For in Mount Sion and in Jerusalem there shall be those who escape, as the LORD has said, and among the survivors shall be those whom the LORD calls.'

The word of the Lord.
Thanks be to God.

RESPONSORIAL PSALM *Psalm 104 (103):1-2a. 24, 35c. 27-28. 29b-30. R. cf. 30*

R. **Send forth your Spirit, O Lord,
and renew the face of the earth.**
or **Alleluia.**

1 Bless the LORD, O my soul!
O LORD my God, how great you are,
clothed in majesty and honour,
wrapped in light as with a robe! R.

2 How many are your works, O LORD!
In wisdom you have made them all.
The earth is full of your creatures.
Bless the LORD, O my soul. R.

3 All of these look to you
to give them their food in due season.
You give it, they gather it up;
you open wide your hand, they are well filled. R.

4 You take away their breath, they die,
returning to the dust from which they came.
You send forth your spirit, and they are created,
and you renew the face of the earth. R.

7 *Joel 3:1-5*

EASTER

PRAYER

Let us pray.
Fulfil for us your gracious promise,
O Lord, we pray, so that by his coming
the Holy Spirit may make us witnesses before the world
to the Gospel of our Lord Jesus Christ.
Who lives and reigns for ever and ever. **Amen.**

GLORIA

The Priest intones the Gloria, and all take up the hymn. ▷ *Music p 316*

COLLECT

Almighty ever-living God,
who willed the Paschal Mystery
to be encompassed as a sign in fifty days,
grant that from out of the scattered nations
the confusion of many tongues
may be gathered by heavenly grace
into one great confession of your name.
Through our Lord Jesus Christ, your Son,
who lives and reigns with you in the unity of the Holy Spirit,
God, for ever and ever. **Amen.**

EPISTLE *Romans 8:22–27*

'The Spirit intercedes for us with groanings too deep for words.'

A reading from the Letter of Saint Paul to the Romans.

Brothers and sisters: We know that the whole creation has been groaning together in the pains of childbirth until now. And not only the creation, but we ourselves, who have the first fruits of the Spirit, groan inwardly as we wait eagerly for adoption as sons, the redemption of our bodies. For in this hope we were saved. Now hope that is seen is not hope. For who hopes for what he sees? But if we hope for what we do not see, we wait for it with patience.

Likewise the Spirit helps us in our weakness. For we do not know what to pray for as we ought, but the Spirit himself intercedes for us with groanings too deep for words. And he who searches hearts knows what is the mind of the Spirit, because the Spirit intercedes for the saints according to the will of God.

The word of the Lord.
Thanks be to God.

ACCLAMATION BEFORE THE GOSPEL

Alleluia, alleluia.
Come, Holy Spirit, fill the hearts of your faithful
and kindle in them the fire of your love.
Alleluia.

GOSPEL *John 7:37–39*

The Lord be with you.
And with your spirit.

A reading from the holy Gospel according to John.
Glory to you, O Lord.

'Rivers of living water will flow.'

On the last day of the feast, the great day, Jesus stood up and cried out,
'If anyone thirsts, let him come to me and drink. Whoever believes in me, as the Scripture has said, "Out of his heart will flow rivers of living water."'

Now this he said about the Spirit, whom those who believed in him were to receive, for as yet the Spirit had not been given, because Jesus was not yet glorified.

The Gospel of the Lord.
Praise to you, Lord Jesus Christ.

▷ *page 11*

PRAYER OVER THE OFFERINGS

Pour out upon these gifts the blessing of your Spirit,
we pray, O Lord,
so that through them your Church may be imbued with such love
that the truth of your saving mystery
may shine forth for the whole world.
Through Christ our Lord. **Amen.**

▷ *page 15*

Preface: The Mystery of Pentecost, p 76.
When the Roman Canon is used, the proper form of the Communicantes (In communion with those) is said, p 20.

COMMUNION ANTIPHON *John 7:37*

On the last day of the festival, Jesus stood and cried out:
If anyone is thirsty, let him come to me and drink, alleluia.

▷ *page 58*

PRAYER AFTER COMMUNION

May these gifts we have consumed
benefit us, O Lord,
that we may always be aflame with the same Spirit,
whom you wondrously poured out on your Apostles.
Through Christ our Lord. **Amen.**

A solemn blessing may be used.

DISMISSAL

▷ *Music p 251*

Deacon or Priest: Go forth, the Mass is ended, alleluia, alleluia.
or
Deacon or Priest: Go in peace, alleluia, alleluia.
People: **Thanks be to God, alleluia, alleluia.**

SIMPLE FORM

ENTRANCE ANTIPHON *Romans 5:5; cf 8:11*

The love of God has been poured into our hearts
through the Spirit of God dwelling within us, alleluia.

The Introductory Rites of the Mass (including the Gloria) are celebrated in the usual way.

▷ *page 7*

COLLECT

Almighty ever-living God,
who willed the Paschal Mystery
to be encompassed as a sign in fifty days,
grant that from out of the scattered nations
the confusion of many tongues
may be gathered by heavenly grace
into one great confession of your name.
Through our Lord Jesus Christ, your Son,
who lives and reigns with you in the unity of the Holy Spirit,
God, for ever and ever. **Amen.**

or

Grant, we pray, almighty God,
that the splendour of your glory
may shine forth upon us
and that, by the bright rays of the Holy Spirit,
the light of your light may confirm the hearts
of those born again by your grace.
Through our Lord Jesus Christ, your Son,
who lives and reigns with you in the unity of the Holy Spirit,
God, for ever and ever. **Amen.**

The readings for the Liturgy of the Word can be found starting on page 279.

One of the Old Testament Readings is chosen followed by the appropriate Responsorial Psalm. This is followed by the Epistle, Gospel Acclamation and Gospel, in the usual way.

Following the Gospel, the Mass is celebrated as in the Extended form. See page 285.

PENTECOST SUNDAY — MASS DURING THE DAY

ENTRANCE ANTIPHON *Wisdom 1:7*

The Spirit of the Lord has filled the whole world
and that which contains all things
understands what is said, alleluia.

or *Romans 5:5; cf 8:11*

The love of God has been poured into our hearts
through the Spirit of God dwelling within us, alleluia.

▷ page 7

COLLECT

O God, who by the mystery of today's great feast
sanctify your whole Church in every people and nation,
pour out, we pray, the gifts of the Holy Spirit
across the face of the earth
and, with the divine grace that was at work
when the Gospel was first proclaimed,
fill now once more the hearts of believers.
Through our Lord Jesus Christ, your Son,
who lives and reigns with you in the unity of the Holy Spirit,
God, for ever and ever. **Amen.**

FIRST READING *Acts 2:1–11*

'They were all filled with the Holy Spirit and began to speak.'

A reading from the Acts of the Apostles.

When the day of Pentecost arrived, the Apostles were all together in one place. And suddenly there came from heaven a sound like a mighty rushing wind, and it filled the entire house where they were sitting. And divided tongues as of fire appeared to them and rested on each one of them. And they were all filled with the Holy Spirit and began to speak in other tongues as the Spirit gave them utterance.

Now there were dwelling in Jerusalem Jews, devout men from every nation under heaven. And at this sound the multitude came together, and they were bewildered, because each one was hearing them speak in his own language. And they were amazed and astonished, saying, 'Are not all these who are speaking Galileans? And how is it that we hear, each of us in his own native language? Parthians and Medes and Elamites and residents of Mesopotamia, Judea and Cappadocia, Pontus and Asia, Phrygia and Pamphylia, Egypt and the parts of Libya belonging to Cyrene, and visitors from Rome, both Jews and proselytes, Cretans and Arabians—we hear them telling in our own tongues the mighty works of God.'

The word of the Lord.
Thanks be to God.

RESPONSORIAL PSALM *Psalm 104 (103):1ab, 24ac. 29b-30. 31, 34. R. cf. 30*

R. **Send forth your spirit, O Lord,**
and renew the face of the earth.

or **Alleluia.**

1 Bless the LORD, O my soul!
O LORD my God, how great you are!
How many are your works, O LORD!
The earth is full of your creatures. R.

2 You take away their breath, they die,
returning to the dust from which they came.
You send forth your spirit, and they are created,
and you renew the face of the earth. R.

3 May the glory of the LORD last for ever!
May the LORD rejoice in his works!
May my thoughts be pleasing to him.
I will rejoice in the LORD. R.

An alternative Second Reading is found below.

SECOND READING *1 Corinthians 12:3b–7, 12–13*

'In one Spirit we were all baptised into one body.'

A reading from the First Letter of Saint Paul to the Corinthians.

Brothers and sisters: No one can say 'Jesus is Lord' except in the Holy Spirit. Now there are varieties of gifts, but the same Spirit; and there are varieties of service, but the same Lord; and there are varieties of activities, but it is the same God who empowers them all in everyone. To each is given the manifestation of the Spirit for the common good.

For just as the body is one and has many members, and all the members of the body, though many, are one body, so it is with Christ. For in one Spirit we were all baptised into one body—Jews or Greeks, slaves or free—and all were made to drink of one Spirit.

The word of the Lord.
Thanks be to God.

ALTERNATIVE SECOND READING *Romans 8:8–17*

'For all who are led by the Spirit of God are sons of God.'

A reading from the Letter of Saint Paul to the Romans.

Brothers and sisters: Those who are in the flesh cannot please God. You, however, are not in the flesh but in the Spirit, if in fact the Spirit of God dwells in you. Anyone who does not have the Spirit of Christ does not belong to him. But if Christ is in you, although the body is dead because of sin, the Spirit is life because of righteousness. If the Spirit of him who raised Jesus from the dead dwells in you, he who raised Christ Jesus from the dead will also give life to your mortal bodies through his Spirit who dwells in you.

So then, brothers and sisters, we are debtors, not to the flesh, to live according to the flesh. For if you live according to the flesh you will die, but if by the Spirit you put to death the deeds of the body, you will live. For all who are led by the Spirit of God are sons of God. For you did not receive the spirit of slavery to fall back into fear, but you have received the Spirit of adoption as sons, by whom we cry, 'Abba! Father!' The Spirit himself bears witness with our spirit that we are children of God, and if children, then heirs—heirs of God and fellow heirs with Christ, provided we suffer with him in order that we may also be glorified with him.

The word of the Lord.
Thanks be to God.

SEQUENCE

The Sequence is said or sung at all Masses.

1 Holy Spirit, Lord of light,
from the clear celestial height
thy pure beaming radiance give.

2 Come, thou Father of the poor,
come with treasures which endure,
come, thou light of all that live.

3 Thou, of all consolers best,
thou, the soul's delightful guest,
dost refreshing peace bestow.

4 Thou in toil art comfort sweet,
pleasant coolness in the heat,
solace in the midst of woe.

5 Light immortal, Light divine,
visit thou these hearts of thine,
and our inmost being fill.

6 If thou take thy grace away,
nothing pure in man will stay;
all his good is turned to ill.

7 Heal our wounds, our strength renew;
on our dryness pour thy dew;
wash the stains of guilt away.

8 Bend the stubborn heart and will;
melt the frozen, warm the chill;
guide the steps that go astray.

9 Thou, on us who evermore
thee confess and thee adore,
with thy sevenfold gifts descend:

10 Give us comfort when we die,
give us life with thee on high;
give us joys that never end.

ACCLAMATION BEFORE THE GOSPEL

Alleluia, alleluia.
Come, Holy Spirit, fill the hearts of your faithful,
and kindle in them the fire of your love.
Alleluia.

An alternative Gospel reading is found below.

GOSPEL *John 20:19–23*

The Lord be with you.
And with your spirit.

A reading from the holy Gospel according to John.
Glory to you, O Lord.

'As the Father has sent me, even so I am sending you. Receive the Holy Spirit.'

On the evening of that day, the first day of the week, the doors being locked where the disciples were for fear of the Jews, Jesus came and stood among them and said to them, 'Peace be with you.' When he had said this, he showed them his hands and his side. Then the disciples were glad when they saw the Lord. Jesus said to them again, 'Peace be with you. As the Father has sent me, even so I am sending you.' And when he had said this, he breathed on them and said to them, 'Receive the Holy Spirit. If you forgive the sins of any, they are forgiven them; if you withhold forgiveness from any, it is withheld.'

The Gospel of the Lord.
Praise to you, Lord Jesus Christ.

ALTERNATIVE GOSPEL *John 14:15-16, 23b-26*

The Lord be with you.

And with your spirit.

A reading from the holy Gospel according to John.
Glory to you, O Lord.

'The Holy Spirit will teach you all things.'

At that time: Jesus said to his disciples, 'If you love me, you will keep my commandments. And I will ask the Father, and he will give you another Helper, to be with you for ever. If anyone loves me, he will keep my word, and my Father will love him, and we will come to him and make our home with him. Whoever does not love me does not keep my words. And the word that you hear is not mine but the Father's who sent me.

'These things I have spoken to you while I am still with you. But the Helper, the Holy Spirit, whom the Father will send in my name, he will teach you all things and bring to your remembrance all that I have said to you.'

The Gospel of the Lord.
Praise to you, Lord Jesus Christ.

▷ *page 11*

PRAYER OVER THE OFFERINGS

Grant, we pray, O Lord,
that, as promised by your Son,
the Holy Spirit may reveal to us more abundantly
the hidden mystery of this sacrifice
and graciously lead us into all truth.
Through Christ our Lord. **Amen.**

▷ *page 15*

Preface: The Mystery of Pentecost, p 76.
When the Roman Canon is used, the proper form of the Communicantes (In communion with those) is said, p 20.

COMMUNION ANTIPHON *Acts 2:4, 11*

They were all filled with the Holy Spirit
and spoke of the marvels of God, alleluia.

▷ *page 58*

PRAYER AFTER COMMUNION

O God, who bestow heavenly gifts upon your Church,
safeguard, we pray, the grace you have given,
that the gift of the Holy Spirit poured out upon her
may retain all its force
and that this spiritual food
may gain her abundance of eternal redemption.
Through Christ our Lord. **Amen.**

A solemn blessing may be used.

▷ *page 59*

DISMISSAL

▷ *Music p 251*

Deacon or Priest:	Go forth, the Mass is ended, alleluia, alleluia.
or	
Deacon or Priest:	Go in peace, alleluia, alleluia.
People:	**Thanks be to God, alleluia, alleluia.**

Easter Time is now concluded.

PROPER OF SAINTS

IMMACULATE CONCEPTION

IMMACULATE CONCEPTION OF THE BLESSED VIRGIN MARY
8 DECEMBER
If the Solemnity falls on a Sunday, it is transferred.

ENTRANCE ANTIPHON *Isaiah 61:10*

I rejoice heartily in the Lord,
in my God is the joy of my soul;
for he has clothed me with a robe of salvation,
and wrapped me in a mantle of justice,
like a bride adorned with her jewels.

▷ page 7

The Gloria is sung (said).

COLLECT

O God, who by the Immaculate Conception of the Blessed Virgin
prepared a worthy dwelling for your Son,
grant, we pray,
that, as you preserved her from every stain
by virtue of the Death of your Son, which you foresaw,
so, through her intercession,
we, too, may be cleansed and admitted to your presence.
Through our Lord Jesus Christ, your Son,
who lives and reigns with you in the unity of the Holy Spirit,
God, for ever and ever. **Amen.**

FIRST READING *Genesis 3:9–15, 20*

'I will put enmity between your offspring and the offspring of the woman.'

A reading from the Book of Genesis.

After Adam had eaten of the tree: The LORD God called to the man and said to him, 'Where are you?' And he said, 'I heard the sound of you in the garden, and I was afraid, because I was naked, and I hid myself.' He said, 'Who told you that you were naked? Have you eaten of the tree of which I commanded you not to eat?' The man said, 'The woman whom you gave to be with me, she gave me fruit of the tree, and I ate.' Then the LORD God said to the woman, 'What is this that you have done?' The woman said, 'The serpent deceived me, and I ate.'

The LORD God said to the serpent, 'Because you have done this, cursed are you above all livestock and above all beasts of the field; on your belly you shall go, and dust you shall eat all the days of your life. I will put enmity between you and the woman, and between your offspring and her offspring; he shall bruise your head, and you shall bruise his heel.' The man called his wife's name Eve, because she was the mother of all living.

The word of the Lord.
Thanks be to God.

RESPONSORIAL PSALM *Psalm 98(97):1. 2-3b. 3c-4. R.1a*

**R. O sing a new song to the LORD,
for he has worked wonders.**

1 O sing a new song to the LORD,
for he has worked wonders.
His right hand and his holy arm
have brought salvation. R.

2 The LORD has made known his salvation,
has shown his deliverance to the nations.
He has remembered his merciful love
and his truth for the house of Israel. R.

3 All the ends of the earth have seen
the salvation of our God.
Shout to the LORD, all the earth;
break forth into joyous song,
and sing out your praise. R.

SECOND READING *Ephesians 1:3–6, 11–12*

'God chose us in Christ before the foundation of the world.'

A reading from the Letter of Saint Paul to the Ephesians.

Blessed be the God and Father of our Lord Jesus Christ, who has blessed us in Christ with every spiritual blessing in the heavenly places, even as he chose us in him before the foundation of the world, that we should be holy and blameless before him. In love he predestined us for adoption to himself as sons through Jesus Christ, according to the purpose of his will, to the praise of his glorious grace, with which he has blessed us in the Beloved.

In him we have obtained an inheritance, having been predestined according to the purpose of him who works all things according to the counsel of his will, so that we who were the first to hope in Christ might be to the praise of his glory.

The word of the Lord.
Thanks be to God.

ACCLAMATION BEFORE THE GOSPEL *cf Luke 1:28*

**Alleluia, alleluia.
Hail, Mary, full of grace, the Lord is with you.
Blessed are you among women.
Alleluia.**

GOSPEL *Luke 1:26–38*

The Lord be with you.
And with your spirit.

A reading from the holy Gospel according to Luke.
Glory to you, O Lord.

'Hail, full of grace, the Lord is with you!'

At that time: The angel Gabriel was sent from God to a city of Galilee named Nazareth, to a virgin betrothed to a man whose name was Joseph, of the house of David. And the virgin's name was Mary. And he came to her and said, 'Hail, full of grace, the Lord is with you!' But she was greatly troubled at the saying, and tried to discern what sort of greeting this might be. And the angel said to her, 'Do not be afraid, Mary, for you have found favour with God. And behold, you will conceive in your womb and bear a son, and you shall call his name

Jesus. He will be great and will be called the Son of the Most High. And the Lord God will give to him the throne of his father David, and he will reign over the house of Jacob for ever, and of his kingdom there will be no end.'

And Mary said to the angel, 'How will this be, since I am a virgin?'

And the angel answered her, 'The Holy Spirit will come upon you, and the power of the Most High will overshadow you; therefore the child to be born will be called holy—the Son of God. And behold, your relative Elizabeth in her old age has also conceived a son, and this is the sixth month with her who was called barren. For nothing will be impossible with God.' And Mary said, 'Behold, I am the servant of the Lord; let it be to me according to your word.' And the angel departed from her.

The Gospel of the Lord.
Praise to you, Lord Jesus Christ.

▷ *page 11*

The Profession of Faith is said.

PRAYER OVER THE OFFERINGS

Graciously accept the saving sacrifice
which we offer you, O Lord,
on the Solemnity of the Immaculate Conception
of the Blessed Virgin Mary,
and grant that, as we profess her,
on account of your prevenient grace,
to be untouched by any stain of sin,
so, through her intercession,
we may be delivered from all our faults.
Through Christ our Lord. **Amen.**

▷ *page 15*

Preface: The Mystery of Mary and the Church, p 76.

COMMUNION ANTIPHON

Glorious things are spoken of you, O Mary,
for from you arose the sun of justice,
Christ our God.

▷ *page 58*

PRAYER AFTER COMMUNION

May the Sacrament we have received,
O Lord our God,
heal in us the wounds of that fault
from which in a singular way
you preserved Blessed Mary in her Immaculate Conception.
Through Christ our Lord. **Amen.**

▷ *page 59*

A solemn blessing may be used.

PRESENTATION OF THE LORD

2 FEBRUARY

If this feast falls on a Sunday, it replaces the Sunday in Ordinary Time.
When the feast is celebrated on a weekday there is only one reading before the Gospel.

THE BLESSING OF CANDLES AND THE PROCESSION
FIRST FORM: THE PROCESSION

The people gather outside the Church or a building other than the Church. Candles are prepared for all who participate. While the candles are being lit, the following antiphon or another appropriate chant is sung.

ANTIPHON

Behold, our Lord will come with power,
to enlighten the eyes of his servants, alleluia.

SIGN OF THE CROSS

All make the Sign of the Cross as the Priest says.

Priest: In the name of the Father, and of the Son, and of the Holy Spirit.
People: **Amen.**

GREETING

Priest: The grace of our Lord Jesus Christ,
and the love of God,
and the communion of the Holy Spirit
be with you all.

or

Priest: Grace to you and peace from God our Father
and the Lord Jesus Christ.

or

Priest: The Lord be with you.
People: **And with your spirit.**

INTRODUCTORY ADDRESS

The Priest gives an introductory address, encouraging the faithful to celebrate the rite of this feast day actively and consciously. He may use these or similar words:

Dear brethren (brothers and sisters),
forty days have passed since we celebrated the joyful feast
of the Nativity of the Lord.
Today is the blessed day
when Jesus was presented in the Temple by Mary and Joseph.
Outwardly he was fulfilling the Law,
but in reality he was coming to meet his believing people.
Prompted by the Holy Spirit,
Simeon and Anna came to the Temple.

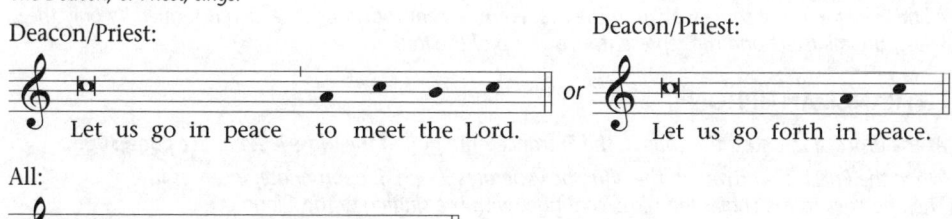

Enlightened by the same Spirit,
they recognized the Lord
and confessed him with exultation.
So let us also, gathered together by the Holy Spirit,
proceed to the house of God to encounter Christ.
There we shall find him
and recognize him in the breaking of the bread,
until he comes again, revealed in glory.

BLESSING OF CANDLES

After the address the Priest blesses the candles, saying, with hands extended:

Let us pray.

O God, source and origin of all light,
who on this day showed to the just man Simeon
the Light for revelation to the Gentiles,
we humbly ask that,
in answer to your people's prayers,
you may be pleased to sanctify with your blessing ✠ these candles,
which we are eager to carry in praise of your name,
so that, treading the path of virtue,
we may reach that light which never fails.
Through Christ our Lord. **Amen.**

or

O God, true light, who create light eternal,
spreading it far and wide,
pour, we pray, into the hearts of the faithful
the brilliance of perpetual light,
so that all who are brightened in your holy temple
by the splendour of these candles
may happily reach the light of your glory.
Through Christ our Lord. **Amen.**

He sprinkles the candles with holy water without saying anything, and puts incense into the thurible for the procession.

PROCESSION

The Deacon, or Priest, sings:

Deacon/Priest:

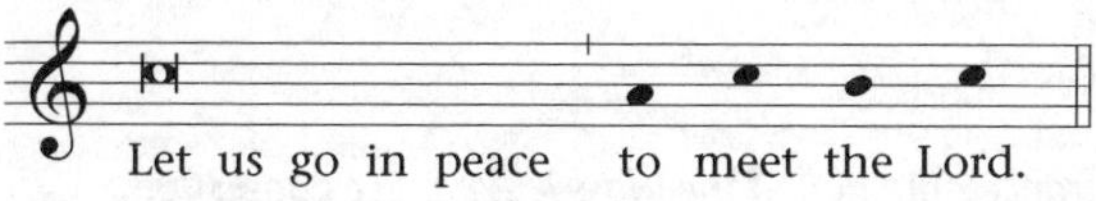

Let us go in peace to meet the Lord.

or

Deacon/Priest:

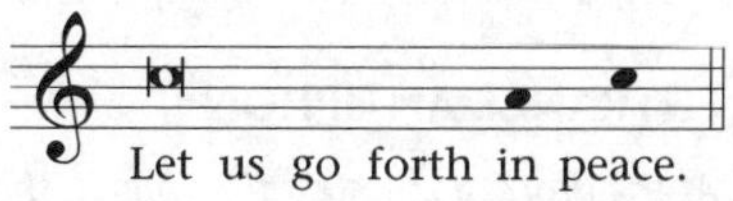

All:

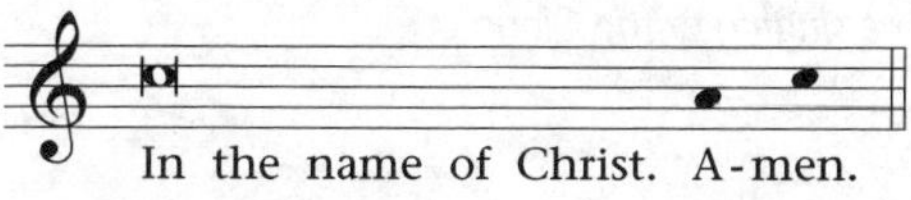

All carry lighted candles.
As the procession moves forward, one or other of the antiphons or another appropriate chant is sung.

Antiphon 1 *Luke 2:29–32*

Ant A light for revelation to the Gentiles
and the glory of your people Israel.

V Lord, now you let your servant go in peace,
in accordance with your word.

Ant A light for revelation to the Gentiles...
V For my eyes have seen your salvation.

Ant A light for revelation to the Gentiles...
V Which you have prepared in the sight of all peoples.

Ant A light for revelation to the Gentiles...

Antiphon II

Sion, adorn your bridal chamber and welcome Christ the King; take Mary in your arms, who is the gate of heaven, for she herself is carrying the King of glory and new light. A Virgin she remains, though bringing in her hands the Son before the morning star begotten, whom Simeon, taking in his arms announced to the peoples as Lord of life and death and Saviour of the world.

ENTRANCE ANTIPHON

As the procession enters the church, the Entrance Antiphon of the Mass is sung. *See p 306.*

When the Priest has arrived at the altar, he venerates it and, if appropriate, incenses it. Then he goes to the chair, and Mass continues with the singing of the Gloria.

THE BLESSING OF CANDLES AND THE PROCESSION
SECOND FORM: THE SOLEMN ENTRANCE

Whenever a procession cannot take place, the faithful gather in church, holding candles in their hands.

The Priest, together with the ministers and a representative group of the faithful, goes to a suitable place, either in front of the church door or inside the church itself, where at least a large part of the faithful can conveniently participate in the rite.

All takes place in the same way as in the First Form, except that the procession is formed by only the Priest, the ministers and the representative group of the faithful

ENTRANCE ANTIPHON

As the procession enters the church, the Entrance Antiphon of the Mass is sung. *See page 306.*

When the Priest has arrived at the altar, he venerates it and, if appropriate, incenses it. Then he goes to the chair, and Mass continues with the singing of the Gloria.

AT THE MASS

ENTRANCE ANTIPHON *cf Psalm 47:10–11*

Your merciful love, O God,
we have received in the midst of your temple.
Your praise, O God, like your name,
reaches the ends of the earth;
your right hand is filled with saving justice.

The Penitential Act is omitted and the Gloria is now sung (said). ▷ Music p 316 ▷ page 9

COLLECT

Almighty ever-living God,
we humbly implore your majesty
that, just as your Only Begotten Son
was presented on this day in the Temple
in the substance of our flesh,
so, by your grace,
we may be presented to you with minds made pure.
Through our Lord Jesus Christ, your Son,
who lives and reigns with you in the unity of the Holy Spirit,
God, for ever and ever. **Amen.**

When this feast is celebrated on a Sunday there are two readings before the Gospel. When it is celebrated on a weekday there is only one reading before the Gospel.

FIRST READING *Malachi 3:1–4*

'The Lord whom you seek will come to his Temple.'

A reading from the Prophet Malachi.

Thus says the LORD God: Behold, I send my messenger, and he will prepare the way before me. And the Lord whom you seek will suddenly come to his Temple; and the messenger of the covenant in whom you delight, behold, he is coming, says the LORD of hosts. But who can endure the day of his coming, and who can stand when he appears? For he is like a refiner's fire and like fullers' soap. He will sit as a refiner and purifier of silver, and he will purify the sons of Levi and refine them like gold and silver, and they will bring offerings in righteousness to the LORD. Then the offering of Judah and Jerusalem will be pleasing to the LORD as in the days of old and as in former years.

The word of the Lord.
Thanks be to God.

RESPONSORIAL PSALM *Psalm 24 (23):7. 8. 9. 10. R.10bc*

**R. The LORD of hosts,
he is the king of glory!**

1 O gates, lift high your heads;
grow higher, ancient doors.
Let him enter, the king of glory! R.

2 Who is this king of glory?
The LORD, the mighty, the valiant;
the LORD, the valiant in war. R.

3 O gates, lift high your heads;
grow higher, ancient doors.
Let him enter, the king of glory! R.

4 Who is this king of glory?
He, the LORD of hosts,
he is the king of glory. R.

SECOND READING *Hebrews 2:14–18*

'He had to be made like his brothers in every respect.'

A reading from the Letter to the Hebrews.

Since the children share in flesh and blood, Jesus himself likewise partook of the same things, that through death he might destroy the one who has the power of death, that is, the devil, and deliver all those who through fear of death were subject to lifelong slavery. For surely it is not angels that he helps, but he helps the offspring of Abraham. Therefore he had to be made like his brothers in every respect, so that he might become a merciful and faithful high priest in the service of God, to make propitiation for the sins of the people. For because he himself has suffered when tempted, he is able to help those who are being tempted.

The word of the Lord.
Thanks be to God.

ACCLAMATION BEFORE THE GOSPEL *Luke 2:32*

**Alleluia, alleluia.
A light for revelation to the Gentiles,
and for glory to your people Israel.
Alleluia.**

GOSPEL *Luke 2:22–40 Shorter form: Luke 2:22–32 (only read text with side line next to it).*

The Lord be with you.
And with your spirit.

A reading from the holy Gospel according to Luke.
Glory to you, O Lord.

'My eyes have seen your salvation.'

When the time came for their purification according to the Law of Moses, the parents of Jesus brought him up to Jerusalem to present him to the Lord (as it is written in the Law of the Lord, 'Every male who first opens the womb shall be called holy to the Lord') and to offer a sacrifice according to what is said in the Law of the Lord, 'a pair of turtle-doves, or two young pigeons.'

Now there was a man in Jerusalem, whose name was Simeon, and this man was righteous and devout, waiting for the consolation of Israel, and the Holy Spirit was upon him. And it had been revealed to him by the Holy Spirit that he would not see death before he had seen the Lord's Christ. And he came in the Spirit into the Temple, and when the parents brought in the child Jesus, to do for him according to the custom of the Law, he took him up in his arms and blessed God and said,

'Lord, now you are letting your servant depart in peace, according to your word; for my eyes have seen your salvation that you have prepared in the presence of all peoples, a light for revelation to the Gentiles, and for glory to your people Israel.'

And his father and his mother marvelled at what was said about him. And Simeon blessed them and said to Mary his mother, 'Behold, this child is appointed for the fall and rising of many in Israel, and for a sign that is opposed—and a sword will pierce through your own soul also—so that thoughts from many hearts may be revealed.'

And there was a prophetess, Anna, the daughter of Phanuel, of the tribe of Asher. She was advanced in years, having lived with her husband seven years from when she was a virgin, and then as a widow until she was eighty-four. She did not depart from the Temple, worshipping with fasting and prayer night and day. And coming up at that very hour she began to give thanks to God and to speak of the child to all who were waiting for the redemption of Jerusalem.

And when they had performed everything according to the Law of the Lord, they returned into Galilee, to their own town of Nazareth. And the child grew and became strong, filled with wisdom. And the favour of God was upon him.

The Gospel of the Lord.
Praise to you, Lord Jesus Christ.

▷ *page 11*

When this Feast falls on a Sunday, the Profession of Faith is said.

PRAYER OVER THE OFFERINGS

May the offering made with exultation by your Church
be pleasing to you, O Lord, we pray,
for you willed that your Only Begotten Son
be offered to you for the life of the world
as the Lamb without blemish.
Who lives and reigns for ever and ever. **Amen.**

▷ *page 15*

Preface: The Mystery of the Presentation of the Lord, p 76.

COMMUNION ANTIPHON *Luke 2:30–31*

My eyes have seen your salvation,
which you prepared in the sight of all the peoples.

▷ *page 58*

PRAYER AFTER COMMUNION

By these holy gifts which we have received, O Lord,
bring your grace to perfection within us,
and, as you fulfilled Simeon's expectation
that he would not see death
until he had been privileged to welcome the Christ,
so may we, going forth to meet the Lord,
obtain the gift of eternal life.
Through Christ our Lord. **Amen.**

▷ *page 59*

SAINT PATRICK

ENTRANCE ANTIPHON *cf Psalm 95:2–3*

Proclaim the salvation of God day by day;
tell among the nations his glory.

▷ page 7

The Gloria is sung (said)

COLLECT

O God, who chose the Bishop Saint Patrick
to preach your glory to the peoples of Ireland,
grant through his merits and intercession,
that those who glory in the name of Christian
may never cease to proclaim your wondrous deeds to all.
Through our Lord Jesus Christ, your Son,
who lives and reigns with you in the unity of the Holy Spirit,
God, for ever and ever. **Amen.**

FIRST READING *Jeremiah 1:4–9*

'To all to whom I send you, you shall go.'

A reading from the Prophet Jeremiah.

In the days of King Josiah: The word of the LORD came to me, saying, 'Before I formed you in the womb I knew you, and before you were born I consecrated you; I appointed you a prophet to the nations.'

Then I said, 'Ah, Lord GOD! Behold, I do not know how to speak, for I am only a youth.'

But the LORD said to me, 'Do not say, "I am only a youth"; for to all to whom I send you, you shall go, and whatever I command you, you shall speak. Do not be afraid of them, for I am with you to deliver you, declares the LORD.'

Then the LORD put out his hand and touched my mouth. And the LORD said to me, 'Behold, I have put my words in your mouth.'

Thanks be to God.

RESPONSORIAL PSALM *Psalm 116 R. Mark 16:15*

R. Go into all the world and proclaim the good news.

1 O praise the LORD, all you nations;
acclaim him, all you peoples! R.

2 For his mercy has prevailed over us;
and the faithfulness of the LORD
endures for ever. R.

ACCLAMATION BEFORE THE GOSPEL *Luke 4:18*

Glory and praise to you, O Christ.
The Lord has sent me to proclaim good news to the poor;
to proclaim liberty to the captives.
Glory and praise to you, O Christ.

GOSPEL *Luke 10:1–12, 17–20*

The Lord be with you.
And with your spirit.

A reading from the holy Gospel according to Luke.
Glory to you, O Lord.

'Your peace will rest upon him.'

At that time: The Lord appointed seventy-two others and sent them on ahead of him, two by two, into every town and place where he himself was about to go. And he said to them, 'The harvest is plentiful, but the labourers are few. Therefore pray earnestly to the Lord of the harvest to send out labourers into his harvest. Go your way; behold, I am sending you out as lambs in the midst of wolves. Carry no money bag, no knapsack, no sandals, and greet no one on the road. Whatever house you enter, first say, "Peace be to this house!" And if a son of peace is there, your peace will rest upon him. But if not, it will return to you. And remain in the same house, eating and drinking what they provide, for the labourer deserves his wages. Do not go from house to house. Whenever you enter a town and they receive you, eat what is set before you. Heal the sick in it and say to them, "The kingdom of God has come near to you." But whenever you enter a town and they do not receive you, go into its streets and say, "Even the dust of your town that clings to our feet we wipe off against you. Nevertheless know this, that the kingdom of God has come near." I tell you, it will be more bearable on that day for Sodom than for that town.'

The seventy-two returned with joy, saying, 'Lord, even the demons are subject to us in your name!' And he said to them, 'I saw Satan fall like lightning from heaven. Behold, I have given you authority to tread on serpents and scorpions, and over all the power of the enemy, and nothing shall hurt you. Nevertheless, do not rejoice in this, that the spirits are subject to you, but rejoice that your names are written in heaven.'

The Gospel of the Lord.
Praise to you, Lord Jesus Christ.

▷ *page 11*

PRAYER OVER THE OFFERINGS

Lord, accept this pure sacrifice
which, through the labours of Saint Patrick,
your grateful people make
to the glory of your name.
Through Christ our Lord. **Amen.**

▷ *page 15*

COMMUNION ANTIPHON *Luke 22:29–30*

I confer a kingdom on you
just as my Father has conferred one on me,
that you may eat and drink at my table in my kingdom, says the Lord.

▷ page 58

PRAYER AFTER COMMUNION

Strengthen us, O Lord, by this sacrament,
so that we may profess the faith taught by Saint Patrick
and proclaim it by our way of living.
Through Christ our Lord. **Amen.**

▷ page 59

IN SCOTLAND

In Scotland, the Antiphons, prayers and Readings are taken from the Common of Pastors: For a Bishop.

The Gloria is sung (or said).

The following Collect is Proper.

COLLECT

O God, who chose the Bishop Saint Patrick
to preach your glory to the peoples of Ireland,
grant through his merits and intercession,
that those who glory in the name of Christian
may never cease to proclaim your wondrous deeds to all.
Through our Lord Jesus Christ, your Son,
who lives and reigns with you in the unity of the Holy Spirit,
God, for ever and ever. **Amen.**

SAINT JOSEPH

SAINT JOSEPH, SPOUSE OF THE BLESSED VIRGIN MARY
19 MARCH

If 19 March falls on a Sunday or in Holy Week the Solemnity is transferred.

ENTRANCE ANTIPHON *cf Luke 12:42*

Behold, a faithful and prudent steward,
whom the Lord set over his household.

▷ page 7

The Gloria is sung (said).

COLLECT

Grant, we pray, almighty God,
that by Saint Joseph's intercession
your Church may constantly watch over
the unfolding of the mysteries of human salvation,
whose beginnings you entrusted to his faithful care.
Through our Lord Jesus Christ, your Son,
who lives and reigns with you in the unity of the Holy Spirit,
God, for ever and ever. **Amen.**

FIRST READING *2 Samuel 7:4–5a, 12–14a, 16*

'The Lord God will give to him the throne of his father David.' [8]

A reading from the Second Book of Samuel.

In those days: The word of the LORD came to Nathan, 'Go and tell my servant David, "When your days are fulfilled and you lie down with your fathers, I will raise up your offspring after you, who shall come from your body, and I will establish his kingdom. He shall build a house for my name, and I will establish the throne of his kingdom for ever. I will be to him a father, and he shall be to me a son. And your house and your kingdom shall be made sure for ever before me. Your throne shall be established for ever."'

The word of the Lord.
Thanks be to God.

RESPONSORIAL PSALM *Psalm 89 (88):2-3. 4-5. 27, 29. R.37a*

R. **His descendants shall continue for ever.**

1 I will sing for ever of your mercies, O LORD;
through all ages my mouth will proclaim your fidelity.
I have declared your mercy is established for ever;
your fidelity stands as firm as the heavens. R.

2 'With my chosen one I have made a covenant;
I have sworn to David my servant:
I will establish your descendants for ever,
and set up your throne through all ages.' R.

continued...

8 *Luke 1:32*

R. His descendants shall continue for ever.

3 'He will call out to me, "You are my father,
my God, the rock of my salvation".
I will keep my faithful love for him always;
with him my covenant shall last.' R.

SECOND READING *Romans 4:13, 16–18, 22*

'In hope he believed against hope.'

A reading from the Letter of Saint Paul to the Romans.

Brothers and sisters: The promise to Abraham and his offspring that he would be heir of the world did not come through the law, but through the righteousness of faith.

That is why it depends on faith; in order that the promise may rest on grace and be guaranteed to all his offspring, not only to the adherent of the law but also to the one who shares the faith of Abraham, who is the father of us all. As it is written, 'I have made you the father of many nations'. In the presence of the God in whom he believed, who gives life to the dead, and calls into existence the things that do not exist; in hope he believed against hope, that he should become the father of many nations— as he had been told, 'So shall your offspring be'. That is why his faith was 'counted to him as righteousness'.

The word of the Lord.
Thanks be to God.

ACCLAMATION BEFORE THE GOSPEL *Psalm 84 (83):5*

During Lent:

Glory and praise to you, O Christ.
Blessed are they who dwell in your house, O Lord,
for ever singing your praise.
Glory and praise to you, O Christ.

In Easter Time:

Alleluia, alleluia.
Blessed are they who dwell in your house, O Lord,
for ever singing your praise.
Alleluia.

GOSPEL *Matthew 1:16, 18–21, 24a*

The Lord be with you.
And with your spirit.

A reading from the holy Gospel according to Matthew.
Glory to you, O Lord.

'Joseph did as the angel of the Lord commanded him.'

Jacob was the father of Joseph the husband of Mary, of whom Jesus was born, who is called Christ. Now the birth of Jesus Christ took place in this way. When his mother Mary had been betrothed to Joseph, before they came together she was found to be with child from the Holy Spirit. And her husband Joseph, being a just man and unwilling to put her to shame, resolved to divorce her quietly. But as he considered these things, behold, an angel of the Lord appeared to him in a dream, saying, 'Joseph, son of David, do not fear to take Mary as your wife, for that which is conceived in her is from the Holy Spirit. She will bear a son, and you shall call his name Jesus, for he will save his people from their sins.' When Joseph woke from sleep, he did as the angel of the Lord commanded him.

The Gospel of the Lord.
Praise to you, Lord Jesus Christ.

Or: **ALTERNATIVE GOSPEL** *Luke 2:41–51a*

The Lord be with you.
And with your spirit.

A reading from the holy Gospel according to Luke.
Glory to you, O Lord.

'Behold, your father and I have been searching for you in great distress.'

The parents of Jesus went to Jerusalem every year at the Feast of the Passover. And when he was twelve years old, they went up according to custom. And when the feast was ended, as they were returning, the boy Jesus stayed behind in Jerusalem. His parents did not know it, but supposing him to be in the group they went a day's journey, but then they began to search for him among their relatives and acquaintances, and when they did not find him, they returned to Jerusalem, searching for him. After three days they found him in the Temple, sitting among the teachers, listening to them and asking them questions. And all who heard him were amazed at his understanding and his answers. And when his parents saw him, they were astonished. And his mother said to him, 'Son, why have you treated us so? Behold, your father and I have been searching for you in great distress.' And he said to them, 'Why were you looking for me? Did you not know that I must be in my Father's house?' And they did not understand the saying that he spoke to them. And he went down with them and came to Nazareth and was submissive to them.

The Gospel of the Lord.
Praise to you, Lord Jesus Christ.

▷ *page 11*

The Profession of Faith is said.

PRAYER OVER THE OFFERINGS

We pray, O Lord,
that, just as Saint Joseph served with loving care
your Only Begotten Son, born of the Virgin Mary,
so we may be worthy to minister
with a pure heart at your altar.
Through Christ our Lord. **Amen.**

▷ *page 15*

PREFACE

THE MISSION OF SAINT JOSEPH

Priest: The Lord be with you.
People: **And with your spirit.**

Priest: Lift up your hearts.
People: **We lift them up to the Lord.**

Priest: Let us give thanks to the Lord our God.
People: **It is right and just.**

It is truly right and just, our duty and our salvation,
always and everywhere to give you thanks,
Lord, holy Father, almighty and eternal God,
and on the Solemnity of Saint Joseph
to give you fitting praise,
to glorify you and bless you.

For this just man was given by you
as spouse to the Virgin Mother of God
and set as a wise and faithful servant
in charge of your household,
to watch like a father over your Only Begotten Son,
who was conceived by the overshadowing of the Holy Spirit,
our Lord Jesus Christ.

Through him the Angels praise your majesty,
Dominions adore and Powers tremble before you.
Heaven and the Virtues of heaven and the blessed Seraphim
worship together with exultation.
May our voices, we pray, join with theirs
in humble praise, as we acclaim:

Holy, Holy, Holy Lord God of hosts…

COMMUNION ANTIPHON *Matthew 25:21*

Well done, good and faithful servant.
Come, share your master's joy.

▷ *page 58*

PRAYER AFTER COMMUNION

Defend with unfailing protection,
O Lord, we pray,
the family you have nourished
with food from this altar,
as they rejoice at the Solemnity of Saint Joseph,
and graciously keep safe your gifts among them.
Through Christ our Lord. **Amen.**

▷ *page 59*

ANNUNCIATION OF THE LORD

25 MARCH

If 25 March falls on a Sunday or in Holy Week, the Solemnity is transferred.

ENTRANCE ANTIPHON *Hebrews 10:5, 7*

The Lord said, as he entered the world:
Behold, I come to do your will, O God.

▷ page 7

The Gloria is sung (said).

COLLECT

O God, who willed that your Word
should take on the reality of human flesh
in the womb of the Virgin Mary,
grant, we pray,
that we, who confess our Redeemer to be God and man,
may merit to become partakers even in his divine nature.
Who lives and reigns with you in the unity of the Holy Spirit,
God, for ever and ever. **Amen.**

FIRST READING *7:10-14; 8:10c*

'Behold, the virgin shall conceive.'

A reading from the Prophet Isaiah.

In those days: The LORD spoke to Ahaz: 'Ask a sign of the LORD your God; let it be deep as Sheol or high as heaven.' But Ahaz said, 'I will not ask, and I will not put the LORD to the test.' And Isaiah said, 'Hear then, O house of David! Is it too little for you to weary men, that you weary my God also? Therefore the Lord himself will give you a sign. Behold, the virgin shall conceive and bear a son, and shall call his name Emmanuel—God is with us.'

The word of the Lord.
Thanks be to God.

RESPONSORIAL PSALM *Psalm 40(39):7-8a. 8b-9. 10. 11. R.8a, 9a*

R. Behold, I have come, Lord, to do your will.

1 You delight not in sacrifice and offering,
but in an open ear.
You do not ask for holocaust and sin offering.
Then I said, 'Behold, I have come.' R.

2 In the scroll of the book it stands written of me:
'I delight to do your will, O my God;
your instruction lies deep within me.' R.

SAINTS

continued...

R. Behold, I have come, Lord, to do your will.

3 Your uprightness I have proclaimed
in the great assembly.
My lips I have not sealed;
you know it, O LORD. R

4 Your saving help I have not hidden in my heart;
of your faithfulness and salvation I have spoken.
I made no secret of your merciful love
and your faithfulness to the great assembly. R.

SECOND READING *Hebrews 10:4–10*

'I have come to do your will, O God, as it is written of me in the scroll of the book.'

A reading from the Letter to the Hebrews.

Brothers and sisters: It is impossible for the blood of bulls and goats to take away sins. Consequently, when Christ came into the world, he said, 'Sacrifices and offerings you have not desired, but a body have you prepared for me; in burnt offerings and sin offerings you have taken no pleasure. Then I said, "Behold, I have come to do your will, O God, as it is written of me in the scroll of the book."'

When he said above, 'You have neither desired nor taken pleasure in sacrifices and offerings and burnt offerings and sin offerings' (these are offered according to the Law), then he added, 'Behold, I have come to do your will.' He does away with the first in order to establish the second. And by that will we have been sanctified through the offering of the body of Jesus Christ once for all.

The word of the Lord.
Thanks be to God.

ACCLAMATION BEFORE THE GOSPEL *John 1:14ab*

During Lent:

**Glory and praise to you, O Christ.
The Word became flesh and dwelt among us,
and we have seen his glory.
Glory and praise to you, O Christ.**

In Easter Time:

**Alleluia, alleluia.
The Word became flesh and dwelt among us,
and we have seen his glory.
Alleluia.**

GOSPEL *Luke 1:26–38*

The Lord be with you.
And with your spirit.

A reading from the holy Gospel according to Luke.
Glory to you, O Lord.

'Behold, you will conceive in your womb and bear a son.'

At that time: The angel Gabriel was sent from God to a city of Galilee named Nazareth, to a virgin betrothed to a man whose name was Joseph, of the house of David. And the virgin's name was Mary. And he came to her and said, 'Hail, full of grace, the Lord is with you!' But she was greatly troubled at the saying, and tried to discern what sort of greeting this might be. And the angel said to her, 'Do not be afraid, Mary, for you have found favour with God. And behold, you will conceive in your womb and bear a son, and you shall call his name Jesus. He will be great and will be called the Son of the Most High. And the Lord God will give to him the throne of his father David, and he will reign over the house of Jacob for ever, and of his kingdom there will be no end.'

And Mary said to the angel, 'How will this be, since I am a virgin?' And the angel answered her, 'The Holy Spirit will come upon you, and the power of the Most High will overshadow you; therefore the child to be born will be called holy— the Son of God. And behold, your relative Elizabeth in her old age has also conceived a son, and this is the sixth month with her who was called barren. For nothing will be impossible with God.' And Mary said, 'Behold, I am the servant of the Lord; let it be to me according to your word.' And the angel departed from her.

The Gospel of the Lord.
Praise to you, Lord Jesus Christ.

▷ *page 11*

PROFESSION OF FAITH

The Profession of Faith is said. All kneel at the words 'and by the Holy Spirit was incarnate.'

PRAYER OVER THE OFFERINGS

Be pleased, almighty God,
to accept your Church's offering,
so that she, who is aware that her beginnings
lie in the Incarnation of your Only Begotten Son,
may rejoice to celebrate his mysteries on this Solemnity.
Who lives and reigns for ever and ever. **Amen.**

▷ *page 15*

PREFACE

THE MYSTERY OF THE INCARNATION

Priest: The Lord be with you.
People: **And with your spirit.**

Priest: Lift up your hearts.
People: **We lift them up to the Lord.**

Priest: Let us give thanks to the Lord our God.
People: **It is right and just.**

It is truly right and just, our duty and our salvation,
always and everywhere to give you thanks,
Lord, holy Father, almighty and eternal God,
through Christ our Lord.
For the Virgin Mary heard with faith
that the Christ was to be born among men and for men's sake
by the overshadowing power
of the Holy Spirit.
Lovingly she bore him
in her immaculate womb,
that the promises to the children of Israel might come about
and the hope of nations be accomplished
beyond all telling.
Through him the host of Angels
adores your majesty
and rejoices in your presence for ever.
May our voices, we pray, join with theirs
in one chorus of exultant praise,
as we acclaim:
Holy, Holy, Holy Lord God of hosts...

COMMUNION ANTIPHON *Isaiah 7:14*

Behold, a Virgin shall conceive and bear a son;
and his name will be called Emmanuel.

▷ *page 58*

PRAYER AFTER COMMUNION

Confirm in our minds the mysteries of the true faith,
we pray, O Lord,
so that, confessing that he who was conceived of the Virgin Mary
is true God and true man,
we may, through the saving power of his Resurrection,
merit to attain eternal joy.
Through Christ our Lord. **Amen.**

▷ *page 59*

MUSIC FOR THE ORDER OF MASS

On occasion, music is not provided for the text which precedes the people's response. In this case a cue is given indicating the last note(s) sung before the response, as in the example opposite:

People:

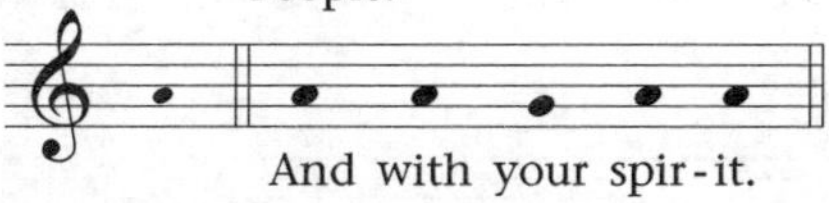

INTRODUCTORY RITES

SIGN OF THE CROSS

All make the Sign of the Cross as the Priest sings:

Priest:

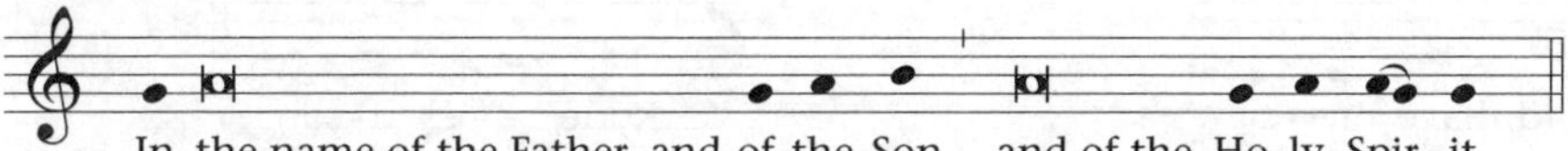

In the name of the Father, and of the Son, and of the Ho-ly Spir-it.

People:

A-men.

GREETING

Priest: The grace of our Lord Jesus Christ,
and the love of God,
and the communion of the Holy Spirit
be with you all.

or

Priest: Grace to you and peace from God our Father
and the Lord Jesus Christ.

or

Priest: The Lord be with you.

A Bishop will say:

Bishop: Peace be with you.

People:

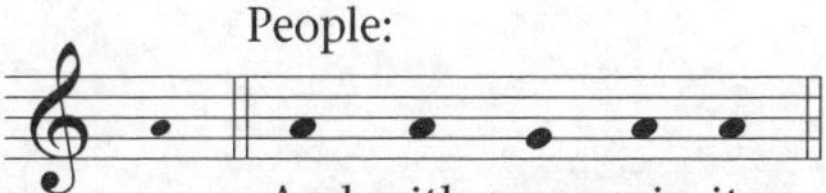

PENITENTIAL ACT

Penitential Act B

Priest: People:

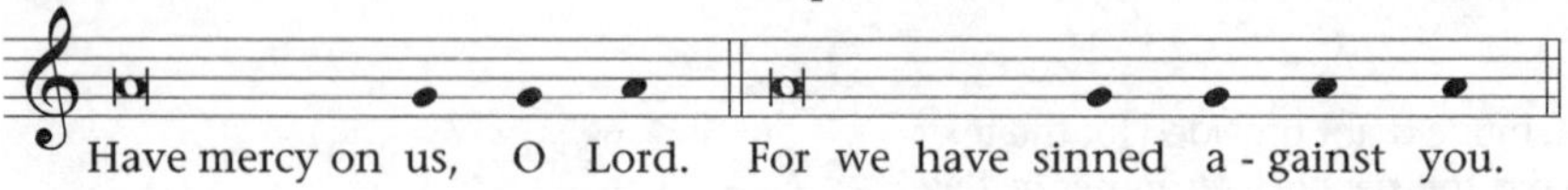

Have mercy on us, O Lord. For we have sinned a - gainst you.

Priest: People:

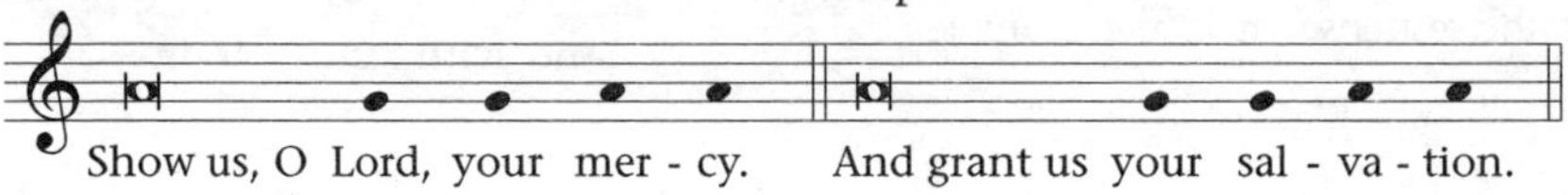

Show us, O Lord, your mer - cy. And grant us your sal - va - tion.

Penitential Act C

Priest or minister: You were sent to heal the contrite of heart:

Repeat after the Priest or minister:

or

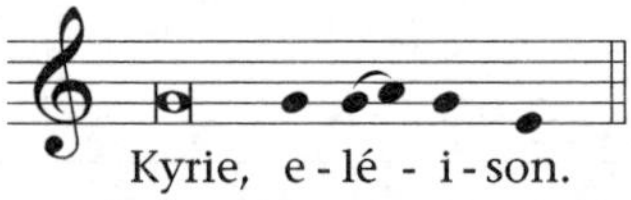

Kyrie, e - lé - i - son.

Priest or minister: You came to call sinners:

Repeat after the Priest or minister:

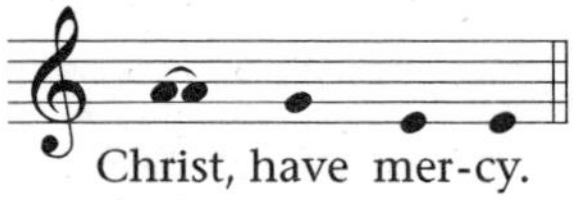

or

Christe, e - lé - i - son.

Priest or minister: You are seated at the right hand of the Father to intercede for us:

Repeat after the Priest or minister:

or

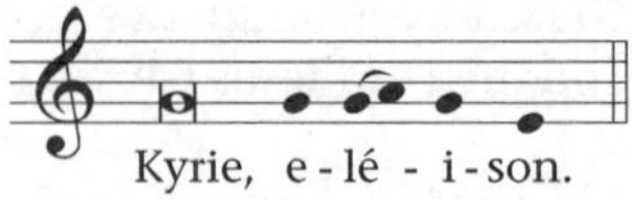

Kyrie, e - lé - i - son.

ABSOLUTION

The absolution by the Priest follows all of the options above

Priest:

May almighty God have mercy on us, forgive us our sins,
People:
and bring us to ever-last-ing life. A-men.

KYRIE

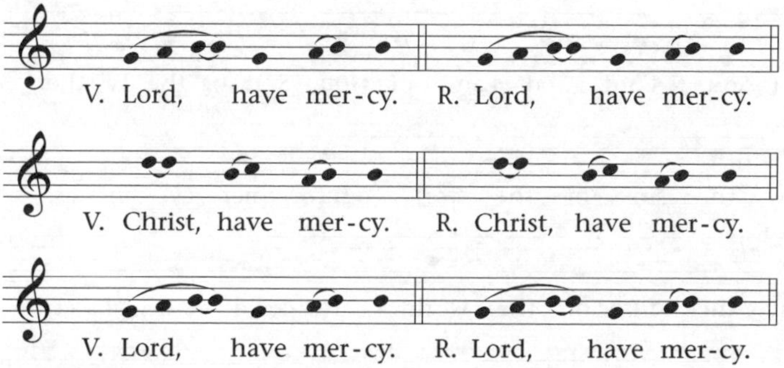
V. Lord, have mer-cy. R. Lord, have mer-cy.
V. Christ, have mer-cy. R. Christ, have mer-cy.
V. Lord, have mer-cy. R. Lord, have mer-cy.

or

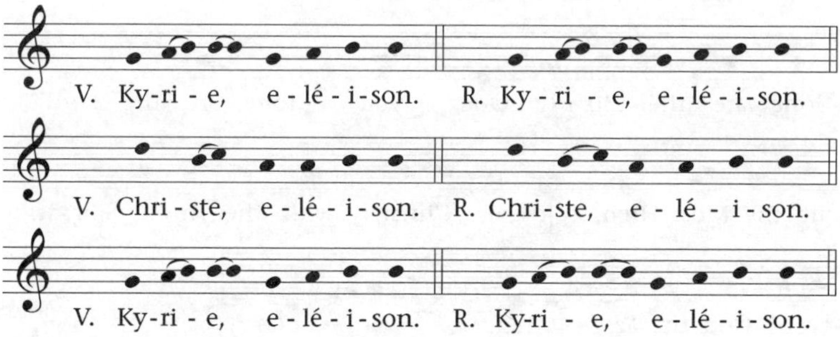
V. Ky-ri-e, e-lé-i-son. R. Ky-ri-e, e-lé-i-son.
V. Chri-ste, e-lé-i-son. R. Chri-ste, e-lé-i-son.
V. Ky-ri-e, e-lé-i-son. R. Ky-ri-e, e-lé-i-son.

or

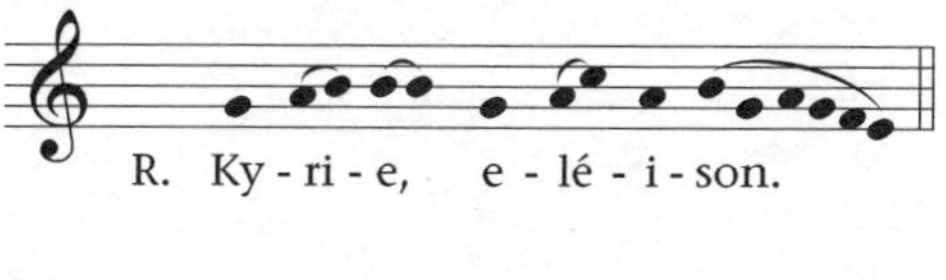
R. Ky-ri-e, e-lé-i-son.

GLORIA

Glo-ry to God in the high-est, and on earth peace to peo-ple of good will.
We praise you, we bless you, we a-dore you, we glo-ri-fy you,
we give you thanks for your great glo-ry, Lord God, heav-en-ly King,
O God, al-migh-ty Fa-ther. Lord Je-sus Christ,
On-ly Be-got-ten Son, Lord, God, Lamb of God, Son of the Fa-ther,
you take a-way the sins of the world, have mer-cy on us;
you take a-way the sins of the world, re-ceive our prayer;
you are seat-ed at the right hand of the Fa-ther, have mer-cy on us.
For you a-lone are the Ho-ly One, you a-lone are the Lord,
you a-lone are the Most High, Je-sus Christ, with the Ho-ly Spir-it,
in the glo-ry of God the Fa - ther. A - men.

LITURGY OF THE WORD

FIRST READING

Acclamation at the end of the reading.

Reader: People:

The word of the Lord.
Thanks be to God.

SECOND READING

Acclamation at the end of the reading.

Reader: People:

The word of the Lord.
Thanks be to God.

GOSPEL

Dialogue at the beginning of the Gospel.

Deacon / Priest: People:

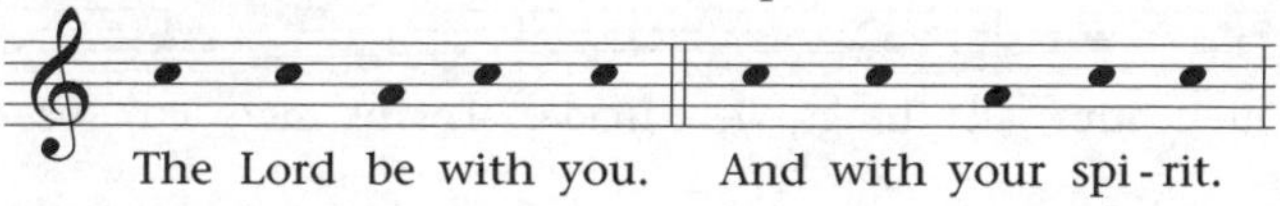
The Lord be with you.
And with your spi - rit.

Deacon / Priest: People:

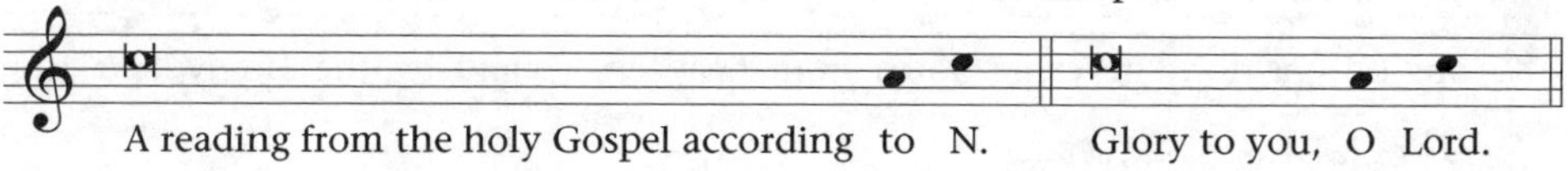
A reading from the holy Gospel according to N.
Glory to you, O Lord.

Acclamation at the end of the Gospel.

Deacon / Priest: People:

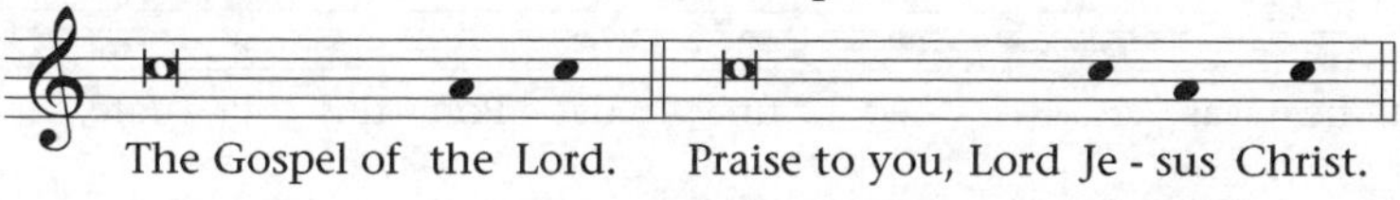
The Gospel of the Lord.
Praise to you, Lord Je - sus Christ.

PROFESSION OF FAITH

Niceno-Constantinopolitan Creed

I be-lieve in one God, the Fa-ther al-migh-ty, mak-er of heav-en
and earth, of all things vis - i - ble and in - vis - i - ble.
I be-lieve in one Lord Je-sus Christ, the Only Be - got-ten Son of God,
born of the Father be - fore all a - ges. God from God, Light from Light,
true God from true God, be - got - ten, not made, con-sub-stan-tial
with the Fa-ther; through him all things were made. For us men and for
our sal - va-tion he came down from heav-en, and by the Ho-ly Spir-it
At the words that follow, up to and including 'and became man', all bow.
was in - car - nate of the Vir - gin Mar - y, and be-came man.
For our sake he was cru - ci - fied un - der Pon - tius Pi - late,
he suffered death and was bur - ied, and rose a-gain on the third day

in accordance with the Scrip - tures. He as - cen - ded in - to heav - en
and is seated at the right hand of the Fa - ther. He will come a - gain in glo - ry
to judge the living and the dead and his kingdom will have no end.
I be - lieve in the Ho - ly Spir - it, the Lord, the giv - er of life,
who pro - ceeds from the Father and the Son, who with the Fa - ther
and the Son is adored and glo - ri - fied, who has spoken
through the proph - ets. I be - lieve in one, ho - ly, cath - o - lic
and a - po - sto - lic Church. I con - fess one bap - tism
for the for - give - ness of sins and I look for - ward to the
res - ur - rec - tion of the dead and the life of the world to come.
A - - - men.

LITURGY OF THE EUCHARIST

ORATE, FRATRES

ALL STAND

Priest:

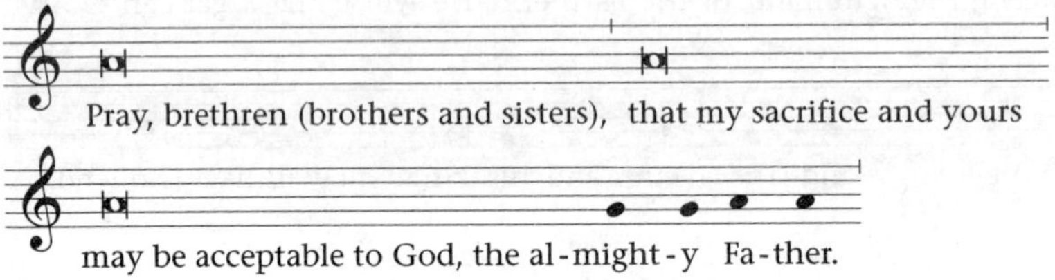
Pray, brethren (brothers and sisters), that my sacrifice and yours
may be acceptable to God, the al-might-y Fa-ther.

People:

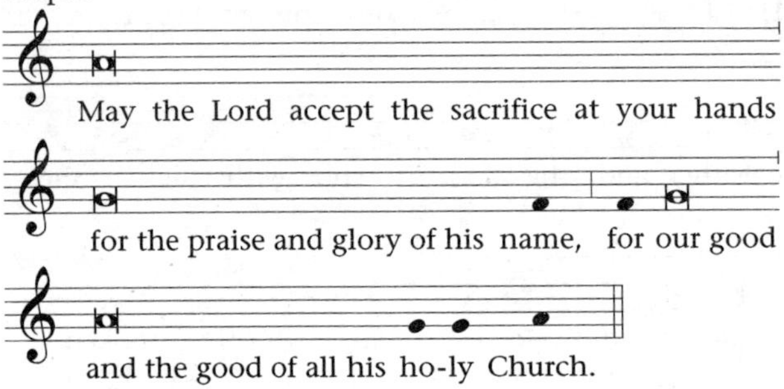
May the Lord accept the sacrifice at your hands
for the praise and glory of his name, for our good
and the good of all his ho-ly Church.

PREFACE DIALOGUE

Priest: All:

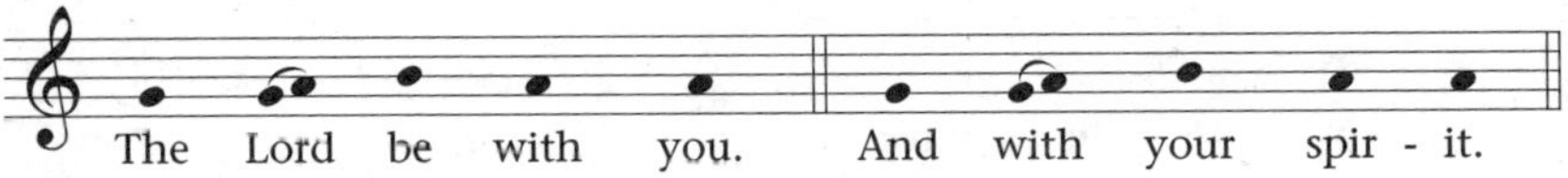
The Lord be with you. And with your spir - it.

Priest: All:

Lift up your hearts. We lift them up to the Lord.

Priest: All:

Let us give thanks to the Lord our God. It is right and just.

SANCTUS

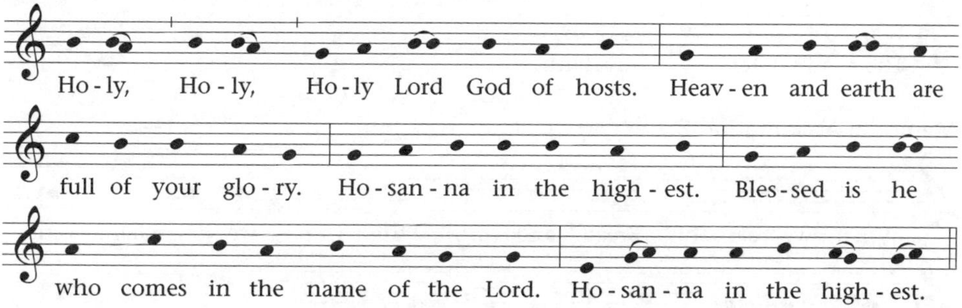
Ho-ly, Ho-ly, Ho-ly Lord God of hosts. Heav-en and earth are
full of your glo-ry. Ho-san-na in the high-est. Bles-sed is he
who comes in the name of the Lord. Ho-san-na in the high-est.

or

San-ctus, San-ctus, San-ctus Dó-mi-nus De-us Sá-ba-oth. Ple-ni sunt cae-li
et ter-ra gló-ri-a tu-a. Ho-sán-na in ex-cél-sis. Be-ne-dí-ctus
qui ven-it in nó-mi-ne Dó-mi-ni. Ho-sán-na in ex-cél-sis.

MEMORIAL ACCLAMATION

Priest:

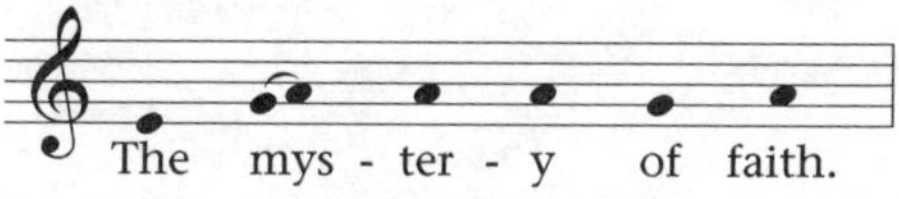
The mys-ter-y of faith.

Memorial Acclamation A

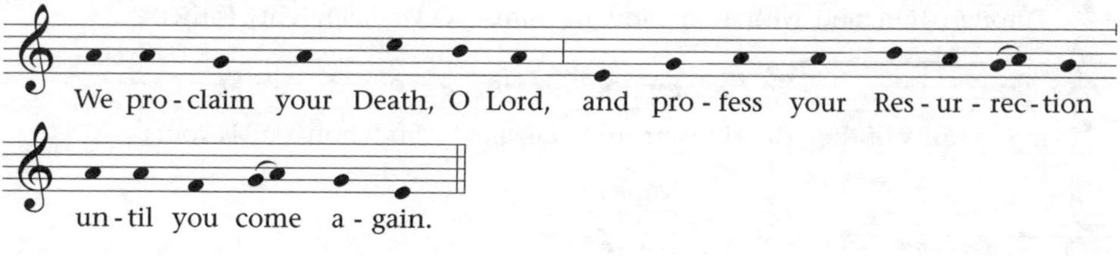
We pro-claim your Death, O Lord, and pro-fess your Res-ur-rec-tion
un-til you come a-gain.

MUSIC

Priest:

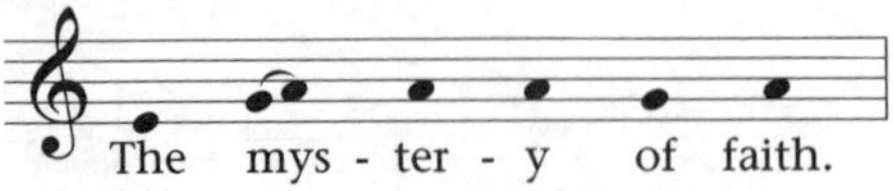
The mys - ter - y of faith.

Memorial Acclamation B

When we eat this Bread and drink this Cup, we pro-claim your
Death, O Lord, un - til you come a - gain.

Memorial Acclamation C

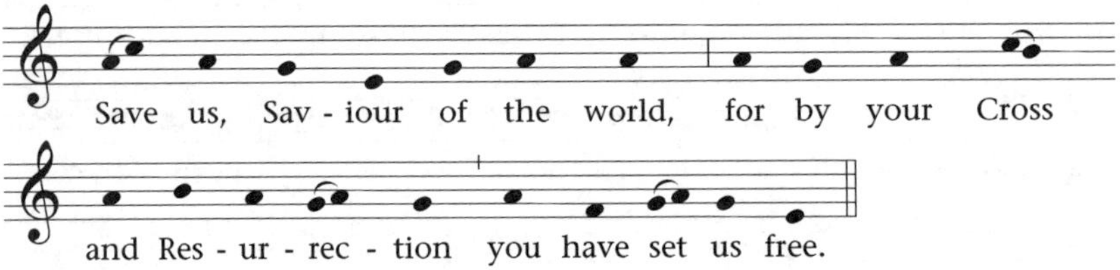
Save us, Sav - iour of the world, for by your Cross
and Res - ur - rec - tion you have set us free.

DOXOLOGY AND GREAT AMEN

Priest:

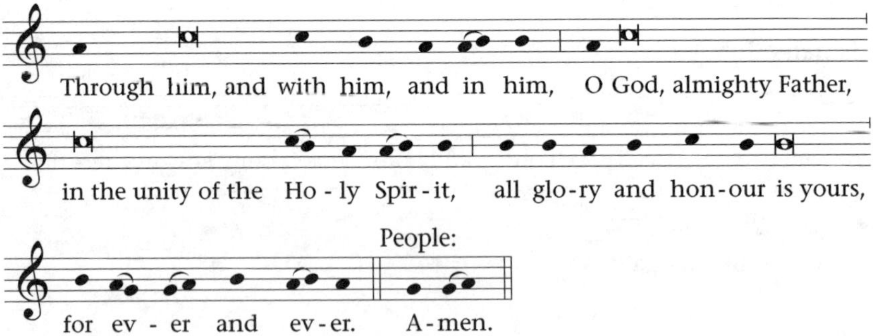
Through him, and with him, and in him, O God, almighty Father,
in the unity of the Ho - ly Spir - it, all glo-ry and hon-our is yours,
People:
for ev - er and ev - er. A - men.

COMMUNION RITE

LORD'S PRAYER

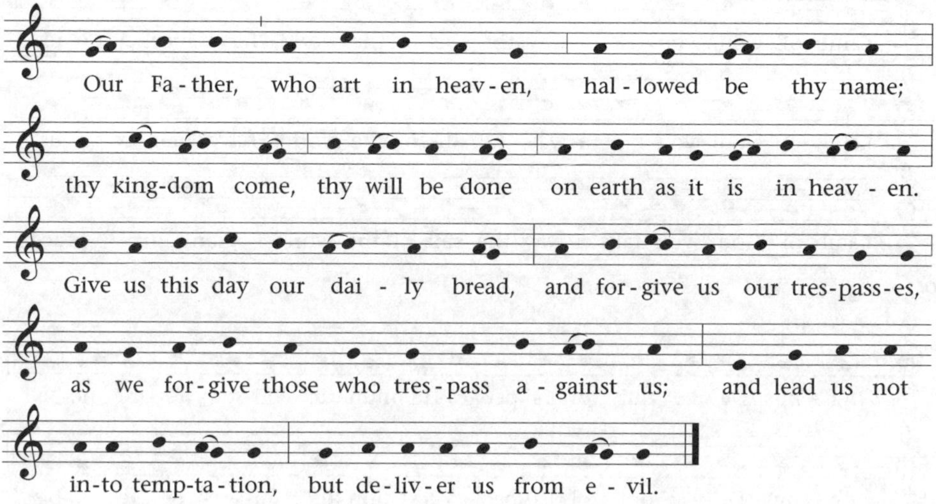
Our Fa - ther, who art in heav - en, hal - lowed be thy name;
thy king - dom come, thy will be done on earth as it is in heav - en.
Give us this day our dai - ly bread, and for - give us our tres - pass - es,
as we for - give those who tres - pass a - gainst us; and lead us not
in - to temp - ta - tion, but de - liv - er us from e - vil.

Priest Deliver us, Lord, we pray, from every evil,
graciously grant peace in our days,
that, by the help of your mercy,
we may be always free from sin
and safe from all distress,
as we await the blessed hope
and the coming of our Saviour, Jesus Christ.

People:

For the king - dom, the power and the glo - ry are yours now and for ev - er.

RITE OF PEACE

Priest: The peace of the Lord be with you always.

People:

And with your spir - it.

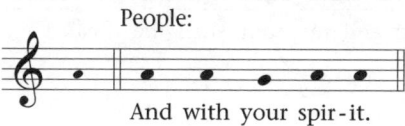

BREAKING OF BREAD

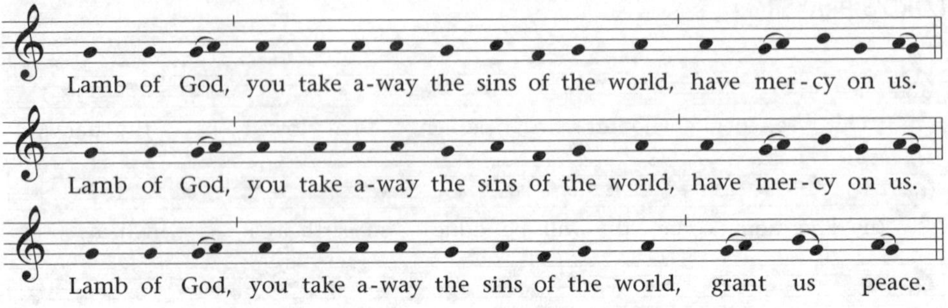

or

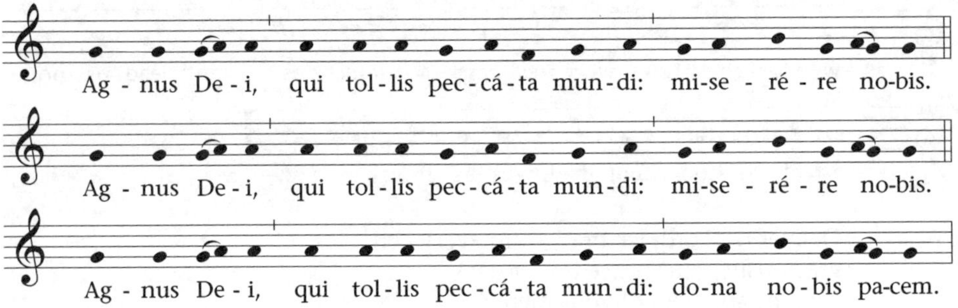

The invocation may be repeated several times if the Breaking of the Bread is prolonged.
The final time always ends 'grant us peace' ('dona nobis pacem').

INVITATION TO COMMUNION

Priest Behold the Lamb of God,
behold him who takes away the sins of the world.
Blessed are those called to the...

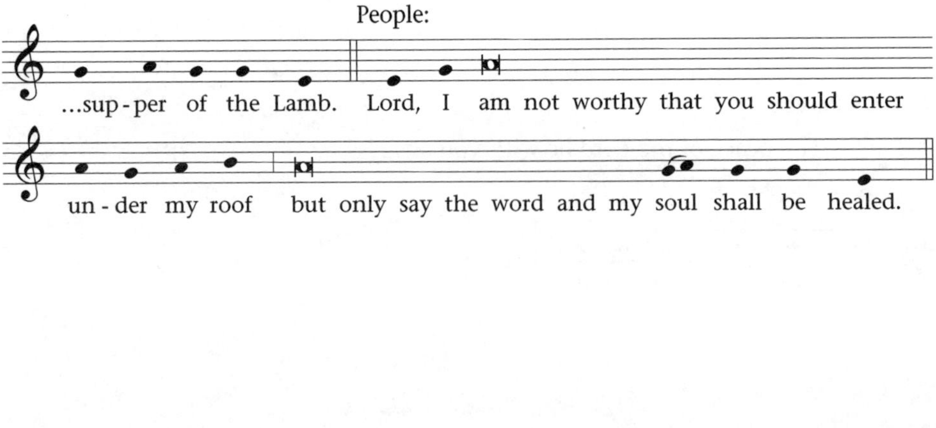

People:
...sup-per of the Lamb. Lord, I am not worthy that you should enter
un-der my roof but only say the word and my soul shall be healed.

CONCLUDING RITES

BLESSING

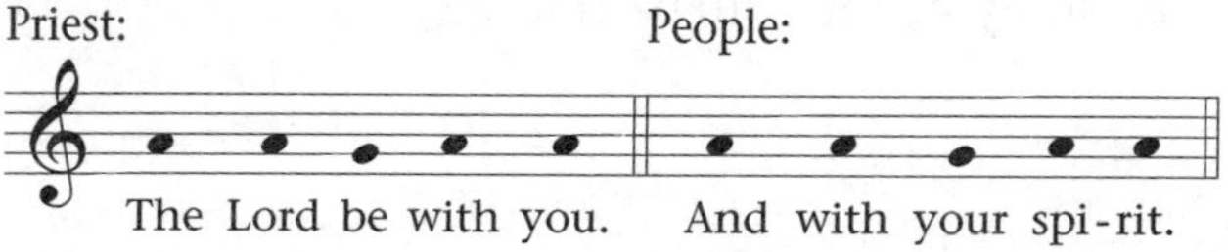

Priest:
People:
The Lord be with you.
And with your spi-rit.

On certain occasions, the following blessing may be preceded by a solemn blessing or prayer over the people. Then the Priest blesses the people, singing:

Priest: May almighty God bless you:
the Father, and the Son, ✠ and the Holy Spirit.

In a Pontifical Mass, the celebrant receives the mitre and sings:

Bishop:
All:
Blessed be the name of the Lord.
Now and for ev-er.

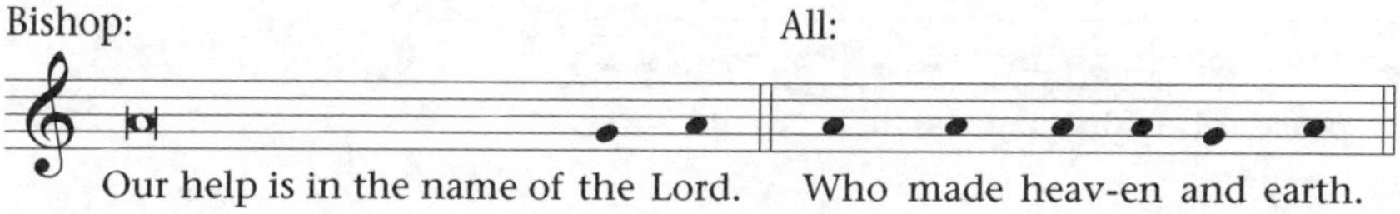

Bishop:
All:
Our help is in the name of the Lord.
Who made heav-en and earth.

On certain occasions the following blessing may be preceded by a more solemn blessing or prayer over the people. Then the celebrant receives the pastoral staff, if he uses it, and sings:

Bishop: May almighty God bless you:
making the Sign of the Cross over the people three times, he adds:
the Father, ✠ and the Son, ✠ and the...

If any liturgical action follows immediately, the rites of dismissal are omitted.

DISMISSAL

Deacon or Priest: Go forth, the Mass is ended.
or Go and announce the Gospel of the Lord.
or Go in peace, glorifying the Lord by your life.

All:

Thanks be to God.

or

Deacon or Priest: All:

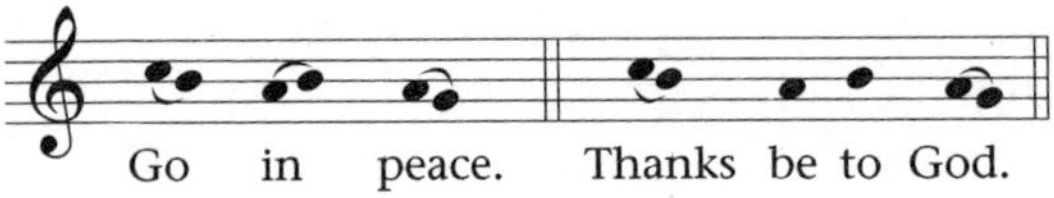
Go in peace. Thanks be to God.

The following dismissal on Easter Sunday, the Octave of Easter, and on Pentecost Sunday.

Deacon/Priest:

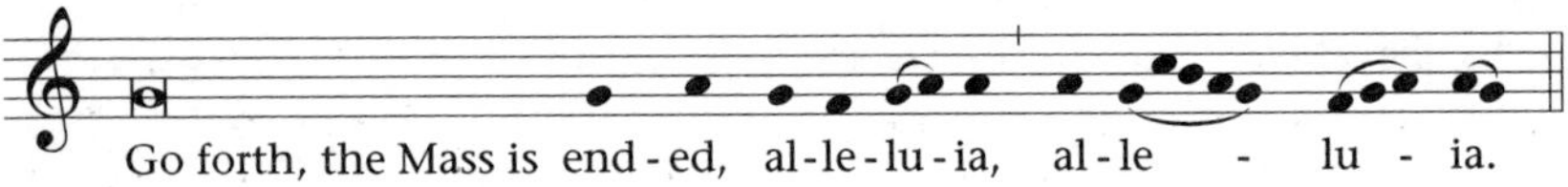
Go forth, the Mass is end - ed, al - le - lu - ia, al - le - lu - ia.

or

Deacon/Priest:

Go in peace, al - le - lu - ia, al - le - lu - ia.

All:

Thanks be to God, al - le - lu - ia, al - le - lu - ia.

INDEX

INDEX

THOUGHTS AND PRAYERS

Prayer Before a Crucifix

Behold, O kind and most sweet Jesus,
I cast myself on my knees in your sight,
and with the most fervent desire of my soul,
I pray and beseech you
that you would impress upon my heart
lively sentiments of faith, hope and charity,
with a true repentance for my sins
and a firm desire of amendment,
while with deep affection and grief of soul
I ponder within myself
and mentally contemplate
your five most precious wounds,
having before my eyes
that which David spoke in prophecy of you,
O good Jesus:
'They have pierced my hands and my feet;
they have numbered all my bones.'

On Silence

We need to find God, and he cannot be found in noise and restlessness,
God is the friend of silence.
See how nature – trees, flowers, grass – grow in silence;
see the stars, the moon and sun, how they move in silence.
Is not our mission to give God to the poor in the slums?
Not a dead God, but a living, loving God.
The more we receive in silent prayer, the more we can give in our active life.
We need silence to be able to touch souls.
The essential thing is not what we say, but what God says to us and through us.
All our words will be useless unless they come from within –
words which do not give the light of Christ increase the darkness.

Mother Teresa

Prayers to Mary

The Memorare

Remember, O most loving Virgin Mary,
that it is a thing unheard of,
that anyone ever had recourse to your protection,
implored your help,
or sought your intercession,
and was left forsaken.
Filled therefore with confidence in your goodness
I fly to you, O Mother, Virgin of virgins.
To you I come, before you I stand,
a sorrowful sinner.
Despise not my poor words,
O Mother of the Word of God,
but graciously hear and grant my prayer.

Hail, Holy Queen

Hail, holy Queen, mother of mercy:
hail, our life, our sweetness, and our hope!
To you do we cry,
poor banished children of Eve.
To you do we send up our sighs,
mourning and weeping
in this vale of tears.
Turn then, most gracious advocate,
your eyes of mercy towards us;
and after this our exile,
show to us
the blessed fruit of your womb, Jesus.
O clement,
O loving,
O sweet Virgin Mary.
Pray for us, O holy Mother of God.
That we may be made worthy
of the promises of Christ.

PRAYERS BEFORE MASS

Prayer to the Holy Spirit

Come, Holy Spirit, fill the hearts of your faithful,
and enkindle in them the fire of your love.
Send forth your Spirit and they shall be created.
And you shall renew the face of the earth.
Let us pray: O God, who has taught the hearts of the faithful by the light of the Holy Spirit, grant that by the gift of the same Spirit we may be always truly wise and ever rejoice in his consolation.

Prayer to Our Lord

Lord Jesus,
I give you my hands to do your work.
I give you my feet to go your way.
I give you my eyes to see as you do.
I give you my tongue to speak your words.
I give you my mind that you may think in me.
I give you my spirit that you may pray in me.

Above all

I give you my heart that you may love in me,
your Father, and all mankind.
I give you my whole self that you may grow in me,
so that it is you, Lord Jesus,
who live and work and pray in me.

Prayer to God the Father

God be in my head, and in my understanding;
God be in mine eyes, and in my looking;
God be in my mouth, and in my speaking;
God be in my heart, and in my thinking;
God be at mine end, and at my departing.

Prayer for Peace

O God, source of holy desires, right counsels and just actions, grant to your servants that peace which the world cannot give, so that our hearts may be wholly devoted to your service, and all our days, freed from dread of our enemies, may be passed in quietness under your protection.

Act of Charity

O my God, I love you with my whole heart and above all things, because you are infinitely good and perfect; and I love my neighbour as myself for love of you. Grant that I may love you more and more in this life, and in the next for all eternity.

Anima Christi

Soul of Christ, sanctify me.
Body of Christ, save me.
Blood of Christ, inebriate me.
Water from the side of Christ, wash me.
Passion of Christ, strengthen me.

Jesus, hear me.
Hide me in your wounds,
that I may never leave your side
and never let me be parted from you.
From the malicious enemy defend me.
In the hour of my death call me,
and tell me come unto you,
that with your saints I may praise you
through all eternity,
for ever and ever. Amen

O Sacrum Convivium

O Sacred Banquet,
in which Christ is received,
and the memory of his Passion is renewed;
where the soul is filled with grace,
and a pledge of future glory is given to us.

PRAYERS AFTER MASS

Prayer of Saint Ignatius

Teach us, good Lord,
to serve you as you deserve;
to give and not to count the cost;
to fight and not to heed the wounds;
to toil, and not to seek for rest;
to labour and to ask for no reward,
save that of knowing
that we do your will;
through Jesus Christ our Lord.

Jesus, Our Brother

Dear Lord,
I believe that Holy Communion joins us all together in union with you and in union with one another.

As we all received you together at the Holy Table, let us remember that we are all members of one family.

Let us help one another and forgive one another, bearing one another's burdens.

You have said that if we do not love our neighbour, whom we can see, how can we love God, whom we cannot see?

Make me careful, therefore, not to despise anyone, as if they were beneath me; not to bear a grudge against anyone who may have done me wrong.

Whenever there is any work to be done for the good of the parish, make me overcome my laziness and my pride and give me the desire to help.

Let me be a good example, not a stumbling block, to those around me.

Prayer of Saint Francis

Lord, make me an instrument of your peace.

Where there is hatred let me sow peace;
where there is injury, pardon;
where there is doubt, let me sow faith;
where there is despair, let me give hope;
where there is darkness, let me give light;
where there is sadness, let me give joy.

O Divine Master, grant that I may not seek
to be comforted, but to comfort;
to be understood, but to understand;
to be loved, but to love.

For it is in giving that we receive,
it is in forgiving that we are forgiven,
and it is in dying
that we are born to eternal life.

Prayer of St Richard

O dear Lord,
three things I pray:
to see thee more clearly,
love thee more dearly,
and follow thee more nearly,
day by day.

A Thought on Thanksgiving

It is very easy to pray to God
when we are in trouble;
even people who do not think
they believe in God
may utter a short prayer in times of crisis.
Fewer people thank God
for the good things which we are given.
Remember how often Jesus said,
'Father, I thank you...'

Etta Gullick